CRITICAL SURVEY OF LONG FICTION

Political Novelists

Editor

Carl Rollyson
Baruch College, City University of New York

SALEM PRESS
Ipswich, Massachusetts • Hackensack, New Jersey

Cover photo:
Nadine Gordimer (© Micheline Pelletier/Corbis)

Copyright ©2012, by Salem Press, A Division of EBSCO Publishing, Inc.
All rights in this book are reserved. No part of this work may be used or reproduced in any manner whatsoever or transmitted in any form or by any means, electronic or mechanical, including photocopy, recording, or any information storage and retrieval system, without written permission from the copyright owner. For information, contact the publisher, EBSCO Publishing, 10 Estes Street, Ipswich, MA 01938.

978-1-4298-3681-4

CONTENTS

Contributors iv

The Political Novel 1

Vicente Blasco Ibáñez 9
Karel Čapek 22
Joseph Conrad 31
Fyodor Dostoevski 50
Nikolai Gogol 67
Nadine Gordimer 78
Maxim Gorky 99
Graham Greene 110
Khaled Hosseini 122
Ismail Kadare 128
Arthur Koestler 134
Milan Kundera 145
Ngugi wa Thiong'o 156
George Orwell 172
Katherine Anne Porter 183
Ayn Rand 193
Salman Rushdie 200
Mikhail Sholokhov 216
Upton Sinclair 225
Aleksandr Solzhenitsyn 239
Yevgeny Zamyatin 254

Bibliography 264
Glossary of Literary Terms 268
Guide to Online Resources 280
Geographical Index 285
Subject Index 286

CONTRIBUTORS

Hallman B. Bryant
Original Contributor

C. F. Burgess
Original Contributor

Suzan K. Burks
Original Contributor

Julian W. Connolly
University of Virginia

Frank Day
Original Contributor

Henry J. Donaghy
Original Contributor

Robert J. Forman
St. John's University

Margot K. Frank
Original Contributor

Peter B. Heller
St. John's University

Abdul R. JanMohamed
Original Contributor

Irma M. Kashuba
Original Contributor

John V. Knapp
Original Contributor

Rebecca Kuzins
Pasadena, California

Norman Lavers
Original Contributor

Leon Lewis
Appalachian State University

Stanley Vincent Longman
University of Georgia

Paul Marx
Original Contributor

Charles E. May
California State University, Long Beach

Laurence W. Mazzeno
Alvernia College

Jeremy T. Medina
Original Contributor

Marion Petrillo
Bloomsburg University of Pennsylvania

Peter Petro
Original Contributor

John D. Raymer
Holy Cross College

DaRelle M. Rollins
Hampton University

Carl Rollyson
Baruch College, CUNY

Robert L. Ross
University of Texas at Austin

Jean M. Snook
Memorial University of Newfoundland

Victor Terras
Original Contributor

Christine D. Tomei
Columbia University

James Whitlark
Texas Tech University

The Political Novel

In the narrowest sense, the political novel is a work of fiction that deals with politicians and the political process. In this category, Robert Penn Warren's *All the King's Men* (1946) and Sinclair Lewis's *It Can't Happen Here* (1935), and the work of British novelists such as Benjamin Disraeli and Anthony Trollope, are paramount examples of fictional narratives that attempt to re-create the business of politics—the speech making, campaigning, lobbying, and governing (both in public and behind-the-scenes). Although such works may derive from historical figures and events (Huey Long is the model for Willie Stark in *All the King's Men*), these novels remain in the realm of the imaginary because they posit outcomes that are hypothetical.

Another form of the political novel is historical fiction. Gore Vidal's *Burr* (1973) and Russell Banks's *Cloudsplitter* (1998)—a novel about John Brown that is narrated by one of his sons—deal directly with the historical record, inventing a voice for their protagonists and portraying a part of history that eludes historians for lack of evidence. These rather traditional political and historical novels have been challenged by postmodern uses of history and politics in works such as Robert Coover's *The Public Burning* (1977), half of which is narrated by an eroticized Richard Nixon, and Ishmael Reed's *Flight to Canada* (1976), featuring nineteenth century figures, including Abraham Lincoln and Harriet Beecher Stowe, who inhabit an anachronistic world of inventions that coexist with slavery. E. L. Doctorow's *Ragtime* (1975) represents a similarly playful and unconventional use of history.

Still another kind of political novel is ideological. Ayn Rand's *Atlas Shrugged* (1957) is a full-scale attack on collectivist societies similar to those established in the Soviet Union and other communist states. An uncompromising individualist, Rand created the future as a dystopia, in which the incentive to produce creatively would be stifled by a centralized government taking over the means of production. The human spirit itself is crushed in Rand's work—as it is in George Orwell's *Nineteen Eighty-Four* (1949), which agrees with Rand on communism, although Orwell shared none of her fervor for capitalism. In Rand's view, current definitions of society—and perhaps society itself—would have to perish for the world to be rebuilt on individualist principles. Other European novelists, such as André Malraux and Ignacio Silone, have portrayed the positive and negative aspects of Marxist and communist revolutions in the twentieth century without resorting to Rand's absolutist rejection of socialist values.

An earlier generation of novelists—Henry James in the *Princess Casamassima* (1886) and Joseph Conrad in *The Secret Agent* (1907)—deal with revolutionaries, anarchist conspiracies, and other underground political activities, which remain staples of the political novel in writers as diverse as Rebecca West in *The Birds Fall Down* (1966) and Russell Banks in *The Darling* (2004).

Still other forms of the political novel focus on espionage and, especially, the Cold

War. Novelists such as Graham Greene, John le Carré, and Charles McCarry explore in considerable depth the cost of the Cold War to those nations that sought to maintain and, in some cases, extend their powers. The nature of covert work in organizations such as the Central Intelligence Agency (CIA) and MI5 (Great Britain's intelligence service) is detailed in Norman Mailer's *Harlot's Ghost* (1991) and le Carré's George Smiley novels.

A separate category might also be applied to the novels of writers such as Arthur Koestler (*Darkness at Noon*, 1940) and Conrad (*Nostromo*, 1904), both of which probe the nature of historical processes and question the course of the modern world. Orwell's fable *Animal Farm* (1945) as well as *Nineteen Eighty-Four* could belong to this category as well. Later novels in this category—Aleksandr Solzhenitsyn's *Odin den' Ivana Denisovicha* (1962; *One Day in the Life of Ivan Denisovich*, 1963) and *V kruge pervom* (1968; *The First Circle*, 1968), for example—explore how Stalinism and Soviet collectivism have attempted to destroy individual consciousness and to command the interpretation of history according to state dogma.

To some extent, all political novels project an idea or philosophy of history, a reading of where humanity is headed. Voltaire's *Candide: Ou, L'Optimisme* (1759; *Candide: Or, All for the Best*, 1759) is perhaps the earliest example of using a fictional narrative to comment on different forms of political organization and the way they impinge on the individual's life. Candide is exposed to an astonishing array of political systems and philosophies of government as well as to the faultiness of his mentor's optimistic claim that this is the best of all possible worlds. Similarly, William Godwin in *Things as They Are: Or, The Adventures Caleb Williams* (1794; also known as *The Adventures of Caleb Williams: Or, Things as They Are*; best known as *Caleb Williams*) used the plight of his protagonist to excoriate a British government bent on punishing dissenters and upholding a class system that threatened individual rights. The political novel yields an impressive panoply of approaches to imagining and assessing the way societies have been organized during the last 250 years.

Politicians and the political process

Both Sinclair Lewis and Robert Penn Warren focused on American forms of fascism that threatened to undermine American political institutions and to bring into disrepute the very nature of democracy. Lewis's *It Can't Happen Here* forecasts a nation so disheartened by the Depression that the calls for the equal distribution of wealth result in a kind of centralized police state. Liberal politicians such as President Franklin D. Roosevelt are unable to effect rapid change so the public turns to more radical solutions—just as the Germans, Italians, and Spaniards had done in Europe. Lewis's protagonist, Doremus Jessup, the liberal owner-editor of a small-town newspaper, heroically tries to resist the new dictatorial regime, but he is also part of the problem. Liberals are slow to heed the onset of evil, Lewis suggests.

In the novel, the country has to suffer a curtailment of liberty before it begins to right itself. As Joseph Blotner observes in his comprehensive study of the political novel, Lewis concludes that it is not outside forces that will subdue American democracy but rather a failure of will from within, of the "conscientious, respectable, lazy-minded Doremus Jessups who have let the demagogue wriggle in, without fierce enough protest." Liberals did not believe a dictatorship could form in the United States—that fascism could prevail in America—and Lewis set out to show just how wrong they might be.

Warren analyzed another weakness of liberalism in his Pulitzer Prize-winning novel *All the King's Men*. While Warren's hero Willie Stark was inspired by the career of Louisiana governor and senator Huey Long, Stark is more complex and tragic than his model. Warren's character begins as a naïve idealist who gradually realizes that he can do good only by becoming a part of the political system. He uses bribery and other forms of corruption to improve the lives of his state's citizens. In other words, he concludes that the end will justify the means—that he must use the corrupt practices in place to build a better world. However, Stark becomes in the process a dictator who does not merely put the idea of democracy in abeyance. On the contrary, he rules by force of personality to such an extent that there is no political system—only his power. This power was called Longism in Louisiana. Like Long in real life, Stark is assassinated, a victim of the unruly political passions that his own drive for power have provoked.

In the novels of Benjamin Disraeli and Anthony Trollope, the focus is on reform, on plots and characters that reveal the corruption at the heart of the British political system and the efforts of their heroes to expose injustice and restore a measure of fairness and truly representative government. Both writers deal with political institutions in a much more concrete fashion than do Lewis or Warren. In *Phineas Finn, the Irish Member* (1867-1869, serial; 1869, book), Trollope explores the career of a Liberal member of Parliament. Disraeli used novels such as *Sybil: Or, The Two Nations* (1845) to show how his Conservative Party could renew itself by addressing the inequities of society. Trollope based his characters on actual politicians and on the parliamentary process in *Phineas Redux* (1873-1874, serial; 1874, book) and *The Prime Minister* (1875-1876, serial; 1876, book).

THE HISTORICAL NOVEL OF POLITICS

Perhaps no novelist has devoted more careful attention to the lives and politics of political figures than has Gore Vidal. In *Lincoln* (1984) and *Burr* he not only creates vivid portraits of historical figures, he also shows them in political combat, so to speak. Thus, Thomas Jefferson becomes, in Aaron's Burr's narrative, a shifty, untrustworthy ally—much more of an opportunist than most historians and biographers are willing to concede. Burr becomes a perceptive dissenter free of the cant that Jefferson and his followers use to cloak their crude desire for power. Vidal's other political novels include *Washington, D.C.* (1967), *1876* (1976), *Empire* (1987), and *Hollywood: A Novel of America in the 1920's* (1990).

Postmodern novels go beyond Vidal's approach of reinterpreting history by also offering alternative scenarios and clearly fictionalized plots that nevertheless attempt to strike at the heart of what certain historical periods signify. Thus, in Robert Coover's *The Public Burning*, convicted American spies Julius and Ethel Rosenberg are publicly burned rather than executed in the electric chair because Coover believes their trial and conviction are part of the paranoid atavistic mood of 1950's America. During this time, tales of communist subversives planning to take over the free world are the equivalent of seventeenth century tales of witchcraft that led to the burning of dissenters or "witches" at the stake. From Coover's perspective, Nixon's anticommunism becomes a projection onto the Rosenbergs of his own perverted desires that he cannot acknowledge but must somehow express. Nixon craves what he condemns.

The ideological political novel

The works of André Malraux and Ayn Rand represent two extremes of the ideological novel, the former seeking in Marxism and collectivism a more just, democratic world based on collective principles (what is best for humanity as a whole), and the latter arguing that human freedom depends on the unfettered energy and creativity of individuals. Unlike Malraux, who portrayed individuals as highly confused about their own natures and lacking in self-knowledge, Rand posited supremely confident individuals who not only knew their own minds but resisted the modern world's tendency to subject powerful minds and achievers to some kind of socially determined core of values. The individual in Rand's view could live only in and for him- or herself. Only by doing so did individuals contribute to the development of the world. So powerful was her notion that the modern world was attempting to enslave its greatest minds that Rand created in *Atlas Shrugged* a colony of superachievers that divorces itself from the world and attempts to create a new one based solely on the desires of its members to work (as artists, businessmen, and industrialists) for their own benefit.

Malraux's most important novel is *La Condition humaine* (1933; *Man's Fate*, 1934; also known as *Storm in Shanghai* and *Man's Estate*). Set during the Shanghai revolution of 1927, the story features an impressive array of characters of different nationalities and ideologies in conflict with themselves. Rather then seeing an intellectual, objective way out of this confusion—as Rand does in her portrayal of heroic individuals—Malraux sees in Marxism a vision of human solidarity, a fraternity of selves that collectively hold out at least the possibility of fighting for a fairer, more egalitarian world. Individuals cannot prevail; indeed the state of individuality is equated with solitude in Malraux's novels, and hence the need for a commitment to a cause greater than oneself.

The underground political novel

In *The Princess Casamassima* (1886), Henry James explores the coterie of revolutionaries residing in late nineteenth century London. Hyacinth Robinson's grandfather died on the barricades in the French Revolution, and Hyacinth has been educated by a man involved in the revolutionary French Commune of 1871. Feeling the pressures of radicalism—a fervent desire to fundamentally change the world—Robinson vows to continue the cause, but then he is smitten by Princess Casamassima and as a result begins to question his devotion to revolution. The idea of obliterating the world the princess represents appalls him and eventually—unable to reconcile his conflicting feelings—he kills himself. James points out the way revolutionary politics tends to obliterate individual rights, even though revolutionaries argue they are fighting for a better, more equal world.

Similarly, in *The Birds Fall Down*, Rebecca West focuses on Kamensky, a double agent who works for a czarist aristocrat but also for the revolutionaries. Based on the case of an actual double agent known as Azeff, West's novel explores the conflicting claims of status quo (tradition) and revolution (change). Individuals torn between the two sides reflect the novelist's own ambivalent attitude about how best to improve the world while also preserving those aspects of government and society that remain essential to securing individual liberty and freedom of conscience. Joseph Conrad heavily influenced West. Her decision to set *The Birds Fall Down* shortly before the Russian Revolution aligns her with her illustrious predecessors, whose novels about the conflicting emotions of revolutionaries seem, in retrospect, prophetic of the confused and ultimately self-defeating ideology that led to the rise and fall of communism and of the Soviet state.

The Cold War espionage novel

Like John le Carré, Charles McCarry uses his characters' biographies to encompass much of twentieth century political history. McCarry, a former employee of the CIA, has published a series of novels about spy hero Paul Christopher, a handsome Yale graduate and a poet. His father also was a spy; he was killed in Berlin in a setup by the Soviets. Christopher's mother, a courageous German woman against Nazi ideology, who aided many Jews to escape the Third Reich, was sent to a concentration camp during the war and then vanished. Each novel is a revelation, delving into Christopher's background and the widening network of contacts that implicate him in the major events of the Cold War. To read the sequence of the Paul Christopher novels is to not only journey through the complexity of contemporary history but also to revise perceptions of Christopher himself, just as perceptions of le Carré's George Smiley evolve from one novel to the next. Thus, biography, history, and psychology are melded into the plots of spy novels that are also contributions to political history.

Although well-known as a critic of American political institutions, Norman Mailer's view of the CIA is curiously positive—even heroic—when compared to McCarry's and le Carré's handling of intelligence agencies. In Mailer's *Harlot's Ghost*, the novel's protagonist, Harry Hubbard, is a protégé of the legendary Hugh Tremont Montague (Harlot) and a key participant in CIA operations in Berlin, Miami, Cuba, Uruguay, and Washington, D.C. Mailer's novel derives from a close reading of nearly one hundred books about the organization; it is also a harping on his well-worn subjects: the murder of Marilyn Monroe, Ernest Hemingway's suicide, and the nature of Fidel Castro's heroism. Mailer portrays the CIA operative as a deceiver, a person who is playing more than one role, an actor whose sense of reality is constantly shifting, making it difficult to maintain loyalties and friendships, never sure of his or her own ground.

Harry Hubbard, the son of a fabled CIA agent, is a typical Mailer hero worried that he is not "tough enough" and takes on risky ventures such as the Bay of Pigs fiasco. As a matter of survival within the agency, he finds himself acting as a double agent—at one point reporting to both his mentor, Harlot, and to his father, Cal. Through Harry's letters, diaries, and first-person narrative, Mailer manages to cover most of the dramatic events involving the CIA from 1955 to 1963.

The political novel and historical process

In *Darkness at Noon*, Arthur Koestler set the pattern of the postwar political novel that examined the trajectory of twentieth century history. The novel is the story of Nicolas Rubashov, an old Bolshevik (a true believer in the Russian Revolution). He has been schooled to believe that the communists are on the right side of history. His Marxism preaches that there are laws of history that the Communist Party follows no matter how they contradict an individual's ideas and convictions. The party, not the individual conscience, rules. Rubashov struggles to maintain his faith even as he himself is incarcerated, a victim of the Stalinist purges, and awaits a public trial for crimes he did not commit. However, Rubashov has been an enforcer of communist dogma and thus realizes that his own blind fealty to an ideology has brought him to this evil end. By forsaking his own moral and ethical codes, he has made it possible for the state to dispose of individuals in accord with its own idea of revolutionary justice and history.

The revolution that is eating its own in *Darkness at Noon* becomes in Orwell's *Nineteen Eighty-Four* a totalitarian state that is constantly at war, rewriting history to suit whatever political line the state currently pursues and treating all individuals as merely tools in a collective enterprise watched over by Big Brother on television screens. The fate of the old Bolsheviks has now become everyday reality for the state's subjects.

From its inception in novels such as *Candide* and *Things as They Are*, the political novel has examined the basis on which modern society is organized. Certain political novelists—such as Conrad and James—do not seek to impose a view of history or of political events, except when they are exploring the inherent ambiguity and cross-purposes of their characters. Other novelists, such as Rand and Malraux, have an agenda, an argument they wish to propose as a solution to political problems. Other novelists, such as Koestler, demonstrate the futility of relying on ideology. West implies that the human character is too complex for a single system of thought to prevail and prove capable of governing the world. Still other novelists, such as McCarry and le Carré, have main protagonists who struggle to make the best of their flawed ideologies. Whereas traditionalists such as Vidal write from a coherent, liberal point of view, postmodernists such as Coover question both liberal and conservative principles, seeking to show that politics is not based on an objective reality, which Rand believed in, but rather on the human power to imagine and fabricate multiple ideologies, a power that leads postmodernists to the point of radical skepticism.

Carl Rollyson

BIBLIOGRAPHY

Blotner, Joseph. *The Political Novel.* 1955. Reprint. Westport, Conn.: Greenwood Press, 1979. Dated but comprehensive and important study of the genre, with short sections on significant political novels published since the eighteenth century. Also focuses on the role of women and on moral problems and values, international communism, proletarian literature, and imperialism. Bibliography divided into sections on American, English, Italian, German, French, Russian, and South African novels.

Boyers, Robert. *Atrocity and Amnesia: The Political Novel Since 1945.* New York: Oxford University Press, 1985. Chapters on Graham Greene, V. S. Naipaul, Aleksandr Solzhenitsyn, Nadine Gordimer, Günter Grass, Milan Kundera, and Holocaust fiction. A wide-ranging interpretation of individual novelists but also of the genre, including its treatment of time and ethics.

Cawelti, John G., and Bruce A. Rosenberg. *The Spy Story.* Chicago: University of Chicago Press, 1987. Examines spy fiction as a way of exploring the complex and bewildering nature of twentieth century political institutions and groups. Argues that the secret agent represents the divided feelings of society. Discusses the work of Graham Greene, John le Carré, and others. Includes several bibliographies of spy novels, films, writers, and themes.

Crossman, Richard, ed. *The God That Failed.* New York: Columbia University Press, 2001. Originally published in 1950, this collection of essays is now a classic. Several distinguished writers, including Arthur Koestler, Ignazio Silone, Richard Wright, and Stephen Spender, describe their attraction to communism and why they ultimately rejected Marxism. An indispensable guide to studying political novels that deal with the development and demise of communism.

Harris, Sharon M, ed. *Redefining the Political Novel: American Women Writers, 1797-1901.* Knoxville: University of Tennessee Press, 1995. Study of American women writers of political novels who crafted their works long before women were assumed to have written such books. Especially valuable for its examination of how women helped to shape the male-dominated genre, despite cultural assumptions that women wrote "social commentaries" rather than political critiques, fictional or otherwise.

Howe, Irving. *Politics and the Novel.* Chicago: Ivan R. Dee, 2002. A classic study of the genre, with chapters on Henry James, André Malraux, Ignazio Silone, Joseph Conrad, and Fyodor Dostoevsky, as well as comprehensive discussions of the genre and the political world its seeks to describe and interpret.

Lord, Ursula. *Solitude Versus Solidarity in the Novels of Joseph Conrad: Political and Epistemological Implications of Narrative Innovation.* Montreal: McGill-Queen's University Press, 1998. Although Lord focuses on Conrad, her introduction is a wide-ranging study of the impact of thinkers such as Karl Marx and Charles Darwin on nineteenth century British political fiction.

Suleiman, S. R. *Authoritarian Fictions: The Ideological Novel as a Literary Genre.* Princeton, N.J.: Princeton University Press, 1983. Focuses on French political novels by André Malraux, Jean-Paul Sartre, and Louis Aragon while exploring the way these ideological narratives challenge the premises of realistic novels.

Woods, Brett F. *Neutral Ground: A Political History of Espionage Fiction.* New York: Algora, 2008. Examines the manner in which contemporary international events have shaped the themes of political novels. Includes a bibliography.

Zinsser, William, ed. *Paths of Resistance: The Art and Craft of the Political Novel.* Boston: Houghton Mifflin, 1989. Essays by Isabel Allende, Robert Stone, Charles McCarry and others explore the role of politics in literature. Although these pieces may be regarded as special pleading for each author's respective work, the volume nevertheless is insightful as the novelists regard such matters as fidelity to fact, to ideas, and to the moral and ethical implications of political writing.

VICENTE BLASCO IBÁÑEZ

Born: Valencia, Spain; January 29, 1867
Died: Menton, France; January 28, 1928

PRINCIPAL LONG FICTION
Arroz y tartana, 1894 (*The Three Roses*, 1932)
Flor de mayo, 1895 (*The Mayflower: A Tale of the Valencian Seashore*, 1921)
La barraca, 1898 (*The Cabin*, 1917; also known as *The Holding*, 1993)
Entre naranjos, 1900 (*The Torrent*, 1921)
Sónnica la cortesana, 1901 (*Sonnica*, 1912)
Cañas y barro, 1902 (*Reeds and Mud*, 1928)
Los muertos mandan, 1902 (*The Dead Command*, 1919)
La catedral, 1903 (*The Shadow of the Cathedral*, 1909)
El intruso, 1904 (*The Intruder*, 1928)
La bodega, 1905 (*The Fruit of the Vine*, 1919)
La horda, 1905 (*The Mob*, 1927)
La maja desnuda, 1906 (*Woman Triumphant*, 1920)
La voluntad de vivir, 1907
Sangre y arena, 1908 (*The Blood of the Arena*, 1911; better known as *Blood and Sand*, 1913)
Luna Benamor, 1909 (includes short stories; English translation, 1919)
Los Argonautas, 1914
Los cuatro jinetes del Apocalipsis, 1916 (*The Four Horsemen of the Apocalypse*, 1918)
Mare Nostrum, 1918 (English translation, 1919)
Los enemigos de la mujer, 1919 (*The Enemies of Women*, 1920)
El paraíso de las mujeres, 1922 (*The Paradise of Women*, 1922)
La tierra de todos, 1922 (*The Temptress*, 1923)
La reina Calafia, 1923 (*Queen Calafia*, 1924)
El papa del mar, 1925 (*The Pope of the Sea: An Historic Medley*, 1927)
A los pies de Venus, 1926 (*The Borgias: Or, At the Feet of Venus*, 1930)
En busca del Gran Kan, 1929 (*Unknown Lands: The Story of Columbus*, 1929)
El Caballero de la Virgen, 1929 (*The Knight of the Virgin*, 1930)
El fantasma de las alas de oro, 1930 (*The Phantom with Wings of Gold*, 1931)

OTHER LITERARY FORMS

In addition to his novels, Vicente Blasco Ibáñez (BLAHS-koh ee-BAHN-yays) wrote early romances, including such works as the novella *El conde Garci-Fernández* (1928), *¡Por la patria! (Romeu el guerrillero)* (1888), *La araña negra* (1928; a collection of short fiction), and *¡Viva la república!* (1893-1894). Blasco Ibáñez later repudiated these early romances as unworthy of preservation. Blasco Ibáñez also wrote short stories and novelettes, including *Fantasías, leyendas, y tradiciones* (1887), *El adiós a Schubert* (1888; stories of a distinctly romantic nature and quite different from the author's mature pieces), and, later *Cuentos valencianos* (1896), *La condenada* (1899), *El préstamo de la difunta* (1921), *Novelas de la costa azul* (1924), and *Novelas de amor y de muerte* (1927). His nonfiction includes *Historia de la revolución española, 1808-1874* (1890-1892), *París: Impresiones de un emigrado* (1893), *En el país del arte* (1896; *In the Land of Art*, 1923), *Oriente* (1907), *Argentina y sus grandezas* (1910), the thirteen-volume *Historia de la guerra europea de 1914* (1914-1919), *El militarismo mejicano* (1920; *Mexico in Revolution*, 1920), the three-volume *La vuelta al mundo de un novelista* (1924-1925; *A Novelist's Tour of the World*, 1926); *Una nación secuestrada: Alfonso XIII desenmascarado* (1924; *Alfonso XIII Unmasked: The Military Terror in Spain*, 1924), *Lo que será la república española: Al país y al ejército* (1925), *Estudios literarios* (1933), and *Discursos literarios* (1966); and one play, *El juez* (pb. 1894). Translations of many of Blasco Ibáñez's short stories have been collected in *The Last Lion, and Other Tales* (1919) and *The Old Woman of the Movies, and Other Stories* (1925).

ACHIEVEMENTS

Vicente Blasco Ibáñez is probably the most widely read Spanish novelist, both in Spain and abroad, except for Miguel de Cervantes. Certainly he was one of the most prolific writers his country ever produced (his collected works run to forty volumes) a result of his extraordinarily dynamic and energetic nature and of his determination to show both the positive and the negative aspects of Spain to his countrymen and to the world.

Blasco Ibáñez has not received a balanced judgment from literary critics. Most have offered exaggerated praise or scorn for his works or have ignored him altogether. For many years, many Spanish critics denied the value of his novels because they rejected his radical political ideas, they envied his financial success, or they held a low opinion of his literary origins. (Blasco Ibáñez did not participate in some of the stylistic renovations of the *generación del 98*, or the Generation of '98, adhering instead to many of the realistic-naturalistic practices of the nineteenth century, thought by many to be out of date.) While Blasco Ibáñez's attacks on the Spanish political scene and eventual millionaire status led to ostracism by his Spanish contemporaries, such English-speaking critics as William Dean Howells, Havelock Ellis, Walter Starkie, Gerald Brenan, A. Grove Day, and Edgar Knowlson, Jr., offered a fairer perspective.

Certainly there are significant defects in some of Blasco Ibáñez's works. Without question, his early Valencian novels represent his greatest achievement, revealing a powerful double legacy that cannot be ignored: a pictorial, concrete, at times poetic style of strength and beauty, and a striking portrayal of human action. Later in his career, as Blasco Ibáñez strayed farther and farther from the format and the setting he knew best, the aesthetic value of his novels declined dramatically. While a definitive study of his total literary production remains to be done, analyses of individual novels have at least offered glimpses into the genuine artistry of his best works.

Biography

Vicente Blasco Ibáñez was born in a room over a corner grocery in Valencia on January 29, 1867. From his parents, he inherited the vigor of the Aragonese peasants, and from an impoverished childhood, he gained the spirit of struggle and defiance. During his early years, the lad of sturdy build, brown eyes, and curly hair could be seen more often walking the beach of nearby Cabañal or talking to fishermen and sailors than sitting at his desk in school. By the age of fourteen, he had written a cloak-and-dagger novel, by age fifteen had published a short story in the Valencian dialect, and by age sixteen had run away from the University of Valencia to Madrid. There, while doing secretarial work for the aging writer Manuel Fernández y González, he gained the inspiration for his first series of lengthy writings—a dozen romances that he later repudiated. By age seventeen, he had published a poem advocating chopping off all the crowned heads of Europe, starting with Spain.

The death of Alfonso XII in 1885 marked the young writer's start as republican conspirator and frequent political prisoner. After completing his law degree in 1888 and his first forced exile in France (brought on by increasingly anticlerical speeches), Blasco Ibáñez married his cousin, María Blasco del Cacho, who was to endure his tempestuous nature and stormy career. They had five children before their separation immediately prior to the outbreak of World War I. On November 12, 1894, Blasco Ibáñez released the first issue of *El pueblo*, a journal that he was to run virtually single-handedly and in which many of his best works would appear in serial form. It was into this enterprise that he poured all of his energy and stamina, as well as the entirety of his parents' inheritance.

Blasco Ibáñez proved to be a born leader of crowds, self-assured, fluent in his oratory, with a booming voice whose warmth quickly dispelled any first impression of coldness that might have been caused by his pointed beard, his mustache, and his aquiline nose. As time passed, he grew to be increasingly impulsive and impatient to eliminate the stupidity, ignorance, and laziness around him. Antireligious in a city venerated as the repository of the Holy Grail, and republican in a region noted for its conservative monarchism, he never avoided the chance for an iconoclastic stance.

Nevertheless, his election as the Valencian representative for the journal *Las cortes* in 1898 was the first of many. To his growing political fame was added an international literary reputation with the French translation of *The Cabin* in 1901. In 1904, he abandoned his home at La Malvarrosa on the Valencian shore to take up residence in Madrid and other Spanish cities.

The year 1909 found Blasco Ibáñez making two trips to Argentina, first to give lectures and subsequently to supervise the development of some new settlements. There he remained, fighting harsh climates and jungle dangers, until economic difficulties led him back to Europe immediately prior to World War I. Shortly afterward, he launched into a campaign to help the Allies, in the form of *Historia de la guerra europea de 1914*, speeches throughout neutral Spain, and several novels, of which *The Four Horsemen of the Apocalypse* had the greatest political and financial impact. When unexpected wealth poured in from this work's reprints, translations, and film rights, he moved to the French Riviera, where most of his last novels were written.

By 1925, Blasco Ibáñez had undertaken a triumphant tour of the United States, composing lengthy travel literature based on a six-month luxury-liner trip around the world, when he received news of the death of his wife. Within months, he married the daughter of a well-known Chilean general and soon thereafter, in failing health, retired to his Riviera home to churn out his final writings. The night before his sixty-first birthday, weakened by pneumonia, diabetes, and overwork, he died uttering the words "my garden, my garden," a reflection of his ardent desire to have his Menton garden resemble those of his beloved Valencia. In his will, he bequeathed his home to "all the writers of the world" and insisted that he not be buried in a nonrepublican Spain. On October 29, 1933, two years after the proclamation of the Second Republic, his body was moved to Valencia amid the impassioned eulogies of those who had scorned him years before. More than forty-seven years later, as renovations were undertaken on the Blasco Ibáñez home at La Malvarrosa, the first international symposium on Don Vicente's works was held, and a determination to rectify the critical neglect of his work was voiced.

Blasco Ibáñez was a man of action first and a writer second. His works bear a profound and constant autobiographical stamp—the mark of a rebel, a revolutionary journalist, a colonizer, a sailor, a fighter for the cause of peasants, fishermen, and slum dwellers, and an exile who attacked his government yet remained loyal to Spanish traditions, as reflected in his tireless efforts to glorify his country's imperial past and to combat the anti-Spanish legend. It is with at least some justification that he is remembered by many of his countrymen more for his life than for his writings.

Analysis

Following Vicente Blasco Ibáñez's first romances, five phases can be distinguished in the course of his prolific career. Into the first fall his Valencian works, from *The Three Roses* (which he considered his first novel) through *Reeds and Mud* and including two collections of stories, *Cuentos valencianos* and *La condenada*. Within this group, three works can be considered the novelist's masterpieces: *The Mayflower*, *The Cabin*, and *Reeds and Mud*. Second are his novels of social protest, written between 1903 and 1905 and dealing with the Catholic Church (*The Shadow of the Cathedral*, set in Toledo, and *The Intruder*, set in the Basque provinces) or with the exploitation of workers in vineyards and in large cities (*The Fruit of the Vine* and *The Mob*, set in Jérez de la Frontera and Madrid, respectively). "Art," the author explains, "should not be simply a mere manifestation of beauty. Art should be on the side of the needy defending forcefully those who are hungry for justice." Nevertheless, interminable didactic monologues, long ideological question-and-answer dialectics, and overtly symbolic characterization lessen the aesthetic worth of these works.

The third phase comprises psychological novels in which the author stresses character development within specific settings: *Woman Triumphant* (Madrid), *La voluntad de vivir* (the aristocracy of Madrid and Paris), *Blood and Sand* (bullfighting in Seville and Madrid), *The Dead Command* (Balearic Islands), and *Luna Benamor* (Gibraltar). While some of these works are admirable for their characterization and for their descriptions of landscape and local customs, they are clearly inferior to the Valencian writings. Fourth are cosmopolitan and war novels, including *Los Argonautas* (a detailed account of a transatlantic journey, envisioned as the first in a series of works dealing with Latin America) and several novels written to defend the Allied cause: *The Four Horsemen of the Apocalypse*, *Mare Nostrum*, *The Enemies of Women*, *The Temptress*, and *Queen Calafia*. These novels proved to be as popular as they were lacking in artistic merit. Finally, Blasco Ibáñez's fifth phase includes historical novels of Spanish glorification, ranging from the account of Pope Benedict XIII's life to the voyages of Columbus and a love story set in Monte Carlo.

In some ways, Blasco Ibáñez is a transitional figure between the age of the realistic novel (1870-1900) and the Generation of '98. Works such as *The Fruit of the Vine* and *The Mob* demonstrate his participation in the ninety-eighters' preoccupation with Spanish social issues, and most of his works, particularly in his early periods, reveal the extraordinary sensitivity to landscape that Pío Baroja's generation would display. Blasco Ibáñez's regionalistic *costumbrismo* and use of descriptive detail are techniques that relate him to the earlier generation of Benito Pérez Galdós and José María de Pereda.

It was Blasco Ibáñez who introduced the *pueblo*, rather than the middle class, as a frequent source for the novel's protagonist, a character who struggles heroically against his environment and his own animal instincts. A convincing narrative action of sharp contrasts; a pictorial, concrete, sensual, often impressionistic realism of strength and beauty; and an admirable tightness and unity of plot are the features that set the Valencian novels apart as his most accomplished works.

Blasco Ibáñez was not a contemplative man, and his themes, while relevant and often powerful, are not complex or subtle. His modes of characterization, his third phase notwithstanding, are a far cry from the probing, individualizing approach of most of the late nineteenth century realists. His figures lack depth, are often excessively masculine and melodramatic, and seldom rise above mere types. They can be divided into two classes: good and bad. These opposites are inevitably caught up in an eternal struggle with each other or with nature. There are few inner battles of conscience, few motivations aside from those of glory, power, sexual gratification, or mere survival. Nevertheless, Blasco Ibáñez's main type—the man of action, passion, animal instinct, and rebellion—is a graphic and powerful creation, made convincing by the sheer force of his portrayal, if not by any unique identity.

Batiste (*The Cabin*), Retor (*The Mayflower*), Toni (*Reeds and Mud*), and, in later novels, Sánchez Morueta (*The Intruder*), Gallardo (*Blood and Sand*), Centauro (*The Four Horsemen of the Apocalypse*), Ferragut (*Mare Nostrum*), and Renovales (*Woman Triumphant*) are such characters, presented in deliberate (albeit artificial) contrast to their opposites; these are weak and lazy types, such as Tonet (*The Mayflower*) and the other Tonet (*Reeds and Mud*). Blasco Ibáñez's women are also one-sided—oppressed and overworked domestics, conventional society figures, or women of action and conquest. The last group would include Dolores (*The Mayflower*), Neleta (*Reeds and Mud*), Leonora (*The Torrent*), Doña Sol (*Blood and Sand*), and la Marquesita (*The Fruit of the Vine*). Finally, one should note that, even if Blasco Ibáñez did not create great characters, he was able to succeed in capturing dramatically the heterogeneity of the masses. Pimentò of *The Cabin*, who represents the people of the region around the Valencian *huerta*, is one striking example of this skillful portrayal.

Although Blasco Ibáñez has often been referred to as the Spanish Zola, he rejected the naturalists' pseudoscientific, analytical approach and emphasis on crude detail, came to mitigate the impression of fatalistic determinism through his admiration of humankind's will to fight and a suggestion of optimism, and, finally, often presented a lighter, less objective, and more poetic tone than is the norm in Émile Zola's novels. Nevertheless, there are many moments in Blasco Ibáñez's work when a strong measure of pessimism and philosophical determinism or the use of unpleasant language and description demonstrate the influence of French naturalism.

Finally, one should not forget that Blasco Ibáñez produced some of the finest Spanish short stories of the modern era. One has only to look at the moving portrait of the protagonist of "Dimoni" to realize the author's skill in this genre. John B. Dalbor, the major critic to have undertaken detailed studies of these pieces, believes that many of the stories are in fact superior to the author's novels and that the very best of these stories are to be found in the collections *Cuentos valencianos*, *La condenada*, and *El préstamo de la difunta*. In the Valencian novels, Blasco Ibáñez's descriptive power—tumultuous, exuberant, dramatic, and exact—is most evident, a talent that sprang from keen observation and an uncanny ability to improvise.

THE MAYFLOWER

These virtues are evident in Blasco Ibáñez's second novel, *The Mayflower*, set in the fishing village of Cabañal; the descriptions of regional scenes and customs and many of the characters are typically drawn from observation at first hand. The plot concerns the struggles of the poor fishermen of the Valencia area. Pascualet, called "El Retor" because of his benign clerical appearance, works and saves so that some day he can afford his own boat and free himself from the demands of another captain. His spendthrift brother, Tonet, is lazy and hates manual labor. When their father is killed at sea, their mother, Tona, cleverly converts her husband's boat into a beach tavern, where she earns a meager but adequate living for the family. El Retor goes to sea as an apprentice, but Tonet turns to drink and women until he leaves for service in the navy. By this time, a child, Roseta, has been born of Tona's affair with a passing *carabinero*. When Tonet returns to find that his brother has married the seductive Dolores, he soon agrees to marry Rosario, who has waited for him for many years. Soon Tonet renews (unbeknown to El Retor) his previous youthful encounters with Dolores, and battles between the sisters-in-law increase in frequency and intensity, despite the attempts at reconciliation managed by the ancient village matriarch, Tía Picores. A boy born to El Retor and Dolores is actually Tonet's child.

After years of hard work and saving, and after a tense smuggling adventure that results in a considerable profit, El Retor is able to arrange for the building of the finest vessel ever seen in the village, named *Flor de Mayo* after the brand of tobacco that had been smuggled into Spain on the earlier trip. Prior to the ship's second sailing, Rosario reveals to El Retor that for years his brother has had an affair with Dolores and that his son is really Tonet's offspring. After a night of shock and humiliation and after refusing for the moment to avenge the affront by his brother, El Retor sets sail in one of the worst storms to afflict the coast of Cabañal. In a suspenseful and tumultuous final chapter, El Retor confronts his brother on board the *Flor de Mayo*, extracts a confession from him, and then refuses to give him the boat's single life jacket. Instead, he puts it on the boy and tosses him overboard. The lad is thrown upon the rocks, and the ship is ripped apart by the fury of the wind. Dolores and Rosario, watching the action from the shore, mourn their loss, and old Tía Picores shouts a final condemnation of the people of Valencia, who are ultimately responsible for the deaths the women have witnessed.

Blasco Ibáñez's viewpoint is usually one of relative neutrality and omniscience, and, as is the case with other Valencian novels, he frequently transports the reader through the minds of the various characters. Some subjective authorial control, however, is evident in the progressively dominant tone of fatalism, the use of situational irony, and moments of open humor.

The style is natural and spontaneous, at times distinctly colloquial. The reader is most impressed by the fresh, graphic, highly sensuous descriptive passages, lyric moments in which a vivid plasticity and an appeal to the senses predominate. Indeed, it seems logical that Blasco Ibáñez dedicated the novel to his childhood friend Joaquín Sorolla, the artist whose vivid transcription and dazzling colors are reflected in the novelist's prose. The reader is immersed in descriptions of Cabañal and of the sea. One can envision the dawn after a night of rain, hear the distant whistle of the first trains leaving Valencia, and smell the wet earth of the village streets and the strong odors (presented in naturalistic fashion) of the local fish market. Animal images abound, and the leitmotifs of human bestiality and the human-sea relationship are the two main elements around which the novel's symbolism is constructed. (The sea itself, for example, represents the inexorable force of destiny.)

The characters are generally flat, since Blasco Ibáñez's frequent suggestion of naturalistic predestination precludes any substantial psychological development. Rather, the author was more interested in description and in constructing a rapid, suspenseful plot line for the daily readers of *El pueblo*, in which the work first appeared. Tonet is pleasure-loving, unrepentant, lazy, and self-centered. His brother El Retor is the first of Blasco Ibáñez's strong heroes, trustworthy, naïve, hardworking, and stubborn. In the last two chapters, an introspective glimpse into his musings is of a kind almost unique among the Valencian novels; a long interior monologue suggestive of Miguel de Unamuno y Jugo's later portraits of inner conflict and uncertainty reveals that, if it were not for the pressures of time and the force of his own tumultuous nature, Blasco Ibáñez might have created psychological portraits of considerable depth. Finally, of some importance is the way in which the author develops the entire *pueblo* as a kind of mass character, accustomed to the hell of life's struggle and to the constant challenge of death.

The central thematic statement of the novel concerns humankind's futile fight against the bestiality of human instincts and the powerful forces of nature. Secondary themes include a condemnation of excessive pride, a parody of religious rituals, and criticism of the villagers' exploitation by the people of Valencia.

The novel's structure is built around two main lines of action: El Retor's attempts to escape from poverty and the adulterous relationship between Tonet and Dolores. As in a number of the later Valencian works, the plot follows a regular, unified pattern: several expository chapters, consisting of an episodic introduction and two chapters of retrospective background; after that, the main action develops as a rectilinear, basically causal progression, within which the main costumbristic "digressions" become integral parts of the whole (the market scene, the Good Friday procession, the smuggling expedition, and the blessing of the boats). The unity of *The Mayflower*, like that of the other novels of the period, derives above all from the fact that Blasco Ibáñez wrote with a clear goal: to capture a people and a region. The powerful descriptions and vigorous, dramatic depiction of the villagers' primitive and difficult existence are the narrative manifestations of this purpose and represent those aspects of the work that are of greatest value.

THE CABIN

Blasco Ibáñez's third Valencian novel, *The Cabin*, was his first universally acclaimed masterpiece. It developed as the final version of a short story that he composed while hiding from the police during four days in 1895. The plot is extremely simple, lacking any kind of secondary complication and moving without distraction toward the final tragedy. In the village of Alboraya, in the *huerta* region north of Valencia, Tío Barret is evicted by a usurious landlord, whom Barret then kills in a burst of anger. For ten years, the villagers prevent anyone from working the land, as revenge for Barret's fate and as a warning to other landowners against mistreatment of the *huertanos*. Nevertheless, Batiste and his family arrive to restore the property and its shack. Pimentô, the village bully and loafer and a local warden for the rationing of irrigation use, causes Batiste to lose his water rights.

Meanwhile, other members of the family suffer: The daughter Roseta's romance with the butcher's apprentice is destroyed, and the three boys must fight their way home from school every day. The youngest son is thrown into a slimy irrigation ditch, which leads to his death. At this point, the villagers seem to repent of their actions and take charge of the funeral. Soon, however, Batiste is lured into a tavern fight with Pimentò, which leads to their shooting each other. On the night Pimentò dies from his wounds, Batiste awakens to find the cabin on fire. As the shack burns, the villagers leave the family to their plight.

The style of *The Cabin* exhibits those attributes already mentioned. Moments of naturalistic delineation and melodramatic animal imagery are perhaps more frequent than in *The Mayflower*, and the color red becomes particularly prominent (linking images of blood, earth, the irrigation water, the fire, the tavern atmosphere, and so on). Batiste (the stoic, hardworking protagonist typical of Blasco Ibáñez's works) and Pimentò (the cowardly incarnation of collective egotism and laziness) are opposite, unidimensional poles of character presentation. The latter figure and the various representatives of the village "chorus" exemplify well the author's powerful glimpses of mass psychology.

Structurally, the novel demonstrates a typical plan: three introductory chapters concerning the arrival of Batiste and then the past tragedy of Tío Barret, four of increasing conflict, and three final chapters in which the boy's funeral suggests a momentary peace and the final disaster is presented. Each of the ten chapters is built tightly into an organic whole, yet each demonstrates a kind of aesthetic autonomy, focusing on a single incident or anecdote. A strict causal line and the careful use of foreshadowing, contrast, and leitmotif add to the impression of structural unity. Finally, cyclical factors are evident, as Barret's story at the start and Batiste's fate at the end are meant to appear similar.

A sense of fatalism and inevitability, similar to that of *The Mayflower*, is created as thematic statements are made in condemnation of the landowners' exploitation and the hypocrisy and pride of the villagers, and in support of the will to struggle for individual liberty and the need to curb one's bestial instincts, to fight against nature and the influence of collective heredity.

The novel, then, is concerned with humankind's courageous attempts to overcome nearly insurmountable obstacles. This struggle is presented on two main levels, one socioeconomic and regional, the other of universal dimensions. Batiste finds work but discovers that he must betray his fellow *huertanos* in breaking the boycott against using forbidden lands. Blasco Ibáñez, however, is ambiguous in his loyalties; one first feels sympathy for the tenant farmers as Tío Barret's eviction is described, only to have one's allegiance shift to a man fighting against the farmer's prejudice and conservatism. The author admires worker solidarity but also respects Batiste's determination to better himself. This confusion, R. A. Cardwell believes, "might be counted the major flaw of the novel." The ending is also ambiguous.

At first glance the ending seems to demonstrate Blasco Ibáñez's pessimism about the power of society and tradition in thwarting individual enterprise, but on a deeper level it may suggest the author's optimism about a person's capacity for courageous struggle and a faint hope for eventual success. This ambiguity, in turn, relates to the universal level of meaning inherent in this and other Valencian novels. Humanity will continue to fight throughout the cyclical pattern of human existence. Blasco Ibáñez's novel thus suggests (albeit subtly) the final stage of the realistic movement of the 1890's, in which the materialistic naturalism of the previous decade gave way to idealistic themes of the need for human understanding and sympathy.

Within the trajectory of the Valencian works themselves, *The Cabin* seems to represent a middle position between the emphasis on socioeconomic concerns of *The Three Roses* and a later emphasis on the way a person acts when confronted by the universal laws of an all-powerful nature. *Reeds and Mud*, with its extraordinary depiction of such natural forces, is the most powerful expression of this subsequent focus.

REEDS AND MUD

While not recognized as such by all the critics, Blasco Ibáñez's last Valencian novel, *Reeds and Mud*, is probably his single greatest literary achievement. "It is the one work," the author confided to his friend Camilo Pitollet, "which holds for me the happiest memories, the one which I composed with the most solidity, the one which I think is the most rounded." The novel is one of the most thorough adaptations by any major Spanish writer of the tenets of French naturalism.

The scene is set between 1890 and 1900 in the swamplike region of the Albufera lake near Valencia, an area known to Blasco Ibáñez's non-Valencian readers for its rice fields and plentiful game birds. The narrative itself is constructed on three levels: first, the story of three generations—the old fisherman Tío Paloma, his hardworking son, Toni, and his rebellious, irresponsible grandson, Tonet; second, the lush, all-pervading atmosphere of the Albufera; and third, a constant, "transcendent" feeling of the power of destiny, the irrevocable pressures of an abstract, deterministic force.

The plot demonstrates the sharp singleness of effect that one generally finds in a short story and traces the love affair between Tonet and Neleta from childhood to disaster, years later. While the lad is away at war, the latter marries a sickly but rich tavern owner, Cañamèl, to escape her impoverished existence. The subsequent illicit love affair between Tonet and Neleta leads to a series of events in which humans are again shown to be defenseless against the destructive forces of nature and animal instinct. Tonet suffers an emotional breakdown. Cañamèl dies after specifying in his will that Neleta cannot retain their property if she remarries or associates in an intimate way with another man. After Neleta gives birth to Tonet's child, she refuses to see her lover openly and orders him to abandon the child in the city across the lake, to escape further suspicion of violating the terms of the will. Instead, fear, remorse, and accidents of fate lead Tonet to throw the infant into the lake. When his dog later discovers the baby's corpse, Tonet seeks escape from life's misery in suicide.

Blasco Ibáñez's skillful shifts in point of view contribute a great deal to the novel's sense of realism. Such shifts frequently reveal a single incident from several different perspectives. Despite the strong measure of objectivity and the relative lack of overt authorial comment, Blasco Ibáñez's humor breaks through now and then as a means of comic relief from the growing tension of the plot line; this is noticeable, for example, in the juvenile enthusiasm of Don Joaquín during a hunting incident and Sangonera's "religious love affair" with the three *pucheros*. Above all, *Reeds and Mud* includes Blasco Ibáñez's most striking descriptive passages, revealing the freshness, the spontaneity, the richness and sensual power that constitute his most significant artistic contribution.

As always with the Valencian novels, no figures are presented in great depth. Each seems to represent dominant passions or vices: laziness (Tonet), drunkenness (Sangonera), avarice (Neleta), the will to work and struggle (Toni), hatred for the changing times (Paloma), and so on. Certainly, all the characters are seen to blend in naturalistic fashion into the landscape around them (although they stand alongside nature rather than being consistently overpowered by it). Tonet is a victim of his own weaknesses: his indifference, his laziness, his hypocrisy, his yearning for adventure, and (under the influence of Neleta) his greed. Caught between the philosophies of his father and grandfather, Tonet is unable to shake off his inertia to make any decision regarding his life. Neleta comes also to represent the force and fecundity of nature. Sangonera, one of Blasco Ibáñez's most memorable types, is at the same time comic and pathetic, a kind of nineteenth century hippie or a modern version of the Golden Age *gracioso*, the comic "servant" who nevertheless is able to utter some very wise convictions. Toni corresponds to Batiste of *The Cabin* and to El Retor of *The Mayflower*, demonstrating the persistence, hard work, self-denial, and undying spirit of struggle that the author so admired.

Thematically, *Reeds and Mud* reveals the fullness of Blasco Ibáñez's acceptance of many tenets of the naturalists' philosophy. The human battle against the bestiality of human instincts and the powerful forces of nature is once again shown to be futile. Precluding an entirely naturalistic interpretation, however, are such factors as the exaltation of Paloma's and Toni's respective kinds of strength, the absence of heredity as a significant force, and a few elements of sheer coincidence in the plot line. (The plot itself does not reveal the strict logic of *The Cabin*; Tonet's suicide, for example, is not really the necessary outcome of causal factors.) Other related but minor thematic concerns again include the condemnation of egotism and envy and a criticism of humankind's drive to accumulate material goods at the expense of nature.

The novel's structure follows Blasco Ibáñez's typical pattern. The main action builds to three peaks, in scenes of adultery, infanticide, and suicide. As usual, a series of techniques is employed to achieve the effect of extraordinary unity: causal links of plot; the skillful integration into the narrative of the main costumbristic scenes (in this case, there are three—the raffle of the best fishing locations, the Fiesta del Niño Jesús, and the hunting expeditions, or *tiradas*); parallels and corresponding incidents; and the skillful use of timing, contrast, and the repetition of leitmotifs. In *Reeds and Mud*, Blasco Ibáñez succeeds most fully in achieving the aim of the Valencian novels: the lifelike rendering (rather than didactic or moralistic evaluation) of a region—its people, its customs, its ambience.

THE FOUR HORSEMEN OF THE APOCALYPSE

Although far inferior artistically to the best of his Valencian novels, Blasco Ibáñez's greatest popular success was *The Four Horsemen of the Apocalypse*. Here the protagonist, Julio Desnoyers, is an elegant young Argentine whose father, a Frenchman, had migrated to Argentina because of the Franco-Prussian War of 1870-1871. After making his fortune in South America, the elder Desnoyers takes his family to Paris. Julio decides to marry Margarita Laurier, a frivolous divorcée, but the outbreak of World War I produces a profound change in the thinking of both. Margarita abandons her interests in fashion and social activities and dedicates herself to the wounded soldiers as a nurse. Julio enlists and sacrifices his life fighting the Germans.

The title derives from the biblical book of Revelation, which describes the four scourges of plague, war, hunger, and death—forces that, the elder Desnoyers prophesies, will walk the earth again. The novel was written as an instrument of propaganda for the Allied cause, and its major weakness is its heavy-handed and exaggerated condemnation not only of the German military establishment but also of the German people and the entirety of German culture. An extraordinarily detailed and vivid account of the Battle of the Marne is the novel's one positive achievement.

Blasco Ibáñez's works are, to say the least, uneven. While his later novels will doubtless continue to be read for years, it is his early masterpieces that earn for him a major place in modern Spanish literature. When adequate studies of his novels are produced and acceptable translations of his best works appear, the world will acknowledge his magnificent descriptions of land and sea and of regional life around Valencia and his powerful portraits of individuals struggling against overwhelming internal and external obstacles.

Jeremy T. Medina

OTHER MAJOR WORKS

SHORT FICTION: *Fantasías, leyendas, y tradiciones*, 1887; *El adiós a Schubert*, 1888; *Cuentos valencianos*, 1896; *La condenada*, 1899; *Luna Benamor*, 1909 (includes the novel of the same title; English translation, 1919); *The Last Lion, and Other Tales*, 1919; *El préstamo de la difunta*, 1921; *Novelas de la costa azul*, 1924; *The Old Woman of the Movies, and Other Stories*, 1925; *Novelas de amor y de muerte*, 1927.

PLAY: *El juez*, pb. 1894.

NONFICTION: *Historia de la revolución española, 1808-1874*, 1890-1892; *París: Impresiones de un emigrado*, 1893; *En el país del arte*, 1896 (*In the Land of Art*, 1923); *Oriente*, 1907; *Argentina y sus grandezas*, 1910; *Historia de la guerra europea de 1914*, 1914-1919 (13 volumes); *El militarismo mejicano*, 1920 (*Mexico in Revolution*, 1920);

Una nación secuestrada: Alfonso XIII desenmascarado, 1924 (*Alfonso XIII Unmasked: The Military Terror in Spain*, 1924); *La vuelta al mundo de un novelista*, 1924-1925 (3 volumes; *A Novelist's Tour of the World*, 1926); *Lo que será la república española: Al país y al ejército*, 1925; *Estudios literarios*, 1933; *Discursos literarios*, 1966.

MISCELLANEOUS: *Obras completas*, 1923-1934 (40 volumes); *Obras completas*, 1964-1965 (3 volumes).

BIBLIOGRAPHY

Anderson, Christopher L. *Primitives, Patriarchy, and the Picaresque in Blasco Ibáñez's "Cañas y barro."* Potomac, Md.: Scripta Humanistica, 1995. Anderson reevaluates the novel *Reeds and Mud*, focusing on the portrayal of its female characters, whom he considers within the context of a male-dominated society.

Anderson, Christopher L., and Paul C. Smith. *Vicente Blasco Ibañez: An Annotated Bibliography, 1975-2002*. Newark, Del.: Juan de la Cuesta, 2005. Extensively annotated compilation of writings by and about Blasco Ibáñez that updates Paul Smith's *Vicente Blasco Ibáñez: An Annotated Bibliography* (1976), which lists works published between 1882 and 1974.

Day, A. Grove, and Edgar C. Knowlton. *V. Blasco Ibáñez*. New York: Twayne, 1972. Survey of Blasco Ibáñez's life and canon that includes a discussion of his revolutionary influences, cosmopolitan experiences, interest in social protest and human psychology, glorification of Spain, and intense dislike of Germans.

Howells, William Dean. "The Fiction of Blasco Ibáñez." *Harper's* 131 (1915): 956-960. Howells, an American novelist and literary critic, praises Blasco Ibáñez's literary skill.

Medina, Jeremy T. *The Valencian Novels of Vicente Blasco Ibáñez*. Valencia, Spain: Albatros Ediciones, 1984. A study of five novels with themes relating to Valencia: *The Three Roses*, *The Mayflower*, *The Cabin*, *The Torrent*, and *Reeds and Mud*. Medina has written two other studies of Blasco Ibáñez's novels, both published by Albatros Ediciones. These studies are *The "Psychological" Novels of Vicente Blasco Ibáñez* (1990) and *From Sermon to Art: The Thesis Novels of Vicente Blasco Ibáñez* (1998).

Oxford, Jeffrey Thomas. *Vicente Blasco Ibáñez: Color Symbolism in Selected Novels*. New York: Peter Lang, 1997. Analyzes the use of color in some of Blasco Ibáñez's novels, arguing that although he was a naturalist, he often depicted life in a subjectively artificial way that belied the naturalists' attempt to objectively portray reality.

Swain, James O. *Vicente Blasco Ibáñez, General Study: Special Emphasis on Realistic Techniques*. Knoxville: University of Tennessee Press, 1959. A critical study of Blasco Ibáñez's work, with one chapter focusing on the realistic images of war in *The Four Horsemen of the Apocalypse*.

KAREL ČAPEK

Born: Malé Svatoňovice, Bohemia, Austro-Hungarian Empire (now in Czech Republic); January 9, 1890
Died: Prague, Czechoslovakia (now in Czech Republic); December 25, 1938

PRINCIPAL LONG FICTION
Továrna na absolutno, 1922 (*The Absolute at Large*, 1927)
Krakatit, 1924 (English translation, 1925)
Hordubal, 1933 (English translation, 1934)
Obyčejný život, 1934 (*An Ordinary Life*, 1936)
Povětroó, 1934 (Meteor, 1935)
Válka s mloky, 1936 (*The War with the Newts*, 1937)
První parta, 1937 (*The First Rescue Party*, 1939)
Život a dílo skladatele Foltýna, 1939 (*The Cheat*, 1941)

OTHER LITERARY FORMS

Apart from long fiction, Karel Čapek (CHAH-pehk) wrote many stories, travelogues, and plays. An important journalist, he published many of his *feuilletons* as well as his conversations with T. G. Masaryk, then president of Czechoslovakia. He also published a book on philosophy, *Pragmatismus* (1918), and a book of literary criticism, *Kritika slov* (1920).

Čapek's collections of short stories include *Zárivé hlubiny* (1916; with Josef Čapek); *Boží muka* (1917; *Wayside Crosses*, 2002); *Krakonošova zahrada* (1918); *Trapné povídky* (1921; *Money, and Other Stories*, 1929; also known as *Painful Tales*, 2002); *Povídky z druhé kapsy* and *Povídky z jedné kapsy* (1929; *Tales from Two Pockets*, 1932); *Devatero pohádek* (1931; *Fairy Tales*, 1933); and *Kniha apokryfů* (1946; *Apocryphal Stories*, 1949).

Among Čapek's most important plays are *R.U.R.: Rossum's Universal Robots* (pb. 1920; with Josef Čapek; English translation, 1923); *Ze života hmyzu* (pb. 1920; with Josef Čapek; *The Insect Play*, 1923; also known as *And So Infinitam: The Life of the Insects*, 1923); *Věc Makropulos* (pb. 1920; *The Macropulos Secret*, 1925); *Bílá nemoc* (1937; *Power and Glory*, 1938; also known as *The White Plague*, 1988); and *Matka* (pr., pb., 1938; *The Mother*, 1939).

ACHIEVEMENTS

Karel Čapek is among the best-known modern Czech writers. He became prominent between the two world wars and was recognized by and acquainted with such eminent figures as George Bernard Shaw, H. G. Wells, G. K. Chesterton, and Jules Romains. Čapek's international reputation earned for him the presidency of the Czechoslovak PEN Club, and he was suggested for the post of president of the International PEN Club, an honor that he declined. Though he was equally versatile in fiction and drama, his fame abroad rests mostly on his science-fiction play *R.U.R.*, written in collaboration with Josef Čapek, which introduced into the world vocabulary the Czech word *robot*, a neologism derived from the Czech *robota*, meaning forced labor.

Despite Čapek's lifelong interest in science and its destructive potential, examined in such novels as *The Absolute at Large* and *Krakatit*, and despite the worldwide fame that such science fantasies brought him, he is remembered in the Czech Republic as a dedicated humanist, a spokesperson for the tolerance, pragmatism, and pluralism best manifested in the philosophy of relativism that his works so creatively demonstrate. He was one of the strongest voices of his time against totalitarianism, be it fascist or communist.

Čapek's work is deeply philosophical, but in a manner that is accessible to a wide readership. He managed to achieve this with the help of a chatty, almost pedestrian style informed by a genuine belief in the reasonable person, one who is open to a rational argument when all else fails. Hence Čapek's humanism; hence, also, his disappointment when, after the infamous appeasement of 1938, he had to acknowledge that the very paragons of the democratic ideal and of Western culture, England and France, had sold out his country to the Nazis.

Such concerns of Čapek as the conflict between humankind's scientific achievements and the very survival of the human race—a conflict illustrated by the fight between the robots and human beings in *R.U.R.*—are not merely alive today but have become more and more pressing as the world is becoming increasingly aware of the threat of nuclear holocaust. Čapek was among the first to see the dangerous potential of humankind's creative ability, not because he was particularly gifted in science, but because he was quite realistic, approaching the tendencies of his time with the far-seeing and far-reaching attitude of one whose relativism was tempered by pessimism derived from his awareness of the past, the tradition from which the imperfect-but-perfectible human departed.

An urbane wit, a certain intimacy with the reader, deft characterization, and concise expression are the hallmarks of Čapek's style. This style heightens the impact of his fictional treatment of profound issues.

Biography

The youngest child of a country doctor, Karel Čapek was born in 1890 in Bohemia, then part of the Austro-Hungarian Empire. A weak and sickly boy, Čapek was pampered by his mother and protected by his older brother, Josef; they, together with his maternal grandmother, inspired him with a love for literature. Karel and Josef prepared themselves for a literary vocation by their prodigious reading in many foreign literatures; among Karel's juvenilia are some verses influenced by Symbolism and the Decadents—French and Czech. Josef was to collaborate with Karel on some of his most celebrated successes, including *R.U.R.*, but he was primarily a gifted artist, illustrator, and designer who gradually established himself as such, leaving Karel Čapek to write alone, though never really drifting spiritually, or even physically, far away.

A brilliant student, Karel Čapek enrolled at Charles University in Prague, though two stints took him to the University of Berlin and the University of Paris. In 1915, he earned his doctorate, having defended his dissertation on objective methods in aesthetics. The next year saw the publication of the short-story collection *Zářivé hlubiny*, written with Josef. This genre was particularly suited to Čapek's talents, and throughout his life he continued to write short stories: philosophical, mystical, detective, and apocryphal. Parody and satire, down to the political lampoon, are not rare among them; they seem to flow naturally from the day-to-day concerns of a journalist sharply reacting to the crises and momentous events of his time.

The first such event was the establishment of the Czechoslovak Republic in 1918, at which time Čapek worked for a National Democrat paper, switching in 1921 to the more liberal *Lindové noviny*, where he stayed to the end of his life. Čapek's youth and his middle age parallel the youth and growing pains of his country's first republic, right down to its (and his) death in 1938. Thus, Čapek is the literary embodiment of the principles of this republic, led by a philosopher-president, Masaryk; among these principles were a distrust of radical solutions, an accent on the small work on a human scale, and a faith in the goodwill of people. In this respect, one can consider Čapek an unofficial cultural ambassador to the world at large.

Čapek was not indifferent to the world: A cosmopolitan spirit, he was drawn toward England in particular, and he traveled widely, reporting on his travels in books on England, Holland, Italy, Spain, and Scandinavia. Indeed, he was a quintessential European, protesting the deteriorating situation in Europe before World War II, which he did not live to witness but the coming of which he foresaw only too clearly. This prescience is particularly evident in his novel *The War with the Newts*, a thinly disguised presentiment of the Orwellian battle of totalitarian superpowers that left Eastern Europe, after years of Nazi occupation, in the stranglehold of the Soviet Union.

Oddly enough, the fact that a Czech writer became known throughout the world did not result in adulation of Čapek by Czech readers and critics. On the contrary, it inspired jealous critical comments to the effect that Čapek in his unusual works was pandering to foreign tastes. In retrospect, this charge seems particularly unfair. Another oddity is that Čapek abandoned the theater after the worldwide success of *R.U.R.* and *The Insect Play*, chiefly producing short stories until his greatest triumph, the trilogy of philosophical novels *Hordubal*, *Meteor*, and *An Ordinary Life*. When, in 1937, he returned to the theater with *Power and Glory*, followed in 1938 by *The Mother*, it was to appeal to the conscience of the world with two timely plays concerned with the catastrophe prepared by Nazism. The plays were designed to counter the spirit of pacifism and appeasement then sweeping Europe; Čapek hoped to salvage Czechoslovakia, destined to be given to the Nazis as a peace offering.

Čapek's last work of great importance was *The Cheat*, written after the tragedy of Munich. Čapek mourned the death of his republic and yet inspired his compatriots not to despair. *The Cheat* breaks with the relativist philosophy common to all of his works: The cheat is a cheat, a fake, a swindler and not a composer, and the novel's many vantage points only underscore this judgment. Death overtook Čapek while he was writing the conclusion of the novel, on Christmas Day, 1938; for political reasons, his grateful readers were not permitted to say good-bye to him in a public ceremony. He was survived by Olga Scheinpflugová, an actor and writer, his companion and wife.

Though Čapek's life was comfortable in material terms, he lived with calcification of the spine, a painful condition that made full enjoyment of those comforts impossible; it also postponed his marriage to only a few years before his death. This physical suffering was accompanied by a spiritual search. For years, as the testimony of his literary works shows, he was content with pragmatism and relativism, though he was not an ethical relativist. Only toward the end of his life, as witness his last novel, did he embrace the idea that, often, people are what they seem, definitely and irrevocably: They are fully responsible for their actions.

Never does Čapek complain or rant against destiny: There is a sunny and humorous side to his work that balances the dark visions. Perhaps his excellence in life and art is explained by his personal heroism in alchemizing his suffering into a quest for a meaningful life.

Analysis

Karel Čapek was a philosophical writer par excellence regardless of the genre that he employed in a given work, but the form of long fiction in particular afforded him the amplitude to express complicated philosophical ideas. Thus, his greatest achievement is the trilogy consisting of *Hordubal*, *Meteor*, and *An Ordinary Life*. These three novels preserve the fruit of Čapek's life's work: the searching and finding of his many short stories, plays, and newspaper columns, as well as his lifelong preoccupation with the philosophy of pragmatism and relativism.

While the trilogy is a complex and at the same time harmonious statement of Čapek's philosophy, his last novel, *The Cheat*, though shorter than either of the three novels of the trilogy, is important for representing a sharp and shocking departure from the trilogy's philosophy. It represents a further development of Čapek's philosophical search.

Hordubal

Hordubal is based on a newspaper story of a crime that took place in the most backward region of prewar Czechoslovakia, the Transcarpathian Ukraine. Juraj Hordubal, an unsophisticated but very sensitive and even saintly peasant, returns from the United States, where he worked and made some money, to his wife Polana and daughter Hafia. He is unaware that in his absence, Polana has fallen in love with Stefan Manya, a Hungarian hired hand. To disguise this affair, Polana forces Manya to become engaged to the eleven-year-old Hafia. When this ruse does not work, the lovers kill Hordubal with a long needle. An investigation uncovers the crime and identifies the criminals, who are caught and punished.

Appropriating the bare facts of the newspaper report with minimal modifications, Čapek invests this simple tale of passion with philosophical depth, first by making Hordubal a rather sensitive man who is aware of the changed circumstances upon his return home. The reader is painfully aware of this when the author lets the reader follow Hordubal's thoughts in beautifully stylized, lyric passages of almost saintly insight and renunciation of violence, leading to the acceptance of his death. The tension develops on several levels simultaneously.

The first level is the *crime passionnelle*, the road that introduces us to the contrasting figures of Hordubal and Manya. A deeper level is attained when the reader perceives the cultural-ethnic contrast: Hordubal, the sedentary agricultural type, is opposed to the Hungarian Manya, the nomadic, violent type. Finally, there is the level on which the tension is between subjective reality, the reality of a given character who sees the world his or her own way, and objective reality. The conclusion, however, undercuts any confident faith in the existence of objective reality. Hordubal is seriously ill when he is murdered, so that a question arises whether the needle of the killer entered his heart before or after his death; if after, there was no murder.

The problem of the interpretation of even simple phenomena is brought to a head in the confrontation between two irreconcilable types of criminal investigations, based on different sets of assumptions and interpretations of events. In the conflict between the young police officer and his seasoned colleague, the deceptively simple case grows more and more complicated. In a plot twist that stresses the evanescent nature of humankind's certainties, the key evidence, Hordubal's heart, is lost in transport, condemning those involved in the investigation to eternal incertitude. The novel shakes the certitudes established in the mystery genre, suggesting that mutually exclusive interpretations are not only possible but also inevitable. More to the point, with the death of Hordubal, the protagonist's internal monologue ceases; the reader no longer sees Hordubal from inside. What the others think about Hordubal is widely off the mark.

METEOR

If the truth is relative and hopelessly compromised by the very fact that it is being approached by different people, the second novel of the trilogy reverses the procedure and asks if different people might not discover the truth on the basis of sharing with one another the human condition and thus having very much in common: first the difference, then the commonality. *Meteor* approaches this further elaboration of Čapek's philosophical quest in an original manner.

Čapek uses three narrators who speculate about the identity of a man fatally wounded in a plane crash and brought to a hospital as "patient X." The three narrators, including a Sister of Mercy, a clairvoyant, and a writer, try to reconstruct his life and the reason for his flight. The first narrator, the Sister, sees X as a young man who runs away from home unaware of the real meaning of love and responsibility. After some peregrinations, he decides to return home, only to crash and die in the process. The clairvoyant sees X as a talented chemist who discovered important new formulas but lacked the patience to see his experiments through and develop them commercially. When he finds that his experiments were founded on a sound basis, he decides to return and claim the discoveries as his own. The writer sees the patient as a victim of amnesia who falls in love with a Cuban girl but is unable to live without memory. When his suffering triggers the recovery of his past, the man flies home to lay claim to his position.

All three accounts differ from one another in approach and in substance, yet each of them identifies an important facet of the victim and provides an insight into the character of the individual narrator. Čapek thus raises the question of self-discovery, the perennial identity problem: What happens when X and the observer are one and the same person? The third novel of the trilogy, *An Ordinary Life*, provides the answer.

AN ORDINARY LIFE

A retired bureaucrat, a self-confessed "ordinary man," decides to write the story of his own life. Looking back, he concludes that he lived an ordinary life governed only by habit and chance; it seems repetitious and predictable to him. There are, however, a few incidents that do not fit this summary generalization of his life, and the more he thinks about them, the more fully he understands that right within his ordinary life, there is a multitude of lives: He as a person is not an individuality but a plurality. He, like a microcosm, mirrors the macrocosm of society. Does he have a stable point of view, or does it too change with each different personality as he comes to adopt it? This is not a case of a pathological disorder; the protagonist is a normal official who, before he settled down to his ways, explored radically different lifestyles. Like all people, he bears within him the potential for many selves, never fully realized.

Thus, the tension between subjective and objective reality that animates *Hordubal* collapses in *An Ordinary Life*. This third novel of the trilogy proposes that even that which is considered a subjective reality (the only accessible one, since the objective escapes forever) is itself a plurality.

As an experiment, as individual novels, and as a philosophical trilogy, these three novels are brilliant. What is difficult to communicate beyond the pale outlines and philosophical underpinnings of these works is their distinctive tone, their often lyric air. This atmosphere of numinous twilight, so difficult to communicate, bathes the novels in an unearthly light and adds to them a certain air of beauty. It comes as a surprise, then, that Čapek's last work, *The Cheat*, makes a departure from the finished whole of the trilogy on philosophical grounds.

THE CHEAT

The trilogy was the culmination of Čapek's work; the relativist philosophy enshrined within it is the summation of findings and beliefs that, for better or worse, animated Čapek's entire oeuvre. *The Cheat* continues with the insights gained in the trilogy—for example, the method of multiple narration is preserved. The several narratives, nine in all, gradually fill out the picture of the fake artist Foltýn, the would-be composer. These multiple narratives, however, do not yield a relativistic perspective: The individual accounts never contradict one another; rather, they gradually illuminate Foltýn and answer some of the questions that the various narrators have raised. The collective finding is damning, and yet there is something admirable in Foltýn: His obsessive love of art saves him from utter condemnation.

In his attempt to express the impossible, Foltýn is like every artist; every artist has a little Foltýn in him or her. It is only fitting, given Čapek's sense of balance, that, after providing in his trilogy examples of the power of art to do good, to express the truth, he should point to the capacity of art to profess evil. Thus, he embraced the totality of the world that his suffering enabled him to know intimately.

Peter Petro

OTHER MAJOR WORKS

SHORT FICTION: *Zářivé hlubiny*, 1916 (with Josef Čapek); *Boží muka*, 1917 (*Wayside Crosses*, 2002); *Krakonošova zahrada*, 1918 (with Josef Čapek); *Trapné povídky*, 1921 (*Money, and Other Stories*, 1929; also known as *Painful Tales*, 2002); *Povídky z druhé kapsy*, 1929 (*Tales from Two Pockets*, 1932); *Povídky z jedné kapsy*, 1929 (*Tales from Two Pockets*, 1932); *Devatero pohádek*, 1931 (*Fairy Tales*, 1933); *Kniha apokryfů*, 1946 (*Apocryphal Stories*, 1949); *Cross Roads*, 2002 (includes *Wayside Crosses* and *Painful Tales*).

PLAYS: *Lásky hra osudná*, pb. 1916 (wr. 1910; with Josef Čapek); *Loupežník*, pr., pb. 1920 (*The Robber*, 1931); *R.U.R.: Rossum's Universal Robots*, pb. 1920 (English translation, 1923); *Věc Makropulos*, pb. 1920 (*The Macropulos Secret*, 1925); *Ze života hmyzu*, pb. 1920 (with Josef Čapek; *The Insect Play*, 1923; also known as *And So Infinitam: The Life of the Insects*, 1923); *Adam Stvořitel*, pr., pb. 1927 (with Josef Čapek; *Adam the Creator*, 1929); *Bílá nemoc*, pr., pb. 1937 (*Power and Glory*, 1938; also known as *The White Plague*, 1988); *Matka*, pr., pb. 1938 (*The Mother*, 1939).

NONFICTION: *Pragmatismus*, 1918; *Kritika slov*, 1920; *O nejbližších vecech*, 1920 (*Intimate Things*, 1935); *Musaion*, 1920-1921; *Italské listy*, 1923 (*Letters from Italy*, 1929); *Anglické listy*, 1924 (*Letters from England*, 1925); *Hovory s T. G. Masarykem*, 1928-1935 (3 volumes; *President Masaryk Tells His Story*, 1934; also known as *Masaryk on Thought and Life*, 1938); *Zahradníkův rok*, 1929 (*The Gardener's Year*, 1931); *Výlet do Španěl*, 1930 (*Letters from Spain*, 1931); *Marsyas*, 1931 (*In Praise of Newspapers: And Other Essays On the Margins of Literature*, 1951); *O věcech obecných: Čili, Zóon politikon*,

1932; *Obrázky z Holandska,* 1932 (*Letters from Holland,* 1933); *Dášeňka,* 1933 (*Dashenka,* 1940); *Cesta na sever,* 1936 (*Travels in the North,* 1939); *Měl jsem psa a kočku,* 1939 (*I Had a Dog and a Cat,* 1940); *Obrázky z domova,* 1953; *Veci kolemnás,* 1954; *Poznámky o tvorbě,* 1959; *Viktor Dyk-S. K. Neumann-bratří Č.: Korespondence z let 1905-1918,* 1962.

TRANSLATION: *Francouzská poesie nové doby,* 1920 (of French poetry).

BIBLIOGRAPHY

Bradbrook, Bohuslava R. *Karel Čapek: In Pursuit of Truth, Tolerance, and Trust.* Portland, Oreg.: Sussex Academic Press, 1998. A critical reevaluation of Čapek's work. Bradbrook discusses Čapek's many intellectual interests, including his search for truth and his appreciation of science and technology. Includes a bibliography and an index.

_____. "Karel Čapek's Contribution to Czech National Literature." In *Czechoslovakia Past and Present,* edited by Miloslav Rechcigl. The Hague, the Netherlands: Mouton, 1968. Clearly places Čapek high on the list of notable Czech authors, demonstrating how much his writing affected other literary production in the country as well as making a political impact. Remarks perceptively on Čapek's inventiveness and on his ability to work in several genres.

Harkins, William E. *Karel Čapek.* New York: Columbia University Press, 1962. This carefully researched and well-written critical biography of Čapek remains one of the best available full-length sources on the author.

Klima, Ivan. *Karel Čapek: Life and Work.* Translated by Norma Comrada. Highland Park, Mich.: Catbird Press, 2002. Catbird Press, an American publisher of Czech literature in English translation, commissioned Klima, a Czech novelist and authority on Čapek, to write this critical biography. Klima analyzes Čapek's work, relating its themes to events in the author's life.

Kussi, Peter, ed. *Toward the Radical Center: A Karel Čapek Reader.* Highland Park, Mich.: Catbird Press, 1990. Kussi's introduction to this collection of Čapek's fiction, plays, and other work provides an excellent brief overview of Čapek's career. Includes a chronology and a helpful list of English translations of Čapek's writings.

Makin, Michael, and Jindrich Toman, eds. *On Karel Čapek.* Ann Arbor: Michigan Slavic Publications, 1992. Collection of conference papers examining Čapek as a modern storyteller, his versions of dystopia, his early work, his short stories, and his reception in the United States.

Mann, Erika. "A Last Conversation with Karel Čapek." *The Nation,* January 14, 1939. Although brief, this account by Thomas Mann's daughter of her last meeting with Čapek comments on the pressures Čapek found building up all around him, causing him to undergo a physical decline that eventually led to his death. She senses and comments on Čapek's sickness of the spirit that left him unwilling to continue living in the face of Adolf Hitler's growing fanaticism and power.

Matuska, Alexander. *Karel Čapek: An Essay*. Translated by Cathryn Alan. London: Allen and Unwin, 1964. An excellent account of Čapek's artistry. Discusses how he develops his themes, shapes his characterization, fashions his plots, and handles the details that underlie the structure of his work. This book remains a valuable resource.

Schubert, Peter Z. *The Narratives of Čapek and Cexov: A Typological Comparison of the Authors' World Views*. Bethesda, Md.: International Scholars, 1997. Although a somewhat difficult work for beginning students, this book proves valuable with its discussion of the themes of freedom, lack of communication, justice, and truth. Includes a separate section discussing the critical views of Čapek. The comprehensive bibliography alone makes this a volume well worth consulting.

Wellek, René. *Essays on Czech Literature*. The Hague, the Netherlands: Mouton, 1963. Wellek's essay, "Karel Čapek," which originally appeared in 1936, is one of the most searching pieces written about the author during his lifetime. Wellek comments on Čapek's relative youth and considers him at the height of his powers. When these words were written, Čapek had less than three years to live.

JOSEPH CONRAD
Jósef Teodor Konrad Nalecz Korzeniowski

Born: Near Berdyczów, Podolia, Poland (now Berdychiv, Ukraine); December 3, 1857
Died: Oswalds, Bishopsbourne, England; August 3, 1924

PRINCIPAL LONG FICTION
Almayer's Folly: A Story of an Eastern River, 1895
An Outcast of the Islands, 1896
The Children of the Sea: A Tale of the Forecastle, 1897 (republished as *The Nigger of the Narcissus: A Tale of the Sea*, 1898)
Heart of Darkness, 1899 (serial), 1902 (book)
Lord Jim, 1900
The Inheritors, 1901 (with Ford Madox Ford)
Romance, 1903 (with Ford)
Nostromo: A Tale of the Seaboard, 1904
The Secret Agent, 1907
The Nature of a Crime, 1909 (serial), 1924 (book; with Ford)
Under Western Eyes, 1911
Chance, 1913
Victory: An Island Tale, 1915
The Shadow-Line, 1917
The Arrow of Gold, 1919
The Rescue, 1920
The Rover, 1923
Suspense, 1925 (incomplete)

OTHER LITERARY FORMS

Joseph Conrad's many short stories were published in seven collected editions. The majority of the stories appeared earlier in magazine form, especially in *Blackwood's Magazine*, a periodical that Conrad referred to as "Maga." Of the short stories, three—"Youth," "The Secret Sharer," and "An Outpost of Progress"—have been widely anthologized and are generally recognized as classics of the genre. Two memoirs of Conrad's years at sea, *The Mirror of the Sea* (1906) and *Some Reminiscences* (1912), which is also known as *A Personal Record*, are prime sources of background information on Conrad's sea tales. Conrad wrote three plays: *The Secret Agent* (pb. 1921), a four-act adaptation of his novel that enjoyed a brief success on the London stage; and two short plays, *Laughing Anne* (pb. 1923) and *One Day More* (pr. 1905), which had no success. His oeuvre is rounded out by two books of essays on widely ranging topics, *Notes on Life and Letters* (1921) and *Last*

Joseph Conrad
(Library of Congress)

Essays (1926); a travel book, *Joseph Conrad's Diary of His Journey Up the Valley of the Congo in 1890* (1926); and the aborted novel *The Sisters*, left incomplete at his death in 1924 but published in fragment form in 1928.

Achievements

In the late twentieth century, Joseph Conrad enjoyed an extraordinary renaissance in readership and in critical attention. Readers and critics alike have come to recognize that although one of Conrad's last novels, *The Rover*, was published in the early 1920's, he is the most modern of writers in both theme and technique.

Conrad is, in fact, the architect of the modern psychological novel, with its emphasis on character and character analysis. For Conrad, people in plot situations, rather than plot situations themselves, are the primary concern. Indeed, Conrad once professed that he was incapable of creating "an effective lie," meaning a plot "that would sell and be admirable." This is something of an exaggeration, but the fact remains that Conrad's novels center on the solitary hero who, either by chance or by choice, is somehow alienated and set apart from his fellow human beings. This theme of isolation and alienation dominates Conrad's novels and spans his work from the early sea tales to the political novels to what Conrad called his "romances."

Conrad's "loners" are manifest everywhere in his work—Jim in *Lord Jim*, Kurtz in *Heart of Darkness*, Razumov in *Under Western Eyes*. This emphasis on the alienated and isolated figure had a considerable impact on the direction of the novel in the twentieth century, and Conrad's influence may be discerned in such disparate writers as Stephen Crane, F. Scott Fitzgerald, and T. S. Eliot.

Conrad made another contribution in shaping the modern novel: He was the forerunner (although not the originator) of two techniques that have found much favor and wide employment in the novel. Conrad was among the first of the modern novelists to employ multiple narrators, or shifting points of view, as he does in *Heart of Darkness* and *Lord Jim*. This technique enabled Conrad to make the probing analyses of characters and their motivations that are the hallmarks both of his work and of the work of so many others to follow. The reader sees both Kurtz and Jim, for example, through several pairs of eyes, some sympathetic, some not, before both tales are turned over to Charlie Marlow, who does his best to sort out the conflicting testimonies and to give the reader objective and rounded views of both men.

The extensive use of the flashback in the modern novel and, indeed, in film, is another technique that Conrad pioneered. In Conrad's case, as is the case with all writers who employ the technique, the flashback creates suspense, but it also serves another and more important function in his work, enabling him to examine more thoroughly the minds and the motivations of his characters. Having presented the crisis or the moment of action or the point of decision, Conrad then goes back in time, in an almost leisurely fashion, and retraces step-by-step the psychological pattern that led to the crisis, to the action, or to the decision.

Finally, Conrad finds a place and a role among the moderns in still another way: He is one of the great Symbolists in English literature. Conrad's use of thoroughly unconventional symbols, related in some way to the metaphysical metaphors to be found in much modern poetry, has had an inestimable influence on the modern novel.

Biography

Joseph Conrad was born Jósef Teodor Konrad Nalecz Korzeniowski on December 3, 1857, near the rural village of Berdyczów in Poland, under Russian domination. Conrad's mother, Ewa Bobrowski, came from an affluent and influential family of landowners who had made their peace, as best they could, with their Russian overlords. Conrad's father, Apollo Korzeniowski, was a would-be poet, a dedicated patriot, and a translator of William Shakespeare into Polish who found no peace in Russian Poland. The marriage of Apollo and Ewa was frowned upon by the Bobrowskis, who felt that Ewa had married beneath herself, and Ewa's brother, Tadeusz, a prominent lawyer and member of the landed gentry, seldom missed an opportunity to remind his nephew, Jósef, that he bore the tainted Nalecz blood.

Apollo Korzeniowski devoted all his energies and, ultimately, his life to the Polish freedom movement. As a result of his political activities, he was labeled an enemy of the state and exiled to Vologda in northern Russia. The five-year-old Jósef and his mother followed Apollo into exile. Three years later, her health ruined by the fierce Russian winters, Ewa Korzeniowski died, and Apollo, equally weakened by the ordeal, succumbed four years after his wife. There is little doubt that Conrad's own lifelong precarious physical state had its genesis in these years in exile.

From these blighted early years, two convictions were impressed in Conrad's consciousness that surfaced in his work: a continuing hatred for all things Russian and for autocratic regimes, and a strong sense of man as victim, instilled by his father's fate, and of man's essential loneliness and isolation, instilled by his own orphanage at the age of twelve. The victimization of the innocent lies at the heart of Conrad's political novels, especially *Under Western Eyes* and *The Secret Agent*, and is a major theme in *Heart of Darkness*. The alienated figure, forced to cope as best he can alone, is the essential Conrad.

With the deaths of Apollo and Ewa Korzeniowski, Conrad came under the tutelage of his concerned but somewhat demanding maternal uncle, Tadeusz Bobrowski. Bobrowski, a man of many affairs and very positive ideas and ideals, sent his young ward to St. Anne's School in Kraków for a brief term and later provided Conrad with a tutor and companion in the hope of creating a proper Polish gentleman. These few years constituted the extent of Conrad's formal education. An avid reader from his early childhood, Conrad was largely self-educated, and the wide knowledge of English, French, and Russian literature apparent in his works (especially in his critical essays) was acquired through his own efforts.

Bobrowski's hopes and plans for Conrad's becoming an accepted member of the right circles in Polish society were not to be realized. Chafing under the regimen of his oversolicitous uncle and, perhaps, convinced that there was no place for Apollo Korzienowski's son in Russian Poland, Conrad finally persuaded his reluctant uncle that his future lay elsewhere: at sea, a dream with which Conrad had been obsessed since seeing the Adriatic during a walking tour of northern Italy in 1873.

In 1874, Conrad left Poland for the port city of Marseilles, France, and the seaman's life to which he would devote the next twenty years. He carried with him his uncle's begrudging blessing and, more important, considerable financial support. The break with his native land was to be more complete than Conrad may have realized at the time, since he returned to Poland on only three occasions during the remainder of his life.

Conrad's adventures and misadventures during his four years in and about Marseilles provided the material, many years later, for the almost lyrical memoir *The Mirror of the*

Sea and the novel *The Arrow of Gold*, the latter of which has been the subject of much critical dispute. With his uncle's backing, Conrad acquired, during that time, part ownership of the bark *Tremolino*, which was then employed in smuggling arms for the Spanish Pretender, Don Carlos. It was a period of much intrigue, and Conrad appears to have been at the center, enjoying it hugely.

What is not clear about the Marseilles years, unless one accepts Conrad's highly fictionalized version of the events in *The Arrow of Gold*, is how his ventures at that time all came to a disastrous end. Conrad apparently invested a considerable sum of money in a quixotic mining venture. Moreover, if the Doña Rita of *The Arrow of Gold* did, in fact, exist as Conrad describes her in the novel, then a particularly painful and hopeless love affair complicated Conrad's desperate financial straits. In any event, in February, 1878, Conrad attempted suicide and almost succeeded by placing a bullet in his chest, very near the heart.

Uncle Tadeusz made a hasty trip to Marseilles and restored some kind of order to Conrad's tangled affairs, and, on April 24, 1878, Conrad signed on to the British ship *Mavis*, bound from Marseilles to England. Conrad's career as a seaman—more particularly, as a British seaman—had begun. In the next twenty years, sailing on a variety of ships on passages that encompassed half the globe, Conrad accomplished an incredible feat. An alien from a landlocked country, bearing an unpronounceable foreign name and speaking English with a strong Slavic-French accent, Conrad rose from able seaman to master mariner in the British Merchant Service. He took great pride in being addressed as Captain Korzeniowski, just as he took great pride in his British citizenship, acquired in 1885.

Many of the ships on which Conrad sailed make appearances in his works. For example, there actually was a *Narcissus* on which Conrad sailed from Bombay to Dunkirk and a *Palestine* that became the *Judea* of "Youth"; the SS *Roi des Belges* was the counterpart of Marlow's "tinpot" steamboat in *Heart of Darkness*. In similar fashion, many of Conrad's characters are based on real-life prototypes, men whom Conrad had encountered or of whom he had heard while at sea. These include the characters Jim, MacWhirr, Almayer, Axel Heyst, and Tom Lingard; the real-life Charlie Marlow was born Józef Korzeniowski.

In 1889, while between ships in London, Conrad began work on the strange tale of Kaspar Almayer. The work continued sporadically during Conrad's six-month tour in the Belgian Congo in 1890, a sojourn that later provided the material for his first major work, *Heart of Darkness*, and also succeeded in further undermining his already unstable health. In 1893, Conrad, then first mate of the ship *Torrens*, showed the nine completed chapters of *Almayer's Folly* to an English passenger and was encouraged to finish the book. *Almayer's Folly* was published in 1895, to be followed by *An Outcast of the Islands* in 1896, *The Nigger of the Narcissus* in 1897, *Heart of Darkness* (in serial form) in 1899, and *Lord Jim* in 1900.

Conrad enjoyed almost immediate critical acclaim, but despite the string of critical successes, he had only a modest public following. In fact, Conrad did not have a best seller until 1913, with *Chance*. Ironically, the reading public did not find Conrad until after he had written his best work. Given this limited popular success, Conrad did not feel secure enough to devote himself entirely to a writing career, and, for a six-year period, 1889 to 1895, he vacillated between the safety of a master's berth aboard ship and the uncertainty of his writing table. Even as late as 1898, when he was well established with a publisher and several reputable magazines were eager for his work, Conrad seriously considered returning to the sea.

With his marriage to Jessie George in 1894, Conrad had, in effect, returned from the sea and settled down to a life of hectic domesticity and long, agonizing hours of writing. Jessie, an unassuming, maternal woman, was the perfect mate for the often unpredictable, volatile, and ailing Conrad, and she cheerfully nursed him through his frequent attacks of malaria, gout, and deep depression. The marriage produced two sons, Borys and John, and lasted until Conrad's death.

Except for a brief trip to his native Poland in 1914, a few holidays on the Continent, and an even briefer trip to the United States in 1923, Conrad was resigned to the endless hours at his desk and content to live the life of an English gentleman in his adopted land. The Conrads were something of a nomadic family, however, moving frequently whenever Conrad tired of one of their rented dwellings. His last five years were spent at Oswalds, Bishopsbourne, near Canterbury.

After World War I, the acclaim and the recognition that he had so richly earned finally came to Conrad—an offer of knighthood (which he declined) and the friendship and the respect of many of the literary greats of the time. Essentially a very private man, Conrad, while never denying his Polish origins or renouncing his Roman Catholic faith, tried to live the quiet life of the quintessential English country squire. There was always, however, something of the foreigner about him—the monocle, the Continental-style greatcoat, the slightly Asian eyes, the click of the heels and the formal bow from the waist—which did not go unnoticed among his English friends and neighbors. Like so many of the characters in his novels, Conrad remained somehow apart and alienated from the mainstream of the life about him.

On August 3, 1924, Conrad succumbed to a massive heart attack at his home near Bishopsbourne. He is buried in the cemetery at Canterbury, in—according to the parish register of St. Thomas's Church—"that part reserved for Catholics." Even in death, Conrad, like so many of his fictional creations, found himself alone and apart.

ANALYSIS

Three themes are dominant among Joseph Conrad's sea tales, considered by most critics as his best work. The first of these themes is an unremitting sense of loyalty and duty to the ship; this quality is exemplified by Conrad's seamen who are successful in practicing their craft. In *The Mirror of the Sea*, Conrad summarizes this necessity for keeping faith, as he also does through Singleton, the exemplar of the faithful seaman in *The Nigger of the Narcissus*, in observing, "Ships are all right. It's the men in them." The note of fidelity is struck again in *A Personal Record*, when Conrad says of his years at sea, "I do not know whether I have been a good seaman, but I know I have been a very faithful one." Conversely, it is the men who break faith—Jim is the prime example—who fail and who are doomed to be set apart.

A second major theme in the sea tales, noted by virtually all of Conrad's critics, is the therapeutic value of work. To Conrad, the ancient adage "Idle hands are the devil's workshop" was not a cliché but a valid principle. The two most damning words in Conrad's lexicon are "undisciplined" and "lazy," and, again, it is the men whose hands and minds are without meaningful employment who get into difficulties, who fail, and who suffer the Conradian penalty for failure, alienation and isolation. Kurtz, in *Heart of Darkness*, is Conrad's chief exemplar here, but Jim's failure, too, partially results from the fact that he has very little to do in the way of work during the crucial passage aboard the *Patna*.

Finally, a sense of tradition, of one's place in the long continuum of men who have gone to sea, is a recurring theme in Conrad's sea tales. Marlow expresses this sense of tradition best when he speaks of the faithful seamen who band together and are bonded together in what he calls "the fellowship of the craft." The Jims, on the other hand, the captains who display cowardice, the seamen who panic under stress, all those who bring disgrace on the men who have kept faith and do keep faith, are dismissed from the fellowship and are set apart, isolated and alienated. Conrad, then, played a central role in setting the stage for the alienated, solitary figures and, ultimately, the rebels-at-arms who people the pages of the modern novel.

HEART OF DARKNESS

In *Heart of Darkness*, the first of Conrad's recognized masterpieces and one of the greatest novellas in the English language, a number of familiar Conradian themes and techniques coalesce: the author's detestation of autocratic regimes and their special manifestation, colonialism; the characteristic Conradian alien figure, isolated and apart; the therapeutic value of work; and the use of multiple points of view and of strikingly unconventional symbols.

Charlie Marlow, the ostensible narrator of the story, finds himself (as Conrad did on occasion during his sea career) without a ship and with few prospects. As a last resort, he signs on to command a river steamboat for a Belgian trading company, then seeking ivory in the Congo. In a curious way, Marlow's venture into the Congo represents a wish fulfillment, since, Marlow recalls, as a child he had placed his finger on a map of Africa and said, "Someday, I will go there," "there" being the Congo. (This is "autobiography as fiction" again in that Conrad himself had once expressed such a desire and in exactly the terms Marlow employs.)

The mature Marlow, however, has few illusions about what he is undertaking. He characterizes his "command" as "a two-penny-half-penny river-steamboat with a penny whistle attached," and he is quite aware that he will be working for a company whose chief concern is turning a profit, and a large one at that. Moreover, the Company's success will come only at the expense of the innocent and helpless natives who have the misfortune of living in an area that has immense possibilities as a colony.

Marlow, like Conrad, abhors the concept of one people dominating another unless, as he says, the colonizing power is faithful to the "idea" that provides the sole rationale for colonialism—that is, the "idea" of actually bringing the benefits of civilization to the colonized. He believes that only in the British Crown Colonies is the "idea" being adhered to, and he has grave reservations about what he will find in the Congo. Despite these reservations, Marlow is hardly prepared for what awaits him.

Marlow finds in the Congo disorder bordering on lunacy, waste, intrigue, inefficiency, and the cruelest kind of exploitation. The "pilgrims of progress," as Marlow calls them, go about their aimless and pointless tasks while the steamboat he is to command sits idle in the river with a hole in its bottom. Mountains are leveled to no purpose, while equipment and supplies rust or rot in the African sun or never reach their destination. As long as the ivory flows from the heart of darkness, however, no one is overly concerned. Marlow is appalled by the hypocrisy of the situation. An entire continent is being ruthlessly ravaged and pillaged in the name of progress, when, in fact, the real motivation is sheer greed. Nor is there the slightest concern for the plight of the natives in the Company's employ. Marlow sees once proud and strong tribesmen, divorced from their natural surroundings and from all that is familiar to them, sickened and weakened, sitting passively in the shade waiting to die.

Herein is Marlow/Conrad's chief objection to colonialism. By taking people from their normal mode of life and thrusting upon them a culture that they neither want nor understand, colonialism places people in isolation and makes them aliens in their own land. The cannibals who serve as woodcutters for Marlow's steamboat have lost their muscle tone and belong back in the jungle practicing the peculiar rites that, however revolting by other standards, are natural for them. The native fireman on the steamboat—"an improved specimen," Marlow calls him—watches the water gauge on the boiler, lest the god inside become angry. He sits, his teeth filed, his head shaved in strange patterns, a voodoo charm tied to his arm, a piece of polished bone inserted through his lower lip. He represents the perfect victim of the white man's progress, and "he ought to have been clapping his hands and stamping his feet on the bank."

The evil that colonialism has wrought is not, however, confined to the natives. The whites who seek adventure or fortune in the Congo are equally uprooted from all that is natural for them, equally isolated and alienated. The doctor who gives Marlow a perfunctory examination in the Company's headquarters in Brussels asks apologetically for permission to measure Marlow's head while, at the same time, noting that the significant changes will occur "inside." To some degree or other, such changes have come to the whites whom Marlow encounters in Africa. The ship on which Marlow sails to the Congo passes a French gunboat firing aimlessly into the jungle as an object lesson to the natives. The accountant at the Central Station makes perfectly correct entries in his impeccable ledgers while just outside his window, in the grove of death, the mass of displaced natives is dying of fever and malnutrition. The Company's brick maker makes no bricks because there has been no straw for more than a year, but he remains placid and unconcerned.

Marlow's summation of what he has seen in the Congo is acerbic, withering in its emotional intensity, but it is also an accurate statement of Conrad's feelings toward this, the cruelest exercise of autocratic power. Marlow says, "It was just robbery with violence, aggravated murder on a great scale . . . and with no more moral purpose at the back of it than there is in burglars breaking into a safe." The voice is Charlie Marlow's, but the sentiments are Joseph Conrad's.

One man alone among the Company's disreputable, if not depraved, white traders appears to be an exception, a man who is faithful to the "idea" and is bringing progress and betterment to the natives in exchange for the ivory he gathers. Kurtz is by far the Company's most productive trader, and his future in Brussels seems assured. At the same time, Kurtz is both hated and feared by all the Europeans in the Company's employ. He is hated because of the unconventional (an ironic adjective) methods he has adopted, and he is feared because these methods are apparently working.

With the introduction of Kurtz into the tale, Conrad works by indirection. Neither Marlow nor the reader is allowed to see Kurtz immediately. Rather, one is exposed to Kurtz through many different viewpoints, and, in an effort to allow the reader to see Kurtz from all perspectives, Conrad brings forth other narrators to take over the story briefly: the accountant, the brick maker, the manager of the Central Station, the Russian. Penultimately, Marlow himself serves as narrator, and ultimately, Kurtz's fiancé, the Intended. In addition to the many shifting points of view that Conrad employs, it should be noted that the story, from beginning to end, is told by a dual narrator. Charlie Marlow speaks, but Marlow's unnamed crony, the fifth member of the group gathered on the fantail of the *Nellie*, is the actual narrator of the story, retelling the tale as he has heard it from Marlow. In some sense, then, it is difficult to say whether *Heart of Darkness* is Kurtz's story or Marlow's story or the anonymous narrator's story, since Marlow's tale has obviously had a significant impact on the silent listener.

Marlow is fascinated by Kurtz and what his informants tell him of Kurtz, and throughout the long journey upriver to the Inner Station, he is obsessed with meeting this remarkable man, but he is destined for a shocking disappointment. Kurtz is perhaps the extreme example among all the isolated and alienated figures to be found in Conrad's works. Philosophically and spiritually alienated from the "pilgrims of progress," he is also physically isolated. He is the only white man at the Inner Station, and, given the steamboat debacle, nothing has been heard from or of him for months. He has been alone too long, and the jungle has found him out. He is, in Marlow's words, "a hollow man" with great plans and hopes but totally lacking in the inner resources vital for survival in an alien environment. As a result, he has regressed completely to the primitive state; he has become a god to the natives, who worship him in the course of "unspeakable rites." He has taken a native woman as a consort, and the Russian trader who tried to befriend him has been relegated to fool and jester in Kurtz's jungle court. Kurtz exercises absolute power of life and death over the natives, and he punishes his enemies by placing their severed heads on poles about his hut as ornaments. The doctor in Brussels, Marlow recalls, was fearful of what physical and spiritual isolation might do to people's minds, and on Kurtz, the effect has been devastating. Kurtz is mentally unbalanced, but even worse, as Marlow says, "His soul was mad."

Marlow has confessed that he, too, has heard the appeal of "the fascination of the abomination," the strange sounds and voices emanating from the banks of the river as the steamboat makes its way to Kurtz. Meaningless and unintelligible as the sounds and voices are, they are also somehow familiar to Marlow and strike deep at some primordial instinct within him. Yet, while Kurtz is destroyed, Marlow survives, "luckily, luckily," as he observes. The difference between the two men is restraint, a recurrent term in the novel: With restraint, a man can survive in isolation. The cannibals on the steamboat have it, and Marlow is at a loss to explain the phenomenon. The manager at the Central Station also has it, largely the result of his unfailing good health, which permits him to serve, virtually unscathed, term after term in the darkness. The accountant has restraint by virtue of concentrating on his correct entries in his meticulous ledgers and, at the same time, by forfeiting his humanity and closing his mind to the chaos around him.

Chiefly, however, restraint (in Conrad's worldview) is a function of work, and Conrad's major statement of the redeeming nature of work comes in *Heart of Darkness*. Marlow confesses that, like most human beings, he does not like work per se. He does, however, respond to "what is in the work," and he recognizes its salutary effect, "the chance to find yourself." Indeed, the fact that Marlow has work to do in the Congo is his salvation. The steamboat must be salvaged; it must be raised from the bottom of the river. No supplies are available, and the boiler is in disrepair. Marlow needs rivets and sheeting to patch the gaping hole in the boat. The task seems hopeless, but Marlow attacks it enthusiastically, almost joyously, because his preoccupation with rescuing his "two-penny, half-penny" command effectively shields him from "the fascination of the abomination." Later, during the trip upriver to the Inner Station, it is again the work of piloting the vulnerable steamboat around and through the myriad rocks and snags of the convoluted river and the intense concentration required for the work that shut Marlow's eyes and, more important, his mind to the dangers to psyche and spirit surrounding him. Marlow does not leave the Congo completely untouched; he has paid a price, both physically and mentally, for venturing into the darkness, but he does escape with his life and his sanity. As he later recognizes, he owes his escape to the steamboat, his "influential friend," as he calls it, and to the work it provided.

Symbols abound in *Heart of Darkness*, many of them conventional: the interplay of light and darkness throughout the novel, for example, carrying essentially the traditional symbolic meanings of the two terms, or the rusting and decaying equipment Marlow comes across at the Central Station, symbolizing the callous inefficiency of the Company's management. More striking, however, is Conrad's use of thoroughly unconventional symbols; dissimilar images are yoked together in a startling fashion, unique in Conrad's time. Kurtz's totally bald head, for example, is compared to a ball of ivory, and the comparison moves beyond metaphor to the realm of symbol, adumbrating the manner in which the lust for and preoccupation with ivory have turned flesh-and-blood human beings into cold, lifeless ivory figures. There are also the shrunken heads fixed as ornaments on the fence posts surrounding Kurtz's hut. These are Kurtz's "rebels," and, notably, all but one are facing inward, so that, even in death, they are compelled to worship their god. The one facing outward, however, is irretrievably damned and without hope of salvation.

LORD JIM

Similar in many ways to *Heart of Darkness*, *Lord Jim* is considered by many critics to be not only Conrad's greatest sea tale but also his greatest novel. *Lord Jim* is not a sea tale, however, in the purest sense, since most of the action of the novel takes place on land. *Lord Jim* is one of Conrad's psychological studies; Jim's mind and his motivations are searched and probed in meticulous detail in an effort to "see Jim clearly." In making this effort, Conrad employs two characteristic techniques: shifting, multiple points of view and the extensive use of flashbacks.

The narrative begins conventionally with an unnamed third-person narrator who brings the reader to the point of Marlow's first encounter with Jim at the Board of Inquiry investigating the strange case of the pilgrim ship *Patna*. At this point, Marlow takes over the tale, recounting his meeting with Jim. Marlow's account, however, is filtered through the consciousness of the anonymous narrator, much as is the case in *Heart of Darkness*. The manipulation of the narrative voices in *Lord Jim* is much more complex, however, since Jim speaks through Marlow and Marlow through the ultimate narrator.

Again, as in *Heart of Darkness*, other narrators enter the scene briefly, and Marlow gives way to a series of speakers, each of whom is qualified to tell the reader something more about Jim. Montague Brierly, captain of the crack ship *Ossa*, is troubled by Jim's failure to meet the demands of "the fellowship of the craft" and is also troubled by his doubts about his own ability to meet those demands. The French lieutenant who boarded the abandoned *Patna* and brought it safely to port is a bit more sympathetic toward Jim's moment of cowardice but is also more rigid in his condemnation of Jim's loss of honor. At the opposite end of the scale, Chester, the preposterous seaman-at-large, dismisses Jim's canceled mate's certificate as nothing more than "a bit of ass's skin" and solicits Marlow's aid in involving Jim in Chester's lunatic scheme of extracting guano from an island that is totally inaccessible. In Chester's view, Jim is the right man for the job, since he is now good for nothing else. Through Chester as interim narrator, Marlow recognizes how desperate Jim's plight is and how equally desperate Jim is for his help.

Marlow does help by putting Jim in touch with Mr. Denver, the owner of a rice mill, and Jim thrives for a time, becoming, in essence, a surrogate son to his employer. The specter of the *Patna* affair overtakes Jim, however, in the form of the fated ship's second engineer, who comes to work at the rice mill. Through Denver, through Egström, who employs Jim briefly as a water clerk, and, finally, through the seedy Schomberg, proprietor of an equally seedy hotel in Bangkok, Marlow learns of Jim's gradual decline and his erratic flight from the *Patna* or, as Marlow puts it, his flight "from himself."

In an attempt to help Jim, Marlow turns to Stein, an extraordinary trader and shrewd judge of both butterflies and people. Stein's eminently "practical" solution is to send Jim to Patusan, virtually the ends of the earth, where the *Patna* has never been heard of and from where Jim need run no more. Marlow's visit to Patusan and to Jim is relayed, as is the bulk of the novel, through the unnamed listener among Marlow's small circle of friends gathered over their evening cigars, to whom Marlow has been addressing his tale. In the final chapters, Conrad's tour de force of narrative technique takes yet another twist. The disaster in Patusan is recounted through the medium of a lengthy letter that Marlow writes to the ultimate narrator, the narration thus coming full circle from third-person narrator, to Marlow, to a series of intermediate narrators, and finally returning to the speaking voice that began the tale.

Adding to the difficulties that Conrad's dizzying shift of narrators presents for the reader is his frequent use of time shifts in the narrative. Jim's long colloquy with Marlow in Marlow's room at the Malabar House, for example, takes the reader back in time to the events aboard the *Patna*, which occurred several months earlier. While observing the seemingly bored Brierly in the courtroom at the Board of Inquiry, Marlow abruptly moves ahead in time to Brierly's suicide, which follows a week after the end of the trial, and then ahead again some two years for the mate's detailed account of Brierly's methodical leap over the side of the *Ossa*. Marlow's letter, which Conrad employs to bring the novel to its close, represents yet another flashback. Examples of this movement back and forth in time in the novel could be multiplied.

Conrad's complex manipulation of his narrators and of the disjointed time sequence of the events of the novel have a single purpose: to give the reader a complete view of a psychologically complex figure. It is an effort, as Marlow insists several times, to "see Jim clearly." Yet, for all Conrad's (and Marlow's) efforts, Jim remains an enigma. Marlow, in fact, confesses at the end of his letter that Jim continues to be "inscrutable."

Two particular problems have plagued critics in coming to grips with Jim. Stein, on whom Marlow relies for enlightenment, pronounces Jim "a romantic," which Stein says is "very bad . . . and very good too." In attempting to resolve the problem of how a romantic may cope with reality, Stein uses the metaphor of a man falling into the sea (the overtones of Jim's leap from the *Patna* are obvious here). Stein continues, "The way is to the destructive element submit yourself, and with the exertions of your hands and feet in the water make the deep, deep sea keep you up." The trouble here is that Stein does not make clear whether it is Jim's dream of heroes and heroics that is the "destructive element" or whether it is the practical and mundane world in which he must endeavor to carry out this dream that is destructive. Does Jim immerse himself in the dream yet keep his head above "water" in the world of reality, or immerse himself in the world of reality and yet keep the dream alive directly above the surface? The critical controversy that Stein's cryptic advice has provoked continues.

Critics are also divided on the meaning of the end of the novel. When Jim presents himself to the old nakhoda, Doramin, and suffers the pistol shot that ends his life, is this the act of a man who has finally accepted that he is capable of failure and who "has mastered his destiny," or is it merely the desperate act of a man who has simply run out of options? The distinction may seem fine, since, in any case, Jim's gesture is a positive act, but it governs the reader's final judgment on whether Marlow is correct in accepting Jim as "one of us."

If Jim is not "one of us," he is clearly one of "them," them being the familiar Conradian figures, the isolated and alienated solitaries, and he is so both spiritually and physically. In abandoning the *Patna*, Jim has violated a cardinal principle of the seaman's code, placing his own safety above that of the pilgrims who have entrusted themselves to him. As Brierly puts it, "We are trusted," and he is unforgiving of Jim's dereliction, as is Marlow, although Marlow is willing to admit mitigating circumstances. To the seamen whom Jim encounters, who raise the specter of the *Patna*, Jim is a pariah who has broken the bond of "the fellowship of the craft." Jim himself is quite conscious of his alienation. When he sails aboard Marlow's ship from Bangkok, he takes no interest in the passage as a seaman would, but instead, in Marlow's words, skulks below deck, "as though he had become a stowaway."

Jim is also isolated physically. In a moving passage, Marlow speaks with great feeling of the seaman's ties with and affection for his native land, for home. Jim, however, can never go home; he has, in effect, no home, and his destiny lies everywhere and anywhere but in the village in Essex where he came into being.

On Patusan, Jim's physical isolation is complete. Except for the unspeakable Cornelius, he is the only white man for hundreds of miles. With the *Patna* safely behind him, as he supposes, Jim thrives in isolation, bringing order and security to the troubled land, and is called by the natives "Tuan Jim," "which is to say, Lord Jim." The years of unparalleled success take their toll. Jim is convinced that "nothing can touch me," and his egotism proves fatal when Gentleman Brown finds him out. Jim spends his last hours isolated, and he dies alone.

In addition to the alienated hero, another familiar Conradian motif may be observed in *Lord Jim*: Conrad's continuing insistence on the redeeming nature of work. Earlier in the novel, the unnamed narrator makes an attempt to sum up Jim, and it comes in the form of Jim's failure to accept or to appreciate the nature of the demands of life at sea. The narrator says that "the only reward [one may expect in the seafaring life] is in the perfect love of the work. This reward eluded him." Notably, throughout the novel, Jim is most vulnerable when he is without work. During his long stay in the hospital at Singapore, he is infected by the malaise of the seamen ashore who have been in the East too long and who have given up all thought of returning to the more demanding Home Service. Under this debilitating influence, Jim takes the fateful step of signing aboard the *Patna*. The ship's passage is deceptively uneventful and undemanding, and Jim has so little to do as mate that his "faculty of swift and forestalling vision," as Marlow calls it, is given free reign. Thus, in the emergency, Jim sees with his imagination rather than with his eyes. In like fashion, after the initial heroics on Patusan, the demands on Jim are minimal. In the absence of anything practical for Jim to do, except carry out his role as Tuan Jim, he is again vulnerable. Gentleman Brown is enabled, as a result, to catch Jim off guard, to find the "weak spot," "the place of decay," and Jim's idyllic but precarious world comes crashing down.

Conrad the Symbolist may also be observed in *Lord Jim*. Again, as in *Heart of Darkness*, some of the symbols are conventional. Jim's retreat from the *Patna*, for example, is always eastward toward the rising sun, and Jim has bright blue eyes—the eyes, one assumes, of the romantic that darken in moments of stress—and wears immaculate white attire during his climactic confrontation with Gentleman Brown across the creek in Patusan.

As in *Heart of Darkness*, however, some of the symbols in *Lord Jim* are thoroughly original. In pronouncing Jim a "romantic," Stein is, in part, also pronouncing judgment on himself. Stein's romanticism, however, is mixed with a strong alloy of the practical, and he is prepared, as Jim is not, to act or to react immediately when action is called for, as is evident when he is ambushed and defends himself with skill and daring. Thus, Stein the romantic collects butterflies, while Stein the practical man collects beetles. The ring that Doramin gives his old "war-comrade" Stein as a talisman of the bond between white and native ultimately assumes symbolic import. Stein, in turn, gives the ring to Jim as his entrée to Patusan, and Jim wears it proudly during his brief days of glory. In the midst of the Gentleman Brown affair, Jim sends the ring to Doramin's son, Dain Waris, as a token of the white man's faith. In the closing scene of the novel, the ring, taken from the finger of the dead Dain Waris and placed in Doramin's lap, falls to the ground at Jim's feet. Jim glances down at it, and, as he raises his head, Doramin shoots Jim. The ring, then, paradoxically, is both a symbol of faith and of a breach of faith.

VICTORY

Victory, one of Conrad's later novels, was published in 1915. As such, it represents in one sense a Conrad who had mastered the techniques of the genre he had made his own, the novel, and in another sense a Conrad in decline as a creative artist. The early experimentation in narrative technique—the multiplicity of narrators and the complex, and sometimes confusing, manipulation of chronology—is behind Conrad. *Victory* is a linear narrative told by a single, first-person speaking voice without interruption of the forward chronological thrust of the tale. For the noncritical reader, this straightforward handling of his material on Conrad's part was a boon and may very well account for the fact that not until *Chance*, in 1913, and *Victory*, two years later, did Conrad enjoy genuine popular success.

At the same time, Conrad made forward strides in narrative technique and in command of the language in the fifteen years between *Lord Jim* and *Victory*. These steps took him past clarity to simplicity. *Victory* is, perhaps, too straightforward a tale, freed of occasional confusion and of the varied and variable speaking voices but also lacking the richness and the range contributed by those same voices. Confined as Conrad is to one point of view, the extensive searching and probing of his characters, seen in Kurtz and Jim, are denied him. Axel Heyst is an interesting character, but he is only that. He is not, like Kurtz and Jim, a provocative, puzzling, and ultimately enigmatic figure.

The other characters in the novel are similarly unimpressive. Heyst finds the heroine, Alma, or Lena, a thoroughly intriguing young woman, but the reader is at a loss to understand the fascination, even the appeal, she seems to have for Heyst. Other than the commitment Heyst has made to Lena in rescuing her from the odious Schomberg, the tie between the two is tenuous. Many critics have noted that Conrad's women are generally lifeless, and it is true that, with the possible exception of Doña Rita in *The Arrow of Gold* (and here Conrad may have been writing from direct emotional involvement), women generally remained mysteries to him. As his greatest work attests, he was essentially a man's writer.

The three other principal characters in *Victory* are male, yet they, too, are wooden and artificial. Much has been made of "plain Mr. Jones," Ricardo, and Pedro's representing Conrad's most searching study of evil. In this construct, Jones stands for intellectual evil, Ricardo for moral (or amoral) evil, and Pedro for the evil of force. On the whole, however, they emerge as a singularly unimpressive trio of thugs. The lanky, emaciated Jones, called the "spectre," is indeed a ghostlike figure whose presence is observed but scarcely felt. Ricardo, with his bluster and swagger, is almost a comic character, and some of his lines are worthy of a nineteenth century melodrama. Pedro's chief function in the novel appears to be his availability to be bashed on the head and suffer multiple contusions. Compared to Gentleman Brown, "the show ruffian of the Australian coast" in *Lord Jim*, they are theatrical, and while they may do harm, the evil they represent pales beside that ascribed by Conrad to Brown, "akin to madness, derived from intense egoism, inflamed by resistance, tearing the soul to pieces and giving factitious vigor to the body."

Victory is a talky novel, with long passages devoted to inconclusive conversations between Heyst and Lena. It is relevant here to contrast the lengthy exchange between Jim and Marlow in the Malabar House and the "getting to know one another" colloquies in which Heyst and Lena engage. In the former, every line is relevant and every word tells; in the latter, the emotional fencing between the two ultimately becomes tedious.

Gone, indeed, in *Victory* are the overblown passages of the earlier works, which can make even the most devout Conradian wince. Gone too, however, are the great passages, the moments of magic in which by the sheer power of words, Conrad moves, stirs, and thrills the reader. On the whole, the style in *Victory*, like the format of the novel itself, is straightforward; the prose is clear, but the interludes of splendor are sadly missing, and missed.

Whatever differences are to be found in the later works in Conrad's technical handling of the narrative and in his style, one constant remains. Heyst—like Kurtz, Jim, and so many of the figures who fill Conrad's pages—is an alien, isolated and apart, both spiritually and physically. He does differ somewhat from his counterparts, however, in that he stands alone by choice. Heyst, following the dying precept of his gifted but idealistic father—"Look-on—make no sound"—proposes to spend his life aloof and divorced from humankind; in this way, he believes, nothing can ever touch him. In general, except for his brief involvement with the unfortunate Morrison, Heyst manages to maintain his role of the amused and detached skeptic, living, as Conrad puts it, an "unattached, floating existence." He accommodates himself to all people but makes no commitments to anyone. Thus, chameleonlike, he is known under many guises; he is called, for example, "Enchanted Heyst" because of his expressed enchantment with the East and, on other occasions by would-be interpreters, "Hard Facts Heyst," "the Utopist," "the Baron," "the Spider," and "the Enemy." A final sobriquet, "the Hermit," is attached to Heyst when, with the collapse of the Tropical Belt Coal Company, he chooses to remain alone on the deserted island of Samburan. Heyst's physical isolation is now of a piece with his spiritual isolation.

The encounter with Lena changes this attitude. With his commitment to Lena, Heyst is no longer the detached observer of the world, and with the flight to Samburan, his wanderings come to an end. Paradoxically, this commitment brings about both his spiritual salvation and his physical destruction. It is a redeemed Heyst, freed at last from the other enchantment of his life (the living presence of his dead father), who, at Lena's death, is able to assert, "Woe to the man whose heart has not learned while young to hope, to love—and to put its trust in life!" Thus, Heyst differs from Conrad's other alien spirits in that he "masters his destiny," as Jim could not and Kurtz, perhaps, would not.

In still another way, Heyst "masters his destiny" as Jim and Kurtz do not. Kurtz dies the victim of his own excesses and of the debilitating effect of the jungle; Jim places his life in the hands of Doramin. Heyst, however, governs his own fate and chooses to die with Lena, immolating himself in the purgative fire that he sets to destroy all traces of their brief idyll on Samburan, a fire that, ironically, blazes over the ruins of a defunct coal company.

Other echoes of the earlier Conrad may be seen in *Victory*. For example, albeit to a lesser degree than in *Lord Jim*, *Heart of Darkness*, *The Arrow of Gold*, and *Almayer's Folly*, *Victory* is another instance of Conrad's writing "autobiography as fiction." In the Author's Note to the novel, Conrad speaks of a real-life Heyst whom he remembers with affection but also with a sense of mystery. So too, Mr. Jones, Ricardo, and Pedro come from Conrad's store of memories, although he encountered each individually and not as the trio they compose in the book. The character of Lena is drawn from a brief encounter in a café in the south of France with a group of entertainers and with one girl in the company who particularly caught Conrad's eye. The settings of *Victory*, exotic names such as Malacca, Timor, and Sourabaya, were, of course, as familiar to the seagoing Conrad as the streets of London, and there is no reason to doubt that somewhere in the tropics, the fictional Samburan has its counterpart.

Finally, in *Victory*, Conrad the Symbolist may again be seen. Noticeably, however, in this later novel, just as Conrad's narrative technique and his style have become simplified and his ability to create vivid characters has declined, the symbols employed lack the freshness and the depth of those of the earlier novels. Conrad makes much of the portrait of the elder Heyst that dominates the sparse living room on Samburan, just as the subject of the portrait has dominated Heyst's existence. In fact, Conrad makes too much of the portrait as a symbol, calling attention to it again and again until the reader can virtually predict that each time Heyst enters the room, the portrait will be brought to his and to the reader's attention. As a symbol, then, the portrait is overdone, overt, and obvious. Similarly, the darkening storm that threatens Samburan as the events of the novel reach their climax is a bit heavy-handed and hardly worthy of Conrad at his best.

Even so, there is a brief moment of the true Conrad shortly before the climactic violence that brings about both Heyst's redemption and destruction. Conrad writes: "The thunder growled distantly with angry modulations of its tremendous voice, while the world outside shuddered incessantly around the dead stillness of the room where the framed profile of Heyst's father looked severely into space." Here the two symbols coalesce in a telling and effective manner. Regrettably, telling and effective instances such as this are rare in *Victory*. Conrad's work as a whole, however, with its stylistic and narrative innovations, testifies to the quality of his contribution to twentieth century literature.

C. F. Burgess

OTHER MAJOR WORKS

SHORT FICTION: *Tales of Unrest*, 1898; *Youth: A Narrative, and Two Other Stories*, 1902; *Typhoon, and Other Stories*, 1903; *A Set of Six*, 1908; *'Twixt Land and Sea, Tales*, 1912; *Within the Tides*, 1915; *Tales of Hearsay*, 1925; *The Sisters*, 1928; *The Complete Short Stories of Joseph Conrad*, 1933.

PLAYS: *One Day More: A Play in One Act*, pr. 1905; *The Secret Agent: A Drama in Four Acts*, pb. 1921; *Laughing Anne: A Play*, pb. 1923.

NONFICTION: *The Mirror of the Sea*, 1906; *Some Reminiscences*, 1912 (also known as *A Personal Record*); *Notes on Life and Letters*, 1921; *Joseph Conrad's Diary of His Journey Up the Valley of the Congo in 1890*, 1926; *Last Essays*, 1926; *Joseph Conrad: Life and Letters*, 1927 (Gérard Jean-Aubry, editor); *Joseph Conrad's Letters to His Wife*, 1927; *Conrad to a Friend*, 1928 (Richard Curle, editor); *Letters from Joseph Conrad, 1895-1924*, 1928 (Edward Garnett, editor); *Lettres françaises de Joseph Conrad*, 1929 (Jean-

Aubry, editor); *Letters of Joseph Conrad to Marguerite Doradowska*, 1940 (John A. Gee and Paul J. Sturm, editors); *The Collected Letters of Joseph Conrad*, 1983-2005 (7 volumes; Frederick R. Karl and Laurence Davies, editors).

BIBLIOGRAPHY

Davis, Laura L., ed. *Conrad's Century: The Past and Future Splendour.* New York: Columbia University Press, 1998. Collection of essays provides context for Conrad's work as it examines the author's life and his times. Includes bibliographical references and index.

Gordon, John Dozier. *Joseph Conrad: The Making of a Novelist.* Cambridge, Mass.: Harvard University Press, 1940. Classic work of Conrad scholarship presents excellent discussion of the author's early novels. This volume was especially important in the revival of interest in Conrad's work in the 1940's and 1950's.

Hawthorn, Jeremy. *Sexuality and the Erotic in the Fiction of Joseph Conrad.* New York: Continuum, 2007. Although Conrad's works are usually thought to be lacking in sexuality, this book opens his writing up to new interpretations by citing passages that support erotic interpretations.

Jordan, Elaine, ed. *Joseph Conrad.* New York: St. Martin's Press, 1996. Excellent introductory study of Conrad focuses on three novels: *Heart of Darkness*, *Nostromo*, and *The Secret Agent*. Discusses the works from postcolonial feminist, Marxist, and other perspectives.

Kaplan, Carola M., Peter Mallios, and Andrea White, eds. *Conrad in the Twenty-first Century: Contemporary Approaches and Perspectives.* New York: Routledge, 2005. Collection of essays examines Conrad's depictions of postcolonialism, empire, imperialism, and modernism. Section 1 contains four essays that discuss *Heart of Darkness*, while other essays focus on *The Secret Agent*, *Nostromo*, *Under Western Eyes*, and other novels.

Karl, Frederick R. *Joseph Conrad: The Three Lives.* New York: Farrar, Straus and Giroux, 1979. This book is, and will likely remain, the definitive Conrad biography, elucidating as it does Conrad's life in Poland, on the seas, and in England. The well-documented study is also replete with generously thorough analyses of Conrad's major works as well as of his artistic development and political orientation.

_____. *A Reader's Guide to Joseph Conrad.* Rev. ed. Syracuse, N.Y.: Syracuse University Press, 1997. Useful handbook for students provides in-depth analysis of Conrad's work. Includes bibliographical references and an index.

Lothe, Jakob, Jeremy Hawthorn, and James Phelan, eds. *Joseph Conrad: Voice, Sequence, History, Genre.* Columbus: Ohio State University Press, 2008. Collection of essays examines Conrad's use of narrative in his fiction and nonfiction, focusing on the four issues listed in the subtitle. Provides several perspectives on *Heart of Darkness* and *Lord Jim*.

Meyers, Jeffrey. *Joseph Conrad: A Biography.* New York: Charles Scribner's Sons, 1991. Briskly moving, no-nonsense biography surveys the key points and themes of Conrad's major works. Very good at placing Conrad within the social and intellectual milieu of his day and offering good insights from other literary figures, such as Ford Madox Ford, who significantly influenced Conrad's literary career.

Najder, Zdzislaw. *Joseph Conrad: A Chronicle.* Translated by Halina Carroll-Najder. Rev. ed. New York: Cambridge University Press, 2007. Thorough and sympathetic biography stresses the influence of Conrad's Polish heritage on his personality and art. Draws many telling and intriguing parallels between Conrad's life and his writing.

Peters, John G. *Conrad and Impressionism.* New York: Cambridge University Press, 2001. Examines the influence of impressionism on Conrad's narrative style and other literary techniques as well as on his philosophy and political opinions. Includes a valuable bibliography.

Stape, J. H., ed. *The Cambridge Companion to Joseph Conrad.* New York: Cambridge University Press, 1996. Collection of essays addresses most of Conrad's major works, including analysis of *Lord Jim*, *Nostromo*, and *Under Western Eyes*. Other topics covered include the Conradian narrative, Conrad and imperialism, Conrad and modernism, and Conrad's literary influence.

Swisher, Clarice, ed. *Readings on Joseph Conrad.* San Diego, Calif.: Greenhaven Press, 1998. Collection features essays on Conrad's works by notable authors such as J. B. Priestley, Robert Penn Warren, and Richard Adams.

FYODOR DOSTOEVSKI

Born: Moscow, Russia; November 11, 1821
Died: St. Petersburg, Russia; February 9, 1881
Also known as: Fyodor Mihaylovich Dostoevski; Feodor Dostoyevsky; Feodor Dostoevsky

PRINCIPAL LONG FICTION
Bednye lyudi, 1846 (*Poor Folk*, 1887)
Dvoynik, 1846 (*The Double*, 1917)
Netochka Nezvanova, 1849 (English translation, 1920)
Unizhennye i oskorblyonnye, 1861 (*Injury and Insult*, 1886; also known as *The Insulted and Injured*)
Zapiski iz myortvogo doma, 1861-1862 (*Buried Alive: Or, Ten Years of Penal Servitude in Siberia*, 1881; better known as *The House of the Dead*)
Zapiski iz podpolya, 1864 (*Letters from the Underworld*, 1913; better known as *Notes from the Underground*)
Igrok, 1866 (*The Gambler*, 1887)
Prestupleniye i nakazaniye, 1866 (*Crime and Punishment*, 1886)
Idiot, 1868 (*The Idiot*, 1887)
Vechny muzh, 1870 (*The Permanent Husband*, 1888; also known as *The Eternal Husband*)
Besy, 1871-1872 (*The Possessed*, 1913; also known as *The Devils*)
Podrostok, 1875 (*A Raw Youth*, 1916)
Bratya Karamazovy, 1879-1880 (*The Brothers Karamazov*, 1912)
The Novels, 1912 (12 volumes)

OTHER LITERARY FORMS

The collected works of Fyodor Dostoevski (dahs-tuh-YEHF-skee) are available in many Russian editions, starting from 1883. The most carefully prepared of these, comprising some thirty volumes, is the Leningrad Nauka edition, which began publishing in 1972. A wide variety of selected works are also available in English. While the novels dominate Dostoevski's later creative period, he began his career with sketches, short stories, and novellas, and he continued to write shorter pieces throughout his working life. These works do not exhibit the same unity of theme as the major novels, though many of them in one way or another involve Dostoevski's favorite topic, human duality.

Dostoevski's nonfictional writing is diverse. In his monthly *Dnevnik pisatelya* (1876-1877, 1880-1881; *The Diary of a Writer*, 1949), he included commentary on sociopolitical issues of the time, literary analyses, travelogues, and fictional sketches. He also contributed many essays to his own journals and other publications. The nonfictional

Fyodor Dostoevski
(Library of Congress)

writings often clash with the views expressed in the novels and consequently enjoy wide circulation among specialists for comparative purposes. Equally popular is his correspondence, comprising several volumes in his collected works. The notebooks for the major novels, as well as other background comments, are also included in the collection. They became available in English in editions published by the University of Chicago Press during the 1960's and 1970's.

Achievements

Both Leo Tolstoy and Fyodor Dostoevski, the giants of the Russian novel during the era preceding the 1917 October Revolution, are firmly part of the Western literary tradition today, but whereas Tolstoy's outlook is solidly rooted in the nineteenth century, Dostoevski's ideas belong to modern times. His novels go far beyond the parameters of aesthetic literature; they are studied not only by literary historians and critics but also by psychologists, philosophers, and theologians the world over. Each discipline discerns a different drift in Dostoevski's work, and few agree on what the author's basic tenets are, but all claim him as their hero. His contemporaries, too, were at a loss to categorize him, primarily because his style and subject matter had little in common with accepted literary norms. Russia's most prominent writing, as espoused by Ivan Turgenev and Tolstoy, was smooth and lyric. While Turgenev analyzed topical social problems in a restrained, faintly didactic manner, and Tolstoy presented panoramic visions of certain Russian social classes and their moral problems, Dostoevski brought an entirely new style and content to Russian writing. He disregarded his colleagues' logically progressing, chronological narrative mode and constructed his stories as mosaics or puzzles, often misleading the audience, experimenting with peculiar narrative voices, allowing his pathological figures to advance the plot in disconcertingly disorienting ways, and in general forcing the reader to reevaluate and backtrack constantly. Dostoevski was also revolutionary in his choice of subjects, introducing characters whose perception of outside reality essentially mirrored their own skewed personalities.

Dostoevski thus rendered obsolete both his contemporaries' classical realism and the prevailing superficial treatment of the human psyche. In his choice of settings, he disdained the poetic landscapes preferred by others and concentrated on the teeming of the city or the starkly barren aspects of the countryside. Because of this preference for the seamy side of life, he is often linked to Nikolai Gogol, but Dostoevski's descriptions of deviant behavior have a decidedly more modern flavor than do Gogol's. During his enforced proximity to criminals, Dostoevski applied his powers of observation to their perverted worldview and, in the process, developed a new approach to literary portraiture; Sigmund Freud praised him for anticipating modern psychological approaches, and twentieth century psychologists on the whole have accepted Dostoevski's observations as valid.

Dostoevski tended to be conservative and didactic in his nonfictional writings, though his often cantankerous and controversial assertions contributed to the lively journalistic interplays of the time; to this day, there is disagreement over whether he affected a conservative public stance in order to be trusted with censorially sensitive material in his fiction or whether conflicting elements were actually integral to his personality. In either case, Dostoevski is responsible for leading Russian literature away from its often tranquilly harmonious narratives, with their clearly discernible authorial points of view, to a polyphonic plane.

During Joseph Stalin's reign as leader of the newly formed Soviet Union, severe censorial strictures limited the average Soviet reader's access to Dostoevski, yet interest in him remained undiminished, and he returned to his prominent place after Stalin's death. Outside his homeland, Dostoevski's influence has been immeasurable. Albert Camus—to cite only one among countless examples of twentieth century writers awed by the power of Dostoevski's metaphysical dialectics—transformed *The Possessed* into a gripping play, *Les Possédés* (pr., pb. 1959; *The Possessed*, 1960), because he saw in Dostoevski's tortured protagonists the forerunners of today's existentialist heroes. Dostoevski's work thus has remained topical and continues to appeal to widely divergent views.

Biography

There was little in the childhood of Fyodor Mihaylovich Dostoevski to presage his achievements as a writer of world-famous novels. Born into a middle-class family of few cultural pretensions, he received a mediocre education. His father, a physician at a Moscow hospital for the poor, ruled the family with a strict hand and enforced observance of Russian Orthodox ritual at home. When Dostoevski entered the St. Petersburg Military Engineering School in 1838, he found himself unprepared for academic life; nevertheless, he enjoyed his first exposure to literature and soon immersed himself in it. The elder Dostoevski's murder at the hands of his serfs (he had in the meantime become a modest landowner) and the first signs of his own epilepsy upset Dostoevski's academic routine, delaying his graduation until 1843.

Dostoevski worked only briefly as a military engineer before deciding to pursue a literary career. When the efforts of acquaintances resulted in the publication of his first fictional work, *Poor Folk*, his excitement knew no bounds, and he envisioned a promising writing career. His initial success led easily to publication of several additional pieces, among them the uncompleted *Netochka Nezvanova* and the psychologically impressive *The Double*. While these works are not considered primary by Dostoevski scholars, they hint at what was to become the author's fascination with humankind's ambiguous inner world.

The perfecting of this artistic vision was interrupted by Dostoevski's encounter with the realities of czarist autocracy under Nicholas I. Dostoevski was active in the Petrashevsky Circle, one of many dissident groups engaged in underground dissemination of sociopolitical pamphlets. Dostoevski's arrest and death sentence in 1849, commuted at the last moment to prison and exile, initiated a terrible period for the young author. On Christmas Eve of that year, he left St. Petersburg in chains to spend four years in the company of violent criminals in Omsk, Siberia. The inhuman conditions of his imprisonment severely taxed his mental stability, especially because he was forbidden to write or even read anything, except religious matter. He later recorded these experiences graphically in *The House of the Dead* (initially translated as *Buried Alive: Or, Ten Years of Penal Servitude in Siberia*), immediately catching public attention for his psychological insight into pathological and criminal behavior. He spent an additional five years (1854-1859) as a political exile in a Siberian army contingent.

In 1857, after recovering somewhat from the ravages of incarceration, which had exacerbated his epilepsy, Dostoevski married a widow, Maria Isayeva, and hesitantly resumed his writing career. Upon his return to St. Petersburg in 1859, he was drawn into a hectic pace of literary activity. Turgenev and Tolstoy occupied first place among writers, leaving the unfortunate ex-convict to rebuild his career almost from scratch. To facilitate the serial printing of his work, he ventured into publishing. Together with his brother Mikhail, he started the journal *Vremya* in 1861, using it as a vehicle to publish his not very successful novel *The Insulted and Injured*, which he had written primarily to alleviate financial pressures. When he visited Western Europe for the first time in 1862, his observations also appeared in *Vremya* as "Zimnie zametki o letnikh vpechatleniyakh" (1863; "Winter Notes on Summer Impressions," 1955). Before he could reap substantial material benefit from his enterprise, government censors closed the magazine in 1863 because a politically sensitive article on Russo-Polish affairs had appeared in its pages.

At this inopportune moment, Dostoevski indulged himself somewhat recklessly by revisiting Europe on borrowed funds in order to pursue a passionate love interest, Apollinaria Suslova, and to try his luck at German gaming tables. Unsuccessful in both pursuits, he returned to Russia in 1864 to risk another publishing venture, the periodical *Epokha*, which folded in less than a year, though he managed to print in it the initial installments of his first successful longer fiction, *Notes from the Underground*, before its demise. His personal life, too, did not proceed smoothly. The deaths of his wife, with whom he had shared seven unhappy years, and of his brother and business partner Mikhail in 1864 brought enormous additional debts and obligations, which led him to make hasty promises of future works. To extricate himself from one such contract, he interrupted work on *Crime and Punishment* and hastily put together a fictional version of his gambling experiences and his torrid love affair with Suslova. To speed the work, he dictated the text to a twenty-year-old stenographer, Anna Snitkina. With her expert help, *The Gambler* was delivered on time. Dostoevski and Snitkina married in 1867, and she is generally credited with providing the stability and emotional security that permitted the author to produce his last four novels at a more measured pace.

Despite the success of *Crime and Punishment*, Dostoevski still ranked below Turgenev and Tolstoy in popular esteem by the end of the 1860's, partly because their wealth allowed them leisure to compose carefully edited works that appealed to the public and their gentry status opened influential doors, and partly because Dostoevski's writings were uneven, alternating between strange psychological portraits and journalistic polemics, all produced in a frantic haste that seemed to transmit itself to the text. Dostoevski spent the first four years after his marriage to Snitkina in Europe, largely to escape creditors but also to feed his gambling mania, which kept the family destitute. He completed *The Idiot* abroad and accepted a publisher's large advance in 1871 to facilitate return to his homeland. His remaining ten years were spent in more rational pursuits.

Between 1873 and 1874, he edited the conservative weekly *Grazhdanin* and initiated a popular column, *Diary of a Writer*, which in 1876 he turned into a successful monthly. The appearance of the politically provocative *The Possessed* and of *A Raw Youth* kept him in the public eye, and he was finally accorded some of the social acknowledgments previously reserved for his rivals Turgenev and Tolstoy. The duality of his writings, at once religiously conservative and brilliantly innovative, made him acceptable to government, Church, and intellectuals alike. This philosophical dichotomy remained characteristic of Dostoevski to the end. In 1880, he delivered an enthusiastically received speech during the dedication of the Alexander Pushkin monument in Moscow, in which he reiterated patriotic sentiments of a rather traditional tenor. At the same time, his last novel, *The Brothers Karamazov*, expressed doubts about a single, traditional view of life. When he died two months after completing the novel, an impressive public funeral attested his stature as a major Russian writer.

ANALYSIS

Fyodor Dostoevski's creative development is roughly divided into two stages. The shorter pieces, preceding his imprisonment, reflect native and foreign literary influences, although certain topics and stylistic innovations that became Dostoevski's trademarks were already apparent. The young author was fascinated by Gogol's humiliated St. Petersburg clerks and their squalid surroundings, teeming with marginal, grotesque individuals. These elements are so abundant in all of Dostoevski's fiction that he labeled himself a disciple of Gogol. Traces of E. T. A. Hoffmann's fantastic tales are evident in the young Dostoevski's preference for gothic and Romantic melodrama. What distinguishes Dostoevski from those influences is his carnivalistically exaggerated tone in describing or echoing the torments of members of the lower classes. He not only imbues them with frantic emotional passions and personality quirks in order to make them strangers to their own mediocre setting but also endows them with precisely the right balance between eccentricity and ordinariness to jar the reader into irritated alertness. While other writers strove to elicit public sympathy for the poor, Dostoevski subtly infused an element of ridiculousness into his portrayals, thereby reducing the social efficacy of the genre while enhancing the complexity of literary expression.

In Dostoevski's later, post-Siberian novels, this delicate equilibrium between empathy and contempt for the downtrodden is honed to perfection. The author supplements his gallery of mistreated eccentrics with powerful, enigmatic, ethically neutral supermen—highly intelligent loners whose philosophies allow simultaneously for self-sacrifice and murder. Other favorite types are passionate females, aborting good impulses with vicious inclinations, and angelic prostitutes, curiously blending religious fanaticism with coarseness.

This multiplicity is the dominant characteristic of Dostoevski's style. It is for the most part impossible to discern in his works an authorial point of view. By using a polyphonic approach, Dostoevski has characters arguing diametrically opposed concepts so convincingly and in such an intellectually appealing fashion that readers are prevented from forming simplistic judgments. Most readers are held spellbound by the detective quality of Dostoevski's writing. On the surface, the novels appear to be thrillers, exhibiting the typical tricks of that genre, with generous doses of suspense, criminal activity, confession, and entrapment by police or detectives. While viewing the works from this angle alone will not yield a satisfactory reading, it eases the way into the psychologically complex subtext. Not the least of Dostoevski's appeal lies in his original development of characters, prominent among them frantically driven types who bare their psyches in melodramatic confessions and diaries while at the same time confusing the reader's expectations by performing entirely contradictory deeds. Superimposed on these psychological conflicts are other metaphysical quandaries, such as passionate discussions about good and evil, church and state, Russia and Western Europe, free will and determinism. These struggles often crowd the plot to the point of symbolic overload, thereby destroying any semblance of harmony.

That Dostoevski is avidly read by the general public and specialists alike attests his genius in fusing banalities with profound intellectual insights. Nevertheless, a certain unevenness in language and structure remains. The constant pressure under which Dostoevski worked resulted in incongruities and dead spots that are incompatible with expert literary craftsmanship, while the installment approach forced him to end segments with suspense artificially built up to ensure the reader's continuing interest. Some of these rough spots were edited out in later single-volume editions, but the sense of rugged style persists, and reading Dostoevski is therefore not a relaxing experience. No reader, however, can easily forget the mental puzzles and nightmarish visions generated by Dostoevski's work.

NOTES FROM THE UNDERGROUND

Notes from the Underground, Dostoevski's first successful longer work, already contained many elements found in the subsequent novels. The nameless underground man is a keenly conscious misogynist who masks excessive pride with pathological submissiveness. In his youth, his need for self-esteem led him into disastrous social encounters from which he usually emerged the loser. For example, his delusion of being ignored by a social superior, who is not even aware of him, has caused him to spend years planning a ridiculous, and in the end miscarried, revenge. Dostoevski liked to use noncausal patterning in his compositional arrangements to enhance a sense of discontinuity. Thus, *Notes from the Underground* begins with the forty-year-old protagonist already withdrawn from society, spewing hatred, bitter philosophy, and ridicule at the imaginary reader of his journals. Only in the second part of the novel, which contains the underground man's actual confrontations, does it become clear that he has no choice but to hide himself away, because his twisted personality is incapable of even a casual positive human interaction. His very pronouncement is a contradiction, uttered in a continuous stream without developing a single argument, so that the overall effect is one of unordered dialectical listing.

On one level, *Notes from the Underground* was written to counter Nikolay Chernyshevsky's *Chto delat'?* (1863; *What Is to Be Done?*, c. 1863), which stresses the benefits of scientific thinking and considers self-interest beneficial to all society. Through the underground man's irrational behavior and reasoning, Dostoevski ridicules Chernyshevsky's assumptions. He makes his hero a living refutation of scientific approaches. If human logic can be corrupted by the mind's own illogic, no strictly logical conclusions are possible. By indulging in actions injurious to himself, the underground man proves that human beings do not act solely out of self-interest, that they are, in part at least, intrinsically madcap. Thus, any attempt to structure society along scientific lines, as suggested by Chernyshevsky, is doomed to failure. The duality of the hero is such, however, that rational assertions, too, receive ample exposure, as the underground man refutes his own illogic and spins mental webs around the imaginary listener. *Notes from the Underground* is difficult to read, especially for those unfamiliar with Chernyshevsky's novel. The unprogressively flowing illogicalities, coupled with an elusive authorial voice, render the narrative undynamic and tax even the intellectually committed reader. Dostoevski himself realized an insufficiency in the work but blamed it partly on censorial editing of an obscure religious reference, according to which the hero saw a glimmer of hope for himself in Christianity. The deleted comments, however, do not carry such a weighty connotation, and Dostoevski made no effort to restore the cut text later, when he might have done so. In its emphasis on the dual qualities of human endeavor, *Notes from the Underground* is firmly linked to the subsequent novels, in which this theme is handled with more sophistication.

CRIME AND PUNISHMENT

The wide appeal of *Crime and Punishment* results partly from its detective-story elements of murder, criminal investigation, evasion, confession, and courtroom drama. Dostoevski immediately broadens the perspective of the genre, however. Readers not only know from the outset who the murderer is but also are at once made part of his thinking process, so that his reasoning, motivations, and inclinations are laid bare from the start. The enigmatic element enters when readers come to realize, along with the murderer, and as slowly and painfully as the murderer, that he cannot assign a purpose to the crime, that human motivation remains, in the end, an unsolved mystery.

The very name of the hero, Raskolnikov, is derived from the Russian word for "split," and his entire existence is characterized by a swiftly alternating, unsettling duality. Raskolnikov is introduced as an intense former student who is about to put a carefully constructed theory into action. The opening chapters chronicle the confused state of his mental processes. He plans to rid the world of an evil by killing a pawnbroker who is gradually ruining her customers, Raskolnikov among them, and plans to use her hoarded wealth for philanthropical purposes in justification of the crime. Almost immediately, other motives call the first into question. Raskolnikov's mother threatens to sacrifice her daughter to ensure his financial well-being. An encounter with a derelict drunkard, Marmeladov, strengthens Raskolnikov in his resolve to kill, for Marmeladov keeps himself in drink and out of work by drawing on the pitiful earnings of his young daughter, Sonia, whom he has sent into prostitution. Raskolnikov notes in horror that he may force his sister into a similar situation through the legal prostitution of a sacrificial marriage. The crime itself renders all of Raskolnikov's musings invalid. He brutally murders a second, innocent victim, takes very little money, does not spend what he does steal, and will have nothing to do with his family.

From this point on, the novel focuses on Raskolnikov's struggle within himself. His prominently present but long repressed humanity asserts itself against his will to demolish arguments against confession provided by the proud part of his personality. Dostoevski uses the device of multiple alter egos in projecting Raskolnikov's dichotomy onto other characters. At one extreme pole stands the personification of Raskolnikov's evil impulses, the suspected killer and seducer Svidrigaïlov. Time and again, Raskolnikov confronts the latter in attempts to develop a psychological affinity with him. Raskolnikov's subconscious moral restraints, however, prevent such a union. Svidrigaïlov, and by extension Raskolnikov, cannot bring himself to perform planned abominations or live peacefully with already committed ones. Svidrigaïlov exits through suicide at about the same time that Raskolnikov is more urgently drawn to his other alter ego, the self-sacrificing, gentle prostitute Sonia.

Whereas Svidrigaïlov is a sensually vibrant figure, Sonia is basically colorless and unbelievable, but as a symbol of Raskolnikov's Christian essence, she turns out to be the stronger influence on him. She is not able to effect a moral transformation, yet she subtly moves into the foreground the necessity of confession and expiation. Raskolnikov never truly repents. He has, however, been forced to take a journey into his psyche, has found there an unwillingness to accommodate murder, and, almost angrily, has been forced to acknowledge that each life has its own sacramental value and that transgression of this tenet brings about psychological self-destruction. The final pages hint at Raskolnikov's potential for spiritual renewal, a conclusion that many critics find artistically unconvincing.

Intertwined with this primary drama are related Dostoevskian themes. Raskolnikov, in one of his guises, imagines himself a Napoleonic superman, acting on a worldwide stage on which individual killings disappear in the murk of historical necessity. On another plane, Dostoevski weaves Raskolnikov's mother, his landlady, and the slain pawnbroker into a triangle that merges the figures in Raskolnikov's confused deliberations, so that murderous impulses toward one are sublimated and redirected toward another. Similarly, the figures of Sonia, Raskolnikov's sister Dounia, and the pawnbroker's sister Lizaveta, also killed by Raskolnikov, are symbolically linked. Raskolnikov directs Dounia away from his lecherous alter ego Svidrigaïlov toward his proper, good-hearted embodiment and friend, Razumihin, while he himself, in expiation for killing Lizaveta, becomes a brotherly friend to Sonia. An important and cleverly presented role is reserved for the detective Porfiry, whose cunning leads Raskolnikov to confess a moral as well as a legal transgression. *Crime and Punishment* remains Dostoevski's most popular novel.

THE IDIOT

The author's narrative mode does not differ drastically in the remaining novels. Though each work is built on a different drama, all are developed along Dostoevski's favorite lines of human duality, alter ego, and authorial ambiguity. These qualities find expression in a most controversial way in *The Idiot*, the incongruous, almost sacrilegious portrayal of a Christlike figure. While the devout and selfless Sonia of *Crime and Punishment* occupies a position secondary to that of the central hero and thus lacks extensive development, Dostoevski makes the similarly self-sacrificing Prince Myshkin into the pivotal character of *The Idiot*. Through him, the author unfolds the notion that compassion and goodness, no matter how commendable on a theological plane, are insufficient to counter the less desirable aspects of reality.

The manner of Myshkin's presentation immediately challenges the reader's expectation of a "perfectly beautiful human being," as Dostoevski called his hero in preparatory notes. Myshkin—the name derives from the root of the Russian word for "mouse"—enters the novel as an insecure, epileptic, naïve young man, characterized by boundless goodwill, an immense capacity for humiliation, and a willingness to take the blame for the loathsome actions of others. He is a rather vapid personality, totally out of tune with existing human realities. Socially inept because of a long absence from Russia, ill at ease and inexperienced in confrontation with women, Myshkin is unable to establish satisfactory relationships. His kindness and empathy with suffering cause him to intervene repeatedly in other affairs, only to run afoul of the intense passions motivating his friends, and his interventions eventually lead to tragedy all around. Far from serving as counselor and redeemer, Myshkin is the cause of several calamities. Unversed in the intricacies of human interaction, created insufficiently incarnate by Dostoevski, the hapless protagonist leaves a path of misery and destruction before sinking totally into idiocy.

As he blunders his way through many unhappy encounters, several other themes emerge. The virginal hero actually has a sexually vicious and otherwise offensive double in Rogozhin, with whom he retains a close bond to the end, when both seemingly merge into one over the body of their mutual love, Nastasya Filipovna, freshly murdered by Rogozhin. Dostoevski assured outraged moralist critics that he had intended to create a perfect saint in Myshkin and implied that he had perhaps failed to create believable separate identities for Myshkin and Rogozhin, but Dostoevski's public assertions often contradicted the thrust of his novels, and it is more likely that here, too, he employed his favorite device of embodying the multifaceted human psyche in diametrically opposed figures.

In most of Dostoevski's novels, male characters are placed at center stage, leaving women to embody a given alter ego, highlight certain aspects of the protagonist, or echo other major concerns. *The Idiot* differs in presenting Nastasya Filipovna as Myshkin's primary antagonist. She is given scope and complexity in bringing to the surface Myshkin's temperamental inadequacy; in revenging herself for having been made concubine to the man appointed to be her guardian; in being torn by pride, guilt, and frustration; in vacillating between Myshkin and Rogozhin; and finally in orchestrating her own destruction. The other major female, Aglaya, receives less psychological expansion, but even here Dostoevski gives an interesting portrayal of a goodly woman unable to accept the humiliations associated with being Myshkin's companion. Dostoevski favored females of devious intensity, as typified by Nastasya Filipovna. In *Crime and Punishment* and *The Brothers Karamazov*, this type is marked by the identical name of "Katerina Ivanovna." Analysts interested in linking biography to plot perceive in these women an echo of Dostoevski's equally cruel and passionate friend, Apollinaria Suslova, as well as traits of his first wife, Maria Isayeva.

The preparatory notes to the novel reveal that Dostoevski changed perspective several times in shaping his guiding theme. In early drafts, Myshkin is a genuine double, possessed of many violent traits later transferred to Rogozhin. As Myshkin is stripped of negative features in later versions, he acquires the characteristics of a "holy fool," a popular type in pre-nineteenth century Russian literature, the mental defective as sweet, innocent, and specially favored by God. In the end, however there emerges the idea that an overflow of goodwill cannot vouchsafe positive results and can easily have the opposite effect. A certain meandering in the second part of the novel still reflects the author's hesitation in deciding on a direction. Earlier scholarship, unwilling to accept the fact that Dostoevski had depicted a failed saint in such a controversial manner, saw in *The Idiot* an unsuccessful attempt to portray a wholly Christian figure, but careful study of the text and background material reveals an intentional and original portrayal of a Christian dilemma. In succeeding works, too, Dostoevski's integrity as novelist took precedence over personal theological convictions.

THE POSSESSED

In *The Possessed*, Dostoevski centered his attention on a very different type, the emerging Russian nihilist-atheist generation of the latter half of the nineteenth century. While the political aspect of the work occupies the general background, metaphysical and moral issues soon find their way into the narrative, as do satiric portraits of prominent Russians, among them a caricature of Turgenev, depicted in the ridiculous figure of Karmazinov. On the political level, Dostoevski demonstrates that revolutionary nihilism inevitably turns into a greater despotism than the order it intends to replace. One unscrupulous gang member, Shigalev, advocates a dictatorship of select revolutionaries and absolute submission on the part of the governed. For this reason, *The Possessed* faced long censorial repression in the Soviet Union, and former Soviet critics still find it awkward to present credible analyses of the novel.

The novelistic conspiracy is headed by a bloodthirsty degenerate, Pyotr Verkhovensky. Like Raskolnikov's murder in *Crime and Punishment*, Verkhovensky's killing is based on an actual event, the extermination of a student by the political terrorist Sergey Nechayev in 1869. Dostoevski's correspondence reveals that he was disturbed by the perverse publicity attending Nechayev's notoriety and intended to incorporate the incident into *The Possessed* for the purpose of deglamorizing such nihilistic misdeeds. In this he succeeded without question. Verkhovensky is shown to manipulate followers whose brutality and narrow-mindedness easily fashion them into blindly obedient puppets.

The focus of the novel, however, is on an enigmatic atheist, Stavrogin, who is only passively interested in external events. Stavrogin has no plans, preferences, illusions, beliefs, or passions, and his actions are accordingly illogical. For example, he engages in duels although he does not believe in them; marries a mental defective on a wager; bites his host, the governor of the province, on the ear; and calmly accepts a slap in the face from a subordinate. His very indifference to everyone and everything has made him into a charismatic figure whom Verkhovensky and his revolutionaries revere as a deity.

Stavrogin is depicted in such a shadowy manner that no coherent portrait emerges. The notebooks for *The Possessed* record the author's difficulties in creating the character: In early versions, Stavrogin is more fleshed out and clarified, but in the end Dostoevski chose to present him as a riddle, to demonstrate that an incorporeal image, by its very nature, exacts the deepest loyalties. Stavrogin's disinterest in the world eventually leads to inner dissatisfaction and suicide. An interesting part of his portrayal, his confession to a priest that he is responsible for the death of a child whom he raped, was excised by the censors and never restored by Dostoevski. Omission of this episode strips Stavrogin of the feeling of regret implied in the confession and intensifies the impression of absolute ethical neutrality assigned to his personality. Stavrogin is the opposite of Prince Myshkin in every respect—uninvolved rather than concerned, bored rather than active, cruel and unpredictable rather than steadfastly compassionate—yet their endeavors lead to the same tragic end. Neither manages to cope with reality and both abandon the world, Myshkin through madness, Stavrogin through suicide.

Another major character carrying a symbolic burden is Kirillov, whose inner conflicts about the existence or nonexistence of God also drive him to self-extinction. Kirillov is Western-educated, influenced by the scientific discoveries of the age; an avowed atheist, he transfers godlike attributes to himself. As Dostoevski traces Kirillov's inner reasoning, he reveals Kirillov to be a philosophical extremist. Because he no longer believes in an afterlife but is inexplicably afraid of death, he conquers that fear by annihilating himself. His opposite, Shatov, a believer in the Orthodox Church and in the special status of the Russian people, ends as a victim of the conspirators; once more, the author's plot line follows two diametrically opposed figures to the same fatal end.

Both *The Idiot* and *The Possessed* lack a hopeful view of the future. The society and mores in which the major figures operate reflect moral confusion and material corruption, a Babylonian atmosphere that Dostoevski subtly ascribes to erosion of faith. As always, it is difficult to say exactly where the author stands. Clearly, he refutes the terrorism exercised by Verkhovensky and his gang. Their political intrigue assumes the metaphysical quality of biblical devils "possessed" by love of ruin and chaos. The grisly demise of the other major characters suggests that Dostoevski also considered their approaches inadequate. The philosophical arguments, however, are presented with such conviction and honesty that no point of view is totally annihilated.

For most of the 1870's, Dostoevski was able to work at a leisurely pace, free from the material wants and deadline pressure of the preceding decades. It is all the more surprising, then, that *A Raw Youth*, composed in those tranquil years, is his least successful major novel. The reasons are painfully clear. The author overloaded the plot with poorly integrated, unrelated themes. What is worse, he let the rhetorical expression of his pet ideas overwhelm the artistic structure. The basic story deals with the illegitimate "raw youth" Arkady Dolgoruky, who is engaged in winning some recognition or affection from his biological father, Versilov. The narrative soon shifts to Versilov, a typical Dostoevskian dual type, motivated simultaneously by cruel passions and Christian meekness. Versilov carries additional symbolic burdens relating to Russia's alleged spiritual superiority over Western Europe. While Dostoevski fails to tie the many strands into a believable or even interesting panorama, he does attempt a symbolic scheme. Arkady's mother, Sofia, embodies "Mother Russia." She is on one side linked by marriage to a traditional peasant, Makar Ivanitch. At the same time, Sofia has been seduced by and continues to be involved with Versilov, the representative of the Western-educated nobility. The hapless Arkady, the disoriented offspring of this unconsecrated union, is driven to drastic schemes in an effort to find his place in life.

THE BROTHERS KARAMAZOV

Together with *Crime and Punishment, The Brothers Karamazov* continues to be Dostoevski's most widely read and discussed work. The author introduces no new concepts or literary devices in the novel, but this time he is successful in casting his themes into a brilliantly conceived construct. The conflict between a cruelly uncaring father and his vengeance-bound sons receives the artistic treatment missing in *A Raw Youth*. The metaphysical arguments, especially the dialectic between atheism and Christianity, are dealt with at length. Finally, the behavioral complexities of bipolar personalities are depicted in a most sophisticated manner.

The plot of the novel revolves around parricide. Four brothers, one illegitimate, have been criminally neglected by their wanton father, Fyodor Pavlovich, and subconsciously strive to avenge this transgression. The abominations of old Karamazov, some brutally indulged in the children's presence and partly involving their respective mothers, settle in the brothers' subconscious and motivate all of their later actions and behaviors. For most of the novel, none of the adult brothers is ever completely aware of the now-sublimated parricidal impulses, but all silently play their parts in seeing the old man murdered. The three legitimate brothers cope by nurturing father substitutes with whom they enter into complicated relationships. The oldest, Dmitri, fights his surrogates, almost murdering one, while the youngest, Alyosha, a novice, faces deep mental anguish in cultivating a father figure in his spiritual superior, Father Zossima. Ivan, the middle brother, has transferred his hatred of his father to a metaphysical plane, where he spars with a cruel God about the injustice of permitting mistreatment of children. In his prose poem "The Legend of the Grand Inquisitor," Ivan creates a benevolent father figure who shields his human flock from such suffering. Only Smerdyakov, the illegitimate offspring, keeps his attention focused on the primary target and actually kills old Karamazov, though his inner understanding of the factors motivating him is equally fuzzy. In desperation at not being fraternally acknowledged by his brothers, even after murdering for them, Smerdyakov implicates them in the crime and removes himself through suicide. The other three undergo painful self-examination from which they emerge as better human beings but not victorious. Dmitri, officially convicted of the crime, faces long imprisonment; Ivan's mind has given way as hallucinations plague him; and Alyosha seeks ways to combine his faith in a merciful God with the catastrophes of his actual experience.

Dostoevski has the major characters respond in different ways to their situation, developing each in terms of a specific psychological or metaphysical problem. Through Ivan, the author demonstrates the inadequacy of intellect where subconscious motivation is concerned. Ivan is educated, rational, atheistic, given to abstraction, loath to enter into close personal relationships, and proud of his intellectual superiority. Yet his wish to see his father dead is so powerful that it leads him into a silent conspiracy with Smerdyakov, whom he despises on a rational plane. The author attaches a higher moral value to Dmitri's type of personality. Dmitri represents an emotionally explosive spirit, quick to engage in melodramatic outbursts and passionate displays of surface sentiment. He instinctively grasps the moral superiority of the earthy, morally lax Grushenka to the socially superior, moralizing Katerina Ivanovna. His reckless nature leads him into many transgressions and misjudgments, but at a crucial point, when he has sought after opportunity to murder his parent, a deeply embedded reverence for life stays his hand. Alyosha acts as Dostoevski's representative of the Christian faith, and, like all other Dostoevskian Christian heroes, he is subjected to severe spiritual torments. His faith is tested as the externals and rituals of religion to which he clings prove elusive, if not false, and he is made to reach for a more profound Christian commitment within himself in order to survive the violence engendered by the Karamazov heritage. He is given the privilege, rare among Dostoevskian heroes, of affecting his environment in a wholesome fashion, especially at the end of the novel.

Each of the three brothers is rendered more complex in the course of his spiritual odyssey. The atheistic Ivan defends the cause of the Orthodox Church in his formal writings and in the end loses all pride and reason as he humbles himself in a futile attempt to save the innocent Dmitri from imprisonment. Dmitri acquires a measure of philosophical introspection as he learns to accept punishment for a murder he ardently desired but did not commit. Alyosha, too, despite largely positive patterning, is shown to let hidden desire neutralize religious conviction. Charged by Father Zossima with acting as Dmitri's keeper, the otherwise conscientious and compassionate Alyosha simply "forgets" the obligation and thereby fails to prevent his father's murder and his brother's entrapment. Dostoevski envisioned a larger role for Alyosha in a sequel to *The Brothers Karamazov* that never materialized. For this reason, Alyosha exits the work somewhat incomplete, incongruously engaged to a cunning, cruel cripple, Liza, who serves as his own unholy alter ego in the parricidal scheme.

The work abounds in secondary plots and figures, all interconnected and echoing the primary drama in intricate ways. Prominent among these plots is the legend of the Grand Inquisitor and the refutation of the legend by Father Zossima. Through the Grand Inquisitor, Dostoevski argues that Christian ideals are set too high for ordinary mortals, who prefer security and comfort to difficult individual choices. The Grand Inquisitor, in a dramatic encounter with Christ, thoroughly defends a benign kingdom on earth as most suitable for the masses. This argument is countered by Zossima's restatement of basic Christian theology, which does not answer the Grand Inquisitor's charges but simply offers traditional belief and practice of Christian tenets as an alternative perspective. The very type of behavior that proved ruinous to Prince Myshkin is in Zossima's actions converted into a richly beneficial model. By presenting the discourse in this fashion, Dostoevski cleverly juxtaposed humanistic and Christian arguments without resolving them. He thus once more implied that all so-called issues contain their own contradictions, that life and truth are indeed multiple.

By devoting his novels to the exploration of the mind, Dostoevski extended the intellectual horizons of his day. Although publicly a conservative of Russian Orthodox conviction, Dostoevski produced works that continuously challenge the notion that atheism inevitably engenders wanton amorality. It is this recognition of human complexity, coupled with a fascinating narrative style, that gives Dostoevski his modern flavor.

Margot K. Frank

Other major works

SHORT FICTION: *Sochineniya,* 1860 (2 volumes); *Polnoye sobraniye sochineniy,* 1865-1870 (4 volumes); *Povesti i rasskazy,* 1882; *The Gambler, and Other Stories,* 1914; *A Christmas Tree and a Wedding, and an Honest Thief,* 1917; *White Nights, and Other Stories,* 1918; *An Honest Thief, and Other Stories,* 1919; *The Short Novels of Dostoevsky,* 1945.

NONFICTION: "Zimniye zametki o letnikh vpechatleniyakh," 1863 ("Winter Notes on Summer Impressions," 1955); *Dnevnik pisatelya,* 1876-1877, 1880-1881 (2 volumes; *The Diary of a Writer,* 1949); *Pisma,* 1928-1959 (4 volumes); *Iz arkhiva F. M. Dostoyevskogo: "Idiot,"* 1931 (*The Notebooks for "The Idiot,"* 1967); *Iz arkhiva F. M. Dostoyevskogo: "Prestupleniye i nakazaniye,"* 1931 (*The Notebooks for "Crime and Punishment,"* 1967); *F. M. Dostoyevsky: Materialy i issledovaniya,* 1935 (*The Notebooks for "The Brothers Karamazov,"* 1971); *Zapisnyye tetradi F. M. Dostoyevskogo,* 1935 (*The Notebooks for "The Possessed,"* 1968); *Dostoevsky's Occasional Writings,* 1963; *F. M. Dostoyevsky v rabote nad romanom "Podrostok,"* 1965 (*The Notebooks for "A Raw Youth,"* 1969); *Neizdannyy Dostoyevsky: Zapisnyye knizhki i tetradi 1860-1881,* 1971 (3 volumes; *The Unpublished Dostoyevsky: Diaries and Notebooks, 1860-1881,* 1973-1976); *F. M. Dostoyevsky ob iskusstve,* 1973; *Selected Letters of Fyodor Dostoyevsky,* 1987.

TRANSLATION: *Yevgeniya Grande*, 1844 (of Honoré de Balzac's novel *Eugénie Grandet*).

MISCELLANEOUS: *Polnoe sobranie sochinenii v tridtsati tomakh*, 1972-1990 (30 volumes).

BIBLIOGRAPHY

Adelman, Gary. *Retelling Dostoyesvky: Literary Responses and Other Observations.* Lewisburg, Pa.: Bucknell University Press, 2001. Provides information on Dostoevski's life and works by examining how nine twentieth century authors re-created *Crime and Punishment* and other Dostoevski novels. Describes how Dostoevski deeply influenced Joseph Conrad, Richard Wright, Vladimir Nabokov, Bernard Malamud, David Storey, Leonid Leonov, J. M. Coetzee, Frank Herbert, and Albert Camus.

Bloom, Harold, ed. *Fyodor Dostoevsky.* New York: Chelsea House, 2005. Collection of essays includes a biography, analyses of Dostoevski's works, and discussions about the characters in *The Brothers Karamazov* and Dostoevski's detractors and defenders. Also reprints "The Idea in Dostoevsky," an essay by Russian philosopher and literary critic Mikhail Bakhtin.

Catteau, Jacques. *Dostoevsky and the Process of Literary Creation.* Translated by Audrey Littlewood. New York: Cambridge University Press, 1989. Excellent resource offers detailed textual analysis and factual information on Dostoevski. Provides a thematic overview of the pressures and inspirations that motivated the author. Includes extensive notes, bibliography, and index.

Frank, Joseph. *Dostoevsky: The Seeds of Revolt, 1821-1849.* Princeton, N.J.: Princeton University Press, 1976.

_____. *Dostoevsky: The Years of Ordeal, 1850-1859.* Princeton, N.J.: Princeton University Press, 1983.

_____. *Dostoevsky: The Stir of Liberation, 1860-1865.* Princeton, N.J.: Princeton University Press, 1986.

_____. *Dostoevsky: The Miraculous Years, 1865-1871.* Princeton, N.J.: Princeton University Press, 1995.

_____. *Dostoevsky: The Mantle of the Prophet.* Princeton, N.J.: Princeton University Press, 2002. Monumental five-volume biography is one of the best sources on Dostoevski's life and art available in English. Frank subordinates details about the writer's private life in favor of tracing his connection to the social and cultural history of his time.

Kjetsaa, Geir. *Fyodor Dostoevsky: A Writer's Life.* Translated by Siri Hustvedt and David McDuff. New York: Viking Press, 1987. Thorough and compelling work on Dostoevski's life seeks to shed light on the creation of his fiction, citing letters and notes as artistic points of departure for the author.

Leatherbarrow, W. J., ed. *The Cambridge Companion to Dostoevskii*. New York: Cambridge University Press, 2006. Collection of essays examines the author's life and works, discussing his relationship to Russian folk heritage, money, the intelligentsia, psychology, religion, the family, and science, among other topics. Includes chronology and bibliography.

McReynolds, Susan. *Redemption and the Merchant God: Dostoevsky's Economy of Salvation and Antisemitism*. Evanston, Ill.: Northwestern University Press, 2008. Argues that readers cannot fully understand Dostoevski's writings without understanding his obsession with the Jews. Analyzes not only the elements of anti-Semitism in his works but also examines his views of the Crucifixion, Resurrection, morality, and other aspects of Christian doctrine.

Miller, Robin Feuer. *Dostoevsky's Unfinished Journey*. New Haven, Conn.: Yale University Press, 2007. Examines Dostoevski's works from numerous perspectives, analyzing the themes of conversion and healing in his fiction, questioning his literary influence, and exploring what happens to *Crime and Punishment* when it is taught in the classroom.

Scanlan, James P. *Dostoevsky the Thinker: A Philosophical Study*. Ithaca, N.Y.: Cornell University Press, 2002. Analyzes Dostoevski's novels, essays, letters, and notebooks to provide a comprehensive account of his philosophy, examining the weakness as well as the strength of Dostoevski's ideas. Concludes that Dostoevski's thought was shaped by anthropocentrism—a struggle to define the very essence of humanity.

Straus, Nina Pelikan. *Dostoevsky and the Woman Question: Rereadings at the End of a Century*. New York: St. Martin's Press, 1994. Argues that Dostoevski's compulsion to depict men's cruelties to women is an important part of his vision and his metaphysics. Maintains that Dostoevski attacks masculine notions of autonomy and that his works evolve toward "the death of the patriarchy."

NIKOLAI GOGOL

Born: Sorochintsy, Ukraine, Russian Empire (now in Ukraine); March 31, 1809
Died: Moscow, Russia; March 4, 1852

PRINCIPAL LONG FICTION
Myortvye dushi, 1842, 1855 (2 parts; *Dead Souls*, 1887)
Taras Bulba, 1842 (revision of his 1835 short story; English translation, 1886)

OTHER LITERARY FORMS

Nikolai Gogol (GAW-guhl) authored many short stories, most of which are part of his "Ukrainian cycle" or his later "Petersburg cycle." He also wrote many plays, including *Revizor* (pr., pb. 1836; *The Inspector General*, 1890) and *Zhenit'ba* (pr., pb. 1842; *Marriage: A Quite Incredible Incident*, 1926), as well as a great deal of nonfiction, much of it collected in *Arabeski* (1835; *Arabesques*, 1982) and *Vybrannye mesta iz perepiski s druzyami* (1847; *Selected Passages from Correspondence with Friends*, 1969). Gogol's *Polnoe sobranie sochinenii* (1940-1952; collected works), which includes unfinished works and drafts as well as his voluminous correspondence, fills fourteen volumes. All of Gogol's finished works, but not his drafts or correspondence, are available in English translation.

ACHIEVEMENTS

Nikolai Gogol's first collection of short stories, *Vechera na khutore bliz Dikanki* (1831, 1832; *Evenings on a Farm near Dikanka*, 1926), made him famous, and his second collection, *Mirgorod* (1835; English translation, 1928), highlighted by the story "Taras Bulba," established his reputation as Russia's leading prose writer. While Gogol's early stories, set in the Ukraine, are for the most part conventionally Romantic, his later Petersburg cycle of short stories, among which "Zapiski sumasshedshego" ("Diary of a Madman") and "Shinel" ("The Overcoat") are two of the best known, marks the beginning of Russian critical realism. Gogol's comedic plays are classics and are as popular on the stage (and screen) today as they were in Gogol's lifetime.

Gogol's novel *Dead Souls* is rivaled only by Leo Tolstoy's *Voyna i mir* (1865-1869; *War and Peace*, 1886) as the greatest prose work of Russian literature. Russian prose fiction is routinely divided into two schools: the Pushkinian, which is objective, matter-of-fact, and sparing in its use of verbal devices; and the Gogolian, which is artful, ornamental, and exuberant in its use of ambiguity, irony, pathos, and a variety of figures and tropes usually associated with poetry. Tolstoy and Ivan Turgenev belong to the Pushkinian school; Fyodor Dostoevski, to the Gogolian. In his historical, critical, and moral essays, but especially in *Selected Passages from Correspondence with Friends*, Gogol established many of the principles of Russian conservative thought, anticipating the ideas of such writers as Dostoevski and Apollon Grigoryev.

Nikolai Gogol
(Library of Congress)

Biography

Nikolai Vasilyevich Gogol, the son of a country squire, was born and educated in the Ukraine. Russian was to him a foreign language, which he mastered while attending secondary school in Nezhin, also in the Ukraine. After his graduation in 1828, Gogol went to St. Petersburg, where he joined the civil service. His first literary effort, "Hans Küchelgarten" (1829), a sentimental idyll in blank verse, was a failure, but his prose fiction immediately attracted attention. After the success of *Evenings on a Farm near Dikanka*, Gogol decided to devote himself entirely to his literary career. He briefly taught medieval history at St. Petersburg University (1834-1835) and thereafter lived the life of a freelance writer and journalist, frequently supported by wealthy patrons. The opening of his play *The Inspector General* at the Aleksandrinsky Theater in St. Petersburg on April 19, 1836, attended and applauded by Czar Nicholas I, was a huge success, but it also elicited vehement attacks by the reactionary press, enraged by Gogol's spirited satire of corruption and stupidity in the provincial administration, and Gogol decided to go abroad to escape the controversy.

From 1836 to 1848, Gogol lived abroad, mostly in Rome, returning to Russia for brief periods only. The year 1842 marked the high point of Gogol's career with the appearance of the first part of *Dead Souls* and the publication of a four-volume set of collected works, which contained some previously unpublished pieces, in particular the great short story "The Overcoat." After 1842, Gogol continued to work on part 2 of *Dead Souls*, but he was becoming increasingly preoccupied with questions of religion and morality. His book *Selected Passages from Correspondence with Friends*, actually a collection of essays in which Gogol defends traditional religious and moral values as well as the social status quo (including the institution of serfdom), caused a storm of protest, as liberals felt that it was flagrantly and evilly reactionary, while even many conservatives considered it to be unctuous and self-righteous.

Sorely hurt by the unfavorable reception of his book, Gogol almost entirely withdrew from literature. He returned to Russia for good in 1848 and spent the rest of his life in religious exercise and meditation. Shortly before his death, caused by excessive fasting and utter exhaustion, Gogol burned the final version of part 2 of *Dead Souls*. An earlier version was later discovered and published in 1855.

Analysis

The cover of the first edition of *Dèad Souls*, designed by Nikolai Gogol himself, reads as follows: "*The Adventures of Chichikov or Dead Souls. A Poem by N. Gogol. 1842.*" "The Adventures of Chichikov" is in the smallest print, "Dead Souls" is more than twice that size, and "A Poem" is twice again the size of "Dead Souls." The word "or" is barely legible. The fact that "The Adventures of Chichikov" was inserted at the insistence of the censor, who felt that "Dead Souls" alone smacked of blasphemy, accounts for one-half of this typographical irregularity. The fact that "A Poem" (Russian *poema*, which usually designates an epic poem in verse) dominates the cover of a prose work that at first glance is anything but "poetic" also had its reasons, as will be seen.

Dead Souls

The plot structure of *Dead Souls* is simple. Chichikov, a middle-aged gentleman of decent appearance and pleasing manners, travels through the Russian provinces on what seems a mysterious quest: He buys up "dead souls," meaning serfs who have died since the last census but are still listed on the tax rolls until the next census. Along the way, he meets various types of Russian landowners: the sugary and insipid Manilov; the widow Korobochka, ignorant and superstitious but an efficient manager of her farm; the dashing Nozdryov, a braggart, liar, and cardsharp; the brutish but shrewd Sobakevich; and the sordid miser Plyushkin. Having returned to the nearby provincial capital to obtain legal title to his four-hundred-odd "souls," Chichikov soon comes under a cloud of suspicion and quickly leaves town. Only at this stage does the reader learn about Chichikov's past and the secret of the dead souls. A civil service official, Chichikov had twice reached the threshold of prosperity through cleverly devised depredations of the state treasury, but each time he had been foiled at the last moment. After his second fiasco, he had been allowed to resign with only a small sum saved from the clutches of his auditors. Undaunted, he had conceived yet another scheme: He would buy up a substantial number of "dead souls," mortgage them at the highest rate available, and disappear with the cash.

The plot of part 1 takes the story only this far. In what is extant of part 2, Chichikov is seen not only trying to buy more dead souls but also getting involved in other nefarious schemes. It also develops, however, that Chichikov is not happy with his sordid and insecure existence and that he dreams of an honest and virtuous life. He would be willing to mend his ways if he could only find a proper mentor who would give him the right start. There is reason to believe that Gogol planned to describe Chichikov's regeneration and return to the path of righteousness in part 3. The whole plot thus follows the pattern of a picaresque novel, and many details of *Dead Souls* are, in fact, compatible with this genre, which was well established in Russian literature even before Gogol's day.

Actually, part 1 of *Dead Souls* is many things in addition to a picaresque novel: a humorous novel after the fashion of Charles Dickens's *Pickwick Papers* (1836-1837, serial; 1837, book), with which it was immediately compared by the critics; a social satire attacking the corruption and inefficiency of the imperial administration and the crudity and mental torpor of the landed gentry; a moral sermon in the form of grotesque character sketches; and, above all, an epic of Russia's abjection and hoped-for redemption. The characters of part 2, while copies, in a way, of those encountered in part 1, have redeeming traits and strike the reader as human beings rather than as caricatures. The landowner Tentetnikov, in particular, is clearly a prototype of Oblomov, the hero of Ivan Goncharov's immortal novel of that title (1859; English translation, 1915), and, altogether, part 2 of *Dead Souls* is a big step in the direction of the Russian realist novel of the 1850's and 1860's. The following observations apply to part 1, unless otherwise indicated.

The structure of *Dead Souls* is dominated by the road, as the work begins with a description of Chichikov's arrival at an inn of an unidentified provincial capital and ends with him back on the road, with several intervening episodes in which the hero is seen on his way to his next encounter with a potential purveyor of dead souls. Chichikov's tippling coachman, Selifan, and his three-horse carriage (*troika*) are often foregrounded in Gogol's narrative, and one of the three horses, the lazy and stubborn piebald, has become one of the best-known "characters" in all of Russian fiction. The celebrated *troika* passage concludes part 1. Vladimir Nabokov has written that critic Andrey Bely saw "the whole first volume of *Dead Souls* as a closed circle whirling on its axle and blurring the spokes, with the theme of the wheel cropping up at each new revolution on round Chichikov's part."

When Chichikov is not on the road, the narrative becomes a mirror, as each new character is reflected in Chichikov's mind with the assistance of the omniscient narrator's observations and elucidations. One contemporary critic said that reading *Dead Souls* was like walking down a hotel corridor, opening one door after another—and staring at another human monster each time.

The road and the mirror by no means exhaust Gogol's narrative attitudes. *Dead Souls* features some philosophical discussions on a variety of topics; many short narrative vignettes, such as when Chichikov dreamily imagines what some of his freshly acquired dead souls may have been like in life; an inserted novella, *The Tale of Captain Kopeikin*, told by the local postmaster, who suspects that Chichikov is in fact the legendary outlaw Captain Kopeikin; repeated apostrophes to the reader, discussing the work itself and the course to be taken in continuing it; and, last but not least, Gogol's much-debated lyric digressions. Altogether, while there is some dialogue in *Dead Souls*, the narrator's voice dominates throughout. In fact, the narrative may be described as the free flow of the narrator's stream of consciousness, drifting from observation to observation, image to image, and thought to thought. It is often propelled by purely verbal associations. A common instance of the latter is the so-called realized metaphor, such as when a vendor of hot mead, whose large red face is likened to a copper samovar, is referred to as "the samovar"; when Chichikov, threatened with bodily harm by an enraged Nozdryov and likened to a fortress under siege, suddenly becomes "the fortress"; or when the bearlike Sobakevich is casually identified as a "fair sized bear" in the role of landowner. It is also verbal legerdemain that eventually turns Sobakevich's whole estate into an extension of its owner: "Every object, every chair in Sobakevich's house seemed to proclaim: 'I, too, am Sobakevich!'"

Hyperbole is another device characteristic of Gogol's style. Throughout *Dead Souls*, grotesque distortions and exaggerations are presented as a matter of course—for example, when the scratching of the clerks' pens at the office where Chichikov seals his purchase of dead souls is likened to "the sound of several carts loaded with brushweed and driven through a forest piled with dead leaves a yard deep." Often the hyperbole is ironic, such as when the attire of local ladies is reported to be "of such fashionable pastel shades that one could not even give their names, to such a degree had the refinement of taste attained!"

A sure sign of the author's own point of view surfaces in frequent literary allusions and several passages in which Gogol digresses to discuss the theory of fiction—for example, the famous disquisition, introducing chapter 7, on the distinction between the writer who idealizes life and the writer who chooses to deal with real life. Gogol, who fancies himself to be a realist, wryly observes that "the judgment of his time does not recognize that much spiritual depth is required to throw light upon a picture taken from a despised stratum of life, and to exalt it into a pearl of creative art" but feels "destined by some wondrous power to go hand in hand with his heroes, to contemplate life in its entirety, life rushing past in all its enormity, amid laughter perceptible to the world and through tears that are unperceived by and unknown to it!" The phrases "to exalt it into a pearl of creative art" and "amid laughter perceptible to the world and through tears that are unperceived by and unknown to it" have become common Russian usage, along with many others in *Dead Souls*.

Dead Souls is studded with many outright digressions. It must be kept in mind, however, that the mid-nineteenth century novel was routinely used as a catchall for miscellaneous didactic, philosophical, critical, scholarly, and lyric pieces that were often only superficially, if at all, integrated into the texture of the larger work. Still, the number and nature of digressions in *Dead Souls* are exceptional even by the standards of a *roman feuilleton* of the 1840's. As described by Victor Erlich, two basic types of digressions are found in *Dead Souls:* "the lateral darts and the upward flights." The former are excursions into a great variety of aspects of Russian life, keenly observed, sharply focused, and always lively and colorful. For example, having observed that Sobakevich's head looks quite like a pumpkin, Gogol, in one of his many "Homeric similes," veers off into a village idyll about a peasant lad strumming a balalaika made from a pumpkin to win the heart of a "snowy-breasted and snowy-necked Maiden."

Gogol's upward flights are of a quite different order. They permit his imagination to escape the prosaic reality of Chichikov's experience and allow him to become a poet who takes a lofty view of Russia and its destiny. In several of these passages, Gogol's imagination becomes quite literally airborne. One of them, at the conclusion of chapter 5, begins with a lofty aerial panorama: "Even as an incomputable host of churches, of monasteries, with cupolas, bulbous domes, and crosses, is scattered all over holy and devout Russia, so does an incomputable multitude of tribes, generations, peoples swarm, flaunt their motley and scurry across the face of the earth." It ends in a rousing paean to "the Russian word which, like no other in the world, would burst out so, from out the very heart, which would seethe so and quiver and flutter so much like a living thing."

Early in chapter 11, Gogol produces another marvelous panoramic vision of Russia, apostrophized in the famous passage, "Russia, Russia! I behold thee—from my alien, beautiful, far-off vantage point I behold thee." (Gogol wrote most of *Dead Souls* while living in Italy.) The conclusion of this, the final chapter of part 1, then brings the most famous lines of prose in all of Russian literature, the *troika* passage in which a speeding three-horse carriage is elevated to a symbol of Russia's historical destiny. The intensity and plenitude of life and emotion in these and other airborne lyric passages stand in stark contrast to the drab world that is otherwise dominant in *Dead Souls*. These lyric digressions were challenged as incongruous and unnecessary even by some contemporary critics who, as do many critics today, failed to realize that Gogol's is a dual vision of manic-depressive intensity.

As a *poema* (epic poem), *Dead Souls* is a work that Gogol perceived as the poetic expression of an important religious-philosophical conception—that is, something on the order of Dante's *La divina commedia* (c. 1320; *The Divine Comedy*, 1802) or John Milton's *Paradise Lost* (1667, 1674). Incidentally, there is one rather inconsequential allusion to Dante in chapter 7, where one reads that a collegiate registrar "served our friends even as Virgil at one time had served Dante, and guided them to the Presence."

Immediately after the appearance of *Dead Souls*, critics were split into two camps: those who, like Konstantin Aksakov, greeted the work as the Russian national epic, found numerous Homeric traits in it, and perceived it as a true incarnation of the Russian spirit in all of its depth and plenitude, and those who, like Nikolai Alekseevich Polevoi and Osip

Ivanovich Senkovsky, saw it as merely an entertaining, though rather banal and in places pretentious, humorous novel. The latter group—which included even the great critic Vissarion Belinsky, who otherwise felt that *Dead Souls* was a perfect quintessence of Russian life—found Gogol's attempts at philosophizing and solemn pathos merely pompous and false. There has never been agreement in this matter. Nevertheless, several passages in part 1, the whole drift of part 2, and a number of quite unequivocal statements made by Gogol in his correspondence (in *Selected Passages from Correspondence with Friends* and in his posthumous "Author's Confession") all suggest that Gogol did indeed perceive *Dead Souls* as a *Divine Comedy* of the Russian soul, with part 1 its *Inferno*, part 2 its *Purgatory*, and part 3 its *Paradise*.

How, then, is part 1 in fact an *Inferno*, a Russian Hell? It is set in a Hades of dead souls, of humans who lead a shadowy phantom existence bereft of any real meaning or direction. Thus, it must be understood that in the Romantic philosophy of Gogol's time, the "normal" existence of a European philistine was routinely called "illusory," "unreal," and even "ghostly," while the ideal quest of the artist or philosopher was considered "substantial," "real," and "truly alive." As Andrey Bely demonstrated most convincingly, all of part 1 is dominated by what he calls "the figure of fiction." Whatever is said or believed to be true is from beginning to end a fiction, as unreal as Chichikov's financial transactions. For example, when the good people of N. begin to suspect that something is wrong with Chichikov, some of them believe that he plans to abduct the Governor's daughter, others conjecture that he is really Captain Kopeikin, a highway robber of legendary fame, and some actually suspect that he is Napoleon escaped from his island exile, but nobody investigates his motive for buying dead souls. As Bely also demonstrated, even time and space in *Dead Souls* are fictitious: The text will not even allow one to determine the season of the year; Chichikov's itinerary, if methodically checked, is physically impossible; and so on. Behind the figure of fiction, there looms large the message that all earthly experience and wisdom are in fact illusory, as Gogol makes explicit in a philosophical digression found in chapter 10.

In this shadowy world of fiction there exist two kinds of dead souls. There are the dead serfs who are sold and mortgaged and who, in the process, acquire a real semblance of life. Mrs. Korobochka, as soon as she has understood that Chichikov is willing to pay her some money for her dead serfs, is afraid that he may underpay her and somewhat timidly suggests that "maybe I'll find some use for them in my own household." Sobakevich, who haggles about the price of each dead soul, insists on eloquently describing their skills and virtues, as though it really mattered. Chichikov himself firmly rejects an offer by the local authorities to provide him with a police escort for the souls he has purchased, asserting that "his peasants are all of eminently quiet disposition." The same night, however, when he returns home from a party thrown by the local police chief to honor the new owner of four hundred souls, he actually orders Selifan "to gather all the resettled peasants, so he can personally make a roll call of them." Selifan and Petrushka, Chichikov's lackey, barely manage to get their master to bed.

The humanitarian message behind all of this is obvious: How could a person who finds the buying and selling of dead souls "fantastic" and "absurd" have the effrontery to find the same business transactions involving living souls perfectly normal? This message applies not only to Russia in the age of serfdom (which ended only in 1861—that is, at about the same time formal slavery ended in the United States) but also to any situation in which human beings are reduced to their social or economic function.

The other dead souls are the landowners and government officials whom we meet in *Dead Souls*. As the critic Vasily Rozanov observed, the peculiar thing about Gogolian characters is that they have no souls; they have habits and appetites but no deeper human emotions or ideal strivings. This inevitably deprives them of their humanity and renders them two-dimensional personifications of their vices—caricatures. Sobakevich is a very shrewd talking bear. Nozdryov is so utterly worthless that he appears to be a mere appendage of his extraordinarily handsome, thick, and pitch-black sideburns, thinned out a bit from time to time, when their owner is caught cheating at cards and suffers a whisker pulling. Plyushkin's stony miserliness has deprived him of all feeling and has turned him, a rich landowner, into a beggar and an outcast of society. *Dead Souls* has many such caricatures, which have been likened to Brueghelian grotesque paintings. This analogy applies to the following passage in chapter 11, for example: "The clerks in the Treasury were especially distinguished for their unprepossessing and unsightly appearance. Some had faces for all the world like badly baked bread: one cheek would be all puffed out to one side, the chin slanting off to the other, the upper lip blown up into a big blister that, to top it all off, had burst."

As early as 1842, the critic Stepan Shevyrev suggested that *Dead Souls* represented a mad world, thus following an ancient literary and cultural tradition (which today is often referred to as that of the "carnival"). The massive absurdities, non sequiturs, and simply plain foolishness throughout the whole text could, for Gogol and for many of his readers, have only one message: That which poses for "real life" is in fact nothing but a ludicrous farce. The basic course of Gogol's imagination is that of a descent into a world of ridiculous, banal, and vile "nonbeing," from which it will from time to time rise to the heights of noble and inspired "being."

TARAS BULBA

While *Dead Souls* is unquestionably Gogol's masterpiece, his only other work of long fiction, *Taras Bulba*, is not without interest. The 1835 version of this work is a historical novella; the 1842 version, almost twice as long and thus novel-sized, has many digressions and is at once more realistic and more gothic but also more patriotic, moralizing, and bigoted. The plot is essentially the same in both versions.

Taras Bulba is a Ukrainian Cossack leader, so proud of his two fine sons recently back from school in Kiev that he foments war against the hated Poles, so that Ostap and Andriy can prove their manhood in battle. The Cossacks are initially successful, and the Poles are driven back to the fortress city of Dubno. The Cossacks lay siege to it, and the city seems ready to fall when Andriy is lured to the city by a messenger from a beautiful Polish maiden with whom he had fallen in love as a student in Kiev. Blinded by her promises of love, Andriy turns traitor. The Cossacks' fortunes now take a turn for the worse. They are pressed hard by a Polish relief force. On the battlefield, Taras meets Andriy (now a Polish officer), orders him to dismount, and shoots him. The Cossacks, however, are defeated, and Ostap is taken prisoner. Old Taras makes his way to Warsaw, hoping to save him, but can only witness his son's execution. Having returned to the Ukraine, Taras becomes one of the leaders of yet another Cossack uprising against the king of Poland. When peace is made, Taras alone refuses to honor it. He continues to wreak havoc on the Poles all over the Ukraine but is finally captured by superior Polish forces. He dies at the stake, prophesying the coming of a Russian czar against whom no power on earth will stand.

There is little historical verity in *Taras Bulba*. Different details found in the text point to the fifteenth, sixteenth, and seventeenth centuries as the time of its action. It is thus an epic synthesis of the struggle of the Orthodox Ukraine to retain its independence from Catholic Poland. The battle scenes are patterned on those in the works of Vergil and Homer, and there are many conventional epic traits throughout, such as scores of brief scenes of single combat, catalogs of warriors' names, extended Homeric similes, orations, and, of course, the final solemn prophecy. Taras Bulba is a tragic hero who expiates his hubris with the loss of his sons and his own terrible death.

The earlier version of *Taras Bulba* serves mostly the glorification of the wild, carefree life at the Cossack army camp. In the later version, this truly inspired hymn to male freedom is obscured by a message of Russian nationalism, Orthodox bigotry, and nostalgia for a glorious past that never was. The novel features almost incessant baiting of Poles and Jews. Gogol's view of the war is a wholly unrealistic and romantic one: The reader is told of "the enchanting music of bullets and swords" and so on. From a literary viewpoint, *Taras Bulba* is a peculiar mixture of the historical novel in the manner of Sir Walter Scott and the gothic tale. The narrator stations himself above his hero, gently faulting him on some of his uncivilized traits, such as the excessive stock Taras puts in his drinking prowess or his maltreatment of his long-suffering wife. Rather often, however, the narrator descends to the manner of the folktale. His language swings wildly from coarse humor and naturalistic grotesque to solemn oratory and lyric digressions. Scenes of unspeakable atrocities are reported with relish, but some wonderful poems in prose are also presented, such as the well-known description of the Ukrainian steppe in the second chapter.

Altogether, *Taras Bulba* contains some brilliant writing but also some glaring faults. It immediately became a classic, and soon enough a school text, inasmuch as its jingoism met with the approval of the czar—and eventually of Soviet school administrators. Several film versions, Russian as well as Western, have been produced.

Although Gogol's production of fiction was quite small by nineteenth century standards, both his novels and his short stories have had extraordinary influence on the development of Russian prose—an influence that was still potent at the end of the twentieth century, as witnessed by the works of Andrei Sinyavsky and other writers of the Third Emigration.

Victor Terras

OTHER MAJOR WORKS

SHORT FICTION: *Vechera na khutore bliz Dikanki*, 1831, 1832 (2 volumes; *Evenings on a Farm near Dikanka*, 1926); *Arabeski*, 1835 (*Arabesques*, 1982); *Mirgorod*, 1835 (English translation, 1928); *The Complete Tales of Nikolai Gogol*, 1985 (2 volumes; Leonard J. Kent, editor).

PLAYS: *Revizor*, pr., pb. 1836 (*The Inspector General*, 1890); *Utro delovogo cheloveka*, pb. 1836 (revision of *Vladimir tretey stepeni*; *An Official's Morning*, 1926); *Igroki*, pb. 1842 (*The Gamblers*, 1926); *Lakeyskaya*, pb. 1842 (revision of *Vladimir tretey stepeni*; *The Servants' Hall*, 1926); *Otryvok*, pb. 1842 (revision of *Vladimir tretey stepeni*; *A Fragment*, 1926); *Tyazhba*, pb. 1842 (revision of *Vladimir tretey stepeni*; *The Lawsuit*, 1926); *Vladimir tretey stepeni*, pb. 1842 (wr. 1832); *Zhenit'ba*, pr., pb. 1842 (wr. 1835; *Marriage: A Quite Incredible Incident*, 1926); *The Government Inspector, and Other Plays*, 1926.

POETRY: *Hanz Kuechelgarten*, 1829.

NONFICTION: *Vybrannye mesta iz perepiski s druzyami*, 1847 (*Selected Passages from Correspondence with Friends*, 1969); *Letters of Nikolai Gogol*, 1967.

MISCELLANEOUS: *The Collected Works*, 1922-1927 (6 volumes); *Polnoe sobranie sochinenii*, 1940-1952 (14 volumes); *The Collected Tales and Plays of Nikolai Gogol*, 1964.

BIBLIOGRAPHY

Bojanowska, Edyta M. *Nikolai Gogol: Between Ukrainian and Russian Nationalism.* Cambridge, Mass.: Harvard University Press, 2007. Analyzes Gogol's life and works in terms of his conflicted national identity. Gogol was born in Ukraine when it was a part of the Russian empire; Bojanowska describes how he was engaged with questions of Ukrainian nationalism and how his works presented a bleak and ironic portrayal of Russia and Russian themes.

Erlich, Victor. *Gogol.* New Haven, Conn.: Yale University Press, 1969. Provides an accessible and evenhanded discussion of Gogol for nonspecialists. Focuses on Gogol's oeuvre, dealing with much of the "myth" about the author, and supplies interesting background to the making of Gogol's works.

Fanger, Donald L. *The Creation of Nikolai Gogol.* Cambridge, Mass.: Belknap Press of Harvard University Press, 1979. Digs deeply into background material and includes discussion of Gogol's works both published and unpublished in an effort to reveal the genius of Gogol's creative power. Worthwhile in many respects, particularly for the wealth of details provided about Gogol's life and milieu. Includes endnotes and index.

Gippius, V. V. *Gogol.* Translated by Robert Maguire. Ann Arbor, Mich.: Ardis, 1981. Originally written in 1924, this famous monograph supplies not only the view of a fellow countryman but also a vast, informed, and intellectual analysis of both the literary tradition in which Gogol wrote and his innovation and contribution to that tradition. Vastly interesting and easily accessible. Includes notes and a detailed list of Gogol's works.

Luckyj, George Stephen Nestor. *The Anguish of Mykola Hohol a.k.a. Nikolai Gogol.* Toronto, Ont.: Canadian Scholars' Press, 1998. Explores Gogol's life and discusses how it affected his work. Includes bibliographical references and index.

Maguire, Robert A. *Exploring Gogol.* Stanford, Calif.: Stanford University Press, 1994. One of the most comprehensive studies of Gogol's ideas and entire writing career available in English. Includes chronology, detailed notes, and extensive bibliography.

———, ed. *Gogol from the Twentieth Century: Eleven Essays.* Princeton, N.J.: Princeton University Press, 1974. Collection of essays represents some of the most famous and influential opinions on Gogol in the twentieth century. Following a lengthy introduction by the editor and translator, the contributors address and elucidate some of the most problematic aspects of Gogol's stylistics, thematics, and other compositional elements. Includes bibliography and index.

Setchkarev, Vsevolod. *Gogol: His Life and Works.* Translated by Robert Kramer. New York: New York University Press, 1965. Standard work on Gogol is still often recommended in undergraduate courses. Concentrates on both the biography and the works, seen individually and as an artistic system. Very straightforward and easily readable.

Spieker, Sven, ed. *Gogol: Exploring Absence—Negativity in Nineteenth Century Russian Literature.* Bloomington, Ind.: Slavica, 1999. Collection of essays focuses on the negativity in *Dead Souls* and Gogol's other works and in the works of other Russian writers. Includes bibliography and index.

Troyat, Henri. *Divided Soul.* Translated by Nancy Amphoux. Garden City, N.Y.: Doubleday, 1973. Provides perhaps the most information on Gogol's life available in English in a single volume. Demonstrates masterfully how Gogol's life and work are inextricably intertwined and does not neglect the important role that "God's will" played in Gogol's life, as the thread that lends the greatest cohesion to the diverse developments in his creative journey. Includes some interesting illustrations as well as bibliography, notes, and index.

Weiner, Adam. "The Evils of *Dead Souls.*" In *By Authors Possessed: The Demonic Novel in Russia.* Evanston, Ill.: Northwestern University Press, 1998. Chapter focusing on *Dead Souls* is included in a wider analysis of nineteenth and twentieth century Russian "demonic novels," defined as novels in which the protagonists are incarnated with the evil presence of the Devil.

NADINE GORDIMER

Born: Springs, Transvaal, South Africa; November 20, 1923

PRINCIPAL LONG FICTION
The Lying Days, 1953
A World of Strangers, 1958
Occasion for Loving, 1963
The Late Bourgeois World, 1966
A Guest of Honour, 1970
The Conservationist, 1974
Burger's Daughter, 1979
July's People, 1981
A Sport of Nature, 1987
My Son's Story, 1990
None to Accompany Me, 1994
The House Gun, 1998
The Pickup, 2001
Get a Life, 2005

OTHER LITERARY FORMS

Nadine Gordimer (GOHR-dih-muhr) is a prolific writer and one of the twentieth century's greatest writers of short stories. Her first collection of stories, *Face to Face* (1949), was published in Johannesburg by Silver Leaf Books. Her first story published in *The New Yorker*, where most of her stories have initially appeared, was "A Watcher of the Dead" (June 9, 1951). Gordimer's first collection of stories to be published in the United States was *The Soft Voice of the Serpent, and Other Stories* (1952). This collection was followed by many others, including *Six Feet of the Country* (1956), *Friday's Footprint, and Other Stories* (1960), *Not for Publication, and Other Stories* (1965), *A Soldier's Embrace* (1980), *Crimes of Conscience* (1991), *Loot, and Other Stories* (2003), and *Beethoven Was One-Sixteenth Black, and Other Stories* (2007). Gordimer has also written teleplays for three of her stories that were adapted for television ("Country Lovers," "A Chip of Glass Ruby," and "Praise").

She has published numerous literary reviews and other essays and short pieces, usually dealing with literature or with the culture or politics of South Africa. Her collections of essays include *The Black Interpreters: Notes on African Writing* (1973), *The Essential Gesture: Writing, Politics, and Places* (1988; edited by Stephen Clingman), *Writing and Being* (1995), and *Living in Hope and History: Notes from Our Century* (1999). With Lionel Abrahams she edited *South African Writing Today* (1967). Gordimer also contributed to and edited *Telling Tales* (2004), a collection of twenty-one short stories by world-re-

Nadine Gordimer
(The Nobel Foundation)

nowned authors; profits from the sale of this volume have been donated to help agencies working to control the spread of human immunodeficiency virus (HIV) and to treat those with HIV and acquired immunodeficiency syndrome (AIDS).

Achievements

Nadine Gordimer won the W. H. Smith Literary Award in 1961 for *Friday's Footprint, and Other Stories*. In 1972, she won the James Tait Black Memorial Prize for her novel *A Guest of Honour*. *The Conservationist* was cowinner of the Booker Prize in 1974. Gordimer also has received the French international literary prize the Grand Aigle d'Or (1975), the Italian Malaparte Prize (1985), and the Nelly Sachs Prize from Germany (1986). She was awarded the Officier de l'Ordre des Arts et des Lettres (1986) and the highest French art and literature decoration, the Commandeur dans l'Ordre des Arts et Lettres (1991). For her 2001 novel *The Pickup*, Gordimer was awarded the 2002 Commonwealth Writers' Prize for the Best Book from Africa. She has been awarded honorary degrees from such American universities as Harvard and Yale (both in 1986) and the New

School for Social Research (1987). In the fall of 1994, Gordimer delivered the Charles Eliot Norton Lectures series at Harvard. In 1991, she was honored with the Nobel Prize in Literature.

Biography

Nadine Gordimer spent her childhood in a gold-mining town near Johannesburg, South Africa. Her father, Isidore Gordimer, was a watchmaker, a Jew who had immigrated from a Baltic town to Africa when he was thirteen; her mother was born in England. In writing about her childhood, Gordimer has referred to herself as a "bolter." She did not care for the convent school to which she was sent as a day student, and she frequently played hooky. When she did attend, she would sometimes walk out. The pressures of uniformity produced revulsion and rebellion in young Nadine. At eleven, Gordimer was kept home from school by her mother on the pretense of a heart ailment, and she received no formal schooling for about a year; for the next three to four years, she was tutored a few hours a day.

Within Gordimer's environment, a white middle-class girl typically left school at about age fifteen and worked for a few years at a clerical job. Ideally, by her early twenties she would be found by the son of a family like her own and would then be ushered through her season of glory—the engagement party, the linen shower, the marriage, and the birth of the first child. There was no point in such a girl's reading books; that would only impede the inevitable process by which she was readied to fit the mold.

Gordimer, however, was an early reader and an early writer. By the age of nine, she was already writing; at fourteen, she won her first writing prize. She read the stories of Guy de Maupassant, Anton Chekhov, W. Somerset Maugham, D. H. Lawrence, and the Americans O. Henry, Katherine Anne Porter, and Eudora Welty. Reading these great artists of the short story helped Gordimer to refine her own story writing, making her work more sophisticated. She found herself becoming increasingly interested in politics and the plight of black South Africans. Unlike other whites who rejected the white South African way of life, Gordimer did not launch into her writing career as a way to bring change. Already a writer, she could not help "falling, falling through the surface" of white South African life.

In her early twenties, Gordimer was greatly influenced by a young male friend. She has written that he did her the service of telling her how ignorant she was. He jeered at the way she was acquiring knowledge and at her "clumsy battle to chip my way out of shell after shell of readymade concepts." Further, she says, "It was through him, too, that I roused myself sufficiently to insist on going to the university." Since she was twenty-two at the time and still being supported by her father, her family did not appreciate her desire to attend the university.

Continuing to live at home, Gordimer commuted to Johannesburg and the University of the Witwatersrand. While at the university, she met the Afrikaans poet Uys Krige, a man who had broken free of his Afrikaans heritage, lived in France and Spain, and served with the International Brigade in the Spanish Civil War. He had a profound effect on Gordimer. She had bolted from school; she was in the process of bolting from family, class, and the superficial values and culture of white South Africa. Uys Krige gave her a final push. She was free to be committed to honesty alone. When she began sending stories to England and the United States, they were well received. Her course was set.

Despite her contempt for the social system and the economic exploitation that prevailed in South Africa, Gordimer continued to make Johannesburg her home. She gave birth to and reared her children there. She married Reinhold Cassirer, a German-born art dealer, who moved to South Africa in the late 1930's. She and her husband would frequently go abroad, to Europe, to North America, to other African countries. She lectured at leading American universities such as Columbia, Harvard, and Michigan State, but she always returned to Johannesburg. For many years some of her writing was censored or prohibited in South Africa.

Gordimer has remained active in promoting South African culture, particularly writing. A member of Southern African PEN (International Association of Poets, Playwrights, Editors, Essayists, and Novelists) in Johannesburg, she also served as vice president for PEN International. She was a founder and has been an executive member of the Congress of South African Writers (COSAW), a political and cultural organization. She has also worked as a board member under the African National Congress's Department of Arts and Culture for cultural reconstruction in South Africa. In 1990, when the African National Congress again became legal, Gordimer joined and supported the new democracy in South Africa.

Analysis

Until 1991, when the last of South Africa's apartheid laws was repealed, to be personally liberated and to be South African was to be doomed to a continuing struggle between the desire for further freedom and development for oneself and the desire for the liberation of the country's oppressed masses. The question was whether one could pursue both effectually. South Africa was a nation in which a white legislature promulgated laws that made it impossible for the overwhelming majority of nonwhite persons to advance themselves. Apartheid, which in Afrikaans means "apartness," was the law of the land. It became codified after the Nationalists came to power in 1948.

In her novels, Nadine Gordimer is engaged in an ongoing examination of the possible combinations of the private life and the public life. She creates a gallery of characters ranging from pure hedonists concerned only with their own pleasure to those who have committed their lives to bringing liberty, equality, and solidarity to South Africa. Her most interesting characters are those who are wracked and torn by the struggle, those who want to be themselves and yet find it impossible to take personal goals seriously in a society built on the exploitation of blacks.

Some great writers—such as James Joyce and Thomas Mann—believe that to write freely one must live in a free country. During the 1920's, numerous American writers disgusted with American values chose to become expatriates. Other writers, such as the great Russians Fyodor Dostoevski, Leo Tolstoy, and Aleksandr Solzhenitsyn, believe that nothing could be more oppressive to them than to be separated from their fellow citizens, however oppressive the government of their country might be. With some of her books banned, with some charge or other always dangling over her head, with her passport liable to be lifted at any time, Gordimer undoubtedly was tempted to go into exile and live in a free country. She always, however, returned to Johannesburg. To her, the accident of being born in a particular place imposed obligations, and having become a writer with an international reputation imposed special obligations. At the cost of the personal freedom and the very air of freedom that could be hers elsewhere, she remained in South Africa during the apartheid years, living with frustration and danger, a witness to the power of compassion and hope.

THE LYING DAYS

A first novel is often a thinly veiled autobiography of the writer's childhood, adolescence, and coming-of-age. Gordimer's *The Lying Days* is of this type, but it is nevertheless special. Full of innocence, tenderness, courage, and joy, it is an unusually mature celebration of a woman's coming-of-age. It is the story of Helen Shaw's growing up in a mining town not far from Johannesburg, the intoxication of her first love affairs, her days at the university, her immersion in the city's bohemian and radical circles, and finally her drawing back to protect herself from being swamped by values, attitudes, and goals that are not her own.

In her life at home, Helen Shaw is under the thumb of a mother who commands and dominates in the name of all that is conventional and trivial. The motivating force in the mother's life is her desire to guide her family through all the planned stops on the middle-class timetable: tea parties and dances, husband's promotions, the big vacation to Europe, and, most important, the molding of offspring to fit the community's notion of success. To celebrate these achievements and in all else to maintain an unruffled surface—such are the goals of Mrs. Shaw and the placid Mr. Shaw, who, important as he may be to the success of the gold-mining company, is completely submissive at home. As Helen comes to realize, both mother and father, their circle of acquaintances, and those in other similar circles are "insensitive to the real flow of life."

The whites of the mining town have blacks in their midst as servants and are surrounded by "locations" where the black mine workers and their families are housed. Helen chooses a lover, Paul Clark, who has committed his professional and personal life to ameliorating the misery of blacks in the townships on the periphery of Johannesburg, on weekdays through his position in the government office dealing with native housing, on weekends through work for the black African National Congress.

Paul meets with frustration at every turn. His inability to get anything done that will have a lasting impact affects the quality of his relationship with Helen. He torments her in small ways, and she reciprocates. He feels ashamed and she feels ashamed, and they become aware of "a burned-out loneliness in the very center of one's love for the other." Helen, who had come to believe that the only way for a man to fulfill himself in South Africa was "to pit himself against the oppression of the Africans" and who had wanted to live with Paul "in the greatest possible intimacy," is compelled to leave him. His political commitments, which made him so attractive to Helen in the first place, have damaged their love irretrievably.

Helen decides to go to Europe. During the few days she spends at the port city, she meets Joel Aron, with whom she had become good friends in Atherton, the town where they grew up. Joel is off to try to make a life for himself in Israel. At first, Helen is envious of Joel; he is headed for a new life in a new country. She feels homeless. South Africa is like a battleground; she cannot join the whites, and the blacks do not want her. She does not want to end up like Paul, "with a leg and arm nailed to each side." In the course of her conversations with Joel, however, she succeeds in coming to a better understanding of her situation. She is not going to be tempted by exile and a new beginning. She accepts South Africa as home and the place to which she must return.

A World of Strangers

Toby Hood, the protagonist of *A World of Strangers*, has grown up in England in a family quite different from Helen Shaw's. Had Toby been a bolter from school and a rebel against bourgeois values, his parents would have loved him all the more. His parents do not care about what other members of the upper middle class think about them; they care about justice. Through his home goes a constant procession of victims of injustice who have come for aid from the Hoods. Thus, there have been bred into Toby "a horror of the freedom that is freedom only to be free" and a consciousness of the need to make every activity in which one engages an act of conscience. Toby, however, is not persuaded. His parents have not been successful in making him into a reformer and protester like themselves. Abstractions such as justice and socialism do not thrill him. Toby wants to live a life oblivious to the suffering in the world; what he feels most inclined to do is enjoy whatever is left of privilege.

Toby is sent to take over temporarily the management of the South African branch of the family-owned publishing company. Arriving in Johannesburg, he is determined to find his own interests and amusements, and not be channeled by the reformers back in England or distracted by the examples of humanity's cruelty to others that will occur before his eyes. Indeed, it seems to Toby that those who would live private lives have become a hunted species, and he resents being hunted. Toby is confirmed in his desire to avoid being a do-gooder by his discovery of a talented black man who also insists on living his own life, regardless of the condition of his people and his country. Toby marvels at the spirit and vitality of Steven Sitole. Steven refuses to allow the chaos and filth of the black townships and the hovels in which he sleeps either to deaden his spirit or to inflame it to rage. He does what he does, seeking pleasure, satisfaction, or quick delight. He has no time for sorrow, pity, guilt, or even anger. He makes his money running an insurance racket, he gets into debt, he gets drunk, he laughs. He fleeces his own people and outwits whites. He is a new kind of man in the black townships; he is of them and not of them. The blacks who know him love him, and Toby Hood loves him as well.

Toby sees in Steven a brother. Drawn to him as if by a magnet at their first meeting, Toby goes into the townships with Steven, meets Steven's friends, gets drunk with him, and sleeps in the same hovels with him. What Steven can do with his life is so severely limited by white authority that he must live without hope or dignity; his life can only be a succession of gestures. That recognition by Toby illumines his own predicament. Steven was born into a South Africa that would not permit him "to come into his own; and what I believed should have been my own was destroyed before I was born heir to it."

Toby undergoes a transformation in the course of the novel. He has had the unusual experience of being able to enter alternately both black township life and the life of upper-crust Johannesburg. As much as he had thought that the privileged life was his natural base, he finds that life—for all its varied forms of recreation, luxury, freedom, and the outward good health of the rich—an empty, superficial existence. The rich, like Helen Shaw's middle-class mining-town family, are out of touch with "the real flow of life." Toby attempts a love affair with the most beautiful available woman among his circle of rich acquaintances. Primarily because the woman, Cecil Rowe, is incapable of expanding her concerns beyond herself, the affair comes to nothing more than a few perfunctory sexual encounters. On the other hand, Toby's relationship with Anna Louw, who is so different, is no more satisfying. She is a lawyer who is a former Communist and whose professional life is devoted to aiding blacks. Hers is anything but the self-centered life of Steven Sitole or Cecil Rowe; always sober, without embarrassment, she is unresponsive to the lure of euphoria. At the end of the novel, Cecil has accepted the marriage proposal of a wealthy businessman. Anna, too, is to begin a new phase—she has been arrested and is to be tried for treason. Anna is a prototype of the committed woman, the full development of whom in Gordimer's fiction does not occur until twenty years later, in *Burger's Daughter.*

Toby decides to stay in South Africa for a second year. His experiences with Cecil and the rich have made him reassess his conception of himself. As different as Steven and Anna are in character and personality, Toby has been greatly affected by both of them, and the effect has been to make him care about the people of the townships. One of Gordimer's great accomplishments in this novel, as it is in her later work, is her rendering of township life. Toby also undergoes his transformation because of what he has seen of township life on his sojourns with Steven. Life in the townships is more real than life among whites. In the townships, the demands of life cannot be evaded through distractions; reality is right on the surface as well as below: "There is nothing for the frustrated man to do but grumble in the street; there was nothing for the deserted girl to do but sit on the step and wait for her bastard to be born; there was nothing to be done with the drunk but let him lie in the yard until he'd got over it." Among the whites, it is different. Frustrations can be forgotten through golf or horse racing, and trips to Europe take away the pain of broken love affairs.

In *A World of Strangers*, Gordimer attempts to show a young man wholly bent on pursuing private concerns who, in the very process of pursuing those concerns, is changed into someone who cannot remain oblivious to South African injustice and unreason. To the extent that the reader can accept the change in Toby, the novel is successful.

OCCASION FOR LOVING

Jessie Stilwell, the protagonist of *Occasion for Loving*, is a well-educated, freethinking socialist of the most enlightened, undogmatic kind. She might well have been arrested and tried for treason, but that would be in a different life from the one that fate has bestowed on her. Her reality is her life as the mother of four children and a helpmate to Tom, a liberal history professor. She could be Helen Shaw fifteen years later, domesticated.

Jessie is content. Her husband, children, and home give continuity to her life; she is in touch with her past, and the future, in five-year blocks at least, seems predictable. She has room to develop; she can pick and choose goals for herself and pursue them to their conclusion. She is a total realist; she knows what is possible and what is not. She is at a point in her life when she will do nothing that is "wild and counter to herself." When someone else in the family causes discord, she will deal with it.

Jessie has a son by a previous marriage who, in his adolescence, has become mildly disruptive. The task she wishes to devote herself to is repairing her relationship with him. Jessie cannot become absorbed in this duty, however, because there are two new presences in her home. Against her better judgment, she has allowed her husband to invite to live with them a colleague and his young wife, Boaz and Ann Cohen. Boaz is a musicologist and is frequently away from Johannesburg to study the music and instruments of tribes. Ann is free to occupy her time as she wishes. What comes to dominate Ann's life is a love affair with a married black man, Gideon Shibalo. The difficulties and dangers of an interracial love affair are such that the lovers necessarily need the help of others; thus the affair between Ann and Gideon, whom Jessie and Tom like, intrudes on the life of the Stilwells, and Jessie resents it.

Even when Jessie goes off with three of her children for a vacation by the sea, she must deal with Ann and Gideon, for they turn up at the remote cottage. Boaz has learned about his wife's affair, and Ann and Gideon decide to be with each other day and night; given South Africa's race laws, that means they must live an underground life. They appeal to Jessie to let them stay. Again, she resents the intrusion, but she yields to their need.

Boaz will not disavow Ann. His freedom to act in response to his wife's adultery is limited by his unwillingness to do anything that would harm a black man. Indeed, the affair itself may owe its birth to its interracial difficulties: "The basis of an exciting sympathy between two people is often some obstacle that lies long submerged in the life of one." After leading Gideon to believe that she was ready to go to Europe or some other African country with him, Ann leaves him and returns to Boaz; the two, reunited, quickly leave South Africa. This action plunges Gideon into alcoholism.

Jessie's meditation on the affair makes clear the meaning Gordimer wants to convey. Race is a force even between lovers; personal lives are affected by society and politics. In South Africa, white privilege is a ubiquitous force; it provides Ann the freedom to go, denying Gideon the same freedom. White privilege is "a silver spoon clamped between your jaws and you might choke on it for all the chance there was of dislodging it." So long as there is no change in South Africa, "nothing could bring integrity to personal relationships." If Jessie were more involved in the plot of the novel or even at the heart of its interest, *Occasion for Loving* would be more satisfying. Jessie, however, remains an objective observer and commentator. It is she with whom the reader identifies, yet not much happens to her; the events belong to Ann and Gideon.

The Late Bourgeois World

Gordimer's fourth novel, *The Late Bourgeois World*, is her least successful. Brief and unconvincing, it is something of a parable, but it does not hit with the impact of the well-told parable. Too much has to be deduced. Without a knowledge of Gordimer's interests from her other works, the reader is hard-pressed to see the meaning and coherence in this work. *The Late Bourgeois World* tells the story, with a great deal of indirection, of a Johannesburg woman whose marriage has broken up and who has responsibility for a teenage son at boarding school. Elizabeth's having to bring her son the news that his father is dead by suicide is what gives the plot its impetus.

Max Van Den Sandt is the scion of one of Johannesburg's best families, but he rejects his heritage and white privilege. He marries Elizabeth, the medical-lab technician whom he has made pregnant. He joins the Communist Party, he participates in marches against the government, and, in the climax to his rebellion, he is arrested on a charge of sabotage. How much of what Max has done is gesture, however, and how much is the result of conviction? After serving fifteen months in prison, Max turns state's evidence and betrays his former colleagues. In return, he is released from prison. Then comes the suicide, which for Elizabeth provides the final answer: Her former husband was a hollow man. It is possible to be a revolutionary without real conviction.

While allowing herself to indulge her contempt for Max, Elizabeth herself turns out to be unwilling to risk very much for the cause. She has the opportunity to respond positively to the plea of a young, handsome black activist for money to help pay for the defense of some of his friends who have been arrested, but Elizabeth equivocates and puts him off. The participation of whites from the middle class in the black revolution, Gordimer seems to suggest, is very unreliable. No matter how strong their sympathies appear to be, for whites the political struggle is not the imperative it is for blacks. The novel's title suggests another, complementary theme. Despite its staunch defense of its own privileges, the bourgeois world is falling apart. Families rupture too easily, and commitments do not count. Elizabeth and Max are case histories.

A GUEST OF HONOUR

Set in an invented nation in central Africa for which she provides a detailed history and geography, *A Guest of Honour* is Gordimer's only novel that does not deal with South Africa. Still, the kinds of events depicted in this novel could very well occur in South Africa at some future time. With independence gained and a native government functioning in the place of the former British colonial administration, there are expectations of dramatic changes: Civil rights will be respected, greater care will be taken in the administration of justice, natural resources will be used for the benefit of the people, the standard of living of the masses will improve. President Mweta believes that these legitimate expectations are being fulfilled in an orderly way and at a satisfactory rate. Edward Shinza, without whom independence might not yet have come, is dissatisfied. He believes that the country is no better off than it would have been under colonial rule. He is seeking a way to have an impact on the course of events. He may even be conspiring with the nation across the border. To Mweta, his former comrade Shinza is "a cobra in the house."

The novel's protagonist is Colonel James Bray, an Englishman who has been a district officer in the colonial administration. Bray is likable and loyal, a wholly sympathetic character. During the struggle for independence, he was of significant assistance to Mweta and Shinza. Now Mweta has invited Bray back to be an honored guest at Independence Day celebrations. Much to his chagrin, Bray discovers that while Mweta is covered with glory as the new nation's leader, Shinza, every bit Mweta's equal if not his better, has no role in governing the country and has not been invited to the celebrations; indeed, Shinza is living in obscurity in the bush. To Bray, this is an ominous sign.

President Mweta sends Colonel Bray on a mission to Gala, the district Bray formerly administered. He is to survey the district's educational needs. With Gala, Gordimer gives the first demonstration of her formidable knowledge of the life and people of rural Africa, of which she gives further demonstrations in *July's People* and, to a lesser extent, in *The Conservationist*. With Gala, she has the opportunity to do a canvas of a whole province. She makes Bray pleased to be back in Gala and curious about what has happened in his absence. He knows the language, he likes the people, and he resonates sympathetically with the daily round of life. While in Gala, Bray will track down Shinza and get his viewpoint on the progress of the nation.

Shinza believes Mweta's principal concern is to consolidate his own power. He has no tolerance for dissent and is quite willing to use the police and torture to stifle it. Mweta allows foreign corporations to extract raw materials and export them rather than finding opportunities to make use of the country's natural wealth at home. Mweta will not allow any changes in the country that might give pause to these foreign interests. Shinza believes that

Mweta's actions, taken together, make up a pattern of betrayal. While Shinza is trying to reassert himself by becoming a force within the trade-union movement, he also may be gathering a counterrevolutionary army, but his present intention is to attack Mweta through the unions and strikes.

Shinza comes onto center stage for the length of his impassioned speech on the ideals of the revolution at the congress of the People's Independent Party (P.I.P.), which has its factions but is still the only political party. Bray, who attends, cannot help but prefer the ideals of Shinza to the charisma and policies of accommodation of Mweta. In presenting the milieu of the party congress and in revealing the subtleties of motivations, alliances, and positions, Gordimer demonstrates a first-rate political intelligence. She has Shinza make use of his union support as the first phase in his scheme to dislodge Mweta; she has Mweta in turn capitalize on the nationalistic fervor of the youth group within the P.I.P. to get the group to attack strongholds of union supporters. Violence breaks out in Gala, and Bray is an accidental victim.

Bray, Shinza, and Mweta are new characters in Gordimer's gallery. She knows them and their social and political contexts exceedingly well. *A Guest of Honour* shows a prescience and knowledge that carry it to the top rank of political novels.

THE CONSERVATIONIST

With *The Conservationist*, Gordimer turns back to South Africa. Again, she chooses a male protagonist, Mehring, who bears no resemblance to anyone in her previous novels. Although this novel is of far larger scope, it is perhaps most similar to *The Late Bourgeois World*, for in both novels Gordimer attempts to delineate the lifestyle of a particular rung of white Johannesburg society. Mehring is a forty-nine-year-old industrialist and financier; he serves on several boards of directors. Given no other name, Mehring is admired and respected by everyone in his business and social circles, but it is clear that his life is essentially without meaning. He is deeply committed to nothing—not to ideology, country, or class, not to a sport, not to a single human being. He is quite the opposite of Colonel Bray.

Mehring has much more money than he needs. On impulse, he decides to buy a farm, very conveniently located only twenty-five miles from the city. Owning a farm will give him a feeling of being in contact with the land; it is something that is expected of a man of his station and wealth. The farm, however, complicates Mehring's life. He is unable to enjoy simple ownership; he must try to make the farm productive. He will practice conservation; he will see to it that buildings are repaired, fences mended, firebreaks cleared. The farm comes to occupy much more of his time and thought than he had intended. Nothing about the land, the weather, or the black people who live and work on the farm can be taken for granted. Something unexpected and unwanted is always occurring.

A dead man is found on the property. The man is black, and so the white police are not particularly concerned. Mehring expects them to remove the body and conduct an investigation, but they do neither. The unidentified body remains in a shallow, unmarked grave on Mehring's property. The presence of that body in the third pasture is troubling both to Mehring and to his black workers, although Mehring is never moved to do anything about it.

Much of the novel consists of Mehring's stream of consciousness. Along with the black man's body, another frequent presence in Mehring's consciousness is the woman with whom he has been having an affair. An attractive white liberal whose husband is away doing linguistic research in Australia, she has been drawn to Mehring because of his power; she is daring enough to taunt him and make light of that power. She is convinced that the reign of the whites in South Africa is nearing its end, yet she is a dilettante. When she gets into trouble with the authorities because of her associations with blacks, she wants to flee the country. She is humbled into asking Mehring to use his connections so that she can leave, and she sets herself up in London. Mehring, however, continues to think about her long after she has gone.

Mehring's relationship with this woman has been entirely superficial; when she is gone he thinks about her but does not really long for her. His relationships with his colleagues and their families are also superficial. These connections are so meaningless to him that he reaches a point where he does not want either their invitations or their concern. On the few occasions each year when he has the company of his son, he has no real interest in overcoming the barriers between them. His son, like his lover, does not believe that apartheid and white privilege can survive for long. The son is contemptuous of what his father represents. He leaves South Africa to join his mother in New York rather than serve his term in the army. In his self-willed isolation, Mehring spends more of his time at the farm. Despite himself, as he discusses routine farm business with his black foreman, Jacobus, and as they deal with the emergencies caused by drought, fire, and flooding, Mehring finds himself feeling more and more respect for Jacobus.

Mehring spends New Year's Eve alone at the farm. As the new year approaches, he wanders across his moonlit field and settles with his bottle against the wall of a roofless stone storehouse. He carries on a convivial conversation with old Jacobus. They talk about their children, the farm, cattle. They laugh a lot. They get along well. Jacobus, however, is not there. For Mehring, such easy, honest talk with a black man can take place only in fantasy.

In the final chapter of the novel, the unidentified body in the third pasture is brought to the surface by flooding. The black workers, under Jacobus's direction, make a coffin, at last giving the man a proper burial. Mehring, in the meantime, is engaged in another of his faceless sexual encounters. He could be killed. If he is killed, where will he be buried? Who are the real owners of the land to which he has title? Gordimer is suggesting that the unknown black man has more of a claim to the land than Mehring has. Mehring and his kind are going to meet ignoble ends. Their claim to the land of South Africa is so tenuous that their bodies will not even deserve burial.

There is little that is sympathetic about Mehring, which leaves Gordimer with the difficult task of keeping the reader interested in his activities. Once he begins to spend more time on the farm, his activities inevitably involve his black workers. Gordimer seizes the opportunity to render in some detail the life of their community. A few of them become minor characters of substance. Gordimer juxtaposes the flow of vital life in the black community with Mehring's isolation and decadence and thereby saves the novel from being utterly unappealing.

Burger's Daughter

Burger's Daughter is Gordimer's best novel. It is set between 1975 and 1977, as important changes are taking place in southern Africa but not yet in South Africa. The independence movements in Angola and Mozambique have succeeded. The Portuguese are in retreat, their colonial rule to be replaced by native governments. South Africa, however, remains firmly in the grip of the white minority. The white South African government will relinquish nothing.

Rosa Burger, the protagonist, is Gordimer's most fully achieved character. The hero of the novel, however, is Rosa's father, Lionel Burger. Just before he is to be sentenced to life imprisonment, Lionel Burger has the opportunity to address the court. He speaks for almost two hours. He explains why he and the Communist Party, of which he is a leader, have been driven to engage in the acts of sabotage for which he has been on trial. For thirty years, to no avail, he and South African Communists had struggled without resort to violence to gain civil rights and the franchise for the country's black majority. The great mass movement that is the African National Congress has been outlawed. In desperation, selected symbolic targets have been sabotaged. If such symbolic actions fail to move the white ruling class, there will be no further careful consideration of tactics. The only way to a new society will be through massive, cataclysmic violence.

Lionel Burger, in his childhood, was already sensitive to the unjust treatment of blacks. Later, as a medical student and doctor, he found it easier to accustom himself to the physical suffering of patients than to the subjection and humiliation forced upon blacks. He could not be silent and simply accept. He joined the Communist Party because he saw white and black members working side by side; there were people who practiced what they preached; there were white South Africans who did not deny the humanity of black South Africans. As a Communist, Lionel Burger came to accept the Marxist view of the dominance of economic relationships; thus, he perceived the oppression of blacks to be rooted in white South Africans' desire to maintain their economic advantages. Burger made a covenant with the victims.

Rosa Burger is very different from her father. She is also different from her mother, who was familiar with prison and who from young womanhood was known as a "real revolutionary." Both her father and her mother regard the family as totally united in their dedication to the struggle. Rosa, who was named in tribute to Rosa Luxemburg, the German revolutionary Marxist, knows that the family is not united. While her parents are free and active, she has no choice but to be an extension of them. Her mother has died, however, and, after three years of his life term, her father dies. When they are gone, Rosa does not take up their work. She is twenty-seven years old and has been in her parents' revolutionary circle since childhood. She has carried out numerous secret missions. Recently, she has pretended to be the fiancé of a prisoner in order to bring him messages. With the death of her father, she cannot deny that she is tired of such a life. She does not want to have anything more to do with the endangered and the maimed, with conspiracies and fugitives, with courts and prisons.

Much more pointedly, *Burger's Daughter* deals with questions first considered in *A World of Strangers* and *Occasion for Loving*: To what extent must individual lives be governed by the dictates of time and place and circumstances not of the individual's choosing? Can a person ignore the facts and conditions that circumscribe his or her life and still live fully, or must a meaningful life necessarily be one that is integrated with the "real flow of life"? Despite his wealth and station, Mehring leads a dismal life, because it has no such integration. Rosa Burger is not devoid of redeeming qualities, however. She already has given much of herself.

Rosa chooses to escape. At first she escapes within the city of Johannesburg, in the tiny cottage of a rootless young white man, a graduate student of Italian literature who survives by working as a clerk to a bookmaker. Rosa and Conrad start out as lovers; after a while they are more like siblings. Conrad, too, is struggling to be free, not of a revolutionary heritage but of his bourgeois heritage. Even after she is no longer with him, Rosa continues to talk to Conrad, silently.

Rosa decides to leave South Africa, but she cannot get a passport because she is the daughter of Lionel Burger. Brandt Vermeulen is a cosmopolitan Boer, a new Afrikaner of a distinguished old Afrikaner family. He has studied politics at Leyden and Princeton and has spent time in Paris and New York. Vermeulen resembles Mehring, but he is rooted, more cultured, and more committed to the status quo. His solution for South Africa is to create separate nations for whites and blacks. Rosa goes to see him because he has friends in the Ministry of the Interior, which issues passports. Playing on the fact that he and Lionel Burger emerged from very similar backgrounds, Rosa succeeds in persuading him to use his influence to get her a passport.

The second part of this three-part novel takes place in Europe. Rosa goes to the French Riviera and looks up the woman who had been Lionel Burger's wife before he met Rosa's mother. The woman, who used to be known as Katya and now is known as Madame Bagnelli, is delighted that Burger's daughter has come to stay with her. Rosa is welcomed by Madame Bagnelli's circle, which consists of unmarried couples, émigrés, homosexuals, persons formerly prominent in Paris—rootless persons for the most part. On the Riviera, life is easy, difference is distinction. Survival is not an issue. Politics seems a waste of time, revolution a form of craziness.

There is great empathy between Rosa and Madame Bagnelli. As Katya, the latter, years before, found it a relief to give up the role of revolutionary that was required of her as Burger's wife. She had not always been able to put private concerns aside; she had been considered a bourgeois or even a traitor and was subjected to party discipline. She has no regrets about leaving that part of her life. Rosa is encouraged about her own course. She allows herself the luxury of a love affair. After a summer of love, Rosa and Bernard Chabalier make plans to live together in Paris, where he is a teacher at a lycée. Rosa visits London while Bernard makes arrangements in Paris. She attends a party for South African exiles and is filled with joy at meeting her black "brother," Baasie, who as a child had been taken into the Burger home but whom Rosa has not seen for twenty years. Rosa is shocked by Baasie's attitude; he is hostile and sullen.

That night in London, Rosa's sleep is broken by a phone call from Baasie. He is angry. He wants her to know that he did not have the life Burger's daughter had. He had been pushed back to the mud huts and tin shanties. His father was a revolutionary who also died in prison, driven to hang himself. No one knows of Isaac Vulindlela, but everyone talks about Lionel Burger. He hates hearing about Burger, the great man who suffered for the blacks. He knows plenty of blacks who have done as much as Burger, but they go unknown. He does not want to be her black brother, he tells Rosa.

Rosa goes back to South Africa. She does not want the soft life Bernard will provide for her in Paris. Defection is not possible. Suffering cannot be evaded. Back in Johannesburg, Rosa takes up the occupation for which she trained, physiotherapy. She also works for the revolution. As the novel ends late in 1977, Rosa is in prison. The authorities have solid evidence that she has committed unlawful acts.

JULY'S PEOPLE

In the brief *July's People* the end has come. Civil war rages; blacks are fighting whites. The whites have discipline, organization, knowledge, and equipment. The blacks have will and numbers. They have the support of the rest of the continent, and the Russians and their Cuban allies are close at hand. Thousands of lives will be lost, but there can be no doubt about the eventual outcome. The artificial society based on apartheid is finished.

Bamford Smales is an architect, an upper-middle-class professional. His wife, Maureen, is, like Jessie Stilwell, an excellent helpmate, a strong, compassionate, intelligent woman. Before the uprisings, Bam and Maureen knew that unless whites, of their own volition, made significant reforms, a conflagration was inevitable. They tried to show the way among their friends and neighbors, treating their male servant, July, with the utmost consideration. They did not, however, go so far as to break their ties with their community. They lived their lives within the pattern they found for their race and their class. Their liberal attitudes had no impact.

When the uprisings begin, the Smaleses flee their Johannesburg suburb. With their three young children, they drive six hundred kilometers in their recreational pickup truck to July's home village. Even though black-white relations are being turned upside down, July is still willing to oblige them; for fifteen years obliging the Smales family has been his life's purpose. Even after their dependence on him is clear, July continues to address Bam Smales as "master." He even moves his mother from her own hut so that the Smales family can settle in it.

When they arrive in the village, the Smaleses are July's people. Over the course of a few weeks, relations change. July has been reunited with his wife and children, whom for fifteen years he has seen only on his vacations every other year. July becomes a presence among the people of his village. *They* become July's people, and his loyalty to the white family is eroded. That erosion occurs slowly through a number of ambiguous situations, for July has no political sensibility. As the relationship between the black servant and the white family loses its structure, July becomes less and less the servant and more and more the master of the family's fate.

When the Smaleses' vehicle, the yellow "bakkie," first pulls in to the village, there is no doubt concerning its ownership, but as July runs errands to the locked bakkie, he comes to be the possessor of the keys to the vehicle. He does not know how to drive, but his young protégé Daniel does. July turns the keys over to Daniel, and they drive off to a store. After this, it is difficult for Bam Smales to claim sole ownership, and it is even more difficult once Daniel has taught July how to drive. Bam Smales has a shotgun. Although he tries to keep its hiding place a secret, the whole village seems to know where the gun is kept. When Bam discovers that the gun is gone, he is beside himself. The loss of the gun emasculates him. On his way to join the freedom fighters, Daniel has helped himself to the gun.

The family's future is completely uncertain. As the villagers begin to break the habit of deference to white skins, the Smaleses become nervous about their safety. They would leave, but they have nowhere to go. The predicament proves too much for Maureen. Sensing an opportunity to save herself, she runs off, frantically, leaving her husband and children. The Smaleses are victims of apartheid. When the tables are turned, as they surely must be, only a miracle will save whites from suffering what they made others suffer.

A SPORT OF NATURE

A Sport of Nature combines elements from several of Gordimer's earlier works. Like Helen in *The Lying Days*, Hillela Capran is a bolter, though not out of obvious rebelliousness. Rather, she is moved by the spirit of the moment in a more unthinking way. The family with whom she lives during her adolescence—her aunt Pauline, uncle Joe, and cousins Sasha and Carole—are similar to the Hoods of *A World of Strangers*, for they also are white liberals, trying ever to be ruled by acts of conscience rather than convenience, as Hillela's Aunt Olga and Uncle Arthur are.

Gordimer's early habit of distancing the reader from her characters is echoed in her treatment of Hillela. The first half of the book has Hillela spoken of mostly in the third person; she does not really come alive until after she meets Whaila Kgomani, a black revolutionary who becomes her first husband and the father of her child. His assassination changes the course of Hillela's life as she inherits his revolution.

Many readers have regarded Hillela's character as amoral and shocking, and even Gordimer has admitted that this creation fascinates her probably as much as anyone else. She does not, however, back down from her portrayal of a revolutionary who accomplishes most of her goals through the use of her feminine wiles. *A Sport of Nature* may not be Gordimer's best book, but it is as thought-provoking as any of her earlier works. Its portrayal of the future, which includes a black African state installed in place of South Africa, has caused some critics to label the work weak and unbelievable.

MY SON'S STORY

Gordimer's novels of the 1990's cover the years from the closing days of apartheid to the new democracy in South Africa. In *My Son's Story* the struggle for freedom is ongoing. Gordimer's recurrent theme of the balance between public and private life is again central. In this novel, the private is sacrificed to the political. Sonny initially seems destined to live under the restrictions of apartheid, but he changes and sacrifices his teaching career to align his life with, and help, those he thinks of as the "real blacks." Sonny moves his family illegally to a white suburb of Johannesburg, one poor enough to ignore the settling of a family of mixed ancestry. The movement claims first Sonny, then his daughter Baby, and finally his wife Aila. Will, the son named for William Shakespeare, remains aloof from political involvement but chronicles the struggle by narrating the disintegration of his family. Before detention and exile claim the three family members and a bomb destroys their home, the family is already disintegrating from Sonny's liaison with Hannah Plowman, a white human rights worker who visited Sonny the first time he was jailed.

Although Gordimer has used such narrators in her short stories, this is her first novel narrated by a young male character from one of the disenfranchised groups in South Africa. The novel fluctuates between the first-person narration by Will and a seemingly third-person account of information the young Will could not possibly know, such as Sonny's thoughts and the details of his intimacy with Hannah. The last chapter of the novel unites the dual point of view, with Will claiming authorship of the whole. He has created—out of his own frustration, experience, and knowledge of the participants—the scenes and thoughts he could not know firsthand. Thrust by the times and by his family into the role of a writer, Will plans to hone his writing skills by chronicling the struggle for freedom in South Africa.

NONE TO ACCOMPANY ME

None to Accompany Me reveals the life of Vera Stark, a lawyer who heads a foundation that during apartheid works to minimize the removal of blacks to crowded, inferior land and after apartheid works to reclaim for them the land they have lost. With some reluctance, Vera leaves the foundation temporarily to join the commission that is drafting a new constitution for South Africa. The novel emphasizes how all aspects of her personal life—her home, children, and husband—become secondary to her work. True to her name, Vera Stark whittles all excess from her life, striving to find her true center through social responsibility.

THE HOUSE GUN

In *The House Gun*, Claudia and Harald Lindgard, privileged South Africans who neither supported nor demonstrated against apartheid, are thrust out of their private lives into the public sphere. Their twenty-seven-year-old son Duncan has killed a man. The parents keep their pledge, made to Duncan in childhood, that no matter the difficulty, he can always come to them for support. Reconciling themselves to his action is no easy matter, however, and dealing with that truth causes them to question their own attitudes about justice. Suddenly, whether South Africa's new constitution outlaws capital punishment is a vital personal issue.

Duncan's is a personal, not a political, crime, but the novel connects his crime to the violence the country has known and still knows. Both the easy access to a gun and the climate of violence in which Duncan grew up play a part in an appeal for a lenient sentence. Even though the novel makes no overt mention of the country's Truth and Reconciliation Commission, after facing the truth, the Lindgards must search for reconciliation just as all South Africans are doing the same under the new democracy. Time must determine whether any of the three Lindgards become reconciled to the brutal truth of the murder.

THE PICKUP

Gordimer's thirteenth novel, *The Pickup*, focuses on the issues of immigration and discrimination. Like her 2005 novel *Get a Life*, *The Pickup* begins in South Africa but moves to other settings, suggesting that the problems faced by individuals in South Africa are of global concern. *The Pickup* opens with reminders of South Africa's apartheid past: Julie Summers has separated herself from her privileged parents' lifestyle. She rents a small cottage apartment, the type inhabited by black workers during apartheid. She begins a relationship with Abdu, a mechanic who works on her car. She soon learns that Abdu is an alias, a name used to shield him from government officials; Ibrahim ibn Musa is an illegal immigrant, a man who has overstayed his permit.

Through the couple's struggle to find a life together, Gordimer reveals that doors that are automatically open to Julie, a white South African, are closed tight to Ibrahim, an Arab immigrant. His university degree in economics provides no practical help, as Ibrahim comes from a country (which remains unnamed) of no prestige, a country rampant with poverty and corruption. Julie wants to abandon what Ibrahim wishes to acquire. Julie's experience in South Africa has taught her that wealth and success are sometimes based on the exploitation of a population; to Ibrahim, wealth and success are a means to live free, to have choices in life.

Forced out of South Africa, Ibrahim marries Julie and takes her to his home village, where they are welcomed by his extended Muslim family. Ibrahim continues his applications to emigrate to some country where he can improve his life; Julie, his opposite in so many ways, surprisingly finds fulfillment in the village. Through meaningful work and the support of a family she respects, she finds a sense of her place in the universe—something she could not have achieved while working in public relations in Johannesburg.

GET A LIFE

Get a Life centers on a family unit similar to that in *The House Gun*—parents and an adult son. Paul Bannerman is quarantined at his parents' house for a few weeks after having radioactive iodine treatment to combat thyroid cancer. Adrian and Lyndsay Bannerman care for him to protect Paul's wife and young son from possible contamination. Paul's brush with early death and his enforced time in near solitude lead the adults to reevaluate their lives. Paul, a member of an independent research team, spends time thinking about his work as an ecologist and about his marriage to Berenice, a successful advertising executive who at times promotes companies that threaten the South African environment. One of Paul's current concerns, ironically, is to stop the construction of a nuclear reactor.

When Paul returns to his family and research, he has changed internally, but not outwardly. His parents change their lives radically: Adrian, a retired businessman, spends time visiting archaeology sites, an avocation he had let lie dormant as he devoted himself to providing for his family; Lyndsay, a civil rights lawyer, adopts a young orphan who was born HIV-positive. The novel ends optimistically, with projects that Paul's research team viewed as dangerous halted and with a new child born healthy to Berenice and Paul. A haunting suggestion remains, however, that while the child is fine and the projects are halted for now, the future comes with no guarantees.

From her first, somewhat autobiographical novel, *The Lying Days*, Gordimer has probed moral and political questions with honesty and unfailing courage, never being dogmatic or predetermining outcomes, allowing vividly imagined characters and communities lives of their own. Her work does more than shed light on the predicament of South Africa; it deals in depth with the problems of individual identity, commitment and obligation, and justice. Gordimer is a novelist who clearly has a place in the great tradition of George Eliot, Fyodor Dostoevski, Joseph Conrad, and Thomas Mann.

Paul Marx
Updated by Marion Petrillo

OTHER MAJOR WORKS

SHORT FICTION: *Face to Face: Short Stories*, 1949; *The Soft Voice of the Serpent, and Other Stories*, 1952; *Six Feet of the Country*, 1956; *Friday's Footprint, and Other Stories*, 1960; *Not for Publication, and Other Stories*, 1965; *Livingstone's Companions: Stories*, 1971; *Selected Stories*, 1975; *A Soldier's Embrace*, 1980; *Something Out There*, 1984;

Reflections of South Africa, 1986; *Crimes of Conscience,* 1991; *Jump, and Other Stories,* 1991; *Why Haven't You Written? Selected Stories, 1950-1972,* 1992; *Loot, and Other Stories,* 2003; *Beethoven Was One-Sixteenth Black, and Other Stories,* 2007.

TELEPLAYS: *A Chip of Glass Ruby,* 1985; *Country Lovers,* 1985; *Oral History,* 1985; *Praise,* 1985.

NONFICTION: *The Black Interpreters: Notes on African Writing,* 1973; *On the Mines,* 1973 (with David Goldblatt); *Lifetimes Under Apartheid,* 1986 (with Goldblatt); *The Essential Gesture: Writing, Politics, and Places,* 1988 (Stephen Clingman, editor); *Conversations with Nadine Gordimer,* 1990 (Nancy Topping Bazin and Marilyn Dallman Seymour, editors); *Three in a Bed: Fiction, Morals, and Politics,* 1991; *Writing and Being,* 1995; *Living in Hope and History: Notes from Our Century,* 1999; *A Writing Life: Celebrating Nadine Gordimer,* 1999 (Andries Walter Oliphant, editor).

EDITED TEXTS: *South African Writing Today,* 1967 (with Lionel Abrahams); *Telling Tales,* 2004.

BIBLIOGRAPHY

Bazin, Nancy Topping, and Marilyn Dallman Seymour, eds. *Conversations with Nadine Gordimer.* Jackson: University Press of Mississippi, 1990. Collection of interviews with Gordimer is invaluable for its scope. Reveals Gordimer's insights and attitudes toward her works and their origins in conversations spanning more than thirty years (1958-1989). Supplemented by bibliography and index.

Clingman, Stephen. *The Novels of Nadine Gordimer: History from the Inside.* 2d ed. Amherst: University of Massachusetts Press, 1992. Interprets Gordimer's novels, through *My Son's Story,* within the context of history in general and the history of South Africa and African literature in particular. A prologue written for this second edition discusses the dismantling of apartheid and Gordimer's Nobel Prize. Includes index.

Ettin, Andre Vogel. *Betrayals of the Body Politic: The Literary Commitments of Nadine Gordimer.* Charlottesville: University Press of Virginia, 1995. Examines all of Gordimer's genres of writing and addresses the recurring themes: betrayal, politics of family, concept of homeland, ethnicity, and feminism.

Head, Dominic. *Nadine Gordimer.* New York: Cambridge University Press, 1994. Provides a comprehensive study of Gordimer's first ten novels. Supplemented by a chronology of Gordimer's career and major South African political events to 1991, a bibliography of works by and about Gordimer, and an index.

King, Bruce, ed. *The Later Fiction of Nadine Gordimer.* New York: St. Martin's Press, 1993. Collection of essays begins with an introduction that surveys the variety in Gordimer's novels from *The Late Bourgeois World* to *My Son's Story.* General essays deal thematically or stylistically with multiple novels; others address one or two novels in depth. Includes index.

Smith, Rowland, ed. *Critical Essays on Nadine Gordimer.* Boston: G. K. Hall, 1990. Excellent selection of sixteen essays, originally published between 1953 and 1988, provides analysis of Gordimer's first ten novels. Includes bibliographical references and index.

Temple-Thurston, Barbara. *Nadine Gordimer Revisited.* New York: Twayne, 1999. Good introductory study of the author and her works. Among the novels discussed are *The Conservationist, July's People*, and *The House Gun.* Includes chronology, selected bibliography, and index.

Uledi-Kamanga, Brighton J. *Cracks in the Wall: Nadine Gordimer's Fiction and the Irony of Apartheid.* Trenton, N.J.: Africa World Press, 2002. Presents a generally chronological discussion of Gordimer's works, with emphasis on the novels. Focuses on Gordimer's use of irony and her work in the context of South African politics.

Uraizee, Joya. *This Is No Place for a Woman: Nadine Gordimer, Nayantara Saghal, Buchi Emecheta, and the Politics of Gender.* Trenton, N.J.: Africa World Press, 2000. Places Gordimer and the other two female novelists within the context of postcolonial writers. Thematically organized chapters address in depth the works of each of the writers. Gordimer's novels *The Conservationist, A Sport of Nature, Burger's Daughter*, and *July's People* receive significant attention.

MAXIM GORKY

Born: Nizhny-Novgorod, Russia; March 28, 1868
Died: Gorki, near Moscow, Russia, Soviet Union (now Nizhny Novgorod, Russia); June 18, 1936
Also known as: Aleksey Maksimovich Peshkov; Maksim Gorky; Maxim Gorki

PRINCIPAL LONG FICTION

Goremyka Pavel, 1894 (novella; *Orphan Paul*, 1946)
Foma Gordeyev, 1899 (English translation, 1901)
Troye, 1901 (*Three of Them*, 1902)
Mat, 1906 (serial), 1907 (book; *Mother*, 1906)
Ispoved, 1908 (*The Confession*, 1909)
Zhizn Matveya Kozhemyakina, 1910 (*The Life of Matvei Kozhemyakin*, 1959)
Delo Artamonovykh, 1925 (*Decadence*, 1927; better known as *The Artamonov Business*, 1948)
Zhizn Klima Samgina, 1927-1936 (*The Life of Klim Samgin*, 1930-1938; includes *The Bystander*, 1930, *The Magnet*, 1931, *Other Fires*, 1933, and *The Specter*, 1938)

OTHER LITERARY FORMS

Maxim Gorky (GAWR-kee) wrote a total of fifteen plays, only three of which were staged during his lifetime: *Na dne* (pr., pb. 1902; *The Lower Depths*, 1912), *Vassa Zheleznova* (pb. 1910; English translation, 1945), and *Yegor Bulychov i drugiye* (pr., pb. 1932; *Yegor Bulychov and Others*, 1937). His other plays include *Meshchane* (pr., pb. 1902; *Smug Citizen*, 1906), *Dachniki* (pr., pb. 1904; *Summer Folk*, 1905), *Deti solntsa* (pr., pb. 1905; *Children of the Sun*, 1906), *Varvary* (pr., pb. 1906; *Barbarians*, 1906), *Vragi* (pb. 1906; *Enemies*, 1945), *Chudake* (pr., pb. 1910; *Queer People*, 1945), *Falshivaya moneta* (pr., pb. 1927, wr. 1913; the counterfeit coin), *Zykovy* (pb. 1914; *The Zykovs*, 1945), *Starik* (pr. 1919, wr. 1915; *Old Man*, 1924), and *Dostigayev i drugiye* (pr., pb. 1933; *Dostigayev and Others*, 1937). All are available in Russian in the thirty-volume *Polnoe sobranie sochinenii* (1949-1955; complete works), in the twenty-five-volume *Polnoe sobranie sochinenii* (1968-1976), and in English in *Seven Plays* (1945), *Five Plays* (1956), and *Plays* (1975). The eight-volume *Collected Works of Maxim Gorky* (1979-1981), is also available.

Gorky wrote about three hundred short stories. Among the most important are "Makar Chudra" (1892; English translation, 1901), "Chelkash" (1895; English translation, 1901), "Starukha Izergil" (1895; "The Old Woman Izergil"), "Malva" (1897; English translation), "V stepi" (1897; "In the Steppe"), "Dvadtsat' shest' i odna" (1899; "Twenty-six Men and a Girl," 1902), "Pesnya o burevestnike" (1901; "Song of the Stormy Petrel"),

Maxim Gorky
(Library of Congress)

"Pesnya o sokole" (1908; "Song of the Falcon"), and the collections *Po Rusi* (1915; *Through Russia*, 1921) and *Skazki ob Italii* (1911-1913; *Tales of Italy*, 1958?). A three-volume collection of his stories, *Ocherki i rasskazy*, was first published in Russian in 1898-1899. The short stories are available in the collected works; some of the best of them are available in English in *Selected Short Stories* (1959), introduced by Stefan Zweig.

Among Gorky's numerous essays, articles, and nonfiction books, the most important are "O Karamazovshchine" (1913; "On Karamazovism"), "Revolyutsia i kultura" (1917; "Revolution and Culture"), *Vladimir Ilich Lenin* (1924; *V. I. Lenin*, 1931), and "O meshchanstve" (1929; "On the Petty Bourgeois Mentality"). The collection *Untimely Thoughts: Essays on Revolution, Culture, and the Bolsheviks* (1968) includes many of these essays in English translation.

Achievements

Hailed by Soviet critics as a true proletarian writer and the model of Socialist Realism, Maxim Gorky is one of few authors to see their native towns renamed in their honor. Many schools, institutes, universities, and theaters bear his name, as does one of the main streets in Moscow. These honors, says Helen Muchnic, resulted from the fact that Gorky, along with Vladimir Ilich Lenin and Joseph Stalin, "shaped and disseminated the country's official philosophy." Stalin admired Gorky greatly, awarding him the coveted Order of Lenin. As chair of the All-Union Congress of Soviet Writers in 1934, Gorky delivered an address in which he defined Socialist Realism, a doctrine that was to be interpreted in a manner different from what he intended or practiced; the *Soviet Encyclopedia* (1949-1958) calls him "the father of Soviet literature . . . the founder of the literature of Socialist Realism."

Although Gorky's novels are not among the best in Russian literature, they did inaugurate a new type of writing, revealing to the world a new Russia. In contrast to the countless fin de siècle evocations of the tormented Russian soul, with their gallery of superfluous men, Gorky offered a new hero, the proletarian, the revolutionary, such as Pavel Vlassov and his mother, Pelagea Nilovna, in the poorly constructed but ever-popular *Mother*. Indeed, Richard Hare argues that even today *Mother* is the prototype for the socially tendentious novel in the Soviet Union, with its crude but determined effort to look into the dynamism of social change in Russia.

Gorky's highest artistic achievements, however, are his literary portraits; the best, says Muchnic, are those that he drew from life, especially of Leo Tolstoy and Anton Chekhov. Also notable is Gorky's affectionate portrait of his grandmother. Gorky had a strong visual sense, the gift of astute observation, and the ability to translate these insights into sparkling dialogue. He created an entire portrait gallery of vignettes, most of which can be traced to people he met in his endless wanderings through Russia and abroad.

The child of a lower-middle-class family that faced rapid impoverishment, a self-taught student, a young man whose universities were the towns along the Volga and the steamers that made their way along its mighty waters, Gorky was nevertheless sympathetic to culture. He devoured books voraciously and indiscriminately and encouraged others to study. From 1918 to 1921, not wholly in favor with the new regime, he worked tirelessly to save writers and intellectuals from starvation and from censorship. He befriended the Serapion Brothers (a group of young Russian writers formed in 1921) and later Mikhail Sholokhov, always encouraging solid scholarship.

Estimates of Gorky even now depend on political ideology, for he is closely associated with the Russian Revolution. His vision, however, is broader than that of any political movement. He repeats often in his autobiographical works his dismay at the ignorance of people and their lack of desire for a better life, and he felt keenly the injustice done to the innocent. His writing is permeated by the desire to bring people from slavery to freedom, to build a good life; he believed in the power of human beings to change their world. Courageous, generous, and devoted to the public good, Gorky was timid, lacking in self-confidence, and infinitely modest. His commitment to social justice is unquestionable. These qualities may be what Chekhov had in mind when he said that Gorky's works might be forgotten, but that Gorky the man would never be.

Biography

Maxim Gorky, champion of the poor and the downtrodden, was born Aleksey Maksimovich Peshkov in Nizhny-Novgorod (a town that would bear the name Gorki after 1932), on March 28, 1868. His father, who died three years later from cholera, was a joiner-upholsterer and later a shipping agent; his mother's family, the Kashirins, were owners of a dyeing establishment. After his father's death, Gorky's mother left young Gorky to be reared by her parents, with whom he lived until the age of eleven, when his recently remarried mother died. Gorky recounts his childhood experiences in brilliant anecdotes and dialogue in his autobiographical *Detstvo* (1913; *My Childhood*, 1915). The influence of his grandparents was great: His grandfather was a brutal, narrowly religious man, while his grandmother was gentle and pious; her own peculiar version of a benevolent God, sharply in contrast to the harsh religiosity of her husband, marked the impressionable child.

The frequent wanderers in Gorky's works are a reflection of his own experience. In 1879, his grandfather sent him "into the world." He went first to the family of his grandmother's sister's son, Valentin Sergeyev, to whom he was apprenticed as a draftsman. Gorky hated the snobbishness and avarice of this bourgeois family, which became the prototype of the Gordeyevs and the Artamonovs in his fiction. For the next ten years, he filled many other minor posts, from messboy on a Volga steamer to icon painter, reading when and where he could. Other than an idealistic admiration for a neighbor whom he named Queen Margot, there were few bright spots in this period, which he describes in *V lyudyakh* (1916; *In the World*, 1917).

In 1889, after an unsuccessful suicide attempt that left him with a permanently weakened lung, Gorky met the Populist revolutionary Mikhail Romas, who helped him to clarify his confused ideas. At the same time, his acquaintance with the writer Vladimir Korolenko aided his literary development, as Tolstoy and Chekhov were to do in later years. In 1892, Gorky published his first story, "Makar Chudra," assuming at that time the pen name Maxim Gorky, meaning "the bitter one," a reflection of his painful childhood. Gorky wandered through Russia, wrote, and began a series of unsuccessful romantic involvements, first with Olga Kaminskaya, an older woman of some sophistication with whom he lived from 1892 to 1894, and then with Ekaterina Pavlovna Volzhina, a proofreader on the newspaper for which he was working. Gorky married Volzhina in 1896; the couple had two children, Maxim and Ekaterina. Imprisoned several times, Gorky was seldom free of police surveillance. In 1899, he became literary editor of the Marxist newspaper *Zhizn* and directed his attention to the problems of social injustice.

In 1905, Gorky's violent protests of government brutality in suppressing the workers' demonstrations on Bloody Sunday once again brought him imprisonment, this time in the Peter-Paul Fortress. By then, however, Gorky was famous, and celebrities all over Europe and the United States protested the sentence. Upon his release, he once again began to travel, both for political reasons and for his health. He visited New York, which he called "the city of the yellow devil," in 1906, where he attacked the United States for its inequalities and the United States attacked him for the immorality of his relationship with Maria Fyodorovna Andreyeva, an actor of the celebrated Moscow Art Theater. After six months in the United States, he spent seven years in Italy, settling in Capri, where his Villa Serafina became a center of pilgrimage for all revolutionaries, including Lenin.

Gorky returned to Russia in 1913. When the Revolution broke out in 1917, he was not at first among its wholehearted supporters, although he served on many committees, working especially to safeguard culture. In 1921, for reasons of health, he went to Sorrento, Italy, where he spent his time writing. Although he made periodic visits to his homeland beginning in 1928, it was not until 1932 that he returned to the Soviet Union for good; in that same year, Stalin awarded him the Order of Lenin. In 1934, he was elected chair of the All-Union Congress of Soviet Writers; during this period, he became increasingly active in cultural policy making. Although he continued to write, he produced nothing noteworthy; his four-novel cycle *The Life of Klim Samgin*, the last volume of which he did not live to complete, is an artistic failure. Gorky's death in 1936 was surrounded by mysterious circumstances, although official autopsy reports attribute it to tuberculosis and influenza.

Analysis

Although Soviet critics tend to exalt the realism of Maxim Gorky's works, D. S. Mirsky said that Gorky never wrote a good novel or a good play, while Tolstoy remarked that Gorky's novels are inferior to his stories and that his plays are even worse than his novels. Maintaining that Gorky's "tremendous heroic emotions ring false," Tolstoy criticized Gorky's lack of a sense of proportion, as Chekhov had noted Gorky's lack of restraint. It is obvious that Gorky did not know how to limit his stories, that he piles up details along with extraneous dialogue. His narrative technique consists in recounting the life story of a single protagonist or the saga of a family. His narratives are always linear, often proceeding from birth to death; the main character yearns for a new life and struggles with a stagnant environment, sometimes experiencing flashes of light. Thus, the typical Gorky novel is a tireless and often tiresome documentary on a single theme.

Gorky's weak narrative technique is counterbalanced by excellent characterization. True, he is guilty of oversimplification—his characters are types rather than individuals, figures from a modern morality play—but he introduced into Russian fiction a wide range of figures from many different walks of life rarely or never treated by earlier novelists. Though not highly individualized, Gorky's characterizations are vivid and convincing, imbued with his own energy.

Gorky sees people as social organisms, and therefore he is especially conscious of their role in society. He was particularly familiar with the merchant class or the *meshchane*, because he grew up among them, in the Kashirin and Sergeyev households. They form some of his most successful portraits, representing not only the petty bourgeoisie but also the barge owners, grain dealers, mill owners, and textile manufacturers, the Gordeyevs, Artamonovs, and Kozhemyakins. Gorky represents them as self-centered individualists, characterized by envy, malice, self-righteousness, avarice, and intellectual and spiritual torpor. Their decadence is symbolic of the malady that ravages prerevolutionary Russia.

In contrast to the merchants are the lonely and downtrodden, not always idealized as in the novels of Fyodor Dostoevski but presented, rather, as the ignorant victims of society and its lethargic sycophants. The corrupt and indifferent town of Okurov in *The Life of Matvei Kozhemyakin* symbolizes Russia's decadence, as do the thieves and vagabonds of Kazan, the flophouse of *The Lower Depths*, and the orgies of the theology students in the houses of prostitution. More Dostoevskian are the *bosyaki*, the barefoot tramps, such as Chelkash and Makar Chudra, who are the heralds of the future. Along with them, yet very different in spirit, is the revolutionary intelligentsia, the new heroes created by Gorky. They are Pelagea Nilovna, the "mother"; her son, Pavel; and his friends, Mansurova in *The Life of Matvei Kozhemyakin* and Derenkov and Romas in Gorky's own life. It is for such characters that Gorky is exalted by the Soviets, though to foreign readers they are usually the least attractive.

Gorky's best characters are presented without excessive ideological trappings. They range from his saintly grandmother, Akulina Kashirina, perhaps his most unforgettable character, to Queen Margot, the idol with clay feet. They include Smoury, the cook on the steamer, who first encouraged Gorky to read, and many other simple people whom Gorky was to meet, "kind, solitary, and broken off from life." They also take the form of figures such as the merchant Ignat Gordeyev, the image of the Volga, vital, seething, creative, generous, and resolute.

Most of Gorky's women are victims of violence, beaten by their husbands and unappreciated by their families, such as Natasha Artamonova and the wife of Saveli Kozhemyakin, who is beaten to death by him. Love in Gorky's novels is either accompanied by violence and brutality or idealized, as in Queen Margot or Tanya in the story "Twenty-six Men and a Girl." It ranges from tender devotion in *Mother* to drunken orgies on Foma Gordeyev's Volga steamer. Gorky's own experience of love was unhappy, and he was ill at ease when portraying sexual scenes. Even his coarsely erotic scenes seem to be tinged with a moralizing intent.

Against a background of resplendent nature, the Volga, the sea, or the steppe, Gorky depicts the eruptions of violence and brutality, the orgies and the squalor, the pain and the harshness that, says Muchnic, are at the heart of his work. One has only to read the opening pages of *My Childhood* to feel its force. His own weight of harsh experience impelled him to force others to look at the bestiality that he saw rampant in Russia and to urge them to exterminate it. Ever the champion of social justice, Gorky felt the need to fight ignorance, cruelty, and exploitation.

FOMA GORDEYEV

Gorky's first and best novel, *Foma Gordeyev*, is set along the banks of the Volga, a region well known to the author. It is the story of the Volga merchants, represented here by the Gordeyev and Mayakin families. Rich, greedy, and passionate, both families represent the iron will and the domination of the merchant class. Gorky's merchants are of peasant origin, unsophisticated and uneducated. In Foma's revolt, Gorky shows the decay of society at the end of the nineteenth century and the impending Revolution, as yet only dimly anticipated. Foma, the only son of Ignat Gordeyev, a self-made barge owner and one of Gorky's richest character sketches, is brought up by his godfather and his father's business colleague, Yakov Mayakin, whose family has owned the local rope works for generations. Foma shows no talent for or interest in business and, after his father's death, wastes his money on debauchery, drink, and wanton destruction. At first dimly attracted to Lyubov Mayakina, he is unable to conform to her educated tastes, and she, in obedience to her father's wishes, marries the respectable and highly Europeanized Afrikan Smolin. Foma continues his wild rebellion, actually a search for self and meaning, not unlike that of Mikhail Lermontov's Pechorin. Finally institutionalized for apparent insanity, Foma becomes an enlightened vagabond.

Foma Gordeyev follows the story line generally adopted by Gorky: the life story of the hero from birth to a crisis. Although it is weak in plot and characterization, it is readable, especially powerful in its evocation of the Volga, the elemental force that intoxicated the wealthy Ignat. Ignat is a finished portrait of the boisterous, dynamic businessman Gorky knew so well—vital, creative, and resolute. He is one of Gorky's most sympathetic portraits, along with Yakov Mayakin, who shows the characteristic traits of the Russian merchant that go back to the sixteenth century *Domostroy* (a book on social conduct). Foma, though not so well drawn, represents the rift in generations and the universally disturbed mood that pervaded Russia on the eve of the abortive Revolution of 1905. The whole novel attempts to assess the flaws in the capitalistic system and thus is very modern in spirit.

MOTHER

Mother, written while Gorky was in the United States after the 1905 Revolution, reflects his disillusionment with both czarist and capitalistic social structures and his desire "to sustain the failing spirit of opposition to the dark and threatening forces of life." The novel was published first in English, in 1906, by *Appleton's Magazine* in New York, and then in Russian in Berlin. It became the symbol of the revolutionary cause and was widely read and acclaimed, even after the Revolution, as a model of the socialist novel. Translated into many languages, it became the basis for other novels and plays, such as Bertolt Brecht's *Mutter Courage und Ihre Kinder* (1941; *Mother Courage and Her Children*, 1941). As a novel, it is one of Gorky's weakest in characterization and plot, yet its optimistic message and accessible style have assured its continuing popularity.

Written in the third person, through the eyes of the courageous mother, Pelagea Nilovna Vlassova, the novel relates her encounter with the Social Democratic Party, inspired by her son, Pavel. Pelagea suffered mistreatment from her husband and seems destined to continue in the same path with her son until his "conversion" to socialism. Pavel becomes a champion of the proletarian cause, the acknowledged leader of a small group of fellow revolutionaries who study forbidden books and distribute literature among the factory workers in their village. After Pavel's arrest, the illiterate Pelagea continues Pavel's work, stealthily distributing pamphlets and becoming a mother to the other members of the group: Sasha, who is secretly in love with Pavel; the "God-builder" Rybin; Andrei, the charming and humorous *khokhol*; the misanthropic Vesovshchikov; and the open-hearted urban intellectual Nikolai. Pavel's release from prison is immediately followed by his bold leadership in the May Day demonstration, for which he is again imprisoned. The mother's work becomes more daring and widespread as she passes to other villages like the holy wanderers so common in Gorky's early work. After Pavel's condemnation to exile in Siberia, Pelagea herself is arrested as she prepares to distribute the speech her son made prior to his sentence.

The best portrait in this weak novel is that of the mother, the only character to show psychological development. Yet Pelagea passes from one type of religious fervor to another, and her socialist convictions are simply the transferral of her Orthodox beliefs to the kingdom of this world. Even the revolutionaries invoke Christ and compare their work to his. The austere Pavel remains remote and unconvincing, while maternal love is the dominant force in the affectionate and almost mystical Pelagea.

THE ARTAMONOV BUSINESS

Written in 1924 and 1925 while Gorky was living abroad in Sorrento, *The Artamonov Business* is a retrospective novel on the causes of the 1917 Revolution. Encompassing three generations and covering the period from 1863 to 1917, it has a much broader base than most of Gorky's works. Although here, as elsewhere, Gorky fills his narrative with extraneous detail, he draws many convincing portraits of the demoralized merchant class at the turn of the century. Frank M. Borras singles out Gorky's interweaving of the historical theme with the characters' personal destinies as one of the merits of the novel.

Ilya Artamonov is the patriarch of the family, a passionate and dynamic freed serf who establishes a linen factory in the sleepy town of Dryomov. His son, Pyotr, inherits his father's sensuality but not his business skill, and the narrative of his debauchery and indifference to his workers occupies the greater part of the novel. The Artamonov family also includes the more businesslike and adaptable Aleksei and the hunchback Nikita, who becomes a monk though he has lost his faith in God. The women in the novel occupy a secondary and passive role, existing mainly for the sensual gratification of the men, both attracting and repelling them.

Pyotr has two sons and two daughters. The eldest son, Ilya, leaves home to study and, as in Chekhov's stories, becomes an unseen presence, presumably joining the revolutionary Social Democratic Party. Yakov, the second son, is a sensualist, indifferent to business, and is killed by revolutionaries as he escapes in fear of them. Miron, Aleksei's son, though physically weak, shows, like his father, an aptitude for commerce. Yet none is strong enough to save the family's ailing business, weakened by the corruption and indifference of its managers.

Gorky's symbolism is evident in his characterization of Tikhon Vialov (the quiet one), an enigmatic ditchdigger, gardener, and ubiquitous servant of the Artamonov family. It is Tikhon who at the very end of the story proclaims the Revolution, calling for revenge for the injustices that he has suffered at the hands of the Artamonovs. Quite obviously he symbolizes the proletariat, victim of the bourgeoisie. Aside from Tikhon, Gorky emphasizes much less the oppression of the workers than the empty, selfish, and superfluous lives of the factory owners. Alternating wild episodes of debauchery, cruelty, and murder with scenes of boredom and superfluous dialogue, *The Artamonov Business* is both a modern novel and a return to Dostoevskian melodrama. Gorky had planned to write the novel as early as 1909 but was advised by Lenin to wait for the Revolution, which would be its logical conclusion. This story of the progressive deterioration of a family is also a profound study in the consequences of the failure of human relationships.

Gorky was less a man of ideas and reason than one of instinct and emotion. His best works are based on intuition and observation. His truth and reality are humanistic, not metaphysical; they deal with the useful and the practical. Unlike Honoré de Balzac, whom he admired, Gorky did not succeed in investing the sordid with mystery or the petty with grandeur. He wrote a literature of the moment, "loud but not intense," as Muchnic describes it. It is, however, a literature of the people and for the people, accessible and genuine. Although some of his works are monotonous to today's Western reader, and no doubt to the Russian reader as well, at their best they are honest portrayals of people, inspiring confidence in humanity's power to change the world.

Irma M. Kashuba

OTHER MAJOR WORKS

SHORT FICTION: "Makar Chudra" (1892; English translation, 1901); "Chelkash," 1895 (English translation, 1901); "Byvshye lyudi," 1897 ("Creatures That Once Were Men," 1905); *Ocherki i rasskazy*, 1898-1899 (3 volumes); "Dvadtsat' shest' i odna," 1899 ("Twenty-six Men and a Girl," 1902); *Orloff and His Wife: Tales of the Barefoot Brigade*, 1901; *Rasskazy i p'esy*, 1901-1910 (9 volumes); *Skazki ob Italii*, 1911-1913 (*Tales of Italy*, 1958?); *Tales of Two Countries*, 1914; *Chelkash, and Other Stories*, 1915; *Po Rusi*, 1915 (*Through Russia*, 1921); *Stories of the Steppe*, 1918; *Zametki iz dnevnika: Vospominaniia*, 1924 (*Fragments from My Diary*, 1924); *Rasskazy 1922-1924 godov*, 1925; *Selected Short Stories*, 1959; *A Sky-Blue Life, and Selected Stories*, 1964; *The Collected Short Stories of Maxim Gorky*, 1988.

PLAYS: *Meshchane*, pr., pb. 1902 (*Smug Citizen*, 1906); *Na dne*, pr., pb. 1902 (*The Lower Depths*, 1912); *Dachniki*, pr., pb. 1904 (*Summer Folk*, 1905); *Deti solntsa*, pr., pb. 1905 (*Children of the Sun*, 1906); *Varvary*, pr., pb. 1906 (*Barbarians*, 1906); *Vragi*, pb. 1906 (*Enemies*, 1945); *Posledniye*, pr., pb. 1908; *Chudake*, pr., pb. 1910 (*Queer People*, 1945); *Vassa Zheleznova* (first version), pb. 1910 (English translation, 1945); *Zykovy*, pb. 1914 (*The Zykovs*, 1945); *Starik*, pr. 1919 (wr. 1915; *Old Man*, 1924); *Falshivaya moneta*, pr., pb. 1927 (wr. 1913); *Yegor Bulychov i drugiye*, pr., pb. 1932 (*Yegor Bulychov and Others*, 1937); *Dostigayev i drugiye*, pr., pb. 1933 (*Dostigayev and Others*, 1937); *Vassa Zheleznova* (second version), pr., pb. 1935 (English translation, 1975); *Seven Plays*, 1945; *Five Plays*, 1956; *Plays*, 1975.

NONFICTION: *Detstvo*, 1913 (*My Childhood*, 1915); *V lyudyakh*, 1916 (*In the World*, 1917); *Vozpominaniya o Lev Nikolayeviche Tolstom*, 1919 (*Reminiscences of Leo Nikolaevich Tolstoy*, 1920); *Moi universitety*, 1923 (*My Universities*, 1923); *Vladimir Ilich Lenin*, 1924 (*V. I. Lenin*, 1931); *Reminiscences of Tolstoy, Chekhov, and Andreyev*, 1949; *Untimely Thoughts: Essays on Revolution, Culture, and the Bolsheviks*, 1968; *Selected Letters*, 1997 (Andrew Barratt and Barry P. Scherr, editors); *Gorky's Tolstoy and Other Reminiscences: Key Writings by and About Maxim Gorky*, 2008 (Donald Fanger, editor).

MISCELLANEOUS: *Polnoe sobranie sochinenii*, 1949-1955 (30 volumes); *Polnoe sobranie sochinenii*, 1968-1976 (25 volumes); *Collected Works of Maxim Gorky*, 1979-1981 (8 volumes).

BIBLIOGRAPHY

Borras, F. M. *Maxim Gorky the Writer: An Interpretation*. Oxford, England: Clarendon Press, 1967. One of the more astute interpretations of Gorky's works, especially his novels and plays. Unlike many other books that concentrate on either biography or political issues, Borras's book emphasizes Gorky's artistic achievements.

Hare, Richard. *Maxim Gorky: Romantic Realist and Conservative Revolutionary*. New York: Oxford University Press, 1962. The first substantial study of Gorky in English since Alexander Kaun's 1931 book. Hare combines the political aspects of Gorky's biography with critical analyses of his works. Contains some interesting observations obtained from anonymous people who knew Gorky well.

Kaun, Alexander. *Maxim Gorky and His Russia*. New York: Jonathan Cape and Harrison Smith, 1931. The first book on Gorky in English, written while Gorky was still alive and supported by firsthand knowledge about him. Covers literary and nonliterary life in Russia and the atmosphere in Gorky's time. Still one of the best biographies, despite some outdated facts later corrected by history.

Levin, Dan. *Stormy Petrel: The Life and Work of Maxim Gorky*. New York: Schocken Books, 1985. This reprint of the author's 1965 work contains the detailed notes he excised from the original edition. An engrossing biographical and literary interpretation of Gorky's life and work.

Morris, Paul D. *Representation and the Twentieth-Century Novel: Studies in Gorky, Joyce, and Pynchon.* Würzburg, Germany: Königshausen & Neumann, 2005. A critical interpretation of Gorky's *Mother*, as well as James Joyce's *Ulysses* and Thomas Pynchon's *Gravity's Rainbow*, discussing how each novel represents a different literary tradition. Morris views Gorky's book as a paradigm of the Socialist Realist novel. For advanced students.

Scherr, Barry P. *Maxim Gorky.* Boston: Twayne, 1988. Chapters on the writer and revolutionary, his literary beginnings, his career as a young novelist, his plays, his memoirs, and his final achievements. Includes a chronology, detailed notes, and an annotated bibliography. Still the best introductory study.

Troyat, Henri. *Gorky.* Translated by Lowell Bair. New York: Crown, 1989. A translation of a French biography, written by a well-regarded literary biographer, which discusses Gorky's life and works. Includes a bibliography and an index.

Valentino, Russell Scott. *Vicissitudes of Genre in the Russian Novel: Turgenev's "Fathers and Sons," Chernyshevsky's "What Is to Be Done?," Dostoevsky's "Demons," Gorky's "Mother."* New York: Peter Lang, 2001. Analyzes Russian fictional works from the 1860's that are examples of the "tendentious novel" of this period. Describes how these novels influenced twentieth century literature.

Weil, Irwin. *Gorky: His Literary Development and Influence on Soviet Intellectual Life.* New York: Random House, 1966. One of the most scholarly books on Gorky in English, skillfully combining biography with critical analysis. Valuable especially for the discussion of Soviet literary life and Gorky's connections with, and influence on, younger Soviet writers. Contains a select but adequate bibliography.

Yedlin, Tova. *Maxim Gorky: A Political Biography.* Westport, Conn.: Praeger, 1999. Yedlin's biography focuses on Gorky's political and social views and his participation in the political and cultural life of his country. Includes a bibliography and an index.

GRAHAM GREENE

Born: Berkhamsted, Hertfordshire, England; October 2, 1904
Died: Vevey, Switzerland; April 3, 1991

PRINCIPAL LONG FICTION
The Man Within, 1929
The Name of Action, 1930
Rumour at Nightfall, 1931
Stamboul Train: An Entertainment, 1932 (also known as *Orient Express: An Entertainment*, 1933)
It's a Battlefield, 1934
England Made Me, 1935
A Gun for Sale: An Entertainment, 1936 (also known as *This Gun for Hire: An Entertainment*)
Brighton Rock, 1938
The Confidential Agent, 1939
The Power and the Glory, 1940 (reissued as *The Labyrinthine Ways*)
The Ministry of Fear: An Entertainment, 1943
The Heart of the Matter, 1948
The Third Man: An Entertainment, 1950
"The Third Man" and "The Fallen Idol," 1950
The End of the Affair, 1951
Loser Takes All: An Entertainment, 1955
The Quiet American, 1955
Our Man in Havana: An Entertainment, 1958
A Burnt-Out Case, 1961 (first published in Swedish translation as *Utbränd*, 1960)
The Comedians, 1966
Travels with My Aunt, 1969
The Honorary Consul, 1973
The Human Factor, 1978
Dr. Fischer of Geneva: Or, The Bomb Party, 1980
Monsignor Quixote, 1982
The Tenth Man, 1985
The Captain and the Enemy, 1988
No Man's Land, 2004

OTHER LITERARY FORMS

In addition to his novels, Graham Greene published many collections of short stories, including *The Basement Room, and Other Stories* (1935), *Nineteen Stories* (1947),

Twenty-one Stories (1954; in which two stories from the previous collection were dropped and four added), *A Sense of Reality* (1963), *May We Borrow Your Husband?, and Other Comedies of the Sexual Life* (1967), and *Collected Stories* (1972). He also wrote plays, including *The Living Room* (pr., pb. 1953), *The Potting Shed* (pr., pb. 1957), *The Complaisant Lover* (pr., pb. 1959), *Carving a Statue* (pr., pb. 1964), and *Yes and No* (pr. 1980). With the exception of his first published book, *Babbling April: Poems* (1925), he did not publish poetry except in two private printings, *After Two Years* (1949) and *For Christmas* (1950). He wrote some interesting travel books, two focusing on Africa, *Journey Without Maps: A Travel Book* (1936) and *In Search of a Character: Two African Journals* (1961), and one set in Mexico, *The Lawless Roads: A Mexican Journal* (1939).

Greene published several books of essays and criticism, including *British Dramatists* (1942), *The Lost Childhood, and Other Essays* (1951), *Essais Catholiques* (1953), *Collected Essays* (1969), and *The Pleasure Dome: The Collected Film Criticism, 1935-40, of Graham Greene* (1972), edited by John Russell-Taylor. He also wrote a biography, *Lord Rochester's Monkey: Being the Life of John Wilmot, Second Earl of Rochester* (1974), and two autobiographical works, *A Sort of Life* (1971), carrying the reader up to Greene's first novel, and *Ways of Escape* (1980), bringing the reader up to the time of its writing. A biographical-autobiographical work, *Getting to Know the General: The Story of an Involvement* (1984), spotlights Greene's relationship with General Omar Torrijos Herrera of Panama. Four children's books are also among Greene's works: *The Little Train* (1946), *The Little Fire Engine* (1950), *The Little Horse Bus* (1952), and *The Little Steam Roller: A Story of Mystery and Detection* (1953).

ACHIEVEMENTS

Graham Greene's style has often been singled out for praise. He learned economy and precision while working for *The Times* of London. More than anything else, he struggled for precision, "truth" as he called it, in form as well as in substance. *The Power and the Glory* won the Hawthornden Prize in 1941. Additionally, Greene's experience as a film reviewer seems to have given him a feel for cinematic technique. What Greene's reputation will be a century hence is difficult to predict. Readers will certainly find in him more than a religious writer, more—at least—than a Catholic writer. They will find in him a writer who used for his thematic vehicles all the pressing issues of his era: the Vietnam War, Papa Doc Duvalier's tyranny over Haiti, the struggle between communism and capitalism, apartheid in South Africa, poverty and oppression in Latin America. Will these issues seem too topical for posterity, or will they prove again that only by localizing one's story in the specifics of a time and place can one appeal to readers of another time, another place?

BIOGRAPHY

Henry Graham Greene was born on October 2, 1904, in the town of Berkhamsted, England. The fourth of six children, he was not especially close to his father, perhaps because of his father's position as headmaster of Berkhamsted School, which Greene attended. Some of the boys took sadistic delight in his ambiguous position, and two in particular caused him such humiliation that they created in him an excessive desire to prove himself. Without them, he claimed, he might never have written a book.

Greene made several attempts at suicide during these unhappy years; he later insisted these were efforts to avoid boredom rather than to kill himself. At Oxford, he tried for a while to avoid boredom by drinking alcohol to excess each day of an entire semester. During these Oxford days, Greene met Vivien Dayrell-Browning, a young Catholic woman who had written to him of his error in a film review in referring to Catholic "worship" of the Virgin Mary. He inquired into the "subtle" and "unbelievable theology" out of interest in Vivien and concluded by becoming a Catholic in 1926. Greene married Vivien, and the couple had two children, a boy and a girl. He separated from his parents' family after the wedding and was scrupulous about guarding his own family's privacy.

In 1926, Greene moved from his first, unsalaried, position writing for the *Nottingham Journal* to the position of subeditor for *The Times* of London. There he learned writing technique, pruning the clichés of reporters and condensing their stories without loss of meaning or effect. Moreover, he had mornings free to do his own writing. When, in 1928, Heinemann accepted Greene's first novel, *The Man Within*, for publication, Greene rashly quit *The Times* to make his living as a writer.

Greene's next two novels, *The Name of Action* and *Rumour at Nightfall*, failed, and he later suppressed them. Still, in trying to understand what went wrong with these works, he discovered that he had tried to omit the autobiographical entirely; as a result, the novels lacked life and truth. He would not make that mistake again.

In 1934, Greene took the first of a seemingly endless series of trips to other parts of the world. With his cousin Barbara, he walked without maps across the heart of Liberia. Recorded in his *Journey Without Maps*, this hazardous venture became a turning point in his life. He had once thought death desirable; in the desert, he became a passionate lover of life. He came even to accept the rats in his hut as part of life. Perhaps more important for his writing, he discovered in Liberia the archetypal basis for his earliest nightmares. The frightening creatures of those dreams were not originally evil beings but rather devils in the African sense of beings who control power. Humankind, Greene came to believe, has corrupted these primitive realities and denied the inherited sense of supernatural evil, reducing it to the level of merely human evil. In doing so, humans had forgotten "the finer taste, the finer pleasure, the finer terror on which we might have built." Greene had found the basis for themes that persistently made their way into his novels.

Greene began his great fiction with *Brighton Rock*, the publication of which, in 1938, followed a trip to Mexico that delighted him much less than the one to Africa. Nevertheless, his observations in Mexico provided the substance of what many consider his finest achievement, *The Power and the Glory*. For the reader interested in a genuine insight into the way Greene moves from fact to fiction, the travel book that emerged from the Mexican journey, *The Lawless Roads*, is very rewarding, showing, for example, how his fictional "whiskey priest" was an amalgam of four real-life priests.

With the outbreak of World War II, Greene was assigned to the Secret Intelligence Service, or MI6, as it was then called. The experience—including his work for the notorious spy Kim Philby—gave him the material for several later works, including *Our Man in Havana* and *The Human Factor*, and nurtured in him that "virtue of disloyalty" that informs his novels.

Greene ceased his writing of explicitly religious novels with *The End of the Affair* in 1951, when people began to treat him as a guru. Although his novels continued to address religious concerns, none—with the possible exception of *A Burnt-Out Case* in 1961—was a religious problem novel. Increasingly, Greene turned to political concerns in novels such as *The Quiet American* and *The Comedians*, but these concerns transcend the topical and speak more enduringly of human involvement.

In his later years, Greene slowed his production somewhat. He continued, however, to write two hundred words every morning, then corrected in great detail in the evening. His practice was to dictate his corrected manuscript into a tape recorder and send the tapes from his home in Antibes, on the French Riviera, to England, where they were typed and then returned. Greene also continued to indulge his taste for travel: He visited dictator Fidel Castro in Cuba, General Omar Torrijos Herrera in Panama, and President Ho Chi Minh in Vietnam. A full catalog of his travels would be virtually endless. Despite the reductive label critics have applied to his settings—"Greeneland"—Greene's novels have more varied settings than those of almost any other novelist, and his settings are authentic. Greene died on April 3, 1991, in Vevey, Switzerland, where he had lived the last years of his life.

Analysis

In an address he called the "Virtue of Disloyalty," which he delivered at the University of Hamburg in 1969, Graham Greene contended that a writer is driven "to be a protestant in a Catholic society, a catholic in a Protestant one," or to be a communist in a capitalist society and a capitalist in a communist one. Whereas loyalty confines a person to accepted opinions, "disloyalty gives the novelist an extra dimension of understanding." Whatever the reader may think of Greene's theory, it is helpful in explaining most of his own novels. From *The Man Within* in 1929, which justified a suicide in the face of Catholic morality's abhorrence for such an act, to *The Human Factor* forty-nine years later, which comes close to justifying treason, Greene practiced this "virtue of disloyalty."

Most of Greene's obsessions originated in his childhood. Where did the desire to be "disloyal," to play devil's advocate, arise? Certainly his serving in MI6 under the authority of Kim Philby was a factor. Greene admired the man in every way except for what appeared to be a personal drive for power. It was this characteristic of Philby that caused Greene finally to resign rather than accept a promotion and become part of Philby's intrigue. Greene later came to see, however, that the man served not himself but a cause, and all his former admiration of Philby returned. Greene continued his friendship even after Philby's treason became known. As he saw it, Philby had found a faith in communism, and he would not discard it because it had been abused by Joseph Stalin, any more than Catholics would discard a faith that had been abused by the Inquisitors or the Roman Curia.

Clearly, however, Greene's "disloyalty" or sympathy for the rebel did not originate here. It too must be traced to his childhood, to his isolation at school, where neither the students nor his headmaster father could treat him unambiguously; it can be traced also to his love of poet Robert Browning, who very early instilled in him an interest in the "dangerous edge of things," in "the honest thief, the tender murderer." It was an influence more lasting, Greene said, than any religious teaching. Religiously, however, Greene's fierce independence manifested itself when, upon conversion to Catholicism, he took the name Thomas, not after the angelic doctor but after the doubter.

Although Greene wrote in many genres, the novel is the form on which his reputation will rest. His strengths in the genre are many. Like all novelists who are more than journeymen, he returns throughout his oeuvre to certain recurring themes. Another strength is his gift for playing the devil's advocate, the dynamics that occur when his character finds himself divided between loyalties. In Greene's first novel, *The Man Within*, that division was handled crudely, externalized in a boy's attraction to two different women; in later novels, the struggle is internalized. Sarah Miles of *The End of the Affair* is torn between her loyalty to God and her loyalty to her lover. Fowler of *The Quiet American* cannot decide whether he wants to eliminate Pyle for the good of Vietnam or to get his woman back from a rival. The characters are shaded in, rendered complex by internal division.

Brighton Rock

Because he was a remarkable self-critic, Greene overcame most of his early weaknesses. He corrected an early tendency to distrust autobiographical material, and he seemed to overcome his difficulty in portraying credible women. In his first twenty-four years as a novelist, he depicted perhaps only two or three complex women: Kate Farrant of *England Made Me*, Sarah Miles of *The End of the Affair*, and possibly Ida Arnold of *Brighton Rock*. His later novels and plays, however, feature a host of well-drawn women, certainly the best of whom is Aunt Augusta of *Travels with My Aunt*. If there is one weakness that mars some of Greene's later novels, it is their prolixity. Too often in his late fiction, characters are merely mouthpieces for ideas.

Brighton Rock was the first of Greene's novels to treat an explicitly religious theme. Moreover, in attempting to play devil's advocate for *Brighton Rock*'s protagonist, Pinkie, the author had chosen one of his most challenging tasks. He made this Catholic protagonist more vicious than he was to make any character in his entire canon, yet Greene demonstrated that Catholic moral law could not condemn Pinkie, could not finally know "the appalling strangeness of the mercy of God."

Pinkie takes over a protection-racket gang from his predecessor, Kite, and must immediately avenge Kite's murder by killing Fred Hale. This murder inspires him to commit a series of other murders necessary to cover his tracks. It also leads to Pinkie's marrying Rose, a potential witness against him, and finally to his attempt to induce Rose to commit suicide. When the police intervene, Pinkie takes his own life.

Vicious as he is, with his sadistic razor slashings, his murders to cover murders, and his cruelty to Rose, Pinkie's guilt is nevertheless extenuated, his amorality rendered somewhat understandable. Pinkie's conscience had not awakened because his imagination had not awakened: "The word 'murder' conveyed no more to him than the word 'box,' 'collar,' 'giraffe.' . . . The imagination hadn't awoken. That was his strength. He couldn't see through other people's eyes, or feel with their nerves."

As with so many of Greene's characters, the explanation for Pinkie's self-destructive character lies in his lost childhood: "In the lost boyhood of Judas, Christ was betrayed." In a parody of William Wordsworth's "Ode: Intimations of Immortality" (1807), Greene said that Pinkie came into the world trailing something other than heavenly clouds of his own glory after him: "Hell lay about him in his infancy." Though Wordsworth might write of the archetypal child that "heaven lay about him in his infancy," Greene saw Pinkie in quite different terms: "Heaven was a word: hell was something he could trust." Pinkie's vivid memory of his father and mother having sexual intercourse in his presence has turned him from all pleasures of the flesh, tempting him for a while with thoughts of the celibate priesthood.

When Pinkie is seventeen, Kite becomes a surrogate father to him. Pinkie's lack of conscience, his unconcern for himself, his sadomasochistic tendencies, which early showed themselves as a substitute for thwarted sexual impulses, stand the youth in good stead for a new vocation that requires unflinching loyalty, razor slashings, and, if necessary, murder. His corruption is almost guaranteed. To say this is not to reduce the novel from a theological level to a sociological one on which environment has determined the boy's character. Rose survives somewhat the same circumstances. Pinkie's guilt is extenuated, never excused.

Pinkie, however, is not the only character in the novel on whose behalf Greene invoked his "virtue of disloyalty." Rose is a prefiguration of the unorthodox "saint" that Greene developed more subtly in his later novels, in the Mexican priest of *The Power and the Glory*, in Sarah Miles of *The End of the Affair*, and to some extent in Scobie of *The Heart of the Matter*. Like Scobie, Rose wills her damnation out of love. She is not so well drawn as Scobie, at times making her naïve goodness less credible than his, but she is motivated by selfless concern for another. When she refuses to reject Pinkie and when she chooses to commit suicide, Rose wants an afterlife with Pinkie. She would rather be damned with him than see him damned alone: Rose will show "them they couldn't pick and choose." This seems unconvincing, until one hears the old priest cite the actual case of Charles Peguy, who would rather have died in a state of sin than have believed that a single soul was damned. In her confession to the old priest, Rose learns of God's mercy and also of the "saintly" Peguy, who, like Rose, preferred to be damned rather than believe that another person had been.

One is asked, then, to be sympathetic both to a character who has willed her own damnation and to one who leads a life of thorough viciousness, to believe that the salvation of both is a real possibility. In asking for this sympathy, for this possibility, Greene is not doctrinaire. As an effective problem novelist, Greene makes no assertions but merely asks questions that enlarge one's understanding. Greene does not equate the Church with Rose's official moral teaching, suggesting that the old priest in this novel and Father Rank in *The Heart of the Matter* are as representative as the teachers of Rose and Pinkie. Still, the moral doctrine provided Greene with the material that he liked to stretch beyond its customary shape.

THE HEART OF THE MATTER

In *The Heart of the Matter*, Greene achieved the genuine tragedy that he came close to writing in many of his other novels. His protagonist, Major Scobie, is a virtuous man whose tragic flaw lies in an excess of pity. In Scobie, pity exceeds all bounds and becomes as vicious as Macbeth's ambition. His pity wrecks a marriage he had wanted to save, ruins a lover he had hoped to help, kills his closest friend—his "boy," Ali—and brings about his own moral corruption. Compared to Aristides the Just by one character and to the Old Testament's Daniel by another, Scobie becomes guilty of adultery, smuggling, treason, lies, sacrilege, and murder before he kills himself.

A late edition of the novel restores to the story an early scene between the government spy, Wilson, and Louise Scobie. Greene had written it for the original, then withdrew it since he believed that, told as it was from Wilson's point of view, it broke Scobie's point of view prematurely. When this scene is restored, Louise is seen in a more sympathetic light, and one can no longer see Scobie as hunted to his death by Louise. Though the reader still likes Scobie and is tempted to exonerate him, it is difficult to read the restored text without seeing Scobie's excess of pity for what it is.

The novel's three final, anticlimactic scenes effectively serve to reduce the grandeur of Scobie's act of self-sacrifice, showing the utter waste of his suicide and the fearful pride contained in his act. It is not that the final scenes make Scobie seem a lesser person. On the contrary, his wife and Helen are made to appear more unworthy of him: Louise with her unkind judgments about Scobie's taking money from Yusef when that very money was borrowed to send her to South Africa as she wanted, and Helen giving her body to Bagster immediately after Scobie's death. Nevertheless, the very criticism of these women makes Scobie's suicide more meaningless and even more effectively shows the arrogance of his action.

Scobie's suicide, then, is not meant to be seen as praiseworthy but rather as the result of a tragic flaw—pity. In this respect, it differs from Elizabeth's suicide in *The Man Within*.

Still, though his suicide is presented as wrong, the final fault in a good man disintegrating spiritually, the reader is compelled to feel sympathy for Scobie. Louise's insistence on the Church's teaching that he has cut himself off from mercy annoys the reader. One is made to see Scobie through the eyes of Father Rank, who angrily responds to Louise that "the Church knows all the rules. But it doesn't know what goes on in a single human heart." In this novel's complex treatment of suicide, then, Greene does not use the "virtue of disloyalty" to justify Scobie's act but rather "to comprehend sympathetically [a] dissident fellow."

THE HUMAN FACTOR

The epigraph for *The Human Factor* is taken from Joseph Conrad: "I only know that he who forms a tie is lost. The germ of corruption has entered into his soul." Maurice Castle's soul is corrupted because a tie of gratitude exists between him and a Communist friend.

The Human Factor may, in part, have been suggested by Greene's friend and former superior in British Secret Intelligence, Kim Philby, although Greene had written twenty-five thousand words of the novel before Philby's defection. When Philby wrote his story, *My Silent War* (1968), Greene put the novel aside for ten years. In any case, Greene anticipated the novel long before the Philby case in his 1930 story, "I Spy," in which a young boy watches his father being whisked off to Russia after the British have detected his spying.

The Human Factor was Greene's first espionage novel since *Our Man in Havana* in 1958. Greene's protagonist, Maurice Castle, works for the British Secret Service in London and has, the reader learns halfway through the novel, become a double agent. He has agreed to leak information to the Russians to help thwart "Uncle Remus," a plan devised by England, the United States, and South Africa to preserve apartheid, even to use nuclear weapons for the purpose if necessary. Castle has not become a Communist and will not support them in Europe, but he owes a Communist friend a favor for helping his black wife, Sarah, escape from South Africa. Also, he owes his wife's people something better than apartheid.

Castle's spying is eventually discovered, and the Russians remove him from England. They try to make good their promise to have his wife and child follow, but the British Secret Service makes it impossible for Sarah to take the boy when it learns that Sam is not Castle's boy, but the boy of an African who is still alive. The novel ends in bleak fashion when Maurice is permitted to phone from Moscow and learns that his family cannot come. He has escaped into a private prison.

The Human Factor exemplifies again the "virtue of disloyalty," but even more, it demonstrates that Greene does not merely flesh out a story to embody that disloyalty. Though he does everything to enlist the reader's sympathies for Castle, demonstrating his superiority to those for whom he works, Greene ultimately condemns his actions as he condemned Scobie's. As Scobie had been a victim of pity, Castle is a victim of gratitude. In chatting with his wife, Sarah, before she learns that he has been spying, Castle defends his gratitude, and his wife agrees it is a good thing "if it doesn't take you too far." Moreover, as Scobie had an excessive pity even as a boy, Maurice Castle had an exaggerated gratitude. At one point, he asks his mother whether he was a nervous child, and she tells him he always had an "exaggerated sense of gratitude for the least kindness." Once, she tells him, he gave away an expensive pen to a boy who had given him a chocolate bun. At novel's end, when Castle is isolated in Russia, Sarah asks him in a phone conversation how he is, and he recalls his mother's words about the fountain pen: "My mother wasn't far wrong." Like Scobie as well, Castle is the most appealing character in the book, and many a reader will think his defection justified.

THE POWER AND THE GLORY

The novels considered above are perhaps extreme examples of Greene's "virtue of disloyalty," but the same quality can be found in most of his novels. In his well-known *The Power and the Glory*, for example, Greene sets up a metaphorical conflict between the powers of God and the powers of atheism, yet it is his "disloyalty" that prevents the allegory from turning into a medieval morality play. The forces of good and the forces of evil are not so easily separated. Although his unnamed priest acquires a real holiness through suffering, the author depicts him as a much weaker man than his counterpart, the atheistic lieutenant. The latter is not only a strong man but also a good man who is selflessly devoted to the people. His anti-Catholicism has its origins in his boyhood memory of a Church that did not show a similar concern for its people.

Perhaps Greene's fairness to Mexico's dusty rationalism, which he actually despised, is made clearer through a comparison of the novel with its first film version. In the 1947 motion-picture adaptation of *The Power and the Glory* directed by John Ford, which was retitled *The Fugitive*, the viewer is given a hero, the priest, played by Henry Fonda, opposed by a corrupt lieutenant.

THE QUIET AMERICAN

That writer's judgment so firmly founded on "disloyalty" also helped Greene to overcome his tendency to anti-Americanism in *The Quiet American*. While Greene is critical of the naïve and destructive innocence of the young American, Pyle, he is even more critical of the English narrator, Fowler, who is cynically aloof. In the end, Greene's "disloyalty" permits him to show Vietnam suffering at the hands of any and all representatives of the Western world.

Greene's painstaking attempt to see the other side, and to be as "disloyal" as possible to his own, animated his fictional worlds and gave both him and his readers that "extra dimension of understanding."

Henry J. Donaghy

OTHER MAJOR WORKS

SHORT FICTION: *The Basement Room, and Other Stories*, 1935; *The Bear Fell Free*, 1935; *Twenty-four Stories*, 1939 (with James Laver and Sylvia Townsend Warner); *Nineteen Stories*, 1947 (revised as *Twenty-one Stories*, 1954); *A Visit to Morin*, 1959; *A Sense of Reality*, 1963; *May We Borrow Your Husband?, and Other Comedies of the Sexual Life*, 1967; *Collected Stories*, 1972; *How Father Quixote Became a Monsignor*, 1980; *The Last Word, and Other Stories*, 1990.

PLAYS: *The Heart of the Matter*, pr. 1950 (adaptation of his novel; with Basil Dean); *The Living Room*, pr., pb. 1953; *The Potting Shed*, pr., pb. 1957; *The Complaisant Lover*, pr., pb. 1959; *Carving a Statue*, pr., pb. 1964; *The Return of A. J. Raffles: An Edwardian Comedy in Three Acts Based Somewhat Loosely on E. W. Hornung's Characters in "The Amateur Cracksman,"* pr., pb. 1975; *For Whom the Bell Chimes*, pr. 1980; *Yes and No*, pr. 1980; *The Collected Plays of Graham Greene*, 1985.

POETRY: *Babbling April: Poems*, 1925; *After Two Years*, 1949; *For Christmas*, 1950.

SCREENPLAYS: *Twenty-one Days*, 1937; *The New Britain*, 1940; *Brighton Rock*, 1947 (adaptation of his novel; with Terence Rattigan); *The Fallen Idol*, 1948 (adaptation of his novel; with Lesley Storm and William Templeton); *The Third Man*, 1949 (adaptation of his novel; with Carol Reed); *The Stranger's Hand*, 1954 (with Guy Elmes and Giorgino Bassani); *Loser Takes All*, 1956 (adaptation of his novel); *Saint Joan*, 1957 (adaptation of George Bernard Shaw's play); *Our Man in Havana*, 1959 (adaptation of his novel); *The Comedians*, 1967 (adaptation of his novel).

TELEPLAY: *Alas, Poor Maling*, 1975.

RADIO PLAY: *The Great Jowett*, 1939.

NONFICTION: *Journey Without Maps: A Travel Book*, 1936; *The Lawless Roads: A Mexican Journal*, 1939 (reissued as *Another Mexico*); *British Dramatists*, 1942; *Why Do I Write? An Exchange of Views Between Elizabeth Bowen, Graham Greene, and V. S. Pritchett*, 1948; *The Lost Childhood, and Other Essays*, 1951; *Essais Catholiques*, 1953 (Marcelle Sibon, translator); *In Search of a Character: Two African Journals*, 1961; *The Revenge: An Autobiographical Fragment*, 1963; *Victorian Detective Fiction*, 1966; *Collected Essays*, 1969; *A Sort of Life*, 1971; *The Pleasure Dome: The Collected Film Criticism, 1935-40, of Graham Greene*, 1972 (John Russell-Taylor, editor; also known as *The Pleasure-Dome: Graham Greene on Film—Collected Film Criticism, 1935-1940*); *Lord Rochester's Monkey: Being the Life of John Wilmot, Second Earl of Rochester*, 1974; *Ways of Escape*, 1980; *J'accuse: The Dark Side of Nice*, 1982; *Getting to Know the General: The Story of an Involvement*, 1984.

CHILDREN'S LITERATURE: *The Little Train*, 1946; *The Little Fire Engine*, 1950 (also known as *The Little Red Fire Engine*, 1952); *The Little Horse Bus*, 1952; *The Little Steam Roller: A Story of Mystery and Detection*, 1953.

EDITED TEXTS: *The Old School: Essays by Divers Hands*, 1934; *The Best of Saki*, 1950; *The Spy's Bedside Book: An Anthology*, 1957 (with Hugh Greene); *The Bodley Head Ford*

Madox Ford, 1962, 1963 (4 volumes); *An Impossible Woman: The Memories of Dottoressa Moor of Capri*, 1975.

MISCELLANEOUS: *The Portable Graham Greene*, 1973 (Philip Stout Ford, editor).

BIBLIOGRAPHY

Bergonzi, Bernard. *A Study in Greene: Graham Greene and the Art of the Novel*. New York: Oxford University Press, 2006. Examines all of Greene's novels, analyzing their language, structure, and recurring motifs. Argues that Greene's earliest work was his best, *Brighton Rock* was his masterpiece, and his novels published after the 1950's showed a marked decline in the author's abilities.

Couto, Maria. *Graham Greene: On the Frontier.* New York: St. Martin's Press, 1988. Well-rounded approach to Greene criticism includes a discussion of the final novels and a retrospective of Greene's career. Contains an insightful interview with Greene and a selection of Greene's letters to the international press from 1953 to 1986.

Falk, Quentin. *Travels in Greeneland: The Complete Cinema of Graham Greene*. 3d ed. New York: Trafalgar Square, 2000. Guide to Greene's association with motion pictures, as a screenwriter and as a reviewer, includes discussion of the numerous adaptations of his novels to film.

Hill, William Thomas. *Graham Greene's Wanderers: The Search for Dwelling—Journeying and Wandering in the Novels of Graham Greene*. San Francisco: International Scholars, 1999. Discusses the themes of dwelling and loss in Greene's fiction, examining how Greene deals with the mother, the father, the nation, and the Catholic Church as the "ground" of dwelling.

Hoskins, Robert. *Graham Greene: An Approach to the Novels*. New York: Garland, 1999. Comprehensive look at Greene's oeuvre features individual chapters providing analysis of fourteen novels, including *Brighton Rock*, *The Quiet American*, and *The End of the Affair*. Also examines the protagonists of Greene's novels in the first and second phases of his career.

Malmet, Elliott. *The World Remade: Graham Greene and the Art of Detection*. New York: Peter Lang, 1998. Focuses on Greene's genre fiction, analyzing the narrative strategies, themes, motifs, and philosophical and theosophical meanings in the author's thrillers and detective novels. Includes bibliography and index.

Miyano, Shoko. *Innocence in Graham Greene's Novels*. New York: Peter Lang, 2006. Addresses innocence as a common theme in Greene's fiction, analyzing the different types of innocence that mark Greene's characters, such as Pinkie Brown in *Brighton Rock*, Harry Lime in *The Third Man*, and Father Quixote in *Monsignor Quixote*.

O'Prey, Paul. *A Reader's Guide to Graham Greene*. New York: Thames and Hudson, 1988. Critical overview of Greene's fiction includes an excellent introduction that serves to familiarize the reader with Greene's major themes. Supplemented by a complete primary bibliography and a brief list of critical works.

Roston, Murray. *Graham Greene's Narrative Strategies: A Study of the Major Novels.* New York: Palgrave Macmillan, 2006. Focuses on seven novels to describe the narrative strategies Greene devised to deflect readers' hostility toward his advocacy of Catholicism and to create heroic characters at a time when the traditional hero was no longer a credible protagonist.

Sheldon, Michael. *Graham Greene: The Enemy Within.* New York: Random House, 1994. Unauthorized biographer Sheldon takes a much more critical view of Greene's life, especially of his politics, than does Norman Sherry, Greene's authorized biographer (cited below). A lively, opinionated narrative. Includes notes and bibliography.

Sherry, Norman. *The Life of Graham Greene.* 3 vols. New York: Viking Press, 1989-2004. Comprehensive, authoritative account of Greene's life was written with complete access to his papers and the full cooperation of Greene's family members, friends, and the novelist himself. Includes a generous collection of photographs, bibliography, and index.

KHALED HOSSEINI

Born: Kabul, Afghanistan; March 4, 1965

PRINCIPAL LONG FICTION
The Kite Runner, 2003
A Thousand Splendid Suns, 2007

OTHER LITERARY FORMS

While Khaled Hosseini (hoh-SAY-nee) is best known for his long fiction, he has written articles for national publications including *The Wall Street Journal* and *Newsweek*. His editorial in defense of Sayed Perwiz Kambakhsh, an Afghan journalism student sentenced to death for distributing information that questions Islamic laws, is the most notable of his writings in nonfiction.

ACHIEVEMENTS

Published in more than forty languages, Khaled Hosseini's *The Kite Runner* has received widespread acclaim from critics and the general public. Awards for the book include the *San Francisco Chronicle* Best Book of the Year for 2003, the American Library Association's Notable Book Award in 2004, and the American Place Theatre's Literature to Life Award in 2005. The novel was adapted for the cinema and released in 2007. *A Thousand Splendid Suns* appeared on many best-seller lists, won a Galaxy British Book Awards—the Richard & Judy Award for Best Read of the Year—and a Book Sense Book of the Year Award in 2008 from the American Booksellers Association.

Hosseini has been honored both for his writing and humanitarian work. In 2006, the United Nations Office of the High Commissioner for Refugees named him its humanitarian of the year. In addition, *Time* magazine included Hosseini in its 2008 list of the most influential people. Former American first lady Laura Bush, an advocate for Afghan women, wrote the *Time* entry about Hosseini and his work.

BIOGRAPHY

Khaled Hosseini was born March 4, 1965, in Kabul, Afghanistan, and spent his boyhood there with his siblings and parents: his mother, a high school teacher, and his father, a diplomat. During that time, the family enjoyed prosperity in a peaceful Afghanistan. In 1976, Hosseini and his family moved to Paris, France, where his father received a new post at the Afghan embassy. The family expected to remain in Paris for only four years, the duration of his father's assignment, and then to return to Afghanistan. However, they found that returning to their country would be too dangerous after it was invaded by the Soviet Union in 1979. Thus, the family applied for and was granted political asylum by the United States. In 1980, they moved to San Jose, California. After graduating from Santa

Clara University with a degree in biology, Hosseini studied medicine at the University of California, San Diego. He graduated in 1993 with a specialization in internal medicine. He was a practicing physician until 2004, shortly after *The Kite Runner* was published.

ANALYSIS

The Kite Runner and *A Thousand Splendid Suns* explore the themes of exile, displacement, immigration, and a person's relationship to one's nation, themes commonly associated with postcolonial literature. Many nations, such as India, Jamaica, and Afghanistan, were once colonies of more powerful countries, including Great Britain, the Netherlands, France, and the United States, seeking to expand their wealth and territories. As the once colonized areas gained independence, they created new national identities, most visibly through art and literature. Theorists have categorized as postcolonial the literature and art that explores the relationships between colonized and colonizer.

Afghanistan has struggled for independence from various invading nations throughout its history; in the twentieth and twenty-first centuries alone, England, the former Soviet Union, and United Nations peacekeeping forces, primarily consisting of U.S. soldiers, have occupied the country. As a result, many Afghans have migrated either by force or by choice to different countries. Both *The Kite Runner* and *A Thousand Splendid Suns* describe the lives of characters who have left their homelands—either to another country or a safer part of their own country—as a result of war.

While far from a direct representation of his childhood in Kabul and young adulthood in California, to which Hosseini's family migrated, the characters in *The Kite Runner* were nevertheless inspired by Hosseini's friends and family. Hosseini acknowledges that his own father inspired the magnanimity of the character Baba, and the mother of another character, Amir, is a professor of Farsi and history, much like Hosseini's own mother, who taught the same subjects in high school. Hosseini said that one of his own family's servants in Kabul, Hossein Khan, and the relationship he had with him, inspired the characterization of Hassan and his friendship with Amir.

One of the most salient ways in which Hosseini examines the tension between selfhood and nationality is through intertextuality—drawing on other literary works to illuminate a novel or poem. In *The Kite Runner*, Amir and Hassan enjoy reading the story of Rostam and Sohrab, which comes from Persian poet Firdusi's *Shahnamah* (c. 1010), the poetic epic of Iran, Afghanistan, and other Persian-speaking countries. Much like the mythologized history of the Greco-Roman world found in classic works of poetry by Homer, the *Shahnamah* poetically narrates the creation of the Persian Empire, of which Afghanistan was once a part. Rostam, a proud and successful warrior, and Sohrab, a champion in his own right, are father and son but have never met. Fighting to protect their country from invaders, they destroy each other and save the nation. Hosseini depicts how the relationships between fathers and sons and the secrets they keep from one another have the potential to determine individual and national characters.

A *Thousand Splendid Suns* borrows its title from a poem by Sā'ib, a seventeenth century Persian poet. A translation of the poem's most pertinent lines reads as follows: "One could not count the moons that shimmer on her roofs/ And the thousand splendid suns that hide behind her walls."

In contrast to the main characters in *The Kite Runner*, Mariam and Laila, protagonists in *A Thousand Splendid Suns*, remain in Afghanistan throughout several invasions. Laila and her father cite the lines of this poem when thinking of the Kabul they knew before the wars. The poem conveys a strong love for the city and nation, but it also serves as a haunting lament for how Afghanistan's troubled history has impacted its peoples.

THE KITE RUNNER

In *The Kite Runner*, Hosseini employs the genre called bildungsroman, or the coming-of-age story, to follow the development of Amir, the protagonist and narrator, from his youth in Kabul through his adulthood in the area of San Francisco, California. Foils and father-son relationships unify the sprawling, yet symmetrical narrative.

As a little boy and preteen, Amir lives with his father Baba; his best friend and servant Hassan; and Hassan's father Ali, also a servant. Amir and Hassan play in Kabul's streets, watch American Westerns at the cinema, run kites together, and live, in many ways, as brothers. Similarly, Baba, a child of the upper class, grew up in the same household with Ali acting as his servant, friend, and brother figure. However, the idyllic surroundings in which Amir matures are troubled by these relationships. Amir desperately seeks Baba's attention, whereas Hassan, despite Baba not claiming him as his son, receives the praise and affection that Amir desires. At once, Amir admires Hassan's goodness, loyalty, bravery, and his relationship with Baba, but he is jealous of him. This creates tension between the two boys, as Amir often resorts to cruelty toward Hassan when he feels inadequate.

While Amir and Hassan are described throughout the novel as "milk brothers," boys who suckled from the same woman as infants, their closeness is frowned upon. Amir is a Pashtun, the majority ethnic group in Afghanistan; Hassan is a Hazara and, as a result, relegated to the servant class in Kabul. Despite their intimacy, the two boys are not supposed to be friends according to cultural beliefs. The tension in their friendship parallels national conflicts between the majority and minority ethnic groups in Afghanistan that have engendered division and war in that country.

After Amir wins a citywide kite-flying tournament, Hassan retrieves the kite for him and encounters a gang who has threatened the two boys before. The gang leader, Assef, physically and sexually assaults Hassan while Amir watches. This act of betrayal affects Amir in myriad ways: He gains Baba's affection, albeit temporarily, by having won the tournament, yet his guilt for failing to protect his best friend Hassan destroys his friendship with Hassan and plagues Amir into adulthood.

Baba and Amir are forced to leave Kabul, escaping to Pakistan and then to the United States as a result of the Soviet invasion. Settling in Northern California, they live relatively tranquil lives in spite of diminished economic circumstances and become members of a vibrant Afghan immigrant culture. After a decade, Baba dies, and Amir, a newly published author, creates a life with his wife Soraya. When Amir receives a telephone call from Baba's best friend from Kabul, Rahim Khan, telling him that "there is a way to be good again," Amir finds that he must return to Kabul. Rahim Khan reveals to Amir that Hassan is his biological half-brother, the son of Baba and Ali's servant wife. He then asks Amir to retrieve Hassan's son Sohrab from one of the underfunded and failing orphanages in Kabul.

Amir's journey to rescue Sohrab acts as a physical and moral journey to redeem himself from guilt and from the cowardice that he and his father shared. Ultimately, he stands up to the men who have brutalized Sohrab and brings him to California. Critics have argued that the symmetrical plot and moralistic theme undercut the novel's realism. In addition, some have claimed that the narrative, if viewed as an allegory of Afghanistan's national crisis and its "redemption" by the West, reads as too simplistic and patronizing. However, it is important to remember that Amir's quest does not paint him as a savior of anyone or any nation. Any fairy-tale endings for Amir, Sohrab, or Afghanistan are quickly dismissed when one takes into account the continuing struggles of survivors and refugees.

A THOUSAND SPLENDID SUNS

Hosseini's second novel has been heralded for its realistic portrayal of Afghanistan during its occupation by the Soviets, the mujahideen—Islamic guerrilla fighters—the Taliban, and U.N. peacekeeping forces. In contrast to *The Kite Runner*, *A Thousand Splendid Suns* examines relationships between women as they are influenced by customs and class.

Spanning a period of nearly thirty years, the novel describes the intertwining lives of Mariam and Laila. Mariam, the daughter of Jalil, a wealthy businessman, and his servant Nana, is raised by her mother in a hut outside Herat, one of Afghanistan's most beautiful cities. Nana, having been ousted by Jalil and disowned by her family, cultivates a pristine bitterness that she tries to pass on to Mariam. Life treated Nana cruelly, and she believes it her job to steal Mariam from the shattered hopes that she will encounter because she is a woman and a *harami*, or illegitimate child.

Despite her mother's admonishments, Mariam relishes the weekly visits Jalil makes to her home. During their time together, Jalil gives Mariam gifts, tells her she's beautiful, and listens to her in a way that Nana cannot. The intimacy between father and daughter, however, is tempered by Jalil having legitimate children and wives in Herat; thus, he cannot publicly accept Mariam as his child—the only gift that Mariam really wants from her father. When she is fifteen years old, Mariam decides to visit Jalil in the city, much to Nana's dismay, and finds that Jalil will not accept her into his home. Still angry from the shame of being forced to sleep on the street in front of her father's house, Mariam returns to her home outside Herat, only to find that Nana has committed suicide. This puts Mariam in extremely precarious circumstances: She is an illegitimate female orphan without a male protector in a culture that values the honor and chastity of women. To rectify the situation, Jalil arranges her marriage to Rasheed, a shoemaker in Kabul who is nearly twice her age.

The early days of their marriage are filled with excitement for Mariam. On the surface, it appears that her life has improved, now that she lives in a house instead of a shack and receives frequent kindnesses from her husband. Rasheed, however, forces her to wear a burka, a garment designed to cover women from head to foot. He also forbids her to leave the house without him. After Mariam miscarries several times, Rasheed begins to beat her consistently. Without a male heir to carry on the family name, he finds Mariam useless. Verses from the Qur'ūn taught by her friend and village mullah, or teacher of Islam, keep Mariam from sinking into despair.

Nearly two decades Mariam's junior, Laila was raised as the daughter of liberal parents in a middle-class household. Her childhood lies in stark contrast to that of Mariam, as she lived in relative freedom and luxury and aspired as a youth to attend the university. However, war infiltrates Kabul and she is left the only survivor of her family. As an act of "mercy," the now-middle-age Rasheed agrees to take adolescent Laila as his second wife. While the relationship between Laila and Mariam is strained at first, the two begin to love one another. The birth of Aziza and the mother-daughter-grandmother relationships that the women share brings purpose and meaning to their otherwise painful existence.

As conditions in Kabul worsen with the Taliban's occupation and as the family increases in size, they suffer from a privation so desperate that Rasheed forces Aziza to live in one of the city's many orphanages while his and Laila's son, Zalmai, continues to live at home. Rasheed continues to abuse Mariam; and, the Taliban, on the lookout for women unaccompanied by male protectors, beats Laila as she makes her way to the orphanage to visit her daughter. When Tariq, Laila's first love and Aziza's birth father, returns to Kabul, the women hope to escape, but it becomes clear that Rasheed will never let them do so. In an act of self-sacrifice, Mariam kills Rasheed and accepts the Taliban's sentence—death by execution—so that Laila, Tariq, Aziza, and Zalmai can live in a loving home. After peacekeeping forces control the Taliban in Kabul, Laila returns to the city and becomes a teacher in an orphanage to honor Mariam's memory and contribute to her country's recovery.

The beauty and sorrow of *A Thousand Splendid Suns* can be seen in the relationship between Mariam and Laila—two women born into vastly different circumstances who find themselves with the same abusive husband. Hosseini presents traditional customs regarding women in a relatively balanced fashion, offering in the novel that some woman accept veiling and the protection it provides. However, the contrast between Mariam's and Laila's expected fates highlights several undeniable issues, most saliently that women and children survivors are the true victims of war and that education and employment are fundamental to individual survival and national redevelopment.

DaRelle M. Rollins

BIBLIOGRAPHY

Ahmed-Gosh, Huma. "A History of Women in Afghanistan: Lessons Learnt for the Future." *Journal of International Women's Studies* 4, no. 3 (2003): 1-14. Study of the history of women in Afghanistan in the late twentieth century that also suggests ways for a freer future.

Bloom, Harold, ed. *Khalid Hosseini's "The Kite Runner."* New York: Bloom's Literary Criticism, 2009. Comprehensive study guide on *The Kite Runner* with essays written especially for students in grades 9 through 12. Part of the Bloom's Guides series of analyses of classic works of literature.

Katsoulis, Melissa. "Kites of Passage: New Fiction." *The Times* (London), August 30, 2003. Brief review of Hosseini's novel *The Kite Runner* in a renowned British periodical.

Lemar-Aftaab. June, 2004. Special issue of this Web-based magazine devoted to Khaled Hosseini and his works. Two articles explore themes in *The Kite Runner*. Also features an interview with Hosseini. Available at http://afghanmagazine.com/2004_06/.

ISMAIL KADARE

Born: Gjirokastër, Albania; January 28, 1936
Also known as: Ismail Dukudu Kadare

PRINCIPAL LONG FICTION

Gjenerali i ushtrisë së vdekur, 1963 (*The General of the Dead Army*, 1971)
Dasma, 1968 (*The Wedding*, 1968)
Kështjella, 1970 (*The Castle*, 1974)
Kronikë në gurë, 1971 (*Chronicle in Stone*, 1987, revised 2007)
Dimri i Madh, 1977
Ura me tri harqe, 1978 (*The Three-Arched Bridge*, 1995)
Gjakftohtësia, 1980
Prilli i Thyer, 1980 (*Broken April*, 1990)
Dosja H, 1981 (*The File on H.*, 1998)
Nëpunësi i pallatit të ëndrrave, 1981 (*The Palace of Dreams*, 1993)
Vepra Letrare, 1981
Kush e solli Doruntinën, 1980 (*Doruntine*, 1988)
Koncert në Fund të Dimrit, 1988 (*The Concert: A Novel*, 1994)
Piramida, 1992 (*The Pyramid*, 1996)
Albanie, 1995
Pallati i ëndërrave, 1996
Tri këngë zie për Kosovën, 1998 (*Elegy for Kosovo*, 2000)
Froides fleurs D'Avril, 2000
Lulet e ftohta të marsit, 2000 (*Spring Flowers, Spring Frost*, 2002)
Jeta, loja dhe vdekja e Lul Mazrekut, 2002
Pasardhësi, 2003 (*The Successor*, 2005)
Vajza e Agamemnonit, 2003 (*Agamemnon's Daughter: A Novella and Stories*, 2006)

OTHER LITERARY FORMS

Ismail Kadare (kah-DAWR) is known primarily for his novels, but he began his writing career as a lyric poet. His stories deal with universal themes and draw on myth and world literature. His nonfiction book *Nga nje dhjetor ne tjetrin: Kronikë, kembim letrash, persiatje* (1991; *Albanian Spring: The Anatomy of Tyranny*, 1994), written after he left Albania and sought political asylum in France, contains his views on Albanian politics and government between 1944 and 1990, when Albania was ruled by a repressive communist regime.

Achievements

In 2005, Ismail Kadare won the inaugural Booker International Prize for literature in English. He was made an honorary member of the Institut de France (1988), was awarded the Prix mondial Cino del Duca (1992), was elected an associate member of l'Academie des Sciences Morales et Politiques (1996), was proclaimed an officer of the Legion of Honor (1996), and was awarded the Herder-Preis in Hamburg, Germany (1998). Winning the Booker International Prize boosted his international reputation considerably. *The New Yorker* published a short story by Kadare on December 26, 2005, and in 2008 he was contracted to write eight columns per year for the New York Times Syndicate. This international attention is in keeping with Kadare's own observation that he is a writer of true literature. He is a keen observer of human nature and his works have universal appeal.

Biography

Ismail Kadare grew up in Gjirokastër, an ancient Albanian city with steep streets. It serves as the setting for his delightful early novel *Chronicle in Stone*, which is about his childhood experiences during World War II. His father, Halit, and his mother, Hatixhe, were nonpracticing Muslims. Kadare studied Albanian language and literature at the state university in Tirana and then attended the Maxim Gorky Literature Institute in Moscow from 1958 to 1961. His sister, Kadrie, studied Russian language and literature, and his brother, Shahin, became an oncologist.

Albania was headed by a strict Stalinist regime, led from 1943 to 1985 by Enver Hoxha, then by his successor, Ramiz Alia, until the collapse of Communist rule in Albania in 1992. Hoxha appreciated Kadare's writing and the positive publicity for the state that followed from Kadare's trips abroad. Kadare's fame outside Albania began when his first novel, *The General of the Dead Army*, appeared in French translation in 1970. Still, Kadare suffered censure and repression at home. In 1975, he was banished from the capital and forbidden to publish for three years. Also in 1981, his novel *The Palace of Dreams* was banned as soon as it appeared. Kadare made the necessary concessions to the state and even served as a member of Parliament, where there was no debate. He continued to write as if he were free, and he smuggled his manuscripts out of the country for later publication. After receiving threats from the Sigurimi, the Albanian secret police, Kadare and his family sought political asylum in France in October of 1990. His subsequent writings were more directly critical of oppressive regimes, including Albania under Hoxha (*The Successor*), China under Mao Zedong (*The Concert*), and ancient Egypt under Cheops (*The Pyramid*).

Kadare and his wife, author Elena Kadare, were married in 1963. In 1970, Elena published the first novel in the Albanian language written by a woman. The couple had two daughters; one earned a doctorate in genetics from the Sorbonne and the other earned a degree in journalism.

Analysis

Most of Ismail Kadare's novels are set in Albania, and the same landmarks appear in many of his books: the three-arched bridge, containing its human sacrifice, and the Inn of the Two Roberts, where travelers both innocent and suspect stop for the night. He frequently refers to the famous and still-debated Battle of Kosovo of 1389 (*Elegy for Kosovo*) and to the official method of Byzantine torture: blinding.

However, Kadare is concerned mainly with human rights, with the lot of the common people throughout history. In fact, he has a standard for assessing the actions of governments—including such things as architectural megaprojects: How will a given action, a government project, affect everyday people? How much will the people, including workers, suffer? These questions frame his novel *The Pyramid*, in which he deals at length with the inhuman treatment of the workers and the general populace during the construction of the largest pyramid in Egypt four thousand years ago; Kadare's analysis is so profound that the edifice itself, the pyramid, pales in comparison. In the final paragraphs of the novel, the pyramid becomes transparent, except for the blemish of a bloodstain that can never be washed clean. For Kadare, brutality devalues products of labor.

Kadare realizes that human nature will never change, and that the behavior portrayed in the Greek myths and in William Shakespeare's dramas continues unabated. There will always be people with a lust for power, and the retention of power will always involve intrigues and misinformation. However, power does not protect those who have it from illness, self-doubts, or senility. Kadare sees everyone's weaknesses, and he writes with compassion for the human condition. He also sees everyone's strengths, and his works contain memorable examples of what the human spirit can achieve against all odds. His beautiful legendary story *Doruntine* portrays the power of love to last beyond the grave.

Kadare considers himself a modern Homer, a storyteller par excellence, and he pays homage in his works to the great tradition of Albanian oral epics. His novel *The File on H.* is an amusing account of the attempts of two Irish American researchers to better understand Homer's working method by studying the few remaining itinerant Albanian rhapsodists who convert contemporary events into epic poetry. The researchers do so at a cost. One of them finds that as he imitates the singing tone of the rhapsodists, he also progressively loses his vision, just like the blind, semilegendary Greek poet.

THE PALACE OF DREAMS

The Palace of Dreams was banned in Albania because it was seen as a thinly veiled portrayal of Hoxha's communist reign of terror. This is a simplistically reductive interpretation of the novel. Although set in an Albanian context, the novel addresses universal aspects of the human condition.

The novel begins slowly and gathers speed. The salient features of the main character, Mark-Alem, are his passivity and uncertainty. He lets his influential family decide where he should work, and they even choose his fiancé. Both at work and at home, he assumes that everything is in someone else's competent hands. When people hint to him that things are not as they should be, he dismisses them as saboteurs. As the novel progresses, Mark-Alem simply watches as his favorite uncle, Kurt, is led away by police, then hears that Kurt has been beheaded. Although Mark-Alem rises rapidly through the ranks and is appointed head of the Palace of Dreams, he does nothing to stop the senseless interrogation of a greengrocer, although he pities the man, and the grocer is eventually carried out in a coffin. While this complacency might seem on the surface to be serious sins of omission, Kadare does not portray them that way. In a novel replete with descriptions of coldness, snow, and ice, Mark-Alem seems permanently frozen with fear. He understands so little about the affairs of his family or the state that he is afraid to act in case he does something wrong that will cause him to plummet from his position of grace. As he comes to incorporate the state by virtue of inexplicably rapid promotions, his lack of compassion and understanding take on symbolic significance.

The Palace of Dreams is about loss: the loss of Mark-Alem's potential for happiness in this world, and the loss of the oral tradition that shaped national identities in the Balkans for centuries. Mark-Alem's family is the subject of a great Bosnian epic, of which there is also an Albanian version. His Uncle Kurt's "crime" was that he arranged for the family to hear a performance of the Albanian version of the epic. Kadare's lyrical description of the rhapsodist's haunting singing, enhanced by the one-stringed *lahuta*, leaves no doubt that the epic represents the soul of the nation. It is all the more tragic, therefore, that the Sovereign, apparently motivated by envy, sent the police to end the performance; instruments were smashed, three rhapsodists were killed on the spot, and Uncle Kurt was led away to his death.

BROKEN APRIL

Broken April is a story of the great loss of life among feuding families in the northern highlands of Albania, families whose lives are governed by the *Kanun*, an ancient code still in force, despite the efforts of Hoxha's Communist regime to put a stop to it. Central to the *Kanun* are the strictly regulated ongoing blood feuds that often wipe out all the men in an extended family. The feuds get started for reasons that, to an outsider, seem unbelievable, and they proceed without personal animosity. The feuds are sorts of business transactions, done in blood for reasons of male honor.

In *Broken April*, Kadare shows the disastrous effect of the *Kanun* on an attractive young Albanian man. Gjorg Berisha does not want to kill anyone and suffers extreme distress and death because of social pressure to follow the rules laid down by *Kanun*. His situation is all the more tragic because he is just beginning to learn about the outer world. He is overtaken by the machinery of the blood feud before he can work out a way of escape from the cycle of violence.

The *Kanun* does not call upon women to kill and be killed. The novel shows that women both inside and outside the family are opposed to the blood feuds. One of Gjorg's married aunts travels many miles to try to persuade his family to seek a settlement rather than sacrificing Gjorg, who is the last of the line, but her efforts are thwarted by an aged uncle. Gjorg is killed, and quite unexpectedly the *Kanun* claims another victim, a beautiful young married woman from the city whose husband takes her to the highlands for their honeymoon. Diana Vorpsi's one brief encounter with Gjorg leads to an obsession to see him again before his time runs out, an obsession that is mutual, because he spends his last days trying to catch another glimpse of her. They do not meet again. He is hunted down and shot on the road, and she is so appalled at his fate that her entire personality changes, as if she had left her soul with him in the highlands. Kadare's moving love story forms the basis for Brazilian filmmaker Walter Salles's award-winning 2001 film *Abril Despedaçado* (*Behind the Sun*).

The final paragraphs of the novel contain Gjorg's dying sensations. He feels his murderer turn him over, then hears his footsteps receding. Then it seems to him that the footsteps are his own, leaving behind his own body, which he, by complying with the *Kanun*, has struck down. It is an eloquent plea for the laying down of arms.

SPRING FLOWERS, SPRING FROST

Twenty years after writing about the *Kanun* in *Broken April*, Kadare dealt with the reactionary resurgence of the *Kanun* in his novel *Spring Flowers, Spring Frost*. After the fall of Communism in Albania in 1992, the new materialism was rejected by some who sought a more austere lifestyle. In the novel, a young idealist is persuaded by his uncle to take up an old blood feud and kill the thoroughly modern, cosmopolitan director of the Arts Center with a single shot. The official announcement is made in archaic language: "Angelin of the Ukaj hath slain Marian of the Shkreli." The reversion to the old customs is the frost that alternates with the warm days of March. In fact, Kadare sees the whole of human history as an ongoing confrontation between the frost and the flowers, between forces of death and forces of life, between tyranny and compassion.

This thematically complex novel places contemporary events in Albania in historical and mythological context. Kadare suggests fascinating reinterpretations of old legends, seeing them from the perspective of someone who spent most of his life under Communist rule, where denunciations and interrogations were routine. It occurs to the main character, Mark Gurabardhi, for example, that Oedipus did not kill his father, nor was he ever his mother's lover, but that those alleged offenses were just standard denunciations, declared to have been committed when Oedipus became a tyrant. To read *Spring Flowers, Spring Frost* is to become aware that hardly anything is as it seems. Kadare follows most chapters with counter-chapters.

In addition to showing that most humans having a dual nature, as illustrated by the legend of the snake-groom who turns into a handsome young man (and by the counter-legend of the man-groom who turns into a snake), Kadare also shows that people often find themselves on a collision course with inhuman forces. He continues the frost imagery by alluding to the sinking of the *Titanic* by an iceberg that, in turn, was presumably destroyed by the ship. The rich texture of this novel by the mature Kadare rewards detailed analysis.

Jean M. Snook

OTHER MAJOR WORKS

POETRY: *Frymëzimet djaloshare*, 1954; *Ëndërrimet*, 1957; *Shekulli im*, 1961; *Përse mendohen këto male*, 1964; *Vjersha dhe poema zë zgjedhura*, 1966; *Koha, vjersha dhe poema*, 1976; *Poezi*, 1979; *Poèmes, 1957-1997*, 1997.

NONFICTION: *Nga nje dhjetor ne tjetrin: Kronikë, kembim letrash, persiatje*, 1991 (*Albanian Spring: The Anatomy of Tyranny*, 1994).

BIBLIOGRAPHY

Bellos, David. "The Englishing of Ismail Kadare: Notes of a Retranslator." *Complete Review Quarterly* 6, no. 2 (2005). An interesting overview of the complicated translation history of Kadare's works.

Guppy, Shusha. "Ismail Kadare." *Paris Review* 40, no. 147 (Summer, 1998): 194-217. An informative interview in which Kadare speaks about the Albanian language, true literature, the novel, writing under a dictatorship, and his opposition to totalitarianism.

Hurezanu, Daniela. "Ismail Kadare: Storytelling and the Power of Myth." *Chattahoochee Review* 27, no. 2 (Winter, 2007): 148-160. Review article that discusses *Chronicle in Stone*, *The Three-Arched Bridge*, *Palace of Dreams*, *The Successor*, *Agamemnon's Daughter*, and *Spring Flowers, Spring Frost*.

Morgan, Peter. "Between Albanian Identity and Imperial Politics: Ismail Kadare's *The Palace of Dreams*." *Modern Language Review* 97, no. 2 (April, 2002): 365-379. Provides background information about the oral epics, and places the writing of the novel in the context of concurrent political events in the Balkans.

_____. "Ismail Kadare: Modern Homer or Albanian Dissident?" *World Literature Today* 80, no. 5 (September/October, 2006): 7-11. Examines Kadare's life as a writer living under an oppressive dictatorship. Considers Kadare "the voice of Albania's modernity *and* the singer of its ancient identity."

Talmor, Sascha. "*The Kanun*: The Code of Honour of Albania's High Plateau." *Durham University Journal*, January, 1993. A good summary and analysis of Kadare's *Broken April*. Includes background information for his later novel, *Spring Flowers, Spring Frost*.

White, Jeffrey. "Breaking the Cycle: Albania Seeks Solutions to Its Blood Feud Problem." *Spiegel*, July 8, 2008. Of relevance to *Broken April* and *Spring Flowers, Spring Frost*. Describes the rules of the ongoing feuds and how the survivors are afraid to leave their homes.

ARTHUR KOESTLER

Born: Budapest, Hungary; September 5, 1905
Died: London, England; March 3, 1983
Also known as: Artúr Kösztler

PRINCIPAL LONG FICTION
The Gladiators, 1939
Darkness at Noon, 1940
Arrival and Departure, 1943
Thieves in the Night: Chronicle of an Experiment, 1946
The Age of Longing, 1951
The Call Girls: A Tragi-Comedy with Prologue and Epilogue, 1972

OTHER LITERARY FORMS

Among his nonfiction works, Arthur Koestler (KEHST-luhr) published four autobiographical volumes—*Spanish Testament* (1937), later abridged as *Dialogue with Death* (1942); *Scum of the Earth* (1941); *Arrow in the Blue: The First Volume of an Autobiography, 1905-1931* (1952); and *The Invisible Writing: The Second Volume of an Autobiography, 1932-1940* (1954)—as well as an autobiographical essay on his disillusionment with Communism found in *The God That Failed* (1950), edited by Richard Crossman and with additional essays by Richard Wright, Ignazio Silone, Stephen Spender, Louis Fischer, and André Gide. Koestler's nonfiction works exceed twenty-five volumes, divided roughly between social-historical commentary and the history of science. He also wrote one play, *Twilight Bar: An Escapade in Four Acts* (pb. 1945). Koestler's first five novels, along with most of his other books, have been reissued in the Danube edition, published in England by Hutchinson and in the United States by Macmillan.

ACHIEVEMENTS

Arthur Koestler will be remembered as an apostate to the Left who dramatized in *Darkness at Noon* and in his autobiographical works the integrity of many Communist intellectuals in the 1930's and the anguish they suffered under Soviet leader Joseph Stalin. As a novelist, he is generally a skilled storyteller, putting conventional techniques to the service of philosophical themes. Although none of his novels were best sellers in the usual sense, *Darkness at Noon*—translated into thirty-three languages—has been reprinted many times, and its appeal shows no sign of slackening. It continues to be read widely in college and university courses and is probably one of the most influential political novels of the twentieth century, despite the fact that comparatively little academic literary criticism has been devoted to it. Indeed, Koestler's novels—even *Darkness at Noon*—are perhaps kept alive more by political scientists and historians than by professional students of literature.

Arthur Koestler
(National Archives)

Aside from being an accomplished novelist of ideas, Koestler was one of the finest journalists of his age, often producing works as controversial as his political fiction. Typical of his best essays is the piece in *The Lotus and the Robot* (1960) on "Yoga Unexpurgated" (noted as being "far too horrible for me to read" by William Empson in his review); like many other of his best essays, "Yoga Unexpurgated" will maintain its readability. *The Sleepwalkers: A History of Man's Changing Vision of the Universe* (1959), a survey of early scientific thought with emphasis on Renaissance astronomy, is part of a trilogy (with *The Act of Creation*, 1964, and *The Ghost in the Machine*, 1967) on the understanding of the human mind, and it ranks as Koestler's most suggestive effort at research and speculation. Even more controversial than his psychological studies, although a wholly different kind of work, is *The Thirteenth Tribe* (1976), which revived the thesis that the Jews of Eastern Europe are descended from the ancient Khazar Empire. Scholarly reviews of Koestler's research tended to be severe. *The Case of the Midwife Toad* (1971) reveals sympathies for neo-Lamarckian philosophy, and *The Roots of Coincidence* (1972) surveys the claims of parapsychology, ending with a plea "to get out of the straitjacket which nineteenth-century materialism imposed on any philosophical outlook."

Although he flirted with crank notions, to the detriment of his credibility, Koestler was neither a crank nor a dilettante. His renegade vision has enlivened contemporary arts and letters for several decades, and it is likely that this force will continue to be felt for several more.

Biography

Arthur Koestler was born Artúr Kösztler on September 5, 1905, in Budapest, Hungary, the only child of middle-class Jewish parents. He was precocious in math and science and closer to his mother than to his father, an eccentric, self-taught businessman. When Koestler was in his teens, the family moved to Vienna, Austria, and he attended the university there as a science student. After four years, he left school without a degree and went to Palestine, where he joined a Zionist movement for a while before obtaining a correspondent's job with the Ullstein newspapers of Germany. He advanced rapidly in journalism, becoming, in 1930, the foreign editor of *B.Z. am Mittag* and the science editor of *Vossische Zeitung* in Berlin, partly as a result of his success as a reporter on the *Graf Zeppelin* flight to the North Pole in 1931.

In December, 1931, Koestler became a member of the German Communist Party, and less than one year later he gave up his position with Ullstein and spent several weeks traveling in the Soviet Union. He then spent three years in Paris working for the Comintern, leaving for Spain at the outbreak of the Spanish Civil War in 1936. His marriage to Dorothy Asher in 1935 lasted only two years before they were separated, eventually to be divorced in 1950. While in Spain for the Comintern in 1937, Koestler was captured by the Nationalists and sentenced to execution. Thanks to the British press, he was freed after three months, and he published an account of his experiences, *Spanish Testament* (1937). By the next year, he was in France again, where he resigned from the Communist Party in disillusionment with Stalinism and the show trials. During that time, he wrote *Darkness at Noon*. After escaping from Nazi internment in France, he fled to Britain and spent 1941 to 1942 in the British Pioneer Corps.

After *Darkness at Noon* was published, Koestler was in Paris at the center of the uproar it caused among members of the French Left. (Simone de Beauvoir's roman à clef, *The Mandarins*, in 1954, makes vivid this period in French intellectual life.) In the late 1940's, Koestler became a leader among anti-Communist voices in the West, twice visiting the United States to lecture, as well as enjoying an appointment between 1950 and 1951 as a Chubb Fellow at Yale University. After his divorce in 1950, he married Mamaine Paget. In 1952, he took up residence in America for two years, during which time he published his autobiographical volumes *Arrow in the Blue* and *The Invisible Writing*. He was divorced in 1953.

One phase in Koestler's career ended in 1955, when he indicated in *Trial of the Dino-*

saur, and Other Essays that he was finished writing about politics. At that time, his interest turned to mysticism and science, and he tried in his writings on extrasensory perception (ESP) to narrow the gap between natural and extrasensory phenomena. He married Cynthia Jefferies in 1965. After World War II, Koestler had become a naturalized citizen of England, and his adopted country honored him by making him a Commander of the Order of the British Empire (C.B.E.) in 1972 and a companion of literature (C.Lit.) in 1974. Koestler and his wife died in London, England, on March 3, 1983, both victims of apparent suicide.

ANALYSIS

All of Arthur Koestler's works, both fiction and nonfiction, reveal a struggle to escape from the oppressiveness of nineteenth century positivism and its later offshoots. *The Yogi and the Commissar, and Other Essays* (1945) sums up the moral paradox of political action. The Yogi, at one extreme, represents a life lived by values that are grounded in idealism. The Yogi scorns utilitarian goals and yields to quietism; his refusal to intervene leads to passive toleration of social evil. The Commissar, committed to dialectical materialism, ignores the shallow ethical concerns of the historically benighted middle class and seeks to function as an instrument of historical progress. History replaces God, and human suffering is seen as an inevitable step toward the ultimate historical synthesis rather than as an element of God's mysterious purpose. For the Commissar, the end justifies the means, and it is this ethical position that is debated most effectively in *The Gladiators*, *Darkness at Noon*, and *Arrival and Departure*.

In his postscript to the Danube edition of *The Gladiators*, Koestler points out that these novels form a trilogy "whose leitmotif is the central question of revolutionary ethics and of political ethics in general: the question whether, or to what extent, the end justifies the means." The question "obsessed" him, he says, during the seven years in which he belonged to the Communist Party and for several years afterward. It was his answer to this question that caused him to break with the party, as he explains eloquently in his essay in *The God That Failed*. The city built by the rebellious slaves in *The Gladiators* fails because Spartacus does not carry out the stern measures necessary to ensure the city's successful continuation. In *Darkness at Noon*, the old revolutionary Rubashov is depicted as trying to avoid the error Spartacus made, but ending up lost in a maze of moral and ethical complications that destroy him.

Behaviorist psychology is congenial to the materialism of Communist revolutionary ethics, and Koestler attacks its claims heatedly. Indeed, Koestler's interest in mysticism, the occult, and parapsychology was an attempt to find an escape route from the deadly rationalism that makes humans a mere clockwork orange. As far back as 1931, Koestler was investigating psychometry with as much curiosity as he brought to his journalistic accounts of the exploding universe. His answer to the behaviorists is laid out in *The Ghost in the Machine*, and it is clearly a theological answer. Koestler implies here that evolution is purposive, hence the theological nature of his understanding of life. A problem remains, however; Koestler argues that the limbic system of the brain is at odds with its neocortex, resulting in irrational decisions much of the time. Humans are thus as likely to speed to their own destruction as they are to their fulfillment. Koestler's unorthodox answer to humans' Manichaean internal struggle is deliberate mutation by chemical agents. The same topic is fictionalized quite successfully in *The Call Girls*.

THE GLADIATORS

Koestler's first novel, *The Gladiators*, was written in German and translated into English by Edith Simon (Koestler's later novels were published in his own English). The source of the novel is the sketchy account—fewer than four thousand words all together—of the Slave War of 73-71 B.C.E. found in Livy, Plutarch, Appian, and Florus. Koestler divides his narrative into four books. The first, titled "Rise," imagines the revolt led by the Thracian gladiator Spartacus and a fat, cruel Gaul named Crixus. They march through Campania looting and adding more defectors to their band. In book 2, "The Law of Detours," after the destruction of the towns Nola, Suessula, and Calatia, the rebels are twenty thousand strong, or more, and approaching the peak of their power. The unruly faction, however, has spoiled the movement's idealism by its ransacking of these towns, and Spartacus is faced with a decision: Should he let this group go blindly into a foolhardy battle with the forces of the Roman general Varinius, or should he counsel them and enforce a policy of prudence? In his deliberations he is aided by a wise Essene, a type of the imminent Christ, who tells him that of all God's curses on man, "the worst curse of all is that he must tread the evil road for the sake of the good and right, that he must make detours and walk crookedly so that he may reach the straight goal." He further tells Spartacus that for what the leader wants to do now, he needs other counselors.

Despite the Essene's warning, Spartacus follows the "law of detours." Later that night, he confers with Crixus, and although no details of their talk are given, it is clear that Crixus is going to lead the lawless to their unwitting deaths in a confrontation with Varinius. This sacrifice of the unruly faction, however justified, is a cynical detour from honor. Later, however, when the Thracian Spartacus, already pressed by food shortages in the Sun State after a double cross by the neighboring city, is faced with a rebellion against his policies by the Celts, he proves to be insufficiently ruthless: He still retains the idealism with which he began the revolution. Koestler sums it up in his 1965 postscript: "Yet he shrinks from taking the last step—the purge by crucifixion of the dissident Celts and the establishment of a ruthless tyranny; and through this refusal he dooms his revolution to defeat." Book 3, "The Sun State," recounts the conflicts that lead up to Spartacus's defeat, and the gladiators' humiliation and crucifixion are narrated in book 4, "Decline." Although Koestler's characters are wooden, *The Gladiators* is a satisfying historical novel; the milieu is well sketched, and Spartacus's dilemmas are rendered convincingly.

DARKNESS AT NOON

Darkness at Noon, Koestler's masterpiece, is the story of an old Bolshevik, Rubashov, who is called before his Communist inquisitors on charges of heresy against the party. He is interrogated first by Ivanov, who is himself executed, and then by Gletkin, and at the end he is killed by the inevitable bullet in the back of the neck. The novel is divided into three sections, one for each hearing Rubashov is given, and a short epilogue titled "The Grammatical Fiction." In addition to the confrontations between Rubashov and his questioners, there are flashbacks from Rubashov's past and extracts from his diary; the latter provide occasions for Koestler's meditations on history. The narrative is tight and fast moving, and its lucid exposition has surely made it one of the most satisfyingly pedagogic novels of all time. Many readers shared the experience of Leslie Fiedler, who referred to *Darkness at Noon* in his review of *The Ghost in the Machine*, admitting that "Koestler helped to deliver me from the platitudes of the Thirties, from those organized self-deceptions which, being my first, were especially dear and difficult to escape."

Speaking of the "historical circumstances" of *Darkness at Noon*, Koestler explains that Rubashov is "a synthesis of the lives of a number of men who were victims of the so-called Moscow Trials." Rubashov's thinking is closest to that of Nikolai Bukharin, a real purge victim, and Rubashov's tormentor, Gletkin, had a counterpart of sorts in the actual trial prosecutor Andrei Vishinsky. (Robert Conquest's *The Great Terror*, 1968, provides useful details of the real trials.)

Two main theses are argued in *Darkness at Noon*: that the end does not justify the means, and that the individual ego, the *I*, is not a mere "grammatical fiction" whose outline is blurred by the sweep of the historical dialectic. The events that cause Rubashov great pain and guilt involve two party workers whose devotion is sacrificed to the law of detours. Little Loewy is the local leader of the dockworkers' section of the party in Belgium, a likable man whom Rubashov takes to immediately. Little Loewy is a good Communist, but he is ill used by the party and eventually destroyed in an act of expediency. When the party calls for the workers to resist the spreading Nazi menace, Little Loewy's dockworkers refuse to handle cargoes going out from and coming into Germany.

The crisis comes when five cargo ships from Russia arrive in the port. The workers start to unload these boats until they discover the contents: badly needed materials for the German war effort. The workers strike, the party orders them back to the docks, and most of the workers defect. Two years later, Mussolini ventures into Africa, and again a boycott is called, but this time Rubashov is sent in advance to explain to the dockworkers that more Russian cargo is on its way and the party wants it unloaded. Little Loewy rejects the duplicity, and six days later he hangs himself.

In another tragedy of betrayal, Rubashov abandons his secretary, Arlova, a woman who loves him and with whom he has had an affair. When Arlova's brother in Russia marries a foreigner, they all come under suspicion, Arlova included. Soon after, she is called back to oblivion in Russia, and all of this happens without a word from Rubashov. As these perfidies run through his mind, Rubashov's toothache rages intensely. Ivanov senses Rubashov's human sympathies and lectures him on the revolutionary ethic:

> But you must allow that we are as convinced that you and they would mean the end of the Revolution as you are of the reverse. That is the essential point. The methods follow by logical deduction. We can't afford to lose ourselves in political subtleties.

Thus, Rubashov's allegiance to the law of detours leads him into a moral labyrinth. He fails to heed that small voice that gives dignity to the self in its resistance to the degrading impersonality of all-devouring history and the behaviorist conception of human beings.

ARRIVAL AND DEPARTURE

In *Arrival and Departure*, Koestler's third novel, Peter Slavek, age twenty-two, stows away on a freighter coming from Eastern Europe and washes up in Neutralia (Portugal) in 1940. He is a former Communist who has been tortured by fascists in his home country, and he is faced in Neutralia with four possibilities: reunion with the party, with whom he is disillusioned; joining the fascists, who present themselves as the shapers of the true brave new world; flight to America; or, finally, enlistment with the British, whose culture is maimed but still represents a "brake" on the madness overtaking Europe.

Homeless and confused, Peter meets two women. Dr. Sonia Bolgar, a native of his country and friend of his family, gives him a room and looks after him while she is waiting for the visa that will take her to America. Her lover, Odette, is a young French war widow with whom Peter has a brief affair until Odette leaves for America. Her departure precipitates a psychosomatic paralysis of one of Peter's legs, symbolic of the paralysis of will brought on by his conflicting urges to follow her and to commit himself again to political action. Sonia, who is an analyst and reduces all behavior to the terms of her profession, leads Peter through a deconstruction of his motives that exposes their origins in childhood guilt feelings. His self-insight cures his paralysis, just as his visa for America is granted. He prepares to leave, but at the last moment he dashes off the ship and joins the British, who parachute him back into his own country in their service.

Much of *Arrival and Departure* is artistically inert, but it does have a solid point to make. Although Fyodor Dostoevski's name is never mentioned in *Arrival and Departure*, the novel is Koestler's response to Dostoevski's *The Possessed* (1871-1872), which depicts revolutionaries as warped personalities, dramatizing their neuroses and grudges in political action. For Koestler, human motives are more complex:

> "You can explain the messages of the Prophets as epileptical foam and the Sistine Madonna as the projection of an incestuous dream. The method is correct and the picture in itself complete. But beware of the arrogant error of believing that it is the only one."

Arrival and Departure is, then, a subtle commentary on the motivation of revolutionaries, rejecting any claims to exclusivity by psychoanalysis and psychobiography.

Thieves in the Night

A far more absorbing novel than *Arrival and Departure* is *Thieves in the Night*, an account of the establishment of the commune of Ezra's Tower in Palestine. Many of the events are seen from the perspective of one of the commune's settlers, a young man named Joseph who was born and educated in England. His father was Jewish, his mother English, and this mixed heritage justifies Koestler's use of him as a voice to meditate on the Jewish character and the desirability of assimilation. As a novelistic study of a single character, *Thieves in the Night* is incomplete, but as a depiction of the personal tensions within a commune and as an essay on the international politics wracking Palestine in the period from 1937 to 1939, it is excellent.

The British policy formulated in the 1939 White Paper is exposed in all its cruelty. This policy—perhaps influenced by romantic conceptions of the Arab world—shut down the flow of immigrants into Palestine, leaving the Jews exposed and helpless in Europe. At the novel's end, Joseph has joined the terrorist movement and is engaged in smuggling Polish Jews off the Romanian cattle boats that are forbidden to unload their homeless cargo. In its musings on terrorism, *Thieves in the Night* seems to back off from the repudiation of the doctrine that the end justifies the means. Koestler always faced these issues honestly, and *Thieves in the Night* is as engrossing—and as cogent—in the twenty-first century as it was in 1946.

The Age of Longing

Published in 1951 and set in Paris in the mid-1950's, *The Age of Longing* describes a time of spiritual disillusionment and longing for an age of faith. The narrative opens on Bastille Day and focuses on three characters: Hydie, a young American apostate from Catholicism, who kneels on her prie-dieu (prayer desk) and laments, "LET ME BELIEVE IN SOMETHING"; Fedya Nikitin, a security officer with a rigid commissar mentality; and Julien Delattre, poet and former party member.

The relationship between Hydie and Fedya occupies much of the novel, with Hydie's ache for religious solace played off against Fedya's unquestioning faith in Communism. Hydie is American, naïve, and innocent; she is seeking experience on which to base faith. Fedya is the son of proletarian revolutionaries from Baku, Azerbaijan, a son of the revolution with the instincts of a true commissar. He seems to have been programmed with party clichés. When the two become lovers, Fedya humiliates Hydie by treating her as a mere collocation of conditioned responses. She then turns against Fedya and, finally understanding his true assignment as a spy, tries to shoot him but botches the job. Regardless of whether their relationship has allegorical significance, the unfeeling commissar is one of Koestler's most effective characterizations. At one point, Fedya asks a young school friend why she likes him, and the answer is, "Because you are clean and simple and hard like an effigy of 'Our Proletarian Youth' from a propaganda poster."

The third main character, Julien Delattre, is in many ways Koestler's self-portrait.

Delattre has given up his allegiance to the "God that failed," and he tells Hydie that "My generation turned to Marx as one swallows acid drops to fight off nausea." He finds his mission in warning others about the ideological traps that he has successfully escaped, and one of the best scenes in the novel comes when he takes Hydie to an evening meeting of the Rally for Peace and Progress. The centerpiece of the session is Koestler's satiric depiction of Jean-Paul Sartre, who appears as the pompous theoretician Professor Pontieux. Author of a fashionable work of postwar despair, "Negation and Position," Professor Pontieux "can prove everything he believes, and he believes everything he can prove."

The Age of Longing ends with an image appropriate to its theme. A funeral party is proceeding past the graves of Jean de La Fontaine, Victor Hugo, and others when air-raid sirens start screaming. "The siren wailed, but nobody was sure: it could have meant the Last Judgment, or just another air-raid exercise."

THE CALL GIRLS

More than twenty years passed between the publication of *The Age of Longing* and that of *The Call Girls*, Koestler's last novel. During those two decades, Koestler's interests had shifted from ideology to science and human behavior. The "call girls" of the title are prominent intellectuals—mostly scientists but including a poet and a priest—nomads of the international conference circuit. Koestler puts them all together in a Swiss mountain setting and sets them to talking about ideas. They have been summoned by one of their members, Nikolai Solovief, a physicist, to consider "approaches to survival" and to send a message to the president of the United States. Unfortunately, the meeting degenerates into a series of uncompromising exchanges between behaviorists and nonbehaviorists. Only Nikolai and Tony, the priest, are able to accommodate themselves to the claims of both reason and faith, and rancor replaces the objective search for truth. *The Call Girls* is an entertaining exposition of the various options available to those seeking enlightenment today.

Readers of *The Ghost in the Machine* and Koestler's work on ESP will recognize in the arguments of Nikolai and Tony those of Koestler himself. Koestler always staged his intellectual dramas in the dress of irreconcilable opposites—the Yogi and the Commissar, ends versus means—and here the protagonist is clearly spirit and the antagonist matter. His call girls demonstrate that there is still life in this old conflict.

Frank Day

OTHER MAJOR WORKS

PLAY: *Twilight Bar: An Escapade in Four Acts*, pb. 1945.
NONFICTION: *Spanish Testament*, 1937; *Scum of the Earth*, 1941; *Dialogue with Death*, 1942; *The Yogi and the Commissar, and Other Essays*, 1945; *Insight and Outlook: An Inquiry into the Common Foundations of Science, Art, and Social Ethics*, 1949; *Promise and Fulfillment: Palestine, 1917-1949*, 1949; *Arrow in the Blue: The First Volume of*

an Autobiography, 1905-1931, 1952; *The Invisible Writing: The Second Volume of an Autobiography, 1932-1940*, 1954; *Trial of the Dinosaur, and Other Essays*, 1955; *Reflections on Hanging*, 1956; *The Sleepwalkers: A History of Man's Changing Vision of the Universe*, 1959; *The Lotus and the Robot*, 1960; *Hanged by the Neck: An Exposure of Capital Punishment in England*, 1961 (with C. H. Rolph); *The Act of Creation*, 1964; *The Ghost in the Machine*, 1967; *The Case of the Midwife Toad*, 1971; *The Roots of Coincidence*, 1972; *The Challenge of Chance: Experiments and Speculations*, 1973 (with Sir Alister Hardy and Robert Harvie); *The Heel of Achilles: Essays, 1968-1973*, 1974; *Life After Death*, 1976 (with Arthur Toynbee et al.); *The Thirteenth Tribe*, 1976; *Janus: A Summing Up*, 1978; *Bricks to Babel: Selected Writings with Comments*, 1981; *Stranger on the Square*, 1984 (with Cynthia Koestler).

EDITED TEXTS: *Suicide of a Nation? An Enquiry into the State of Britain Today*, 1963; *Drinkers of Infinity: Essays, 1955-1967*, 1968 (with J. R. Smythies); *Beyond Reductionism: New Perspectives in the Life Sciences*, 1969 (with Smythies).

BIBLIOGRAPHY

Cesarani, David. *Arthur Koestler: The Homeless Mind*. New York: Free Press, 1999. A thorough reassessment of Koestler's ideas and writings that also explores, among other subjects, his Jewish background, relationships with women, and political activities. Includes a bibliography and an index.

Goodman, Celia, ed. *Living with Koestler: Mamaine Koestler's Letters, 1945-1951*. New York: St. Martin's Press, 1985. A vivid personal view of Koestler, documented by Koestler's second wife, Mamaine Paget.

Hamilton, Iain. *Koestler: A Biography*. Reprint. New York: Macmillan, 1985. This lengthy biography, favorable to Koestler, is arranged year by year in the fashion of a chronicle and breaks off around 1970. Many events have been retold partly on the basis of interviews, Koestler's papers, and firsthand accounts.

Harris, Harold, ed. *Astride the Two Cultures: Arthur Koestler at Seventy*. London: Hutchinson University Library, 1975. This collection of essays by authors sympathetic to Koestler provides nearly equal coverage of the writer's involvement in literary and in scientific activities. The essays include discussions of the Koestler the novelist and his book *Darkness at Noon*.

Judt, Tony. "Arthur Koestler, the Exemplary Intellectual." In *Reappraisals: Reflections on the Forgotten Twentieth Century*. New York: Penguin Press, 2008. Judt includes a discussion of Koestler in this book, which seeks to inform twenty-first century readers about the social thought and socially motivated activism of the twentieth century.

Koestler, Cynthia. *Stranger on the Square*. New York: Random House, 1984. A joint memoir by Cynthia and Arthur Koestler, left unfinished at their deaths.

Marton, Kati. *The Great Escape: Nine Jews Who Fled Hitler and Changed the World*. New York: Simon & Schuster, 2006. Koestler was among the Hungarian Jews who left

Hungary between World War I and II to escape Fascism. Marton recounts Koestler's journey to the United States and his accomplishments as an author.

Pearson, Sidney A., Jr. *Arthur Koestler.* Boston: Twayne, 1978. Although a bit sketchy on matters of biography, this work deals with basic issues in Koestler's writings and has some trenchant and interesting discussion of political themes. Also helpful are the chronology and a selected annotated bibliography.

Perez, Jane, and Wendell Aycock, eds. *The Spanish Civil War in Literature.* Lubbock: Texas Tech University Press, 1990. References Koestler throughout. Peter I. Barta's essay "The Writing of History: Authors Meet on the Soviet-Spanish Border" specifically discusses *Darkness at Noon*, providing an excellent grounding in the political history from which Koestler's fiction evolved.

Sperber, Murray A., ed. *Arthur Koestler: A Collection of Critical Essays.* Englewood Cliffs, N.J.: Prentice-Hall, 1977. Both positive and negative reactions appear in this fine sampling of critical work about Koestler's literary and scientific writings. Among those commentators represented by excerpts here are George Orwell, Saul Bellow, Edmund Wilson, Stephen Spender, and A. J. Ayer.

Sterne, Richard Clark. *Dark Mirror: The Sense of Injustice in Modern European and American Literature.* New York: Fordham University Press, 1994. A substantial discussion of *Darkness at Noon* is included in this book, which analyzes literature that treats the conflict between "natural" ethical law and more "realistic" concepts of justice.

MILAN KUNDERA

Born: Brno, Czechoslovakia (now in Czech Republic); April 1, 1929

PRINCIPAL LONG FICTION

Žert, 1967 (*The Joke*, 1969, revised 1982)
La Vie est ailleurs, 1973 (*Life Is Elsewhere*, 1974; in Czech as *Život je jinde*, 1979)
La Valse aux adieux, 1976 (*The Farewell Party*, 1976; in Czech as *Valčik no rozloučenou*, 1979; revised as *Farewell Waltz*, 1998)
Le Livre du rire et de l'oubli, 1979 (*The Book of Laughter and Forgetting*, 1980; in Czech as *Kniha smíchu a zapomnění*, 1981)
L'Insoutenable Légèreté de l'être, 1984 (*The Unbearable Lightness of Being*, 1984; in Czech as *Nesnesitelná lehkost bytí*, 1985)
Nesmrtelnost, 1990 (*Immortality*, 1991)
La Lenteur, 1995 (*Slowness*, 1996)
L'Identité, 1997 (*Identity*, 1998)
La Ignorancia, 2000 (*Ignorance*, 2002)

OTHER LITERARY FORMS

Apart from his novels, Milan Kundera (koon-DEHR-uh) has published three linked volumes of short stories, *Směšné lásky* (1963; laughable loves), *Druhy sešit směšných lásek* (1965; the second book of laughable loves), and *Třetí sešit směšných lásek* (1968; the third book of laughable loves), which were published together in a definitive edition, *Směšné lásky* (1970); seven of these stories appear in English translation in *Laughable Loves* (1974). Kundera started his literary career with poetry, publishing three collections of that genre. His first important contribution to literary criticism was his study of the Czech novelist Vladislav Vančura, *Umění románu: Cesta Vladislava Vančury za velkou epikou* (1960; the art of the novel: Vladislav Vančura's search for the great epic). Kundera contributed to the revival of Czech drama with *Majitelé klíčů* (pr. 1961; the keys), *Ptákovina* (pr. 1968), and *Jacques et son maître: Hommage à Denis Diderot* (1970; *Jacques and His Master*, 1985). Kundera's speech to the Union of Czechoslovak Writers' Congress of 1967 was one of the high points of the cultural-political movement known as the Prague Spring; the essayistic talent revealed there has since been put to use in a series of striking essays, among the best known of which are "The Tragedy of Central Europe" (*The New York Review of Books*, April 26, 1984) and "The Novel and Europe" (*The New York Review of Books*, July 19, 1984). Two important essays that Kundera has published on the subject of fiction are *L'Art du roman* (1986; *The Art of the Novel*, 1988) and *Le Rideau: Essai en sept parties* (2005; *The Curtain: An Essay in Seven Parts*, 2007). He has also cowritten, with Costa-Gavras and Christopher Frank, the screenplay for the 1979 motion-picture adaptation of Romain Gary's novel *Clair de femme*.

Achievements

Milan Kundera became well known quite early in his career on account of his poetry. In his novel *Life Is Elsewhere*, however, he denounces poetry, and he later switched to prose, experimented in drama, and, finally, took a lively interest in the literary-political scene in Prague at the time of great excitement caused by the liberalization of the Czechoslovakian Communist regime. As far as Kundera was concerned, the time of his great breakthrough in literature and on the cultural scene that involved him also in politics came in 1967, following the publication of *The Joke*, a novel exemplifying the cultural and political sophistication of its author as well as of his country. This confluence of art and life, private and public, and philosophical and political domains is the principal characteristic of Kundera's fiction, refined and finely honed in his subsequent novels.

Kundera has been the recipient of many prestigious literary prizes, including the Czechoslovak State Prize (1964), the Union of Czechoslovak Writers' Prize (1968), the Czechoslovak Writers' Publishing House Prize (1969), the Prix Médicis (1973), the Premio Mondello (1978), the Common Wealth Award for Distinguished Service in Literature (1980), the Jerusalem Prize (1985), the Académie Française Prize (1986), the Nelly Sachs Prize (1987), and the Austrian State Prize (1987). He has also received nominations for a Nobel Prize. Awarded an honorary doctorate by the University of Michigan (1983), in 1986 Kundera became a foreign honorary member of the American Academy of Arts and Letters. In 1990, he was made a Knight of the Légion Etrangère in France. He won the Jaroslav-Seifert Prize for his novel *Immortality* in 1994, and the next year he received the Czech Medal of Merits for his contribution to the renewal of democracy. The University of Vienna awarded him the Herder Preis in 2000, and in 2007 he was honored with the Czech Republic's State Award for Literature.

Biography

Milan Kundera was born into a highly cultured and sophisticated family of a Brno pianist, Milada Janosikova, and a distinguished professor of Janáček's Academy of Music, Ludvík Kundera. Thus, in addition to literature, among those early interests that he took seriously was music. In 1948, the year of a Communist coup in Czechoslovakia, Kundera began his study at the Charles University in Prague and simultaneously attended the famous film school of the Prague Academy of Music and Dramatic Arts, from which he graduated in 1958 after being forced to withdraw from 1950 to 1956 because of his expulsion from the Communist Party. During that hiatus, he composed poetry (a genre in which he had been publishing since 1949) and music, including "Composition for Four Instruments" and a setting of verses by Guillaume Apollinaire, an author who much influenced Kundera's own poetry. The Prague film school also became his employer: There, he taught world literature. In 1963, he married Vera Hrabankova and joined the editorial board of the journal *Literarni noviny*.

Having associated himself strongly with the movement known variously as the Prague

Spring and "socialism with a human face," Kundera fell into disfavor following the 1968 invasion of Czechoslovakia by the Soviet Union. His works were put on the censor's index and withdrawn from the libraries, and he was left without any means of support when forced out of his professorship in 1970. Because of a request by the president of the French parliament, Kundera was allowed to go to France, in 1975, as a visiting professor at the university in Rennes, and it was in France that he learned, in 1979, of the Czechoslovak government's decision to take his citizenship from him. Kundera continued to teach and write in Paris, and he became a French citizen in 1981.

Beginning in 1985, Kundera spent much time revising French and English translations of his work. His 1990 sojourn in Martinique and Haiti led to his publishing a 1991 essay on the culture of French-speaking Caribbean natives of African descent. A victim of explosive politics from Czechoslovakia to the Caribbean, he strove to detach himself from public life, as he demonstrated in the address he delivered in 1985 when he received the Jerusalem Prize. He said that the novel can rise to more than personal and national wisdom only through novelists' humbly absenting themselves from celebrity, so that they can ridicule the kitsch and sentimentality spread by public figures, who fear offending the masses.

ANALYSIS

None of Milan Kundera's novels fits into the traditional concept of the novel. Each is an experimental foray into the unknown, although well prepared and supported by the literary legacy of Jaroslav Hašek, Karel Čapek, and Vančura. This is particularly visible in the structure of a Kundera novels, which strikes one as that of a loosely organized group of short stories that have in common not so much recurring characters as a central theme, of which each story illustrates a single facet.

Each of his novels—as well as his cycle of short stories, *Laughable Loves*—is a fresh approach to his abiding concern: the search for authenticity defined as an unmasked, demythologized, yet philosophical parable of the existence of a Czech intellectual in a given historical time. Against the background of modern Czech fiction, Kundera appears as a worthy follower of the three main directions of Czech prose, associated with the names of Jaroslav Hašek, Karel Čapek, and Vladislav Vančura. It is the mark of Kundera's genius that he has been able to alchemize the best that these authors had to offer him into his own original prose, surpassing them all.

THE JOKE

Kundera's first novel, *The Joke*, seems to grow out of the short-story collection *Laughable Loves*. They have in common the central device of a "joke"—that is, an intended and performed hoax, a prank—that misfires and, like a boomerang, hurts the perpetrator rather than the intended victim. For example, in one of the stories in *Laughable Loves*, "I, the Mournful God," the narrator wants to punish a pretty girl who has resisted his advances by punishing her vanity. He approaches his Greek friend, who acts the role of a foreign impresario attracted by the talent of the girl, who happens to be a music student. The girl is easily seduced, and the affair is consummated the same day on the narrator's couch, to the narrator's wrenching and never-ending dismay. Hoist with his own petard, the narrator waxes philosophical about the important lesson he has learned about life.

This device is central in the novel *The Joke*, wherein it is enriched and used to probe deeply into the realms of character motivation past and present, the political order (with the attendant zigzags of the Communist Party line), and the sensitive area of emotional and erotic relationships, the highs and lows of which Kundera captures with singular detachment bordering on misanthropy and misogyny.

The Joke consists of four narratives of the same event, or rather a set of events, centering on the "joke": Ludvík Jahn, the central character, sends his naïve activist girlfriend a postcard that is politically compromising; his intention is to make fun of her seriousness and steer her toward erotic rather than political interests. The girlfriend reports him to the Communist Party organization, and Ludvík is thrown out of the university as a politically unreliable element, his life derailed for years, during which he has to work as a mine laborer, first as a draftee in a punishment battalion, then as a volunteer without much choice. In revenge, the "rehabilitated" Ludvík, now a scientist in Prague, decides to seduce the wife of his archenemy who engineered his dismissal from the university. Like the first joke, the second misfires: The enemy's wife falls in love with Ludvík at a time when her husband is estranged from her; to add insult to injury, the enemy, Zemánek, is a thoroughly reformed man, now as fond of ideas as is Ludvík and embarrassed for his past—all in all, a different man, one who is involved with a young woman and glad that Ludvík is interested in his unwanted wife. Philosophically, the novel explores the fluidity, the inconstancy of people's characters and ideas; Kundera also suggests that the nature of justice is undermined by the element of time. Perhaps in some timeless corner of the universe, an exact justice prevails, but how can one implement it in a world crucified by time?

Ludvík Jahn is also an ideal personification of the reformist ideas sweeping Czechoslovakia in 1967 and 1968. Historically, the novel is a literary summing up of the Czechoslovak experience with socialism from its very outset, in 1948. The sensational quality of *The Joke*, from the political point of view—and it is clear that this point of view is relevant to an understanding of the novel—stems from the near-documentary quality with which Kundera depicts successive stages of modern Czech history, taking into account the many different moves and countermoves of cultural, social, and existential aspects of the Czech reality. What each of the four character-narrators documents, Kundera the author transcends, so powerfully does one feel the controlling intelligence behind the scene pulling the strings that direct the literary "god game."

While *The Joke* was immediately praised for its literary qualities when it appeared, it also served to polarize Czech critics along political lines, dividing them into dogmatists and reformists: The former decried Kundera's wholly irreverent attitude toward Communist taboos, while the latter praised his candor. Kundera himself has noted the danger of ideological interpretations of the novel that obscure the more subtle love story between Ludvík and the tender girl, Lucie, whom he meets while he is a laborer—a love story at the center of the complex novel but for that very reason easily overlooked when weightier and more topical concerns clamor for attention. In the novel's first reception, few critics noted Ludvík's failure to lead an authentic existence. Imprisoned by his grudge and his ambiguous attitude toward women as a result of the decisive, treacherous act by the female Communist Party activist, Ludvík blinds himself even to such timeless aids as Moravian folk music—which, in a key passage omitted from the original English translation, opens his eyes to the authenticity he has missed.

LIFE IS ELSEWHERE

Kundera develops this powerful concern with authentic life masterfully in *Life Is Elsewhere*. Where, then, is life? Rather, what is life? Kundera's second novel answers this question by way of a negative example of a young poet living the life of precocious maturity conventionally found admirable in the works of Arthur Rimbaud, Vladimir Mayakovsky, Sergei Esenin, and the Czechs Jiří Wolker and Jiří Orten, embodying Romantic conventions of the genius and of the indivisibility of art and life. Is it then possible for the Poet, this higher being, to become a wretched masturbator and police informer as well as a clumsy bungler of everything but his verses?

Kundera magisterially answers these and other questions by giving an indecent history of the young poet Jaromil: his life, beginning with his conception, all the way up to his pathetic and bathetic death. On the way, Kundera demolishes the Romantic myth of the poet as the truth seeker, or truth sayer. Instead of a prophet, he shows us a pervert. That, however, is only the consequence of Jaromil's inability to lead an authentic life, precisely because he is and remains all the time a poet. The lyric quality so necessary for a poet is seen as the greatest obstacle to authenticity, to life as it should be lived.

The unlikely counterpart of Jaromil is a man with whom Jaromil shares a girlfriend. The authentic man, however, is selfless, whereas Jaromil is possessive; he is attached to timeless traditional art, whereas Jaromil seeks absolute modernity. Needless to say, in the political sphere, Jaromil repeats Communist inanities, though he is sufficiently intelligent to see how flawed they are. Lyricism contra logic: This is the conflict at the heart of the painful demolition of the poet. He, the poet Jaromil, even dies without understanding the harm he has done to others and himself through his fateful lyricism.

THE FAREWELL PARTY

So much for the poet—but what if Jaromil's condition is generally present among people at large? Kundera turns to this question in the wry, tragicomic novel *The Farewell Party*. Instead of following one causal chain, he traces several, crisscrossing them in order to show how, like billiard balls, individual fates meet and are bounced in yet further unexpected directions. The plot of the novel is too complex to recount in detail; in simplified form, however, *The Farewell Party* deals with the issue of self-deception on a group scale, up from the previous novel's individual scale.

A musician is arranging his mistress's abortion with a doctor who heads a fertilization clinic in an unorthodox manner: He impregnates his patients artificially, using his own semen. The man whose mission it is to fertilize then kills, and the man who wants to free himself supplies poison to a woman, the same musician's mistress, who, not knowing about the poison, kills herself. Further complications follow. This novel is far more dramatic than anything else Kundera has published, but it does have the operatic quality of some of his early tales. The obvious tragic aspect of the happenings is countered step by step with genuinely comic happenings, accidents, and a jovial set of characters, almost all of whom preclude the kind of tragic tension that the mere plot implies.

Without any doubt, *The Farewell Party* is Kundera's most cynical and misanthropic literary performance. At the same time, it announces the arrival of supernatural elements in his fiction, in the guise of an American, Bartleff. Without the somewhat absurd supernaturalism of Bartleff, which injects a modicum of warmth, the novel would be hard to bear. Thematically, it is possible to place the work within the tense, Kafkaesque atmosphere of postinvasion Bohemia, with its ever-growing demoralization.

THE BOOK OF LAUGHTER AND FORGETTING

Kundera's next novel was like a breath of fresh air. A daring experiment, *The Book of Laughter and Forgetting* features the return of a more aggressive narrative with documentary elements, more authorial intrusion and manipulation of the narrative with autobiographical elements, quotations from an eccentric array of thinkers, attempts at the theory of laughter, and incursions into the domains of musicology and philosophy of history.

First, Kundera manages to introduce and establish very successfully the plight of a dissident and an émigré, though in ways that run contrary to political clichés. There is then a considerable dose of "reality": Historical events are recounted; politicians—dead and alive—are quoted and described; and snippets of what purports to be Kundera's life are offered in a very appetizing smorgasbord, where the wound of history is treated with the balm of a new mythology, created by Kundera in a feat of magic to vanquish the old—people dance the hypnotic circle and rise into thin air. Finally, there is a "theory of laughter" that distinguishes between the laughter of the Devil and the laughter of angels. At the same time, structurally, the novel solidifies around seven key tales with a limited number of characters, some of whom are present in more than one tale; the tales themselves are introduced as variations (in musical fashion) on the common themes of laughter and forgetting. The dangers of forgetting and the necessity of laughter are often illustrated roughly, subtlety being reserved for a sustained criticism of the modern malaise of indifference, lack of compassion, and the frittering away of a precious cultural heritage.

Above all, Kundera's concern with authenticity is present here in force, as is his attempt to do away with the sentimental glorification of youth, of childhood even—as if he believed that he had not finished the job properly in *Life Is Elsewhere*. To get his message across in a definitive fashion, he places his favorite heroine, Tamina, on an island inhabited by children who ogle her, pounce on her, take away her privacy, rape her, and finally kill her—naïvely, sincerely, purely, without malice, but full of curiosity. The island of children, the children's paradise, is a beautiful parable of the horrors of totalitarianism.

Kundera wanted to impress the Western reader with the issue of totalitarianism, and the avenue he chose was a parable. The totalitarian system, however imperfect, tries to turn adults into children in yet another parody of a perfectly legitimate and profound traditional idea found in many sacred traditions—above all, in Christianity. The primitivism of the totalitarian ideology, the simplicity of its propaganda, has thus acquired a profound meaning: It harks back to the children imprisoned within adults, and therein lies its success, no matter how banal, how simple, how trivial.

To resist the totalitarian temptation, to become a "dissident," is desirable, but in Kundera's world, the dissident is a person who exemplifies in miniature the larger political processes existing on a large scale in society, for one is but a part of the whole. Thus, even the dissident feels the need to tamper with the past in order to bring it more in line with his or her present: The past embarrasses the dissident. Kundera justifiably resents labels such as "dissident" and "émigré" as applied to him, for he has spent his entire adult life peering at what is hidden behind the labels, behind the masks, knowing that a label—any label— does not absolve one of anything. At the depths at which Kundera operates, such labels are meaningless.

THE UNBEARABLE LIGHTNESS OF BEING

It is curious to see, then, in Kundera's *The Unbearable Lightness of Being*, his attempt to present a character who, according to all indications, does lead an authentic life. When Kundera portrays someone who is living an authentic life, as his main character Tomas and Tomas's love Tereza do, it is only to suggest that ultimately life itself has been emptied of meaning, of authenticity. The novel begins by stating that if humanity believed (as in German philosopher Friedrich Nietzsche's idea of eternal return) that everything, including the horrors of the past, would occur again and again forever, every act would be "heavy" with consequence. Instead, however, many people now assume that their acts will have no eternal result (in heaven or hell); thus, life becomes "light"—perhaps unbearably so.

Tomas and Tereza, as authentic and as unobjectionable as Kundera could make them, are frustrated by the accidents of history. They understand the personal and the social tragedy that they witness. They feel compassion. When the great traumatic event of their life happens, the Soviet invasion of Czechoslovakia in 1968, they decide to emigrate to Switzerland. Because Tomas is a natural Don Juan, Tereza, who loves him deeply, decides to return to Czechoslovakia, as she is unable to share Tomas with other women. Tereza's absence weighs heavily on Tomas, and he returns to Czechoslovakia to join her, though the price is high: A skillful surgeon, he is fired from his hospital and forced to work as a window washer. He does not mind, however; he feels even more free, and the new occupation seems especially useful from the point of view of his easier access to potential erotic adventures. Finally, Tomas and Tereza move into a benighted village, where Tomas works as a truck driver. During a weekend outing, Tomas and Tereza are accidentally killed in the truck.

Far away from Tomas, in the United States, lives his former love, Sabina, who also suffers from the burden of "lightness." She influences one of her lovers, Franz, a Swiss professor, into adopting a more authentic life and then drops him. Franz looks for a cause, is attracted to a humanitarian mission in Southeast Asia, and while there is killed in a mugging. Tomas, Sabina, and Franz all have something in common, irrespective of their accomplishments as authentic beings, inasmuch as the meaning has been decanted from life itself. This common feature is the Nietzschean *amor fati*, love of life as it is in all its merciless fatefulness. Kundera never announces this theme, but after his Nietzschean opening, it is only logical to translate the surrender of all these characters to life as it is, without preconditions, as a literary adaptation of this Nietzschean conceit.

Mention should be made of Kundera's superlative satire of leftism and its kitsch in this novel. In this connection, the conclusion serves as a magnificent counterpoint to Kundera's discussion of many varieties of kitsch, including the political. What could promise more in the way of kitsch than the death of a dog improbably named Karenin? After all, pets, whatever kind, are the beneficiaries of the most absurd type of maudlin sentimentality and kitsch. It takes courage to lecture about kitsch and then, in a truly inspired and unforgettable passage, after showing why the deaths of millions of human beings no longer have power to move people, describe the death of Tomas and Tereza's dog Karenin as a genuinely moving event that restores, through acceptance of tragedy, meaningfulness to life. This is the most unbearable event of the novel. As such, it pokes a hole through the all-embracing curtain of Tomas's *amor fati* and reestablishes the primary importance of authenticity.

Slowness

In all of Kundera's major works there is complex counterpoint between essaylike lecture and narrative. The distance between the two, however, narrows beginning with *Slowness*. This novel juxtaposes a leisurely, eighteenth century journey through beautiful countryside with a modern motor trip, where people distance themselves from nature and time in an "ecstasy" of speed. Representing the earlier century is a character simply called the Chevalier, who enjoys a night of love at the climax of Vivant Denon's 1777 novella *Point de lendemain (No Tomorrow)*. Wandering out of that book and into Kundera's, this Chevalier meets Vincent, a man who also spends a night with a beautiful woman but who is rendered impotent by trying to perform in public. Indeed, throughout *Slowness*, one modern character after another behaves in a ridiculous fashion because of exhibitionism, a metaphor for quickly traversed open spaces in contrast to the unhurried pace and privacy cherished in the eighteenth century. A Czech scientist, for instance, rushes to a foreign conference only to forget to give his lecture because he is deeply moved by the grandstanding remarks he makes as his introduction. More comically lamentable is a French politician so addicted to ostentatious globe-trotting that he long ago renounced any private life.

IDENTITY

Even more than *Slowness*, Kundera's next novel, *Identity*, takes advantage of a French milieu, where ideas permeate conversation. In the former work, the essays have been reduced to short asides by a narrator who witnesses the events. In *Identity*, however, the essayistic elements are confined to the dialogue and thus are integrated into the action. They all spring from a vision of life as boring because people are no longer distinguished from one another by passionate attachment to their occupations. Instead, there has been homogenization, even of gender: The women occupy previously male-dominated professions, in which they feel detached and two-faced, and the men become effeminate "daddies" instead of authoritative "fathers." Kundera's assignment of these ideas to his characters leaves tantalizingly open the question of whether male chauvinism is part of his defense of Old World values or a satire of the stereotypes into which European culture has crumbled.

The character Chantal first laughs at the "daddies" she meets because they lack the masculinity to give her a second glance. Almost immediately, however, their neglect makes her feel old and unattractive. She tries to joke about this depression to her lover, Jean-Marc, but her blush betrays to him that she is deeply hurt. To rekindle her self-esteem, he begins writing her anonymous letters, as from a secret admirer. He then becomes jealous of their success, and the couple's life slips toward a nightmare of identity loss and boredom. According to Jean-Marc, boredom is the direct experience of time without the protection offered by friendship and occupation (both of which modern life vitiates). In fifty-one short sections, the novel provides so many variations on the theme of identity loss that *The New York Times Book Review* likened it to a fugue. Kundera has always achieved a musiclike structure in his works, but his later novels have attained a new delicacy and harmony, even if perhaps with some loss of volume.

IGNORANCE

As in Kundera's other novels, there is one more character in *Ignorance* beyond the fictional characters. The narrative is essentially the story of two Czech émigrés, Irena living in Paris and Josef in Denmark. Many years earlier, they had an encounter that Irena remembers fondly and that Josef has forgotten entirely. Memory, nostalgia, forgetting, and ignorance all play a role in this. The additional character is the author himself—he steps in to make general observations and to comment on the lives of his characters. In a device not unlike the intrusions of the narrator in *Slowness* and *The Unbearable Lightness of Being*, the author launches into an essay on perception of time and place after the narrative has barely begun.

The narrative itself is a fascinating account of characters engaging momentarily and forgetting, much like ships passing in the night. The story begins in 1989 with Sylvie telling her friend, Irena, that she ought to go home. Home for Irena is Paris, where she has lived the past twenty years; for Sylvie, however, Irena's home ought to be her native Czechoslovakia, just now freed from Communist rule. The author interrupts, and for the remainder of the chapter and through the next two chapters he explores the idea of belonging, with all the attendant concerns about memory, nostalgia, history, expectation, disappointment, and other states of mind that isolate or alienate the individual. The narrative then resumes (with occasional commentary form the author), tracing the paths of Irena and Josef as they return to their homeland after twenty years' absence (much like Odysseus's return to Ithaca). They meet at the Paris airport, where Irena recognizes Josef at once from a pleasant and romantic encounter years ago, when he gave her an ashtray as a memento. Josef, however, does not remember Irena at all, although he pretends to.

Back in Prague, they try individually to make connections with the world they had left behind, but the effort frustrates them. People have different memories, and in any event they have no interest in what the returned émigrés may have experienced while they were away. At times they seem to make connections, only to see them fall apart. One of these involves Milada, who tells Irena that she remembers Josef from the time he jilted her when they were teenagers. She attempted suicide by taking sleeping pills and waiting to freeze in the subzero mountains, but only her ear was frozen, and it had to be cut off. She does not meet Josef again, but Irena does at his hotel. In their loneliness they end up making love, after which Irena realizes that he does not remember her, not even when she shows him the ashtray she has kept as a souvenir. He cannot even speak her name. There is a palpable sadness in the journey they have taken, especially for Irena, who is left totally alone and friendless.

Peter Petro; James Whitlark
Updated by Stanley Vincent Longman

Other major works

SHORT FICTION: *Směšné lásky: Tri melancholicke anekdoty*, 1963; *Druhy sešit směšných lásek*, 1965; *Třetí sešit směšných lásek*, 1968; *Směšne lásky*, 1970 (partial translation *Laughable Loves*, 1974).

PLAYS: *Majitelé klíčů*, pr. 1961; *Ptákovina, čili Dvojí uši—dvoji svatba*, pr. 1968; *Jacques et son maître: Hommage à Denis Diderot*, pr. 1970 (*Jacques and His Master*, 1985).

POETRY: *Člověk zahrada širá*, 1953; *Poslední máj*, 1955 (revised 1963); *Monology*, 1957 (revised 1964).

SCREENPLAY: *Clair de femme*, 1979 (adaptation of Romain Gary's novel; with Costa-Gavras and Christopher Frank).

NONFICTION: *Umění románu: Cesta Vladislava Vančury za velkou epikou*, 1960; *L'Art du roman*, 1986 (*The Art of the Novel*, 1988; revised 2000); *Les testaments trahis*, 1993 (*Testaments Betrayed: An Essay in Nine Parts*, 1995); *Le Rideau: Essai en sept parties*, 2005 (*The Curtain: An Essay in Seven Parts*, 2007).

BIBLIOGRAPHY

Aji, Aron, ed. *Milan Kundera and the Art of Fiction: Critical Essays*. New York: Garland, 1992. Collection of critical essays addresses Kundera's contribution to the novel form.

Banerjee, Maria Nemcová. *Terminal Paradox: The Novels of Milan Kundera*. New York: Grove Weidenfeld, 1990. Critical study of Kundera's long fiction presents in-depth discussion of individual novels. Includes bibliography.

Bloom, Harold, ed. *Milan Kundera*. New York: Chelsea House, 2003. Collection of essays represents a wide range of critical responses to Kundera's work. Includes an informative introductory overview.

Kundera, Milan. *Testaments Betrayed: An Essay in Nine Parts*. New York: HarperCollins, 1995. Discussion of the novel as a genre throws much light on Kundera's fiction, both long and short. Kundera argues for a fiction of moral judgment, discusses the importance of humor in fiction, and examines the ways in which critics have misunderstood great works of fiction.

Misurella, Fred. *Understanding Milan Kundera: Public Events, Private Affairs*. Columbia: University of South Carolina Press, 1993. Lays out an approach to Kundera's novelistic forms and examines such topics as the human possibilities of Kafka and Diderot and the longing for paradise in *The Unbearable Lightness of Being*. Includes a chronology and a comprehensive bibliography.

Petro, Peter, ed. *Critical Essays on Milan Kundera*. New York: G. K. Hall, 1999. Collection of essays provides informative exploration of Kundera's fiction. Includes bibliography and index.

Ricard, François. *Agnès's Final Afternoon: An Essay on the Work of Milan Kundera*. Translated by Aaron Asher. New York: HarperCollins, 2003. Examines Kundera's novels by focusing on their themes, motifs, characters, and structures.

Steiner, Peter. "Ironies of History: *The Joke* by Milan Kundera." In *The Deserts of Bohemia: Czech Fiction and Its Social Context*. Ithaca, N.Y.: Cornell University Press, 2000. Discussion of *The Joke* is part of a larger work that examines the political nature of Czech fiction in the twentieth century. Provides a close reading of Kundera's novel.

Weeks, Mark. "Milan Kundera: A Modern History of Humor Amid the Comedy of History." *Journal of Modern Literature* 28 (Spring, 2005): 130-148. Focuses on Kundera's ongoing pursuit of the subjects of laughter and humor in his fiction.

Woods, Michelle. *Translating Milan Kundera*. Clevedon, England: Multilingual Matters, 2006. Presents an account of Kundera's writing practices and discusses the challenges inherent in translating his works. Supplemented by an extensive bibliography.

NGUGI WA THIONG'O

Born: Kamiriithu village, near Limuru, Kenya; January 5, 1938
Also known as: James Ngugi

PRINCIPAL LONG FICTION
Weep Not, Child, 1964
The River Between, 1965
A Grain of Wheat, 1967
Secret Lives, 1974
Petals of Blood, 1977
Caitaani Mutharaba-Ini, 1980 (*Devil on the Cross*, 1982)
Matigari ma Njiruungi, 1986 (*Matigari*, 1989)
Murogi wa Kagogo, 2004 (*Wizard of the Crow*, 2006)

OTHER LITERARY FORMS

In addition to his novels, Ngugi wa Thiong'o (ehn-GEW-gee wah tee-ONG-goh) has published short stories, numerous plays, and several works of nonfiction. His plays include *The Black Hermit* (pr. 1962); *The Trial of Dedan Kimathi* (pr. 1974), written with Micere Githae-Mugo; and, with Ngugi wa Mirii, *Ngaahika Ndeenda* (pr. 1977; *I Will Marry When I Want*, 1982) and *Maitu Njugira* (pb. 1982; *Mother, Sing for Me*, 1986). Ngugi has expressed his commitment to his political responsibility as a writer in numerous works of literary, political, and social criticism, including *Homecoming: Essays on African and Caribbean Literature, Culture, and Politics* (1972), *Writers in Politics* (1981; enlarged, revised, and subtitled *A Re-engagement with Issues of Literature and Society* in a 1997 edition), *Detained: A Writer's Prison Diary* (1981), *Decolonising the Mind: The Politics of Language in African Literature* (1986), and *Penpoints, Gunpoints, and Dreams: Toward a Critical Theory of the Arts and the State in Africa* (1998). In the 1980's, he pursued his interest in African-based educational curricula by recasting stories of the Mau Mau resistance, many of which had appeared in his novels, as works for children, written first in his native Kikuyu and later translated into English. A collection of Ngugi's essays and talks written between 1985 and 1990 appeared in 1993 under the title *Moving the Centre: The Struggle for Cultural Freedoms*.

ACHIEVEMENTS

With the publication of his first three novels, Ngugi wa Thiong'o quickly established himself as the major East African writer of the anglophone literary movement that began in Africa in the late 1950's and early 1960's. This anglophone literary school, which must be distinguished from the preceding romantic francophone movement called "negritude" because of its different political assumptions and its stress on realism, coincided with the bitter political and at times military struggle and the eventual achievement of independence by most African countries that had been under British colonial rule. Given the political situation, this literary movement was naturally preoccupied with assessing the impact of colonialism and with defining independent and syncretic African cultures. With a handful of other African writers, Ngugi stands out as a literary pioneer in this movement.

Ngugi's systematic examination of the manner in which indigenous cultures were destroyed by colonialism has distinguished him from many of his colleagues, while his depiction of these cultures' attempts to reconstitute themselves has made him unique. His refusal to divorce literature from politics and his acerbic portrayal of corruption in independent Kenya—first in *Petals of Blood* and then in his play *Ngaahika Ndeenda*, which was considered more dangerous by the government because it was performed in an indigenous language—earned him the wrath of political leaders and a year in prison without a trial. Building on his reputation as a fearless critic of African dictatorships, Ngugi produced *Wizard of the Crow*, which takes up where *Petals of Blood* left off—sparing readers nothing by graphically depicting the carnage wrought by these murderous regimes, yet all the while employing his characteristic whimsy and humorous satire to highlight the surreal world the dictators create for their subjects.

Ngugi has also been concerned with the implications entailed in the use of English language by African writers, and he has supplemented his theoretical reflections by switching to Kikuyu as his primary literary language. Ngugi is widely recognized as Africa's foremost revolutionary writer and is one of the world's most read African writers.

Biography

Ngugi wa Thiong'o, who published as James Ngugi until 1970, was born in 1938 near Limuru, a Kikuyu region of Kenya. He received a varied education, alternating between mission schools and an institution that grew out of the independence schools movement, the aim of which was to prepare Kenya's young people for freedom from British rule. The Mau Mau war disrupted Ngugi's education and had a profound impact on his family: His brother Walter fought with the Mau Mau, and his parents were detained as subversives. Ngugi's experiences during the war made a lasting impression on him and served as the basis for his first three novels.

In 1955, Ngugi entered Alliance High School, a missionary institution from which he graduated. His literary career developed rapidly once he became a student at Makerere University College in Kampala, Uganda. There he edited the student literary magazine, *Penpoint*, and wrote *The Black Hermit*, a play celebrating Uganda's independence.

In 1964, Ngugi published his first novel, which won two prizes, one from the 1965 Dakar Festival of Negro Arts and one from the East African Literature Bureau. After working for the *Sunday Nation*, a Nairobi newspaper, he attended graduate school at the University of Leeds in England. He returned to Kenya in 1968 to take up a lectureship in the English department at University College, Nairobi, and in 1969 he resigned that post in protest against government interference with academic freedom and in sympathy with a student strike. That same year, he accepted a teaching position at Northwestern University in Illinois, where he remained until 1971, when he returned to University College in Nairobi.

On December 31, 1977, the police detained Ngugi for his political views, a charge stemming from his involvement with an educational theater project in a Kenyan village. He remained in prison until December 12, 1978. On his release, he went back to teaching and again worked with a theater group, which was banned by Kenyan authorities in 1982. Ngugi, anticipating further restrictions on his artistic freedom, entered self-imposed exile, first in London, then in the United States. He took a teaching job at Yale University. In the following decade, he taught at New York University and traveled back to Nairobi, where he and his wife were attacked by progovernment forces. In 2002, he became director of the International Center for Writing and Translation at the University of California at Irvine.

Although Ngugi wrote little in the 1990's, he continued to speak against and write about the widespread corruption and injustice in Kenya. In particular, he stresses what he calls "the politics of language," insisting that the continued use of English, French, and Portuguese in Africa rather than the native languages separates the people from their culture.

ANALYSIS

Ngugi wa Thiong'o's fiction, like that of many contemporary African novelists, is highly political: It portrays the traumatic transition from colonized culture to an independent African society. His novels illustrate with unmatched clarity the problems created by this period of rapid change. Superior European technology introduced into Africa at the beginning of the twentieth century undercut traditional cultural values, and colonial domination (denunciation of indigenous cultures and religions, appropriation of native lands, forced labor) led to a disintegration of indigenous societies.

The major themes of Ngugi's novels derive from his characters' attempts to overcome the confusion caused by the peripeteia of values and to reintegrate and revitalize their new syncretic culture. Faced with the drastic dissolution of his family in the Mau Mau war from 1952 to 1958, Njoroge, the protagonist of *Weep Not, Child*, tenaciously adheres to his beliefs in education and messianic deliverance in a vain attempt to maintain some cohesion in his life. Waiyaki, the hero of *The River Between*, believing that he is the new messiah, also attempts in vain to reunite the Christian and traditional Kikuyu factions of his village. *A Grain of Wheat* is experimental in form: The novel's meaning is available not through the character and experiences of a single protagonist but through the complex interrelationships of five major and many minor characters. The theme, however, remains the same—the attempt of the members of a Kikuyu village to reintegrate themselves and to reorder their priorities after the devastation of the Mau Mau war. *Petals of Blood*, set in postcolonial Kenya, once more depicts a group of peasants who are trying to fashion a meaningful life for themselves in the context of economic exploitation by the new black leaders of the country.

Ngugi's preoccupation with this theme is best understood in the historical context of the conflict between the Kikuyus and British colonizers that culminated in the Mau Mau war of 1952 and that was provoked by three important factors: the economic and cultural effects of land appropriation, the importance of education for the Kikuyus and consequently the impact of its deprivation, and the messianic fervor that characterized Kikuyu politics at the time. Ngugi focuses on various combinations of these three factors in his novels, and his repeated concern with these issues is largely determined by his traumatic experiences during the war.

When the British settled in Kenya, they expropriated large areas of the best arable land from the Kikuyus (who were then crowded into reserves). The land was given, at little or no cost, to English syndicates, investors, and farmers. Piecemeal appropriation of Kikuyu land was finally systematized by a 1921 court ruling in which all land, even that which had been put aside for "reserves," was declared to be owned by the British government. The natives were thus considered squatters on land they had owned for generations. In exchange for squatting "rights," the Kikuyus had to provide 180 days of free labor per annum. Such manipulation, along with coercive tax laws and punitive raids, put tremendous pressure on the Kikuyus and eventually led to the Mau Mau war. Although independence was achieved in 1962, the war was a particularly bitter experience for the Kikuyus because they were divided—some fought for and some against the British.

While being deprived of their land, the Kikuyus focused their attention on education, only to find themselves once more at odds with the colonial government, which, with the aim of promoting agricultural and vocational training, limited African education to the primary level and prohibited the use of English as the medium of instruction. The Kikuyus, however, preferred liberal, humanistic secondary education because it permitted access to civil service jobs and, more important, because English was the language of technology and power. They reasoned, quite accurately, that mastery of English was crucial for their nationalistic aspirations. The Kikuyus responded by mercilessly taxing themselves in order to build their own schools, only to have them shut down repeatedly by the government. This struggle continued until the outbreak of the Mau Mau war, when all Kikuyu schools were closed for several years.

Knowledge of another element of Kenyan history is also important to an appreciation of Ngugi's fiction. Mugo wa Kibiro, a Kikuyu prophet, predicted that a messianic leader would come to deliver the tribe from colonial bondage. Jomo Kenyatta, the leader of the independence movement and the first president of Kenya, skillfully used this prophecy to coalesce the social and religious sentiments of the Kikuyu around himself during the Mau Mau war. Hence the atmosphere at that time was charged by powerful contradictory feelings: Fear, uncertainty, bitterness, and despair produced by colonial oppression were balanced by fervent feelings of loyalty, sacrifice, and elation resulting from messianic expectations and hopes for independence, freedom, and recovery of the land.

At the age of fifteen, Ngugi was caught up in this historical and emotional drama, and its effects on him were profound. He had experienced extreme poverty and thus clearly sympathized with the economic and political predicament of the peasants. At the age of ten or eleven, he witnessed the forced evacuation of Kikuyu farmers from their land. As they were being moved, they sang about their hopes of reclaiming their property and about their educated children who might attain this goal some day. Ngugi's memory of this scene explains his preoccupation with the war: "They sang of a common loss and hope and I felt their voice rock the earth where I stood literally unable to move." Ngugi's burden was exacerbated by the closing of schools. Young Kikuyus were being exhorted to master Western knowledge and use it as a weapon of liberation, but the political and military crises blocked access to education and therefore to the possibility of leadership. This deprivation was rendered even more painful by the sustained messianic fervor that reemphasized the role of leadership.

This, then, was the nexus of forces that composed the sociopolitical and religious ambience in which Ngugi reached maturity. Because he was so young when he began writing, his early fiction shows an imperfect understanding of his predicament. His first two novels graphically depict his entanglement in the peripeteia of values, whereas his third and fourth novels, written after he had studied Frantz Fanon's psychopolitical analysis of colonialism, show a sudden and clearer understanding of the ambiguities and contradictions of colonial society.

WEEP NOT, CHILD

Set in Kenya in the 1940's and 1950's and ending in the midst of the Mau Mau war, *Weep Not, Child* is Ngugi's most autobiographical novel; Njoroge, its child protagonist, is about the same age as Ngugi would have been at that time. The novel is an anticlimactic, truncated bildungsroman in that it follows the development of a child into adolescence but does not adequately resolve the question of what precisely the hero has learned by the end.

The novel rapidly and cogently focuses on Njoroge's preoccupation with education and messianism. Ngotho, Njoroge's father, is confused and emasculated by his inability to comprehend and resist the appropriation of his land by an English settler named Howlands, so the family begins to disintegrate, reflecting in microcosm the general social fragmentation. The family's burden passes to Njoroge, who is fortunate enough to be receiving a formal education (which annually consumes the wages of two brothers). When Njoroge graduates into secondary school, the entire village contributes to his tuition, and thus the hero is transformed from the "son of Ngotho to the son of the land." He begins to feel that through his education he will become a great leader, and Kenyatta's imprisonment further fuels his grandiose fantasies: He even envisions himself as the new messiah.

Njoroge's self-image, however, remains insubstantial. His love of "education" is abstract: He does not care for particular subjects, nor does his vision encompass specific goals or projects. His messianic delusions are equally empty, and his egocentric world crumbles as soon as he is confronted with the reality of the war. When his father dies as the result of severe torture and castration, when his brothers are either imprisoned or killed, and when he too is tortured in spite of his innocence, his illusions are shattered. Finally, the girl he loves rejects him, and he attempts suicide but is easily dissuaded by his mother. The novel ends with his recognition that he is a coward.

Ngotho's rapid descent from the height of self-importance to the nadir of self-negation is enacted against the backdrop of a society in violent turmoil, which Ngugi depicts in effective detail. The complex social entanglements and contradictions—the different political views and the conflict between generations within Ngotho's family; the enmity between Ngotho and Jacobo, whose loyalty to the British is rewarded with wealth and political power; the mixture of fear, hatred, and respect that Howlands harbors for Ngotho because he has occupied the latter's land; the Englishman's desire to torture and kill Ngotho, which leads to the retaliatory murder of Howlands by Ngotho's son; Howlands's contempt for Jacobo's collaboration; Njoroge's love for Mwihaki, Jacobo's daughter, and his brief friendship with Howlands's son—as well as the descriptions of torture and summary executions by the British and the Mau Mau—create a powerful microcosmic picture of a whole society being ripped apart by economic and political conflict. The novel brilliantly depicts the trauma and the ambiguities of a revolution. Njoroge's actual experience is not derived from active involvement in this upheaval, however; rather, he functions as a passive, reluctant witness. His experience is that of a highly suggestible and solitary adolescent who easily internalizes the hopes, frustrations, and anguish of his society and then soothes his own trauma with self-aggrandizing fantasies.

The violence and trauma to which Njoroge is subject only partially account for the oscillation of his self-image. The rest of the explanation lies in the abrupt change of values that engulfs the hero and the narrator. Njoroge's early subscription to English values includes a naïve belief in biblical messianic prophecies that supplement the Kikuyu myth. As a self-styled messiah, he attempts to soothe the fears of a "weeping child"; thus his attitude toward others exactly parallels the narrator's depiction of Njoroge as the weeping child. This profound sympathy and parallelism between the narrator's and the hero's views underscore the complete absence of irony in Ngugi's portrayal of Njoroge.

The denouement of the novel also confirms this underlying problem. Without any justification, Njoroge assumes all the guilt of the trauma suffered by several families and accuses the girl he loves of betraying him before he tries to commit suicide. He is thus still following the model of Christ, of a messiah who assumed all human guilt, was betrayed, and was then turned into a scapegoat. By allowing his hero to transform his self-image from that of a savior to that of a scapegoat, Ngugi allows him to retain his original egocentricity. This essential continuity in Njoroge's characterization testifies to the powerful influence of Christianity on Ngugi himself. If Njoroge's fantasies are a product of the sociopolitical and religious factors in this specific colonial situation, then the ambiguity in the narrative attitude toward Njoroge can be ascribed to the same forces. In the final analysis, it is Ngugi's inability to define adequately his stand toward these factors that is responsible for the narrative ambiguity. The novel, then, can be seen simultaneously as a portrayal and a product of changing values. The persistence of this confusion led Ngugi to a reworking of the same issues in his next novel.

THE RIVER BETWEEN

The plot of *The River Between*, set in the late 1920's and 1930's, is centered once more on a combination of education and messianism, while the subplot examines the clash of values through the emotionally and culturally charged controversy over female circumcision. The geographic setting is allegorical: The events take place in the "heart and soul" of Kikuyu land and culture among the communities on two ridges ranged on either side of the river Honia (which means "regeneration" in Kikuyu). Both ridges, Kameno and Makuyu, claim to be the source of Kikuyu culture, but as the novel progresses, Kameno, home of the Kikuyu prophet Mugo wa Kibiro and his descendant Waiyaki, the novel's protagonist, becomes the base for those who want to retain the purity of Kikuyu culture, whereas Makuyu becomes the home of those who have converted to Christianity and have renounced various "evil" aspects of their original tradition. The ensuing conflict thus becomes emblematic of the problems of upheaval experienced by the entire culture. The stylized characterization reflects this antagonism between the desire for cultural purity and the desire to abrogate traditional values.

Among the older generation, which provides the secondary characters, the opposition is embodied in Chege and Joshua. Chege, Waiyaki's father, a minor prophet embittered by the people's disregard for his claims, is realistically aware of the specific cultural and technological superiority of European society and thus, in spite of inherent dangers, commands his son to attend the missionary school and master Western knowledge without absorbing its vices. He is simultaneously concerned with preserving Kikuyu purity and with ensuring its survival through the absorption of clearly efficacious aspects of Western culture. On the other hand, Joshua, a zealous convert who has become a self-righteous, puritanical minister, renounces Kikuyu culture as dirty, heathen, and evil. He has entirely dedicated himself to his own and other people's salvation through Christianity. Ngugi balances these static and absolute oppositions with the dynamic and relativistic attitudes of Waiyaki and Joshua's two daughters, Muthoni and Nyambura, who attempt in their different ways to synthesize the two cultures.

The subplot depicts Muthoni's disastrous attempt to combine what she considers to be the best aspects of both cultures. Even though her parents will not permit her to undergo circumcision because the church has forbidden this rite of purification and rebirth in Kikuyu culture, Muthoni decides that she must be circumcised. By becoming a circumcised Christian she hopes to combine the two cultures within herself. Unfortunately, an infection contracted during the ceremony kills Muthoni. In addition to radicalizing the two factions, her apostasy and death reveal the more profound problems of cultural transition. The fact that her notion of womanhood is predicated on circumcision shows that peripeteia involves not only physical and social changes but also ontological ones; specific modifications of a culture become meaningless unless the entire cultural gestalt is altered to accommodate particular infusions. Waiyaki sees Muthoni as a sacrifice to the clash of cultures, and when he falls in love with her uncircumcised sister, Nyambura, the subplot is deftly woven into the main plot—Waiyaki's attempt to become a messiah and an educator.

Unlike *Weep Not, Child*, where the messianic possibility is entirely confined to Njoroge's fantasies, *The River Between* presents it as an actual, unambiguous fact: While Waiyaki is still a child, his "mission" to master Western knowledge and unite the Kikuyus is revealed to him. When, along with many other students, he resigns from the Christian mission school, he gets his chance to fulfill his destiny. With the help of the people and his colleagues he establishes an independent Kikuyu school that flourishes and thus earns him the respect befitting a messiah; by successfully mediating between the English and Kikuyu cultures and by making the positive aspects of the former available to the latter, he seems to have fulfilled the prophecy. His success, however, is short-lived. Jealousy and political ambition spur a faction from Kemano to accuse him of treason and spiritual contamination because he loves an uncircumcised woman. Since he is unwilling to renounce Nyambura, Waiyaki is forced to relinquish his leadership, and his personal fate remains ominously ambiguous at the end of the novel.

The River Between is a better bildungsroman than Ngugi's first novel because Waiyaki does realize that he is a product of shifting values and that cultural synthesis is an ambiguous, complex, and even dangerous undertaking. This education of the hero is not sufficient, however, to save the novel from the confusion caused by a double narrative intention. Overtly, the narrator clearly intends to present Waiyaki as a man constantly concerned with communal welfare, yet the rhetoric of Waiyaki's contemplation demonstrates that he is entirely engrossed in his own messianic potentiality: All his dealings with people always revert to questions about his status and leadership. Furthermore, the divine source of his authority, by providing him with *transcendent* knowledge, severs him from the Kikuyu to the extent that his vision of the future, and actions based on that vision, need not rely on mundane familiarity with the people's social and political desires.

The major problem of the novel is that Ngugi seems unable to decide whether to treat his protagonist as a real messiah or to portray him as a character whose prophetic calling is a self-delusion: Waiyaki is simultaneously subjected to divine surety and human fallibility. At the end of the novel, Ngugi seems to sympathize with two incompatible feelings— with Waiyaki's decision to choose a personal relationship over communal obligation, a private cultural synthesis over a larger social synthesis, and with the people's decision to protect their culture by sacrificing a promising individual. The persistent ambiguity about

Waiyaki and the final recourse to scapegoating, which resembles so closely the pattern of grandiose self-delusion and vindication through persecution in *Weep Not, Child*, reveal once more that *The River Between* is a product of subjective anxiety. Waiyaki's insight into the anxiety caused by the peripeteia of values is applicable to the novel as a whole. According to him, this anxiety can cause a person to cling fanatically to whatever promises security. For Waiyaki and Ngugi, messianism provides that security. If one considers Ngugi's predicament at the age of fifteen, when he internalized the social preoccupation with education, leadership, and messianism, one can see that the ambiguity and ambivalence of *The River Between* are a literary transformation of the author's own traumatic experience.

A Grain of Wheat

Before writing his next novel, *A Grain of Wheat*, Ngugi studied Frantz Fanon's *The Wretched of the Earth* (1961), an experience that unmistakably altered his understanding of the psychological and cultural changes that take place in the process of anticolonial revolutions. The view that education and messianism are panaceas is entirely displaced by a clear and deep comprehension of the way out of the psychological bind produced by colonial subjugation. In *A Grain of Wheat*, Ngugi is still concerned with the reintegration of Kikuyu society, but his method has changed drastically. Instead of focusing on a single protagonist, Ngugi uses five major characters—Mugo, Karanja, Kihika, Gikonyo, and Mumbi—and a host of minor ones to contrast different kinds of personal isolation, love, and sympathy for others, and then he orchestrates a complex pattern wherein some characters move from isolation to community, some move in the opposite direction, and still others remain relatively static. By contrasting and interweaving these movements, Ngugi creates a polyphonic novel in which the experience of social regeneration and communal cohesiveness lies not in the awareness of any single character but in the interactions between various individuals and in the reader's experience of these interactions.

The novel's plot concerns an intriguing search for the traitor who betrayed Kihika, a leader of the Mau Mau guerrillas. The war is over, and, just prior to independence day, Kihika's comrades emerge from the forests in order to seek the traitor. The search, however, is really a vehicle for investigating various characters' motives and actions during the war that has destroyed the village of Thabai. The actual time encompassed by the novel is only six days, but through retrospection the reader is allowed to experience the whole Mau Mau revolution and even the prerevolutionary childhood of the protagonists as well as the mythic past of the Kikuyus. The multiplicity of viewpoints through which the reader is led to understand the characters conveys admirably Ngugi's notion that an organic community can be apprehended only through its historical and interpersonal interactions.

Ngugi's investigation of patterns of isolation and communality is focused on four men and one woman. Two of the men, Mugo and Karanja, are motivated by an almost pathological desire for isolation, and the other two, Kihika and Gikonyo, are deeply dependent on their different views of communality. Mugo, deprived of human warmth since childhood, attempts in vain to avoid all involvement. His isolation is repeatedly shattered, first by Kihika, who is seeking shelter from the colonial soldiers and whom Mugo betrays, and then by the whole village of Thabai, which, having mistaken Mugo for a supporter of Kihika and a staunch patriot, ironically invites him to become the village chief on independence day.

While Mugo gradually journeys from isolation to social integration, Karanja moves in the opposite direction. In order to remain with Mumbi, who had earlier rejected him for Gikonyo, Karanja joins the colonial police when Gikonyo is sent to a concentration camp. His collaboration with the British naturally earns him the enmity of the entire village, which expels him on independence day. While Karanja betrays the community as an abstract entity in order to remain with a specific woman, Kihika abandons his pregnant lover in order to become a guerrilla fighter and plays an important part in winning the freedom of his society. In contrast to Kihika, Gikonyo has always been dependent on concrete relationships with his mother and Mumbi. His personality and the very meaning of existence crumble when he is forcibly isolated from them. He confesses his involvement with the Mau Mau so that he can return to his village, only to find when he arrives that Mumbi has given birth to Karanja's child.

Ngugi explores these labyrinthine relationships with great skill. The retrospections, juxtapositions, and multiple interpretations of events, and the gradual, interrupted revelation of the truth represent in a concrete and poignant manner the actual reintegration of a community that has been destroyed. Ngugi's main objective, admirably realized, is to show that strength in one character can be a weakness in another and that what is constructive and desirable at one stage in a community's history is harmful at another—that all forms of fortitude and lapses are necessary for social cohesion. Even Mugo's betrayal performs a vital function in the end. His confession of the betrayal fits into the pattern of complementary wills that is essential for the cohesion of a community. Thus, where Kihika's callousness toward individuals may be undesirable in itself, its reverse, his concern for abstract humanity, proves invaluable for the freedom of his country. Where Kihika's self-sacrifice, in spite of its eventual usefulness, causes a great deal of pain to the community (because of his assassination of a British district officer, Thabai is burnt to the ground), Mugo's self-sacrifice, through his confession, is ultimately soothing. It comes to symbolize the depth of misunderstanding and the renewal of honest and open communication.

In a different manner, Kihika and Gikonyo form a complementary unit that is equally vital for the society. Kihika's disregard for the individual and concern for people in general are balanced by Gikonyo's lack of concern for an abstract conception of community, his betrayal of the Mau Mau covenant, and his powerful desire for concrete individual relations with Mumbi and his mother. Whereas Kihika's attitude is necessary for society's struggle to free itself, Gikonyo's attitude is necessary for its survival. Similarly, even Karanja's defection can be seen as a complementary necessity because he is responsible for keeping Mumbi alive while the rest of the men are either guerrillas hiding in the forests or prisoners in the camps. People are thus tied to one another in ways that they themselves fail to understand. By focusing on these interconnections, Ngugi demonstrates that relationships between individuals are more important than individual character.

The bulk of *A Grain of Wheat* represents the reintegration of Thabai through keen and accurate realism, but in order to emphasize that he is depicting the entire Kikuyu culture, Ngugi resorts to symbolism at the end of the novel. Gikonyo and Mumbi clearly symbolize the mythic ancestors of their society, Kikuyu and Mumbi. Gikonyo feels that his "reunion with Mumbi would see the rebirth of a new Kenya." In light of this symbolism, Karanja's protection of Mumbi and Mugo's confession, which is responsible for the reunion of Gikonyo and Mumbi, become significant contributions to their society. Finally, the iconography—a father, a pregnant mother, a child, a field ready for harvest, and a stool that Gikonyo intends to carve and present to Mumbi as a gift of reconciliation—implies the regeneration of community that is so central to all Ngugi's fiction. The formal structure of *A Grain of Wheat*, a perfect emblem of an actual viable society, and Ngugi's definition of community make this a unique novel in African fiction.

PETALS OF BLOOD

Toward the end of *A Grain of Wheat* there are signs that after political "independence" has been won, the struggle between British colonizers and Africans that has dominated the country and the novel will be displaced gradually by a conflict between the native political-economic elite and the peasants, who will be disinherited once again. *Petals of Blood*, set in independent Kenya in the mid-1970's, examines in depth the problem that Ngugi's previous novel has accurately predicted. In *Petals of Blood*, Kenya is drastically, perhaps too schematically, divided between the rich capitalists, portrayed as two-dimensional, greedy, conniving predators, and their peasant victims, depicted as complex individuals who become prey to a modern world they cannot control. The problem with this dichotomy is that the opposition between the poor and the rich lacks any dramatic tension, because the latter are shallow characters minimally and symbolically represented through their expensive automobiles, lavish parties, and deceptive contracts. Thus, even though Ngugi's portrayal of the economic and political situation in Kenya is broadly accurate, it is not entirely convincing.

The center of *Petals of Blood* is a powerful, fecund woman, Wanja, a prostitute who is many things to the different men around her like petals of blood. If the novel is read as an allegory, she can be seen as the protean substance of Kenya, which entices the lechery of the capitalists and sustains and inspires the resistance of the peasants. Kimeria, one of the three successful entrepreneurs in the novel, seduces Wanja while she is a teenager and then abandons her only to lust after her again when she has become the successful madam of a house of prostitution. Munira, an introspective, religious schoolteacher, is initially liberated from his repressions through her, but, after his guilt has overwhelmed him, he sees her as an incarnation of Satan. Karega, a young, nascent revolutionary, has an idyllic affair with her and finds in her the inspiration for his rebellion. Finally, Abdulla, a crippled Mau Mau warrior, treats her as a comrade and eventually fathers the child that she has desired throughout the novel.

The plot of *Petals of Blood* is similar to a Charles Dickens plot in its labyrinthine relationships and its reliance on coincidence. Ostensibly, the novel is a detective story; it begins with the arrest of three major characters, Munira, Abdulla, and Karega, who are under suspicion for the murder of three wealthy directors of the Theng-eta Breweries, Kimeria, Chui, and Muzigo. After being ignored for the vast bulk of the novel, the mystery is suddenly solved at the end by Munira's admission that he set fire to Wanja's brothel, in which the directors were trapped. The relations between characters are revealed in an equally sudden and summary fashion, with the result that the plot becomes a mere vehicle for the political substance of the novel—a detailed examination of the manner in which the rightful inheritance of the peasants and idealists has been stolen from them.

Once more this is accomplished through a series of retrospective scenes that reveal the past in the light of the present struggle. The peasants undertake an epic journey to Nairobi, the capital city, in order to confront their parliamentary representative, who has in fact ignored and even tried to plunder his constituency. The climax of this spatial journey—that is, the confrontation in the city—allows the peasants to understand the economic opposition between them and the new African elite, but through the various personal and communal stories told by the peasants to one another during their journey, they also realize that they are a part of a temporal "journey"—that they are the current embodiment of a long historical tradition. As Karega says, "The history that he had tried to teach as romantic adventures, the essence of black struggle apprehended in the imagination at the level of mere possibilities, had tonight acquired immediate flesh and blood."

Petals of Blood is at its best when it explores the lives and sensibilities of these people. Through Munira and Karega, Ngugi shows the radically different effects of similar causes. Both are expelled from Siriana high school at different times (they are a generation apart) for leading student strikes. Whereas the resultant shock and confusion experienced by Munira turns into depression and later into a pathological preoccupation with spiritual purity, the initial confusion felt by Karega is gradually displaced by an increasingly clear understanding of his place in the sociopolitical system of the country and eventually turns into a radical opposition to the new elite. Thus Munira treats people such as Wanja or Abdulla as mere objects of his lust or indifference, whereas Karega sees them as subjects whose personal histories make him aware of his own predicament and potential. The novel makes a dramatic distinction between individuals lost in their own subjectivity and those who through circumstances, personal courage, and fidelity are able to understand themselves in terms of an objectively determined social and political reality.

Unfortunately, Ngugi's sensitive representation of the inner lives of his politically oppressed characters is not matched by an equally sensitive management of the novel's structure. The caricature of the capitalists and the plot's reliance on brief, mechanical coincidences deprive the novel of a demonstrated and felt struggle between the exploiters and the exploited. Instead of using viable fictive embodiments of oppressive forces, Ngugi relies heavily on discursive delineation of capitalist exploitation. At times, the novel sounds like a leftist pamphlet. In contrast to *A Grain of Wheat*, where Ngugi's political concerns are perfectly interlocked with a well-wrought and ingenious structure, *Petals of Blood* is overwhelmed by the writer's sensitive and moving depiction of the peasants' lives and by his justified anger over callous exploitation and broken promises.

Devil on the Cross

Devil on the Cross is another passionate denunciation of postcolonial abuses. Written on stolen bits of toilet paper during Ngugi's year in prison, the novel features, again, several protagonists—mostly peasants—who are grievously wronged by the corrupt politicians and bureaucrats of modern Kenya. With this novel and the nonfiction works that followed, Ngugi solidified his commitment to a revolutionary African literature—outraged, combative, and uncompromising.

Matigari

In *Matigari* Ngugi continues to record Kenya's postcolonial struggle, but in this novel he moves away from realism and adopts a fluidity of time and space that is mythological in tone. At the outset, he warns the "Reader/Listener" that the narrative is purely imaginary in its action, characters, and setting. It follows the adventures of the mythical Matigari, who embodies the virtues, values, and purity of the betrayed and abused people he sets out to rouse from their apathy. Whether Ngugi succeeds in mythologizing remains questionable, for the landscape, characters, circumstances, and historical events are obviously Kenyan. In fact, when the 1986 edition appeared in the original Kikuyu language, so many Kenyans were talking about Matigari that officials ordered his arrest. When they discovered that the suspected rabble-rouser was fictional, they banned the book.

Matigari denounces contemporary Kenya, where a privileged few, in connection with representatives of overseas interests, rule and exploit the masses, thereby reversing the hard-fought struggle for independence. Matigari ma Njiruungi, whose name means "he who survived the bullets," emerges from the forest, sets his weapons aside, and dons the belt of peace to move through the countryside to rediscover his true family—a free Kenyan people who live in a just society and who share its wealth. Along the way he meets the downtrodden and dispossessed, and he faces all the ills the contaminated society has produced: homeless children, dissidents harassed and murdered by the police, young women forced into prostitution, and much more. In opposition to the suffering masses stand the black politicians and their cronies, who have grown rich through collaboration with international business interests.

The novel also contains variations on familiar themes, such as the role of Christianity in oppression and the failure of Western education. At the same time, Ngugi subverts the Christian myth by turning Matigari into a modern Jesus who moves among the people and faces rejection. The biblical allusions become especially evident in the prison scenes. For example, Matigari's fellow detainees resemble Jesus' disciples; one even betrays Matigari. The novel also contains the Swiftian elements of satire that characterize *Devil on the Cross*. *Matigari* finally emerges as a powerful account of the postcolonial state, however—an indictment not only against the corruption in Kenya but also against the conditions that prevail in numerous African nations.

WIZARD OF THE CROW

Wizard of the Crow, which is set in a fictional East African country named the Free Republic of Aburiria, artfully and satirically delineates the inner workings of that most pernicious, toxic, and notorious of twentieth and twenty-first century African institutions, the strong-arm dictatorship. Ngugi sees the institution as both vulnerable and thriving, buoyed as it is by credible threats of torture and death aimed at those who oppose it as well as by the power-seeking Western world's collusion with it. In Aburiria, the mad leader known simply as the Ruler is eventually deposed, only to give way to another thug with the usual dictatorial traits of incompetence, brutality, and toxicity. At novel's end, however, Ngugi does supply readers with some trace of hope for the future of Aburiria, albeit a highly ambiguous one, the hope being that freedom will come to those nations beset by one-person rule—but down the road a bit.

This lengthy political novel features the corrupt world of an archetypal power-hungry gangster, the self-proclaimed First Ruler of the Free Republic of Aburiria, a venomous though intelligent paranoid who surrounds himself with such ridiculous and yet dangerous toadies as Wonderful Tumbo, minister of police; Machokali, minister for foreign affairs; Julius Caesar Big Ben Mambo, minister of information; Silver Sikiokuu, governor of the Central Bank; and Titus Tajirika, minister of defense. These bumbling but still often terrifying agents will sell out anyone—including the Ruler himself—for personal gain. Opposing their self-serving machinations are two unlikely proponents of democracy and change: Kamiti, an unemployed university business major and graduate, and Kamiti's lover and fellow conspirator, the beautiful and accomplished Nyawira, a former bar hostess.

Kamiti rises to become the legendary Aburirian man of powerful magic, "Wizard of the Crow," and Nyawira becomes the Wizard's consort, the so-called Limping Witch. Together, using their powerful wit and imagination, the Wizard and the Witch find clever "magical" ways to trick the government officials who oppose them and, in the process, undermine the officials' lucrative positions. Soon the two lovers find themselves the stuff of Aburirian folk legend—ones who can take on the establishment and never be caught. In addition to Kamiti and Nyawira, the author includes in his cast two characters, the saintly Maritha and Mariko, who labor against what they see as the works of the devil in their country. In *Wizard of the Crow*, Ngugi provides an entertaining, although at times somewhat long-winded, commentary on one of the chief reasons sub-Saharan African nations are not as well-off as they should be, given their natural resources and their lively and potentially resourceful populations.

Abdul R. JanMohamed; Robert L. Ross
Updated by John D. Raymer

OTHER MAJOR WORKS

SHORT FICTION: *Secret Lives, and Other Stories*, 1975.

PLAYS: *The Black Hermit*, pr. 1962; *This Time Tomorrow: Three Plays*, 1970 (includes *The Rebels*, *The Wound in My Heart*, and *This Time Tomorrow*); *The Trial of Dedan Kimathi*, pr. 1974 (with Micere Githae-Mugo); *Ngaahika Ndeenda*, pr. 1977 (with Ngugi wa Mirii; *I Will Marry When I Want*, 1982); *Maitu Njugira*, pb. 1982 (with Ngugi wa Mirii; *Mother, Sing for Me*, 1986).

NONFICTION: *Homecoming: Essays on African and Caribbean Literature, Culture, and Politics*, 1972; *Detained: A Writer's Prison Diary*, 1981; *Writers in Politics*, 1981 (revised 1997); *Barrel of a Pen: Resistance to Repression in Neo-colonial Kenya*, 1983; *Decolonising the Mind: The Politics of Language in African Literature*, 1986; *Writing Against Neocolonialism*, 1986; *Moving the Centre: The Struggle for Cultural Freedoms*, 1993; *Penpoints, Gunpoints, and Dreams: Toward a Critical Theory of the Arts and the State in Africa*, 1998.

MISCELLANEOUS: *The World of Ngugi wa Thiong'o*, 1995 (Charles Cantalupo, editor).

BIBLIOGRAPHY

Booker, M. Keith. "Ngugi wa Thiong'o: *Devil on the Cross*." In *The African Novel in English: An Introduction*. Portsmouth, N.H.: Heinemann, 1998. Discussion of *Devil on the Cross* addresses many of Ngugi's preoccupations, including the brutality of class distinctions, his connections with and problems concerning the Western literary tradition, Kenya's resistance to British economic and political forces, and the future of Africa itself.

Cantalupo, Charles, ed. *Ngugi wa Thiong'o: Texts and Contexts*. Edinburgh: Edinburgh University Press, 1997. Selection of contributions from a major conference held in 1994 to honor and examine Ngugi's work. Focuses primarily on the prose works, examining issues such as Ngugi's status as an exile and his use of the Kikuyu language.

Gikandi, Simon. *Ngugi wa Thiong'o*. New York: Cambridge University Press, 2001. Examines each of Ngugi's works in the context of its historical background and in the light of Ngugi's life. Asserts that Ngugi's novels are of primary importance to Ngugi himself, and that the author's drama and criticism are meant to supplement the novels.

Lovesey, Oliver. *Ngugi wa Thiong'o*. New York: Twayne, 2000. Provides a good introduction to Ngugi's life and work for the general reader. Presents five chapters of criticism and analysis as well as a chronology of the author's life and an annotated bibliography.

Nazareth, Peter, ed. *Critical Essays on Ngugi wa Thiong'o*. New York: Twayne, 2000. Collection of essays offers a wide range of discussion of Ngugi's work. Topics addressed include themes, language use, and use of the oral tradition in Ngugi's novels.

Parker, Michael, and Roger Starkey, eds. *Postcolonial Literatures: Achebe, Ngugi, Desai, Walcott*. New York: St. Martin's Press, 1995. Presents thoughtful examination of the works of Ngugi, Chinua Achebe, Anita Desai, and Derek Walcott. Includes bibliographical references and index.

Sewlall, Harry. "Writing from the Periphery: The Case of Ngugi and Conrad." *English in Africa* 30 (May, 2003): 55-69. Offers a thoughtful appraisal of Ngugi's strong debt to and ties with English novelist Joseph Conrad's anti-imperial vision of Africa. Also addresses the difficulties faced by both Ngugi and Conrad in writing in languages other than those to which they were born.

Sicherman, Carol. *Ngugi wa Thiong'o: A Bibliography of Primary and Secondary Sources, 1957-1987*. London: Hans Zell, 1989. A treasure for the scholar, with citations of Ngugi's works in the original languages, manuscripts and other unpublished material, translations, secondary sources, undated material, nonprint media, and indexes of authors, editors, translators, titles, interviews, and subjects. Includes a brief introduction and preface.

Williams, Patrick. *Ngugi wa Thiong'o*. Manchester, England: Manchester University Press, 2000. Presents analysis and interpretation of all of Ngugi's writings through *Penpoints, Gunpoints, and Dreams*.

GEORGE ORWELL
Eric Arthur Blair

Born: Motihari, Bengal, India; June 25, 1903
Died: London, England; January 21, 1950
Also known as: Eric Arthur Blair

PRINCIPAL LONG FICTION
Burmese Days, 1934
A Clergyman's Daughter, 1935
Keep the Aspidistra Flying, 1936
Coming Up for Air, 1939
Animal Farm, 1945
Nineteen Eighty-Four, 1949

OTHER LITERARY FORMS

Since the mid-1940's, George Orwell has been considered one of the world's premier essayists. Combining reportage, the polemical essay, fictional techniques, and refracted autobiographical detail, his works defy precise generic definition. Orwell's numerous nonfiction works have been compiled in *The Collected Essays, Journalism, and Letters of George Orwell* (1968), edited by Sonia Orwell and Ian Angus.

ACHIEVEMENTS

Although George Orwell is widely recognized as one of the best essayists of the twentieth century, his reputation as a novelist rests almost entirely on two works: the political allegory *Animal Farm* and the dystopian *Nineteen Eighty-Four*. Both have been translated into so many other languages and have been read so widely that the adjective "Orwellian" has international currency—synonymous, as Bernard Crick has put it, with the "ghastly political future." Indeed, Jeffrey Meyers has asserted that Orwell, the writer of essays, political tracts, and fiction, "is more widely read than perhaps any other serious writer of the twentieth-century."

BIOGRAPHY

George Orwell was born Eric Arthur Blair, the son of Richard Walmesley Blair and Ida (Limouzin) Blair. Orwell was born in India and lived there for four years, until his father moved the family back to England, to a small house named Nutshell, located in Henley-on-Thames. After a short leave, Orwell's father returned alone to India; his wife and children remained in England, where he rejoined them later, upon his retirement. With his father's return, Orwell, like most male members of the upper middle class, was sent away to boarding school, St. Cyprian's, located at Eastbourne on the Sussex coast. After several

George Orwell
(Library of Congress)

miserable years, as Orwell describes them in his autobiographical *Such, Such Were the Joys* (1953), he won a scholarship to Eton, the public school that would forever set him apart from the working classes about which he was so concerned during most of his adult life.

Considered rather unacademic at Eton, Orwell graduated in December, 1921, and, after a decision not to attend university, he applied to the India Office for the position of imperial police officer. Five years in Burma, from 1922 to 1927, shaped the impressionable young man so as to make him forever sympathetic to individuals victimized by governmental bureaucracy and imperialistic power. Orwell left Burma in the summer of 1927, ostensibly on sick leave (he suffered from a lung condition most of his life). At some point early in his leave, Orwell wrote a letter of resignation to the India Office and explained to his skeptical parents that all he really wanted to do was to write.

In 1928, Orwell commenced a long, five-year apprenticeship as a writer, time spent as a tramp in both Paris and London and in the writing and rewriting of countless manuscripts. By 1933 he had assumed the name by which he is known and had produced, in addition to at least two destroyed novels, the nonfictional *Down and Out in Paris and London* (1933) and his first novel, *Burmese Days*, published one year later.

From 1933 to 1937, Orwell continued to develop his literary talents, producing two more novels, a nonfiction book about his experiences with poverty-stricken coal miners in Wigan (*The Road to Wigan Pier*, 1937), and several essays, occasional pieces, and book reviews. By the end of this period, he had also married for the first time and, within a year or so of that, gone to Spain. In perhaps the most singular experience of his life to date, the Spanish Civil War found Orwell on the front lines, a member of a Partido Obrero de Unificación Marxista (a Marxist worker's party) brigade; from that time on, Orwell passionately declared himself a fighter for "democratic Socialism." In that context, he wrote his most famous nonfictional work, *Homage to Catalonia* (1938). After being wounded (and nearly imprisoned), Orwell escaped Spain with the help of his wife, returned to England, and continued his literary career. Within another year, his lungs still causing him problems, Orwell moved to the dry climate of Morocco, where he wrote much of *Coming Up for Air*.

His fourth novel was buried under mounting war concerns and preparations. Orwell, unable to join the military because of his health, became a spokesman for the British Broadcasting Corporation (BBC). During the last years of the war, Orwell finished writing *Animal Farm*, only to see it rejected by almost every major publisher in England and the United States. Finally brought out in August, 1945, during the last days of the Pacific War, *Animal Farm* was a work of near perfection, making Orwell's name internationally known, so that when *Nineteen Eighty-Four* was published four years later, the world came to realize that both works would henceforth be considered literary classics, satires ranking with Sir Thomas More's *De Optimo Reipublicae Statu, deque Nova Insula Utopia* (1516; *Utopia, 1551*) and Jonathan Swift's *A Tale of a Tub* (1704). Orwell's death in 1950 at the age of forty-six was a tragic loss to the world of letters and to the larger world with which he always kept in touch.

Analysis

Excepting *Animal Farm*, most critics view George Orwell's fictions as aesthetically flawed creations, the work of a political thinker whose artistry was subordinate to his intensely didactic, partisan passions. This reaction to Orwell's novels was generally promoted posthumously, since his fiction in the 1930's was often ignored by the larger reading public and panned by those reviewers who did pick up one of his books. The early academic critics—up to the late 1960's—were often Orwell's personal friends or acquaintances, who tended to see his early novels as conventionally realistic and strongly autobiographical. Even his masterpieces, *Animal Farm* and *Nineteen Eighty-Four*, were viewed as formally undistinguished, however powerful their message. It was not until the second generation of critics began looking at Orwell's fiction that a more balanced assessment was possible.

Burmese Days

Orwell's first published novel, *Burmese Days*, concerns the life of John Flory, an English policeman in Burma during the early 1920's. The plot is fairly straightforward. After a lengthy introduction to Flory's personality and daily life, Orwell dramatizes him as a man blemished with a physical stigma, a birthmark, and puzzled by moral dilemma—how to deal with the increasingly rebellious natives, to whom he is secretly sympathetic but against whom he must wield the club of imperialistic authority. In the middle of this dilemma, Elizabeth arrives, a young English woman who is fresh faced but decidedly a traditional "burra memsahib." Flory attempts to win both her heart and mind—much to the dismay of his Burmese mistress, Ma Hla May—and succeeds in doing neither, even though he manages to half succeed in proposing marriage during an earthquake. With a mind too closed to anything not properly British, and a heart only to be won by someone very English, Elizabeth forgets Flory's attentions with the arrival of Verrall, an English military policeman, who will in turn reject her after his billet is completed. A humble Flory waits for Elizabeth, and after Verrall has left takes her to church services, confident that he has outlasted his rival. Unfortunately, Flory is humiliated by Ma Hla May, is repulsed yet again by Elizabeth, and, in a mood of despair, commits suicide, killing both his dog and himself.

In such a world, Flory is emphatically not meant to be a sympathetic character, but rather a victim of the very political order he has sworn to uphold. In effect, Orwell has laid a trap for the unwary reader. Too close an identification with Flory, too intense a desire to have him succeed in marrying Elizabeth—an unholy alliance of imperialistic Englishwoman and revolutionary, thinking pariah—will prevent the reader from recognizing the irreconcilable contradictions inherent in the British presence in Burma.

Coming Up for Air

Orwell's fourth published novel, *Coming Up for Air*, was written in Marrakesh, Morocco, shortly after the author had recovered from yet another bout with tubercular lesions of the lungs. Although the novel sold moderately well for the time (a first printing of two thousand copies and a second printing of one thousand), many critics were vaguely condescending toward the hero, George Bowling, a middle-class insurance salesman who longs for the golden country of the past while simultaneously dreading the horrors of a second world war, then only months away. Many of the themes more fully developed in *Nineteen Eighty-Four* find their initial expression in Orwell's last conventional novel, set before the outbreak of the devastation that the next six years would bring.

Coming Up for Air is set in London during the late 1930's; Orwell employs a first-person narrative to describe the life of George Bowling, a middle-aged, middle-class salesman, whose first set of false teeth marks a major milestone in his life. Musing in front of a mirror while he prepares for work one morning, George's mind wanders back to the past, the golden England of thirty years earlier when he was growing up. As he goes about his day, disgusted with all the evidence of modern life in front of him—the casual brutalities, the tasteless food, the bombers overhead—George forms a plan to return to Lower Binfield, his childhood home, and, by extension, the simple life he had once led. Unfortunately, his return only confirms the all-pervasive slovenliness of the modern world: Lower Binfield has been swallowed by a sprawling suburb, his adolescent sweetheart has become a frowsy old married woman (she is all of two years older than he), and the fishing hole (once filled with huge finny dreams) has been emptied of water and filled with trash. Shocked and completely disenchanted, Bowling makes plans to get at least a relaxing few days from the trip when a bomber accidentally drops a bomb close by, killing and wounding several people. In thorough disgust, Bowling packs, leaves, and returns home to face his wife, who has somehow found out where he has gone, although his motives for going will be forever incomprehensible to her.

A plot summary of the novel fails to do justice to the subtle tonal shifts and complicated psychological changes Orwell employs in presenting his portrait of the average man waiting for the Apocalypse. Orwell uses the ancient theme of the double (or doppelgänger) to illustrate the self-fragmentation of European man prior to the outbreak of the war. George Bowling is divided into two "selves." Tubby is the outwardly fat, insensitive insurance tout who is able to function successfully in a fast-paced, competitive world that would eat up less hardened personalities, but his character can survive only at the cost of any sort of satisfying inner life. Georgie, on the other hand, would be lost in the modern rat race and so is protected by Tubby; nevertheless, Georgie can give expression to the memories, the sensitivities, the love for natural pleasures that Tubby (and George Bowling) would have to forgo to remain functional. Thus, George Bowling devised a strategy for living both materially successfully and psychologically well in the modern world, doing so by splitting his identity into Tubby and Georgie. *Coming Up for Air* details the ongoing dialogue between these two "selves"—a conversation that reflects the strains of modern living as well as any other novelist has done in the twentieth century.

Furthermore, Orwell has modified the literary conventions of the doppelgänger to suit his own needs. Whereas the death of one-half of the double usually means the destruction, ultimately, of both, Orwell has Tubby live on after Georgie is symbolically destroyed by the bombing plane. The tonal change at this point, rather like the tonal change in Joseph Heller's *Catch-22* (1961) with the death of Kid Sampson, shows the reader the world that Orwell envisioned between 1938 and 1939, one horrible enough to prevent total escape even by death. It is, however, typically Orwellian that however horrible human bondage can make the cultural world, nature, of which humankind is a part, has enough ebullient energy to wait out any social mess—a wait without immediate hope, without idols, but also without hopeless despair. George Bowling leaves Lower Binfield, returning to his scold of a wife, Hilda; to the everlasting round of bills, worries, war clouds on the horizon, and a death-in-life without Georgie—but, as the novel's epigraph states, "He's dead, but he won't lie down."

Animal Farm

Animal Farm is one of those rare books before which critics lay down their pens. As a self-contained "fairy story," the book can be read and understood by children not old enough to pronounce most of the words in an average junior high school history text. As a political satire, *Animal Farm* can be highly appreciated by those who actually lived through the terrible days of World War II. As an allegory concerned with the limitations and abuses of political power, the novel has been pored over eagerly by several generations of readers.

The novel is built around historical events in the Soviet Union from before the October Revolution to the end of World War II; it does this by using the frame of reference of animals in a farmyard, the Manor Farm, owned by a Mr. Jones. Drunk most of the time and, like Czar Nicholas II of Russia in the second decade of the twentieth century, out of touch with the governed, Jones neglects his farm (allegorically representing the Soviet Union, or by extension, almost any oppressed country), causing much discontent and resentment among his animals. One day, after Jones does his nightly rounds, Major, an imposing pig (Vladimir Ilich Lenin), tells the other animals of a dream he has had concerning theories about the way they have been living. Animals have been exploited by Mr. Jones and humankind generally, but Major has dreamed of a time when they will throw over their yokes and live free, sharing equally both the profits and the hazards of their work. Major teaches the animals the words to a song, "Beasts of England" (The Internationale), and tells them to look to the future and the betterment of all animals; three days later he dies.

The smartest of the animals, the pigs, are aroused by his speech and by the song; they secretly learn to read and write, developing a philosophical system called animalism (Communism, Bolshevism) whose principles are taught to all the animals. When Jones forgets one day to feed them (as Russians starved near the end of their involvement in World War I), the animals revolt spontaneously, driving out Jones, his wife (Russian nobility), and Moses, the raven (the Russian Orthodox Church). The animals rejoice, feeling a sense of camaraderie and esprit de corps, and set about to build a new life.

The pigs, however, by taking on the responsibility of organization, also take over certain decision-making processes—as well as all the milk and apples; in fact, Orwell has himself stated that the first sign of corruption, the taking of the cow's milk, led to the inevitable destruction of everything else. Two pigs in particular, Snowball (Leon Trotsky) and Napoleon (Joseph Stalin), argue constantly, while a third, Squealer (*Pravda*, Tass) appears more than happy to endorse any course of action with his adroit use of language and his physical habit of skipping from side to side as he speaks. After changing the name from Manor Farm to Animal Farm, the pigs paint on the side of the barn the seven commandments of animalism, the most important being: "All animals are equal." Meanwhile, Napoleon has been privately raising puppies born on the farm after the overthrow of Jones, puppies that develop into savage attack dogs (secret police, People's Commissariat of Internal Affairs, or NKVD); with these, he will one day drive off the farm all of his personal enemies, especially the brilliant theoretician Snowball. Also soon to be lost to Animal Farm is Mollie (the bourgeoisie), who shows up at Pilkingtons (the West, England).

At this point, the work becomes more difficult, the pigs assume practical control, and the arguments become more intense. Even though Benjamin, the donkey (Tolstoyan intellectuals), remains cynical about the supposed heaven on earth, Boxer, the horse (the peasantry), vows to work harder; nevertheless, the animals continue to lose their spirit and cohesiveness until attacked by Farmer Jones, who tries to regain the Farm. Because of Snowball's brilliant strategy, Jones is driven off in what is thereafter called the Battle of the Cowshed (the Civil War).

Following the victory celebration, Snowball and Napoleon move toward a decisive parting: The former wants to move full speed ahead with the building of the windmill (permanent revolution), while the latter thinks the most important task immediately ahead is the increase in food production (develop socialism in Russia first). After much debate and just before what could be an affirmative vote for Snowball's policies, Napoleon unleashes his secretly kept dogs on his rival, chasing him out of Animal Farm forever. Henceforth, the unchallenged leader abolishes Sunday meetings, increasingly changes rules at will, and even announces that the building of the windmill was his idea.

The animals continue to work hard, still believing that they are working for themselves. The changes Napoleon institutes, however, are so at variance with the initial rules of Animal Farm, and life gets to be so much drudgery, that no one has the memory to recall the ideals of the past, nor the energy to change the present—even if memories were sound.

Very soon, life at Animal Farm seems indistinguishable from the life the animals led at Manor Farm. Orwell is not so much ultimately pessimistic as he is realistically moral: Institutionalized hierarchy begets privilege, which begets corruption of power. The first mistake of the animals was to give over their right to decide who got the milk and apples. Lord Action's famous statement could not be more appropriate: "Power tends to corrupt; absolute power corrupts absolutely."

NINETEEN EIGHTY-FOUR

Nineteen Eighty-Four is Orwell's most famous work. As a fantasy set in the future, the novel has terrified readers for more than thirty years—frightened them into facing the prospect of the ultimate tyranny: mind control. As a parody of conditions in postwar England, it is, as Anthony Burgess argues in his novel *1985* (1978), a droll, rather Swiftean exaggeration of then current trends straining the social and political fabric of British culture. As a critique of the way in which human beings construct their social reality, the novel has so affected the modern world that much of its language (like that of its predecessor, *Animal Farm*) has entered into the everyday language of English-speaking peoples everywhere: "doublethink," "newspeak," "thoughtcrime," and "Big Brother." Bernard Crick has argued that *Nineteen Eighty-Four* is intimately related to *Animal Farm* and that both works convey Orwell's most important message: Liberty means telling people what they do not want to hear. If the vehicle for the telling gets corrupted, then the message itself will always be corrupted, garbled; finally, the very thoughts that led to the utterances in the first place will be shackled, constrained not only from the outside but also from the inside. To think clearly, to speak openly and precisely, was a heritage Englishmen received from their glorious past; it was a legacy so easily lost that it needed to be guarded fiercely, lest those who promulgated ideologies of right or left took away what had been won with such difficulty. That was where the danger lay, with those who practiced the "smelly little orthodoxies" that are still "contending for our souls."

The story begins with a man named Winston Smith, who is hurrying home on a cold, windy April day as the clocks are striking thirteen. With this ominous beginning, the reader is quickly plunged into a gritty, decaying world where the political order so dominates everyday life that independent thought is a crime, love is forbidden, and language seems to say the opposite of what one has normally come to expect. As Winston's daily life unfolds, the reader quickly learns that the whole world has been divided into three geographical areas: Oceania, Eurasia, and Eastasia. All are engaged in perpetual warfare with one or both of the others, not for territorial or religious reasons but primarily for social control. At some point, atomic warfare had made total war unthinkable, yet it suits the political leaders of Oceania (the same is also true of the other two political areas) to keep the population in a general state of anxiety about foreign attack. Under the guise of national concern, Oceania's leaders keep the population under their collective thumb through the use of propaganda (from the Ministry of Truth), through outright, brutally applied force (from the Ministry of Love), through eternally short rations (Ministry of Plenty), and through the waging of perpetual war (Ministry of Peace). The ruling elite, called the Inner Party, make up only 2 percent of the population; the Outer Party, the next 13 percent. The remainder, some 85 percent of the population, make up the oppressed masses; those in this group are called Proles.

Winston, a member of the Outer Party, has been disturbed by strange thoughts of late, and one day he purchases a small, bound volume of blank paper, a diary in which he can record his most private thoughts without being observed by the omnipresent telescreen manned by members of the Thought Police. In his diary, he records his first thought: "Down with Big Brother!" To compound such a heinous thoughtcrime, he begins a liaison with a pretty young woman, a member of the Anti-Sex League, named Julia. After their affair has progressed for some time, they are contacted by a man named O'Brien, who enlists their aid in combating Big Brother by joining a group called the Brotherhood. O'Brien gives Winston a book, written by a man named Emannuel Goldstein, called *The Theory and Practice of Oligarchical Collectivism*. Having made love to Julia in a room rented from an old Prole (secretly a member of the Thought Police), Winston begins reading to her from Goldstein's book, actually an exposition of the theory that Orwell has used to construct *Nineteen Eighty-Four*.

Although Winston is fascinated, Julia, a rebel from the waist down only, falls asleep, and, after a while, so does Winston. They awake many hours later, are captured by the Thought Police, who apparently knew of their hideaway from the first, and are taken to rooms in the Ministry of Love. There, they find that O'Brien is in reality a member of the Thought Police; he alternately tortures and debates with Winston, trying to convince him that he must love Big Brother.

When torture fails, Winston is taken to Room 101, where he will be subjected to that which he fears most—in his case, rats. He gives in, begs them to "do it to Julia," and is ultimately convinced that he loves Big Brother. The novel ends as Winston, having exchanged mutual conversations of betrayal with Julia, sits at the Chestnut Café drinking Victory Gin, completely brainwashed and committed to Big Brother.

Much has been said about the ultimate pessimism of *Nineteen Eighty-Four* being related to Orwell's fatal illness, which he fought unsuccessfully during the composition of the novel. If, however, one thinks of Orwell's fiction less in biographical terms and more in relation to artistic intention, then such a conclusion could be subject to argument. Although the novel ends with Winston in what Northrop Frye called the sixth level of irony, unrelieved bondage, one should draw a distinction, as Orwell does in his other writings (most notably in the essay "A Good Word for the Vicar of Bray"), between humans' actions as cultural beings and their activities as creatures of planet Earth, natural beings.

As political creatures, humans and their purely cultural institutions could, Orwell believes, develop a world such as the one portrayed in *Nineteen Eighty-Four*. This would be impossible, however, for humans as biological residents of the planet Earth. Humankind never displays hubris more graphically than does O'Brien in his speech about the party's supposed control of nature. In Orwell's view, human beings will never fully control nature, because they are only a part of what they wish to control. The great chestnut tree blossoming over Winston and his degeneration as a free being is Orwell's symbol indicating that the natural world can outlast humankind's cultural and political aberrations. "The planting of a tree," says Orwell, "if [it] takes root . . . will far outlive the visible effect of any of your other actions, good or evil." If there is hope for Oceania in the Proles, perhaps it is because they are instinctively closer to the natural world symbolized by the chestnut tree. Nevertheless, whether one thinks there is any hope for the people of that world or not, their existence has served as a warning to the larger world: The price of the right to tell people what they do not want to hear is never too high to pay.

John V. Knapp

Other major works

NONFICTION: *Down and Out in Paris and London*, 1933; *The Road to Wigan Pier*, 1937; *Homage to Catalonia*, 1938; *Inside the Whale, and Other Essays*, 1940; *The Lion and the Unicorn*, 1941; *Critical Essays*, 1946 (also known as *Dickens, Dali, and Others*); *Shooting an Elephant, and Other Essays*, 1950; *Such, Such Were the Joys*, 1953; *The Collected*

Essays, Journalism, and Letters of George Orwell, 1968 (4 volumes; Sonia Orwell and Ian Angus, editors); *Orwell: The War Broadcasts*, 1985 (also known as *Orwell: The War Commentaries*, 1986); *The Lost Orwell*, 2006 (Peter Davison, editor).

MISCELLANEOUS: *Orwell: The Lost Writings*, 1985; *The Complete Works of George Orwell*, 1986-1998 (20 volumes; Peter Davison, editor).

BIBLIOGRAPHY

Bloom, Harold, ed. *George Orwell*. Updated ed. New York: Chelsea House, 2007. Collection of essays provides analyses of Orwell's works, including the novels *Animal Farm*, *Nineteen Eighty-Four*, and *Coming Up for Air*. Includes bibliography, chronology, and index.

Bowker, Gordon. *Inside George Orwell*. New York: Palgrave Macmillan, 2003. Biography presents the "human face" of Orwell, describing his inner emotional life and its relationship to his political activities and ideas. One of the better books about Orwell to be published in the centenary year of his birth.

Crick, Bernard. *George Orwell: A Life*. Boston: Little, Brown, 1980. Important full-scale biography considers all phases of Orwell's career, drawing on extensive use of the writer's archives and other manuscript sources as well as numerous publications. Crick was the first biographer of Orwell to benefit from unlimited rights of quotation from Orwell's works held under copyright.

Davison, Peter. *George Orwell: A Literary Life*. New York: St. Martin's Press, 1996. Follows the course of Orwell's career as a writer. Includes background chapters explaining Orwell's origins, but focuses chiefly on his literary influences and relationships, such as those with his publishers and editors.

Hitchens, Christopher. *Why Orwell Matters*. New York: Basic Books, 2002. Emphasizes Orwell's criticism of Nazism and Stalinism—philosophies toward which he never softened his view in order to sell books. Argues that Orwell's analyses of those two governmental systems continue to apply in the early twenty-first century.

Holderness, Graham, Bryan Loughrey, and Nahem Yousaf, eds. *George Orwell*. New York: St. Martin's Press, 1998. Collection of essays on Orwell's novels covers topics such as his use of allegory, his politics, his view of England, and his handling of form, character, and theme. Includes bibliography.

Meyers, Jeffrey. *Orwell: Wintry Conscience of a Generation*. New York: W. W. Norton, 2000. Well-researched biography provides a balanced look at Orwell's life and work. Vividly describes the contrast between Orwell the writer and Orwell the man.

Reilly, Patrick. *"Nineteen Eighty-Four": Past, Present, and Future*. Boston: Twayne, 1989. Spirited defense of Orwell's last novel upholds the author's conceptions against the claims of modern detractors. Contains a detailed chronology and an annotated bibliography.

Rodden, John, ed. *The Cambridge Companion to George Orwell*. New York: Cambridge

University Press, 2007. Collection of essays provides information on a wide range of Orwell's works and literary influences. Some of the essays analyze *Animal Farm* and *Nineteen Eighty-Four*; others discuss Orwell's response to the political events of his time.

Sandison, Alan. *George Orwell After "Nineteen Eighty-Four."* New York: Macmillan, 1986. Interpretive work views Orwell's writings as a reflection of a long intellectual tradition of religious and philosophical individualism. A lengthy postscript presents Sandison's views on other works about Orwell.

Saunders, Loraine. *The Unsung Artistry of George Orwell: The Novels from "Burmese Days" to "Nineteen Eighty-Four."* Burlington, Vt.: Ashgate, 2008. Offers reappraisal of all of Orwell's novels, arguing that the novels published in the 1930's deserve as much credit as the subsequent works. Examines the influences of writer George Gissing and of 1930's politics on Orwell's work, and also discusses Orwell's depictions of women.

Shelden, Michael. *Orwell: The Authorized Biography.* New York: HarperCollins, 1991. Extensive, detailed work helps to place Orwell's works within the context of the events of his life. Includes notes and a bibliography.

KATHERINE ANNE PORTER

Born: Indian Creek, Texas; May 15, 1890
Died: Silver Spring, Maryland; September 18, 1980
Also known as: Callie Russell Porter

PRINCIPAL LONG FICTION
Noon Wine, 1937 (novella)
Old Mortality, 1937 (novella)
Pale Horse, Pale Rider, 1938 (novella)
Pale Horse, Pale Rider: Three Short Novels, 1939 (includes the 3 novellas above)
Ship of Fools, 1962

OTHER LITERARY FORMS

Katherine Anne Porter is best known for her short fiction. Her stories appear in *Flowering Judas, and Other Stories* (1930), *The Leaning Tower, and Other Stories* (1944), and *The Old Order* (1944) and were gathered in *The Collected Stories of Katherine Anne Porter* (1965). Criticism, essays, and poems were collected in *The Days Before* (1952) and *The Collected Essays and Occasional Writings* (1970).

ACHIEVEMENTS

Katherine Anne Porter's solid and lasting reputation as a writer is based on a very small output of published work: one novel, a handful of novellas, and fewer than two dozen stories. This slender output, however, represents only a small portion of the fiction she wrote during her lifetime. Exacting and self-critical, she discarded many more stories than she published. By the time her first story appeared in print, she had already developed her fictional techniques to near perfection, and the maturity and craft of her style in *Flowering Judas, and Other Stories*, her first published collection, never was surpassed by her later fiction. Porter early established her reputation with literary critics and only later became widely known and read. In 1931, one year after the publication of her first volume, she was granted a Guggenheim Fellowship, an award she received again in 1938. The Society of Libraries of New York University awarded her its first annual gold medal for literature in 1940 upon the publication of *Pale Horse, Pale Rider*. A Modern Library edition of *Flowering Judas, and Other Stories* appeared that same year. In 1943, she was elected a member of the National Institute of Arts and Letters, and in 1949, she accepted her first appointment as writer-in-residence and guest lecturer at Stanford University. In later years, she held similar positions in many other colleges and universities, including the University of Chicago, the University of Michigan, Washington and Lee University, the University of Liège, and the University of Virginia.

By the time she published *Ship of Fools* in 1962, Porter had received three more honors: a Ford Foundation grant in 1959, the O. Henry Memorial Award in 1962 for her story "Holiday," and the Emerson-Thoreau bronze medal of the American Academy of Arts and Sciences. *Ship of Fools* became a Book-of-the-Month Club selection and an immediate best seller. In the face of its overwhelming popular success, some critics charged that Porter had forsaken her artistic standards in favor of writing a book that would appeal to a large audience. *Ship of Fools* also was criticized for its pessimism and for its failure to conform neatly to the structure of a novel, a supposed flaw especially irksome to those who had admired the formal perfection of Porter's earlier works. Porter herself was surprised by the book's popularity. She had abandoned the form of her earlier work—with its tight plots centered on the fate of a single character—but she had moved deliberately on to something else. She was still writing "honest," she said, a quality that characterized all her fiction. First and last, she was still an artist, a label she applied to herself unhesitatingly.

Though Porter published no new fiction after *Ship of Fools*, her critical and public acclaim grew. It reached its peak when she received both the Pulitzer Prize and the National Book Award in fiction in 1966.

BIOGRAPHY

Katherine Anne Porter was born Callie Russell Porter in Indian Creek, Texas, on May 15, 1890. She was the third of five children born to Harrison and Mary Alice Jones Porter. When her mother died in 1892, she and her brothers and sisters moved to Kyle, Texas, where they were cared for by their paternal grandmother, Catherine Anne Porter. When Grandmother Porter died in 1901, Harrison Porter sold the farm in Kyle and moved with his family to San Antonio.

Facts about Porter's early life and education have been difficult to substantiate, partly because Porter's own accounts were evasive or inconsistent. Although her family apparently was Methodist, Porter attended convent schools, possibly for a time in New Orleans, which may be why later researchers have reported that she was a Roman Catholic from birth. Porter denied this allegation when it appeared in a biographical sketch published by the University of Minnesota series on American writers. Precocious as a child and rebellious as a teenager, she ran away from school at age sixteen to marry. The name of her first husband is not known, although the marriage lasted three years.

After the divorce, Porter moved to Chicago, already cherishing the ambition of becoming a professional writer. She worked as a reporter on a Chicago newspaper for a time and signed on as an extra with a motion-picture company for a few months. Passing up the opportunity to travel to Hollywood with the film company, she returned to Texas, where she reported that she made a living as a traveling entertainer, singing Scottish ballads, dressed in a costume she made herself. Thereafter, she wrote drama criticism and society gossip for a Fort Worth weekly, *The Critic*. One year later, she moved to Denver, Colorado, and became a reporter for the *Rocky Mountain News*. In Denver, during the influenza epidemic of 1918, she became severely ill and almost died. This experience, which she fictionalized in *Pale Horse, Pale Rider,* affected her profoundly. "I really had participated in death," she said years later in an interview with Barbara Thompson of *The Paris Review.* She had had "what the Christians call the 'beatific vision'"; she was no longer "like other people."

In 1919, Porter moved to New York City, where for a brief time she worked as a hack and ghostwriter. The following year she went to study in Mexico. Again she stayed only a short time, but for the next ten years Mexico was to be the center of her intellectual and imaginative life. Returning to Fort Worth, she began to write the stories based on her experiences there. During the next decade she traveled extensively, reviewed books for leading national magazines and newspapers, and worked and reworked the stories that were published in 1930 in *Flowering Judas, and Other Stories.*

Supported by a Guggenheim Fellowship granted that year, Porter returned to Mexico. In 1931, she sailed aboard a German ship from Veracruz to Bremerhaven. This voyage gave her the setting for *Ship of Fools,* which was not to be published for another thirty years. She lived until the mid-1930's in Paris, marrying and later divorcing Eugene Pressly, a member of the American Foreign Service, and working on her fiction. After her divorce from Pressly, she married Albert Erskine, Jr., of the Louisiana State University faculty. Until her divorce from Erskine in 1942, she lived in Baton Rouge. During this time, she continued to work on her short fiction, but not until the late 1950's did she begin sustained effort on her only full-length novel, *Ship of Fools.* Although by that time many of her acquaintances believed she never would finish it, fragments of the novel appeared in magazines. In 1962, *Ship of Fools* was published. Porter wrote no more new fiction after that, although *The Collected Essays and Occasional Writings* appeared in 1970. On September 18, 1980, at the age of ninety, Porter died in Silver Spring, Maryland.

Analysis

Katherine Anne Porter once suggested that when she sat down to write about her life as accurately as possible, it turned into fiction; indeed, she knew no other way to write fiction. Whether this anecdote is true, it is certain that capturing the past with great detail was an important ingredient in her writing. In a number of the short stories, and in two of the best short novels, Miranda, the central character, is very close to being Porter herself. These stories follow Miranda's life from infancy in her grandmother's house in South Texas to her scrape with death from influenza in Colorado at the age of twenty-four—her first major step toward maturity.

Concerning the time of her illness, Porter has said that it was as though a line were drawn through her life, separating everything that came before from everything that came after. She had been given up and then had survived, and in some ways all her time after that was borrowed. Perhaps that is why her overtly autobiographical stories deal with the time before that line, the time when she was "alive" and therefore had a life to record. The stories that take place after that incident present her, if at all, as an observer, as someone slightly distant and alienated from life. (It is a question of degree: Miranda is also, of course, an acute observer in the stories in which she takes part. Her name, in fact, means "observer" in Spanish.) Porter was in real life a passenger on the ship about which her novel *Ship of Fools* was written, but she speaks of herself as purely an observer, who scarcely spoke a word on the entire voyage. She does not appear directly as a character in the novel.

OLD MORTALITY

Miranda, the girl in the short novel *Old Mortality*, runs away from school to get married, in part to escape from her family, so suffocatingly steeped in its own past. At the conclusion of the novella, she is determined to free herself once and for all from that past, so that she can begin to consider her own future; but she determines this, the reader is told in the ironic concluding lines, "in her hopefulness, her ignorance." The irony is that Miranda (Porter) herself became so obsessed with that past that much of her best work is devoted to it. The explanation for Porter's obsession with the past can perhaps be guessed from the conclusion of *Pale Horse, Pale Rider*. Everything of importance to Miranda has died; only her ravaged body, her spark of a soul somehow survives. She finds that she has no future, only the slow progression to death once again. The past, then, is all she has, yet the past is finally intangible, as the girl in *Old Mortality* discovers as she sifts through all the evidence. At last no truth can be discovered, no objectivity, only the combined and contradictory subjectives: The only truth, once again, is the truth of fiction.

Porter said that in her fiction she is not interested in actions so much as she is interested in the various and subtle results of actions. Certainly, of all her works, *Old Mortality* deals directly with the ramifications of past actions. This short novel spans ten years in the life of the protagonist, Miranda, from the age of eight to the age of eighteen. In that time, the reader learns little of Miranda's life, except that she is bad tempered and that, unlike many of the young women in her widely extended family, she is not going to be a "beauty." She is, rather, the recording center of the novel: The events are brought to her and have their effect on the person she is becoming.

The crucial actions have occurred in the preceding generation. Miranda's family is obsessed by a past event. Miranda's aunt, Amy, was a great beauty, the measure, in fact, against which all the current crop of beauties are found wanting. She was glamorous, racy, even though tubercular, and for a long time spurned Gabriel's devoted courtship. Gabriel was himself wild, ran a string of racehorses, and was heir to the fortune. Only when he was disinherited and Amy found herself in the terminal stage of her illness did she consent to marry him. The couple went to New Orleans on their honeymoon, and almost immediately Amy died. Miranda tries to sift out the truth of the story. She looks at the photograph of Amy and does not find her so impossibly beautiful and indeed thinks she looks silly in her out-of-fashion dress. Later, she is introduced to Gabriel, and instead of the dashing young man who had once challenged a rival to a duel over Amy, she finds him fat and drunken, down on his luck; the woman whom he married after Amy is bitter and depressed from living with a ne'er-do-well who has spent their whole married life talking about Amy. Later still, Miranda meets Eva, a homely spinster cousin from Gabriel's generation, and Eva says the real truth is that Amy was a lewd woman, who married only because someone else got her pregnant, and took her own life with an overdose of drugs.

After a moment of shock, Miranda realizes that Eva's version, in its negative way, is just as romantic as the others. Miranda does not want to know where the truth lies. By this time, she has left school and has run off to get married. Her father is cool with her, thinking she has deserted the family; indeed she has, and deliberately. She refuses to be trapped in the past, represented by this unknowable woman whose brief life still haunts the family. She wants instead to discover who she—Miranda—is; she wants her own life to exist in the present and future. This is what she determines—in the novel's ironic final line—"in her hopefulness, her ignorance."

In her ignorance, Miranda learns that her past is what she is, the result of those past actions. She has been touched by Amy even more than the others, for she has become Amy, the Amy who refused to live by the others' rules, and at last ran off, married, and never returned—just as Miranda has done. In so doing, Amy and Miranda become separated from the rest of the family, freezing its members in their moment of history just as Porter herself became separated from her family so that she could re-create them forever in her stories.

NOON WINE

Noon Wine is set in the rural southern Texas of Porter's childhood but does not deal with her family. The characters in this short novel, set at the turn of the twentieth century, are poor and uneducated farmers, but this does not stop the story from being an intricate and subtle moral allegory. The lingering effect of past actions is not the central theme, as it was in *Old Mortality*, but a sense of the cumulative force of a man's actions gives the story a tragic inevitability.

Mr. Thompson is a proud man, and as a result he marries above himself. Instead of a strong woman to help him in the strenuous operation of his farm, he marries a delicate and genteel woman who quickly becomes a near invalid. Further, she insists that they have a dairy, a bit higher class than an ordinary row-crop farm. In the end, Thompson is left with a wife who cannot help him and a kind of farmwork that he does not feel is masculine and that he therefore shirks. The farm is deteriorating, and the couple is about to go under entirely, when a strange taciturn Swede from North Dakota arrives, asking for work. Instantly there is a revolution. The Swede fixes, paints, repairs everything, and shortly the failing farm becomes productive. As the years go by, the couple is able to buy such luxuries as an icebox, and Mr. Thompson is able to sit on the porch while the work is being done. One day Hatch arrives, a thoroughly evil man. He is a bounty hunter; the Swede, it is revealed, is an escaped homicidal maniac who in a berserk fury stabbed his own brother to death. Thompson refuses to give up the Swede. There is a scuffle; the Swede suddenly appears and steps between them; Thompson, believing he sees Hatch stabbing the Swede in the stomach, smashes Hatch's skull with an ax.

The confrontation is remarkably complex. Hatch, as he is presented in the story, seems a pure manifestation of evil, and so perhaps he should be killed, but ironically he has in fact done nothing. The Swede is a primal murderer, a brother-killer like Cain, and is a threat to murder again. Thompson believes Hatch has stabbed the Swede and acts to defend him, but after he has killed Hatch, the Swede does not have a mark on him, not even, perhaps, the mark of Cain, which has been transferred to Thompson.

Thompson is easily acquitted of the crime in court, but his fundamentalist neighbors in the close-knit community look on him as a murderer. Most important, he must examine his own motives. Was he defending the Swede, or was he defending the success of his farm, which, he must have guiltily realized, was not the result of his work, but of the work of another, a sinner, a primal murderer? With his mark of Cain, Thompson goes the rounds of his neighbors, trying to tell his side of the story, believing it less each time himself, until he kills himself, the final consequence of his original pride.

PALE HORSE, PALE RIDER

Porter has called sleep "that little truce of God between living and dying." If dreams, therefore, take place in a landscape somewhere between life and death, it is appropriate that *Pale Horse, Pale Rider* begins with one of Miranda's many dreams to be recorded. Although the story is set during World War I in a small town in Colorado where Miranda is working for a newspaper, symbolically the story takes place in the dreamlike zone between life and death. In that initial dream, Death rides alongside Miranda, but she tells him to ride on ahead; she is not quite ready to go with him. She wakes up only to be reminded of the war, which is poisoning the lives of many people, who are full of despair because of their inability to control their destinies. The streets are filled with funerals, as the influenza epidemic kills people like a medieval plague. Miranda's work on the paper is hateful, and her only release is when, after work, she meets Adam. Adam, as his name suggests, is the man who should be her companion, her mate in life. He is a soldier, however, on his way to war and committed wholly to death, and so Miranda struggles to withhold her love from him.

The war and the plague, as presented in the novel, are symbols of the struggle of life and its vulnerability. Miranda and Adam differ from others in being existentially aware; all that exists for them is the present tense of their lives. They dance together in a cheap café, knowing that it is all they will ever have. Because they have so little—a brief moment of troubled life, and then death—the integrity of their actions becomes their only value. Miranda tells Adam that he is stupid to fight in a war in which old men send young men to die. He agrees, saying, however, that if he does not go, he can no longer face himself. Miranda has her own costly sense of integrity: As a reporter for the paper, she witnesses a pathetic scandal, and when the victims beg her not to write the story, she does not. The rival papers do, however, and her editor is furious; her colleagues think she is senseless. She is demoted to writing entertainment reviews. Even there, when she writes an unfavorable review of a vaudeville act, she is confronted by the old, broken, has-been actor, and her subsequent compassion struggles against her dedication to her job. Her colleagues counsel her to fake the reviews and make everyone happy, but writing honest reviews is an important value to her.

Miranda gets the flu, and in a long delirious dream comes to the point of death and has a beatific vision. The doctor and nurse fighting to preserve her, working with their own existential integrity, bring her back, but it is so painful being taken away from her vision and back to life, that when life-giving drugs are injected into her, she feels them like "a current of agony."

Miranda had fought, with her tiny spark of consciousness, to survive, to survive for Adam. Then she learns that Adam, perhaps having caught flu from her, has himself died. Her dream of heaven had been so brilliant that the real world seems to her a monochrome, a bleak field in which, with Adam gone, she has nothing. The reader, however, can see beyond this point. Earlier, Miranda and Adam had sung an old spiritual together, of a pale horse with a pale rider, who takes a girl's lover away, leaving her behind to mourn. Miranda is the singer who is left behind to mourn and to record the story for the rest of the world.

SHIP OF FOOLS

Porter has described her fiction as an investigation of the "terrible failure of the life of man in the Western World." Her one full-length novel, *Ship of Fools*, is a bleak cross section of modern civilization. It follows the lives of literally dozens of characters, from all levels of the particular society it is observing. More than forty characters of various nationalities are presented in some detail: American, Spanish, Mexican, Cuban, German, Swiss, Swedish. The time is 1931, and chaos is spreading. Soon Adolf Hitler will be in power, the extermination camps will be in operation, and another world war will be under way. The title *Ship of Fools* is a translation of Sebastian Brant's medieval moral allegory, *Das Narrenschiff* (1494). The ship is the world; the time of the journey is the lifetime of the characters. They, of course, do not see it that way. They think of it as a temporary voyage. The lies they tell, the treacheries they enact, the hopeless relationships they form, are only temporary, have nothing to do with the course of their real lives, with the objectives they mean to obtain, the moral codes by which they mean to live.

The ship, the *Vera* (truth), leaves Veracruz, Mexico, for the nearly monthlong journey to Bremerhaven. It is a German ship, and the German passengers sit at the captain's table. From the pompous and second-rate captain on down, they are comic grotesques, guzzling their food swinishly and looking suspiciously at everyone who does not eat pork, or who has a slightly large nose, as potentially Jewish. The only seemingly human Germans are Wilhelm Freytag, concealing as long as he can his Jewish wife, and Dr. Schumann, the ship's doctor and the novel's most sympathetic character. He is urbane, gentle, and wise, and to his own horror, commits perhaps the basest act of anyone on board. The American characters are only slightly less grotesque. William Denny, the Texan, is pure caricature: To him everyone but a white Texan is a "nigger," "spick," "wop," or "damyankee." He devotes all his time to pursuing sexual pleasures but is fearful that he will be cheated into paying too much for it. The comic result is that he pays out everything and gets nothing in return but a severe drubbing.

Mrs. Treadwell, a forty-five-year-old divorcé, is utterly selfish, yet she wonders why she gets nothing from life. David Scott and Jenny Brown, who live together and fight constantly, are, with Dr. Schumann and Freytag, the novel's main characters. David Scott is tied up within himself and will give up nothing to another. Jenny Brown sporadically gives up everything to mere acquaintances yet seems to have nothing of her own within.

One character after another debates humanity's nature: Are all people basically good? Are all people naturally depraved? Are the pure races good and the mongrel races evil? The characters seem intent on acting out all these possibilities. The most disciplined of them regularly lapse into helpless sentimentality. Freytag thinks that each woman he meets is the beautiful love of his life. One of these women is a Jew, whom he married during a period of extreme romanticism, and now he is déclassé among his German compatriots and cannot admit to himself how regretful he is. David and Jenny, needing everything from each other, have only gone as far as learning each other's weaknesses, of which they take full advantage to lacerate each other. They continue to cling together, always saying they will separate at some later time. Most painful is the folly of the sympathetic Dr. Schumann. He convinces himself that he is in love with a neurotic Spanish countess (he has a wife at home), and under pretense of caring for her as her doctor, he turns her into a hopeless and helpless drug addict in order to keep his power over her.

The most purely evil characters on the ship are the shoddy Spanish dance troupe. Through herculean efforts they almost take control of the ship and certainly take control of the lives of the characters, bringing out their deepest and worst traits, but at the end they sit listless and exhausted, as though the effort were immensely greater than any return they have had from it. This troupe of carnival performers cheats, steals, blackmails, and even kills right before the others, who remark on it, but do nothing to stop them, each character feeling it is not his place to do anything. At length, the troupe is sitting confidently at the captain's table, having rearranged everyone's position on the ship. In a kind of Walpurgis Night, they bring the many characters to some sort of climax in an eruption of drunken violence. It is Porter's vision of how World War II began: low thugs and gangsters taking power with the casual, half-intentional connivance of the world.

In the middle of this bleak and pessimistic picture of the Western world, there is one possibility of redemption. The rare positive moments in the novel are when the characters suddenly, often to their own surprise, come together in the act of sex—Porter emphasizing the sensuality of the contact rather than any spiritual qualities. Perhaps Porter is saying that in their fallen state human beings must start at the bottom, with earthly sensuality, in order to slowly acquire a knowledge of spiritual beauty.

Norman Lavers

OTHER MAJOR WORKS

SHORT FICTION: *Flowering Judas, and Other Stories*, 1930; *Hacienda*, 1934; *The Leaning Tower, and Other Stories*, 1944; *The Old Order*, 1944; *The Collected Stories of Katherine Anne Porter*, 1965.

POETRY: *Katherine Anne Porter's Poetry*, 1996 (Darlene Harbour Unrue, editor).

NONFICTION: *My Chinese Marriage*, 1921; *Outline of Mexican Popular Arts and Crafts*, 1922; *What Price Marriage*, 1927; *The Days Before*, 1952; *A Defence of Circe*, 1954; *A Christmas Story*, 1967; *The Collected Essays and Occasional Writings*, 1970; *The Selected Letters of Katherine Anne Porter*, 1970; *The Never-Ending Wrong*, 1977; *Letters of Katherine Anne Porter*, 1990.

BIBLIOGRAPHY

Bloom, Harold, ed. *Katherine Anne Porter*. Bromall, Pa.: Chelsea House, 2001. A book of essays interpreting Porter's fiction, with a biography and chronology of her life. Includes a bibliography.

Brinkmeyer, Robert H., Jr. *Katherine Anne Porter's Artistic Development: Primitivism, Traditionalism, and Totalitarianism*. Baton Rouge: Louisiana State University Press, 1993. Brinkmeyer traces Porter's development as a writer, dividing her work into three stages: the early work written in Mexico, the rediscovery of her southern identity, and a period of cynicism and obsession that resulted in *Ship of Fools*. Argues that she achieved her height as an artist when she created a memory-based dialogue with her southern roots.

Givner, Joan. *Katherine Anne Porter: A Life*. Rev. ed. Athens: University of Georgia Press, 1991. Givner, Porter's chosen biographer, provides a well-balanced account of the author's life. This revision of the biography originally published in 1982 includes updated information, as well as previously embargoed material.

Hartley, Lodwick, and George Core, eds. *Katherine Anne Porter: A Critical Symposium*. Athens: University of Georgia Press, 1969. A collection of seminal essays, this book includes an interview with Porter conducted in 1963, as well as a personal assessment by Porter's friend, Glenway Wescott. A group of five essays provide general surveys of her writing. Includes a bibliography and an index.

Hendrick, George. *Katherine Anne Porter*. New York: Twayne, 1965. A biographical sketch precedes studies grouped according to settings from Porter's life: The first group from Mexico, the second from Texas, and the third from New York and Europe. After a chapter on *Ship of Fools*, this book surveys Porter's essays and summarizes major themes. Includes notes, an annotated bibliography, an index, and a chronology.

Liberman, Myron M. *Katherine Anne Porter's Fiction*. Detroit, Mich.: Wayne State University Press, 1971. In his study of the techniques and intentions of Porter's fiction, Liberman devotes seven chapters to an analysis of *Ship of Fools*. Includes notes and an index.

Stout, Janis. *Katherine Anne Porter: A Sense of the Times*. Charlottesville: University Press of Virginia, 1995. Contains chapters on Porter's background in Texas, her view of politics and art in the 1920's, her writing and life between the two world wars, and her relationship with the southern agrarians. Also addresses the issue of gender, the problem of genre in *Ship of Fools*, and the quality of Porter's "free, intransigent, dissenting mind." Includes notes and a bibliography.

Titus, Mary. *The Ambivalent Art of Katherine Anne Porter*. Athens: University of Georgia Press, 2005. A look at the ways in which Porter confronted issues of gender in her work and life. Includes a study of some of her unpublished papers.

Unrue, Darlene Harbour. *Katherine Anne Porter: The Life of an Artist*. Jackson: University Press of Mississippi, 2005. The first biography written since Givner's book. A comprehensive account that offers insight into Porter's turbulent personal life and her writing.

Walsh, Thomas F. *Katherine Anne Porter and Mexico: The Illusion of Eden*. Austin: University of Texas Press, 1992. Contains chapters on Porter and Mexican politics, her different periods of residence in Mexico, and *Ship of Fools*. Includes notes and a bibliography.

AYN RAND

Born: St. Petersburg, Russia; February 2, 1905
Died: New York, New York; March 6, 1982
Also known as: Alisa (Alice) Zinovievna Rosenbaum

PRINCIPAL LONG FICTION
We the Living, 1936
Anthem, 1938 (revised 1946)
The Fountainhead, 1943
Atlas Shrugged, 1957
The Early Ayn Rand: A Selection from Her Unpublished Fiction, 1984 (Leonard Peikoff, editor)

OTHER LITERARY FORMS

In addition to her three novels and one novelette, Ayn Rand published a play and several philosophical disquisitions. An early critique, *Hollywood: American Movie City*, was published in the Soviet Union in 1926 without Rand's permission.

ACHIEVEMENTS

Ayn Rand won the Volpe Cup at the Venice Film Festival in 1942 for the Italian motion-picture dramatization of *We the Living*, a novel about the failures of the Soviet system. She was awarded an honorary degree, a doctor of humane letters, by Lewis and Clark College in Portland, Oregon, in 1963, but this sole award does not reflect the significance of her influence on America's philosophical and political economic thought.

BIOGRAPHY

Ayn Rand was born Alisa (Alice) Zinovievna Rosenbaum, the eldest of three children, into a Russian Jewish middle-class family in czarist Russia. When her father's pharmacy was nationalized following the Bolshevik Revolution of 1917, Rand, who had been writing stories since she was nine, found a calling: She turned against collectivism, and she elevated individualism—personal, economic, political, and moral—into a philosophy that eventually attracted a large, occasionally distinguished, following. Early in her career she declared herself to be an atheist.

At the University of Petrograd (now St. Petersburg), Rand studied philosophy, English, and history, graduating with highest honors in history in 1924. By then the works of French writers Victor Hugo and Edmond Rostand, and of Polish writer Henryk Sienkiewicz, had inspired her passion for the heroic and the ideal. Fyodor Dostoevski and Friedrich Nietzsche also left their mark.

Unhappy because the Soviet system was not moving in the direction of her republican

Ayn Rand
(Library of Congress)

ideals and because she had a dead-end job, Rand accepted an invitation from relatives and went to Chicago in 1926. It was while in the United States that she restyled herself Ayn Rand, and within a few months moved to Hollywood, California.

Working as a film extra, a file clerk, and a waiter and doing other odd jobs from 1926 to 1934, Rand perfected her language skills and became a screenwriter at various motion-picture studios. In 1937, she worked as an unpaid typist for Eli Jacques Kahn, a well-known New York architect, in preparation for her first major novel, *The Fountainhead*. Given her early experience in totalitarian Russia, Rand soon became known as the most driven of American anticommunists. She had acquired U.S. citizenship in 1931. In 1947, she appeared as a "friendly witness" before the House Committee on Un-American Activities (HUAC) during the period of the communist witch-hunts—an action she later admitted regretting. Along the way, in 1929, Rand married Charles Francis (Frank) O'Connor, a minor actor and amateur painter. He died in 1979.

After her major literary successes, Rand devoted herself exclusively to philosophizing, writing, and lecturing. She spoke on numerous Ivy League university campuses. She became a regular at the Ford Hall Forum and a columnist for the *Los Angeles Times*. She was coeditor or contributor to several philosophical publications. She was active in the

Nathaniel Branden Institute, created to spread her philosophy of objectivism, until her personal and professional break with Nathaniel and Barbara Branden in 1968. This triangular relationship had played an important part in Rand's life, because the Brandens formed the nucleus of a close group of followers, ironically known as the collective.

Rand, a chain smoker whose loaded cigarette holder had become a symbol of her persona, was diagnosed with lung cancer in her seventies. She died in March, 1982, in the New York City apartment in which she had lived since 1951. Her wake was attended by hundreds of people, including Alan Greenspan, an early Rand devotee and later chair of the Federal Reserve Board Bank. Philosopher Leonard Peikoff, Rand's intellectual and legal heir, also was present.

Rand's publications have sold well over twenty million copies in English and in translation even as literary critics generally dismissed her ideas as reactionary propaganda or pop philosophy. Rand was a paradox. She was a writer of romantic fiction whose ideas were often taken seriously, but she was also a controversial individualist and a contrarian who defied the moral, political, social, and aesthetic norms of her times.

Analysis

In her two major works of fiction, Ayn Rand explicated her philosophy of objectivism in dramatic form. Thus, in *The Fountainhead* and especially in *Atlas Shrugged*, Rand argues that reality exists independent of human thought (objectively), that reason is the only viable method for understanding reality, that individuals should seek personal happiness and exist for their own sake and that of no other, and that individuals should not sacrifice themselves or be sacrificed by others. Furthermore, unrestricted laissez-faire capitalism is the political economic system in which these principles can best flourish. Underlying this essence is the philosophy of unadulterated individualism, personal responsibility, the power of unsullied reason, and the importance of Rand's special kind of morality.

In her long fiction, the philosopher-novelist spells out her concept of the exceptional individual as a heroic being and an "ideal man," with "his" happiness as the highest moral purpose in life, with productive achievement the noblest activity, and reason the only absolute. Rand advocates minimal government intrusion and no initiation of physical force in human interactions. She represents such a system as enshrining the highest degree of morality and justice.

Because Rand also focuses on the denial of self-sacrifice and altruism, a staple of conventional morality and welfarism, she opposes both Christianity and communism. She finds it irrational to place the good of others ahead of one's own rational self-interest. Likewise, she denies mysticism and promotes the Aristotelian view that the world that individuals perceive is reality, and there is no other. Both her major novels can be considered elitist and antidemocratic in that they extol the virtues of a few innovative, far-thinking individuals over the mediocre majority, which is either ignorant and uncaring or, even worse, actively striving to destroy the brilliant individuals of great ability. Besides disparaging mediocrity, Rand also decried the power of connections, conformity with what has been done before, a trend she found far too evident in the American welfare state, and the intellectual bankruptcy she deemed it to have fostered.

Rand considered herself a practitioner of Romanticism, who was concerned with representing individuals "in whom certain human attributes are focused more sharply and consistently than in average human beings." Accordingly, in both these novels the characters of the heroes, sharply drawn, are idealized creations—not depictions of real individuals—who are in control of their own destinies despite major odds.

THE FOUNTAINHEAD

The Fountainhead is the story of Howard Roark, Rand's ideal man, an architect who has a vision of how buildings should really be designed. He is innovative and efficient; he also has a strong aesthetic sense and has integrity—in short, he is a man of principle and artistic individuality. Roark is contrasted with Peter Keating, a former classmate and fellow architect but a "secondhander," constantly replicating conventional styles because he has no originality of his own. He achieves a seeming success by manipulating others. Unlike Roark, whom he envies, Keating does not know who he really is.

Another of Roark's adversaries is Ellsworth Toohey. He writes a column for the *Banner*, arguing that architecture should reflect the art of the people. Gail Wynand is the *Banner*'s owner and newspaper magnate; he appreciates Roark's creativity but buckles under societal pressures, disregards his vision, and thereby engineers his own downfall as a worthy human being. The love interest is embodied in Dominique Francon, the daughter of Guy Francon, the principal owner of the architectural firm that employs Peter Keating. She is a typical Rand heroine, a self-reliant idealist alienated by the shallow conventions of her day in interwar America and convinced that a life of principle is impossible in a world ruled by mediocrity. Her affair with Roark is motivated not by physical or emotional passion but by the recognition that he is a man of great worth. Along the way, in between and sometimes during other affairs, she marries Keating and then Wynand before finally marrying Roark. Dominique seems inconsistent in her ideals, attitudes, and critiques of architectural designs, but the inconsistencies are all part of her effort to spare Roark from ultimate destruction.

Roark, long professionally unsuccessful because he is unwilling to compromise the integrity of his creations, preferring not to work at all or to do menial tasks, eventually overcomes not only financial difficulties but also numerous intrigues by the likes of Keating. For instance, through the mean-spirited Toohey, Roark is assigned to build an interdenominational temple for a patron, Hopton Stoddard, a traditionalist who is abroad at the time. Toohey knows that Stoddard will hate Roark's radically innovative design. Roark makes the building's centerpiece Dominique's nude figure. Toohey incites public condemnation and persuades the patron to sue Roark for breach of contract. Stoddard wins the case, as Roark fails to defend himself in court.

Paradoxically, a friendship develops between Roark and Wynand, attracted to each other for different reasons. Wynand helps Roark in his defense at a second trial, which follows Roark's dynamiting a low-income housing project that Keating had commissioned. The latter had agreed not to alter Roark's design in any way in exchange for Roark's allowing Keating to claim credit for the former's innovative and cost-effective blueprint. When Keating fails to keep his promise and adulterates the design, Roark, with Dominique Francon's assistance, destroys the structure. The trial gives Roark the opportunity to spell out his—that is, Rand's—defense of ethical egoism and opposition to a world perishing from an "orgy of self-sacrifice" and conventional morality. After Roark's exoneration, Wynand commissions him to build the tallest skyscraper in New York City despite Wynand's losing Dominique to Roark.

Ultimately, *The Fountainhead* is a novel of ideas, of heroic characters who are the fountainhead of human progress and of their opposites, who live secondhand, second-rate lives and constantly seek social approval for their beliefs. The philosophy in the novel alternates with the action, and neither can be understood without the other.

ATLAS SHRUGGED

Rand's philosophy extolling the myth of absolute, rugged individualism and its relationship to society is most fully explicated in what proved to be her last work of fiction, several years in the making: the twelve-hundred-page *Atlas Shrugged*. In this novel, Rand tries to answer the question raised by one of her earlier heroes: "What would happen to the world without those who do, think, work, produce?" In this apocalyptic parable, it is John Galt of Twentieth Century Motors, a physicist, engineer, inventor, and philosopher, who is Rand's ideal man and leads the other "men of the mind" on a strike against the exploitation of the genuine creators of wealth by all the leeches and parasites—the nonproducers—whom they had been sustaining.

Rand's philosophy is played out through the stories of the four heroes, the authentic moneymakers. They are the Argentine Francisco d'Anconia, heir to the world's leading copper enterprise; the Scandinavian Ragnar Danneskjold, a onetime philosopher who turns pirate in order to steal wealth back from the looters and return it to the producers of legitimate values; Henry (Hank) Rearden, an American steel magnate and inventor of a metal better than steel; and finally, the other American, John Galt, who, with the others, stops the ideological motor of the world in a strike before rebuilding society. The heroine, rail heir Dagny Taggart, wonders where the individuals of ability have gone.

Confronting them is an array of villains, manipulative appropriators, enemies of individualism and free enterprise, scabs, and moochers profiting from the achievements of the producers and united by their greed for unearned gains. Especially, there is Dr. Robert Stadler, the counterpart of Gail Wynand in *The Fountainhead*. Stadler, once the greatest physicist of his time, fully cognizant of the value of the human mind, fails to stand up for his principles. The progressive decay of James Taggart, Dagny's brother and the titular president of Taggart Transcontinental Railroad, parallels that of the society in which he lives.

In the novel, set some time in the vaguely defined future, the United States is following Europe down the long, hopeless path of socialism, government regulation, and a predatory state into a new Dark Age. The heroes join forces with other intelligent, freedom-loving leaders of commerce, industry, science, and philosophy to reverse the slide. They do this as Atlas may have done had he grown tired of holding the world on his shoulders without reward.

Eventually, the heroes repair to a secret Colorado mountain citadel, where they wait for their time to rebuild the decaying collectivist society whose end their "strike of the mind" against productive work is hastening. Galt, arrested and tortured by the looters but finally freed by the other heroes, delivers a thirty-five-thousand-word oration via a commandeered radio, epitomizing Rand's objectivism and views of the ideal man. Galt's (Rand's) philosophy then becomes that of the new society: "I swear by my life and my love of it that I will never live for the sake of another man, nor ask another man to live for mine." By the end of the novel, socialism has produced a bankrupt world pleading for the return of the men of the mind, who, after a confrontation with the parasites, start to rebuild society. *Atlas Shrugged* is Rand's most thorough exploration of the social ramifications of politics, economics, psychology, metaphysics, epistemology, aesthetics, religion, and ethics.

Peter B. Heller

OTHER MAJOR WORKS

PLAYS: *Night of January 16th*, pr. 1934 (also known as *Woman on Trial* and *Penthouse Legend*); *The Unconquered*, pr. 1940 (adaptation of her novel *We the Living*).

SCREENPLAY: *The Fountainhead*, 1949.

NONFICTION: *For the New Intellectual: The Philosophy of Ayn Rand*, 1961; *The Virtue of Selfishness: A New Concept of Egoism*, 1964; *Capitalism: The Unknown Ideal*, 1966; *Introduction to Objectivist Epistemology*, 1967, second enlarged edition, 1990 (Harry Binswanger and Leonard Peikoff, editors); *The Romantic Manifesto*, 1969; *The New Left: The Anti-Industrial Revolution*, 1971; *Philosophy: Who Needs It?*, 1982; *The Ayn Rand Lexicon: Objectivism from A to Z*, 1984 (Peikoff, editor); *The Voice of Reason: Essays in Objectivist Thought*, 1988 (Peikoff, editor); *The Ayn Rand Column*, 1991; *Letters of Ayn Rand*, 1995 (Michael S. Berliner, editor); *Journals of Ayn Rand*, 1997 (David Harriman, editor); *The Art of Fiction: A Guide for Writers and Readers*, 2000 (Tore Boeckmann, editor); *The Art of Nonfiction: A Guide for Writers and Readers*, 2001 (Robert Mayhew, editor); *Ayn Rand Answers: The Best of Her Q and A*, 2005 (Mayhew, editor).

MISCELLANEOUS: *The Objectivist Newsletter*, 1962-1965 (later known as *The Objectivist*, 1966-1971, edited by Rand); *The Ayn Rand Letter*, 1971-1976 (published by Rand).

Bibliography

Baker, James T. *Ayn Rand.* Boston: Twayne, 1987. A brief introductory overview of Rand's life and work, written in an objective and highly readable style. Includes a chronology, references, a bibliography, and an index.

Branden, Nathaniel. *My Years with Ayn Rand.* Reprint. San Francisco, Calif.: Jossey-Bass, 1999. A personal account by Rand's disciple, organizer, spokesman, lover, and, ultimately, enemy. Includes photographs and an index. Originally published in 1989 as *Judgment Day: My Years with Ayn Rand.*

Branden, Nathaniel, and Barbara Branden. *Who Is Ayn Rand?* New York: Random House, 1962. This book contains three essays on objectivism's moral philosophy, its connection to psychological theory, and a literary study of Rand's methods in her fiction. It contains an additional biographical essay, tracing Rand's life from birth to her mid-fifties.

Britting, Jeff. *Ayn Rand.* Woodstock, N.Y.: Overlook Press, 2005. A readable biography of Rand's literary and personal life but lacking in scholarly analysis.

Gladstein, Mimi Reisel. *The New Ayn Rand Companion.* Rev. and expanded ed. Westport, Conn.: Greenwood Press, 1999. Provides biographical information, a summary of Rand's fiction and nonfiction, information about her characters, criticism of her writing, and a comprehensive bibliography. This revised edition contains newly discovered information about Rand's posthumous publications, updated biographical data, and summaries of books and articles published since her death.

Gladstein, Mimi Reisel, and Chris Matthew Sciabarra, eds. *Feminist Interpretations of Ayn Rand.* University Park: Pennsylvania State University Press, 1999. Collection of essays examining Rand's life and work from a feminist perspective. Includes pieces by cultural critics Susan Brownmiller and Camile Paglia and analysis of *Atlas Shrugged.*

Peikoff, Leonard. *Objectivism: The Philosophy of Ayn Rand.* New York: Dutton, 1991. A comprehensive overview of objectivist philosophy, written by the philosopher who was closest to Rand during her lifetime. Includes a discussion of Rand's ideas about reason, the good, virtue, happiness, government, art, and capitalism.

Pierpont, Claudia Roth. *Passionate Minds: Women Rewriting the World.* New York: Alfred A. Knopf, 2000. Evocative, interpretive essays on the life paths and works of twelve women, including Rand, connecting the circumstances of their lives with the shapes, styles, subjects, and situations of their art.

Sciabarra, Chris M. *Ayn Rand: The Russian Radical.* University Park: Pennsylvania State University Press, 1995. Sciabarra charts the evolution of the author as a philosopher, of her dialectics, and of her philosophy. Includes a bibliography and photographs.

Younkins, Edward W., ed. *Ayn Rand's "Atlas Shrugged": A Philosophical and Literary Companion.* Burlington, Vt.: Ashgate, 2007. Collection of essays discussing *Atlas Shrugged* as a work of literature and philosophy. Includes discussions of the novel's ideas about aesthetics, economics, and human relationships, the novel as a work of science fiction, and its characterization.

SALMAN RUSHDIE

Born: Bombay (now Mumbai), India; June 19, 1947
Also known as: Ahmed Salman Rushdie

PRINCIPAL LONG FICTION
Grimus, 1975
Midnight's Children, 1981
Shame, 1983
The Satanic Verses, 1988
Haroun and the Sea of Stories, 1990 (fable)
The Moor's Last Sigh, 1995
The Ground Beneath Her Feet, 1999
Fury, 2001
Shalimar the Clown, 2005
The Enchantress of Florence, 2008

OTHER LITERARY FORMS

In addition to his novels, Salman Rushdie (ROOSH-dee) has produced short stories and works of nonfiction. *The Jaguar Smile: A Nicaraguan Journey* (1987) is a book of travel and political observations written following Rushdie's visit to Nicaragua in July, 1986, as a guest of the Sandinista Association of Cultural Workers. Among his short stories; the best known is "The Prophet's Hair," which appeared originally in the *London Review of Books* in 1981 and has been reprinted in *The Penguin Book of Modern British Short Stories* (1987). A fable in the style of *The Arabian Nights' Entertainments*, *Haroun and the Sea of Stories* was published in 1990, and the collection of short stories *East, West: Stories* (1994) includes "The Prophet's Hair" and the dazzling "At the Auction of the Ruby Slippers." The essays in Rushdie's *Step Across This Line: Collected Nonfiction, 1992-2002* (2002) deal with a variety of subjects, including popular culture, politics, and soccer.

ACHIEVEMENTS

Although furor and indignation have followed the publication of a number of Salman Rushdie's novels, the works have also received critical praise and rave reviews. *Midnight's Children* won the James Tait Black Memorial Prize, the English Speaking Union Literature Award, and the Booker Prize; it has been translated into twelve languages. Although *Shame* was banned in Pakistan, as *Midnight's Children* had been in India, it too received critical plaudits for its seriocomic portrait of Pakistani life. No writer since English satirist Jonathan Swift has aroused as much ire from so many sources, notwithstanding the notoriety of *The Satanic Verses*, which won the Whitbread Award as best novel of 1988.

On February 14, 1989, the Ayatollah Ruhollah Khomeini, the fundamentalist spiritual leader of Iran, issued a fatwa (a proclamation concerning a matter of Muslim faith) that called for Rushdie's death as an enemy of Islam and sanctioned similar reprisals against those who published or distributed *The Satanic Verses*. Rushdie became a Knight of the British Empire in 2007. Ironically, this royal honor served to rekindle the hatred and many of the threats that haunted him following publication of *The Satanic Verses*.

Rushdie's novels, actually modern picaresques, explore the tragicomic results of lost identity; they portray in exuberant, highly inventive, satirical style what the author considers to be the consequences of living in cultures that have become mixed, distorted, and diluted through combinations of expediency, political ineptitude, and exploitative religion.

Biography

Ahmed Salman Rushdie was born in Bombay (now Mumbai), India, on June 19, 1947, less than two months before the end of the British Raj. His father, Anis Ahmed Rushdie, and his mother, Negin Butt Rushdie, were Muslims with ties to the region that would become Pakistan. The family did not at first join the Muslim exodus to Pakistan that began after partition in September, 1947. Even so, they became increasingly aware of their minority status as Muslims in a predominantly Hindu state.

Although the Rushdies were nominally Muslim, they also identified with India and with Great Britain. Rushdie's father had been educated in England, at Cambridge University, and had determined to rear his son and three daughters to appreciate their multicultural background. As a result, Rushdie had, from boyhood, access to a variety of works in his father's library. It became a recurring argument between father and son, however, that the boy did not make adequate use of this wealth of books. His private reading during boyhood was generally limited to an English translation of the fifteenth century collection of stories known as *The Arabian Nights' Entertainments* (or *The Thousand and One Nights*). His mother, considered "keeper of the family stories," regaled young Rushdie and his sisters with a wealth of anecdotes on their family history; he remembered them all and would later adapt many of them in his writings.

Rushdie was sent to the Cathedral and John Connon School, a British-administered primary school with Anglican affiliation located in Bombay. As his sister Sameen has recalled, "He mopped up all the prizes," was not very adapt at games, read extensively in both serious and popular literature, and loved both American B films and Hindu hit films. In 1961, at the age of thirteen, he was sent to the prestigious Rugby public school in England. At Rugby, however, although the masters were generally fair-minded, Rushdie felt alienated from his classmates, the "old boys" from British established families, who subjected him to cruel pranks. Rushdie compensated for the pranks and racial taunts by excelling at debates, appearing in theatrical productions, and thriving in academic areas, winning the Queen's Medal for history and securing (but refusing) a scholarship at Balliol College, Oxford.

In 1964, the Rushdie family had emigrated to Karachi, Pakistan, and while Rushdie was not enthusiastic about returning to England, he had been offered a scholarship at his father's university, King's College, Cambridge, and amid the India-Pakistan war in 1965, his father literally pushed him onto an airplane bound for the United Kingdom. Rushdie's attitude toward his father was often argumentative, and there was a serious rupture in their relationship when he entered Cambridge. Shortly before the elder Rushdie's death in 1987, there was a rapprochement between the two men.

At Cambridge, Rushdie decided to read for a degree in history, and he eventually attained a 2.2 (that is, "second-rate") degree, but he thrived in the social atmosphere of the mid-1960's. "It was a very good time to be at Cambridge," he has stated. "I ceased to be a conservative snob under the influence of the Vietnam War and dope." He continued his involvement in theater, and upon his graduation in 1968, he attempted to work in the entertainment industry in Pakistan. He found that censorship was inescapable there, however, and returned to London, where he worked in amateur theatricals and supported himself as a copywriter at the J. Walter Thompson advertising agency. He had already begun to think of himself as a writer, however, and he completed a never-published novel in 1971, "The Book of the Pir," which he has described as "post-Joycean and sub-Joycean."

Grimus was Rushdie's first published novel, written while he was still working irregularly in advertising to earn an income. It was a commercial failure and never was published in the United States, but it was favorably reviewed in London's *The Times Literary Supplement* (January 21, 1975), and it attracted notice and the beginnings of an audience for Rushdie. It took several short stories and five years before Rushdie produced his next novel, *Midnight's Children*. This work won rave reviews on both sides of the Atlantic, but it also offended a great many people, among them the family of Indira Gandhi, then prime minister of India. Rushdie made a public apology for the cutting satirical references to her and specific members of her family in the novel, but he made no changes in subsequent editions. The affair was exacerbated by the fact that Rushdie's accusations coincided with the Indian army's assault on the Golden Temple of the Sikh Muslims. The assassination of Mrs. Gandhi in 1984 brought a tragic end to this series of events.

Having offended large numbers of Indians with *Midnight's Children*, Rushdie published *Shame*, his portrayal of the blood feuds that led to the deposing and execution of Pakistan's prime minister Zulfikar Ali Bhutto by his former protégé, Mohammad Zia-ul-Haq. The same pattern followed publication of this novel, but this time Rushdie had offended the Pakistanis, India's enemies. Again Rushdie had great commercial success and received critical plaudits, but *Shame*, which Rushdie has called *Midnight's Children's* "antisequel," was denied publication in Pakistan just as *Midnight's Children* had been banned in India.

By 1985, Rushdie was sought after by every major publisher. Viking Penguin offered him an advance of $850,000 for rights to his work then in progress, leading to a rancorous break with Liz Calder, an old friend trying to establish her own publishing firm. Everyone in publishing circles knew that the new book would cause a sensation, but no one, not even Rushdie, could have known that *The Satanic Verses* would make him a marked man.

After February 14, 1989, with the Khomeini decree of death, Rushdie's life came to resemble the plots of his novels. The threat of assassination forced him to close his London home and go into hiding. Viking Penguin received thousands of threatening letters. Bookstores that did not remove *The Satanic Verses* from their shelves were threatened with bombings. Riots related to the book broke out in Bombay; at least five people were killed and dozens injured in Islamabad, Pakistan; and two Muslim leaders were killed in Brussels, Belgium, after they expressed opposition to censoring the book. Two bookstores in Berkeley, California, were firebombed, and a bomb blast in London, which killed the terrorist who had placed the bomb, was attributed to the anti-Rushdie campaign. Rushdie's Japanese translator was murdered, his Italian translator was wounded in a knife attack, and his Norwegian publisher was almost killed in a shooting.

Although some members of the British political establishment expressed a personal distaste for Rushdie, and authors such as John le Carré and Roald Dahl (who called him a "dangerous opportunist") claimed that Rushdie deserved his predicament, Scotland Yard was assigned the task of protecting him.

The fatwa on Rushdie's life inevitably continued as the bane of his existence. Writers such as William Styron, Milan Kundera, and Norman Mailer called upon the governments of democratic nations to exert pressure on Iran, and, without making his position public, horror writer Stephen King insisted that any bookstore chain that gave in to threats and removed Rushdie's books from its shelves would have to remove King's as well. In 1990, Rushdie issued a statement that he had "converted" to Islam to show "people who viewed me as some kind of enemy that I wasn't one," but he realized that he had acted out of "despair and disorientation" and "made strenuous steps to get out of the false position."

When Rushdie made a secret trip to the United States in 1992, President George H. W. Bush's administration avoided contact with him, but in 1993 he was able to arrange a brief meeting in the White House with President Bill Clinton. The British government of Prime Minister John Major was more supportive, albeit discreetly, than its predecessor. In the third year of his concealment, Rushdie began to write again, remarking "If I can't write, then, in a way, the attack has been successful." His fable *Haroun and the Sea of Stories*, written as a means of speaking to his son, whom he could not contact while in hiding, was published in 1990, and a collection of short fiction, *East, West*, was released in 1994. After five years of labor, *The Moor's Last Sigh* was published in 1995.

The fatwa and life in hiding ended Rushdie's marriage to his second wife, the American novelist Marianne Wiggins; they divorced in 1993 (his first marriage, to Clarissa Luard, with whom he had a son, ended in divorce in 1985). His third marriage, to Elizabeth West, produced one son and ended in divorce in 2004. Rushdie's *The Enchantress of Florence* was written even as his fourth marriage, to actor Padma Lakshmi, was unraveling (they divorced in 2007) and contains, amid much else, a meditation on an ideal wife conjured in dream.

During the mid-1990's, Rushdie appeared in public more often, unannounced but usually greeted with considerable enthusiasm, and was active in encouraging international resistance to the fatwa. In 1998, some more moderate members of the Iranian government moved toward a withdrawal of the fatwa, but Rushdie's safety was still not entirely guaranteed, and he remained cautious in terms of his movements into the early years of the twenty-first century.

ANALYSIS

Many Western readers, ignorant of Islam and Hinduism, the 1947 partition of the Indian subcontinent and the creation of Pakistan, the India-Pakistan war of 1965, and the Pakistani civil war of 1974, may tend to read Salman Rushdie's novels as bizarre entertainments. This is unfortunate, since each is a picaresque allegory into which the author has inserted details from his own life in order to prove that myth is history, today is yesterday, and the life of one person is integral to the history of nations. Rushdie masks events here and there and relentlessly mixes Persian and Hindu myths, but the hiatus in logic that this method creates is merely to prove his contention that an Anglo-Indian-Pakistani is a person with a hole in the body, a vital place in which there is a haunting void.

MIDNIGHT'S CHILDREN

Midnight's Children is Rushdie's allegorical picaresque on the history of the modern state of India. Its narrator, Saleem Sinai, is one of those whose birth coincided with the hour and day India achieved independence: midnight, August 15, 1947. He and many others, including Jawaharlal Nehru, India's first prime minister, considered these "midnight's children" singled out, privileged by the hopeful hour at which they began their lives. Saleem discovers that he does indeed have special powers; he can, in his mind, summon all the other children born during the midnight hour of August 15, 1947, and, when a boy, he does so nightly, establishing the "Midnight Children's Conference," a forum he hopes will augur well for organizing the leaders of the new state.

Saleem's family is prosperous; they reside in one of Bombay's more affluent sections on an estate of homes once owned by an Englishman, William Methwold, who left India on the very day the Raj ended. Through a bizarre series of events (an accident at school that reveals that his blood type corresponds to neither parent and the subsequent confession of Mary Pereira, a nurse who had worked at the hospital at which Saleem was born), Saleem's family discovers that Mary had intentionally switched children, giving the Sinais a child of one of Bombay's poorest families. Only Saleem, through his telepathic powers, knows that the Sinais's real son, reared as a street urchin named Shiva, is actually an illegitimate child of the Englishman Methwold. Though the Sinais make no attempt to locate their own boy and do accept Saleem as their own, Saleem recognizes Shiva as his nemesis and realizes that Shiva may well destroy him.

Each of the children of midnight has some special talent or ability by virtue of time and date of birth: Saleem's telepathic skills, Shiva's extraordinarily strong knees (which he uses to kill the Indian street entertainer he believes is his father), and the abilities of Parvati-the-witch, who seeks to use her talents only for good. All the children become caught up in the political machinations that follow upon India's independence and the creation of Pakistan. Saleem's family, aware that they are part of India's unwanted Muslim minority, immigrate to Pakistan. This event, plus the fact that Saleem no longer wishes to have any contact with Shiva, the rightful heir of the Sinais, ends Saleem's nightly summoning of the Midnight Children's Conference. Once in Pakistan, Saleem discovers that his telepathic powers do not work. He tries, instead, to develop his exceptional power of smell, utilizing his huge nose to smell danger, injustice, unhappiness, poverty, and other elements of Pakistani life.

Saleem and his family become caught up in Pakistan's 1965 war with India. Saleem's former countrymen become his enemies, and all of his family are killed in the war, except his sister, who has taken the name Jamila Singer and has become famous as a singer of patriotic songs. When the east wing of Pakistan secedes in 1973 and declares itself the independent state of Bangladesh, Saleem enlists in Pakistan's canine patrol, the Cutia, performing the function of a dog to sniff out traitors. Pakistan's devastating loss in the war leaves Saleem without a country. Ultimately, it is Parvati-the-witch who uses her magic to make him disappear and return him to India.

Saleem marries Parvati but is unable to consummate the marriage. Whenever he tries to do so, he sees the decaying face of Jamila, the woman who had been reared as his sister. Saleem had loved Jamila, but he also had come to recognize that their nominal brother-sister relationship would not allow her to be his. Out of frustration, Parvati takes Shiva, now a major in India's army, as her lover. She gives birth to his child, named Aadam, whom Saleem acknowledges as his own son.

Shiva, the destroyer, supervises the slum clearance project that not only eliminates the Bombay quarter in which the magicians had lived but also kills Parvati and many of her magician colleagues who had refused to leave their homes. Saleem is one of those arrested and brought to Benares, the town of the widows. Here he is imprisoned, forced by Shiva to name and identify the skills of the children of midnight; he is released only after he has been forcibly sterilized. Oddly, those arrested as a result of Saleem's information do not blame him; they, too, are sterilized.

Much more happens in *Midnight's Children*. The novel is structured as a family history that reaches back to Saleem's grandparents and describes the political circumstances in India after World War I, through World War II and the end of the Raj, to the war with Pakistan and the Pakistani civil war. It is also highly mythic. Sinai, the surname of the narrator, masks the name of the Arabian philosopher Avicenna (Abū ʿAlī al-Husain ibn ʿAbdallāh ibn Sīnā; 980-1037), who saw the emanations of God's presence in the cosmos as a series of triads of mind, body, and soul. The triads appear in the three generations of Sinais who appear in the novel, but the three religions of India—Hinduism, Islam, and

Christianity—which also appear, do nothing to reverse the downward course of India's fortunes after 1947. Sin is the ancient moon god of Hadhramut, who acting at a distance can influence the tides of the world. He is represented by the letter *S* and is as sinuous as the snake. Appropriately, Saleem discovers his son Aadam in the care of a master snake charmer, Picture Singh. Sinai is both the place of revelation, of commandments and the golden calf, and the desert of barrenness and infertility that is Rushdie's view of modern India.

Saleem's nose resembles the trunk of the elephant deity, Kali, who is the god of literature, and the huge ears of Saleem's son Aadam carry the motif into India's future. Shiva is the Hindu god of destruction and reproduction, a member of the trinity that includes Brama and Vishnu. The closing chapters of the novel find Saleem the manager of a Bombay pickle factory owned by his former nurse, Mary Pereira, the woman who had originally exchanged him for the true son of the Sinais, underscoring the motif of absurd continuity, pickled history, and Saleem's huge nose, which is called a cucumber as often as it is an elephant's trunk.

The most savage satire of the book is reserved for Indira Gandhi, daughter of Nehru and, until her 1984 assassination, prime minister of India. Rushdie repeatedly cites a famous newspaper photograph in which her hair is white on one side and black on the other to symbolize her hypocrisy. He ridicules Sanjay Gandhi, her son, now also dead, as the mastermind of India's slum clearance and birth-control plans. Specific members of Gandhi's cabinet appear in the novel with appendages to their titles, such as "Minister for Railroads and Bribery." Gandhi's campaign slogan "Indira is India, and India is Indira," which Rushdie often quotes in these contexts, thus becomes a dire prophecy. It is little wonder that distribution of *Midnight's Children*, published during India's state of national emergency, was prohibited in India. The novel also made Rushdie persona non grata in the country of his birth.

SHAME

Rushdie has called *Shame* his "antisequel" to *Midnight's Children*. It has picaresque and seriocomic elements that resemble those of the earlier novel, but its characters are Pakistanis, members of the power elite that had its historical counterpart in the circle of deposed prime minister Zulfikar Ali Bhutto and Bhutto's protégé, the man who engineered the coup and Bhutto's trial and execution, Mohammad Zia-ul-Haq. *Shame* created as much consternation in Pakistan as *Midnight's Children* had in India, with precisely the same result: The novel was banned in Pakistan, and Rushdie was considered subversive.

The title of *Shame* derives from the Urdu word *Sharam*, and it contains an encyclopedia of nuance the English barely suggests: embarrassment, discomfiture, indecency, immodesty, and the sense of unfulfilled promise. Rushdie thus explores in this work themes that are similar to those of his first novel. All the characters experience shame in one or another of these forms as well as some its converse, shamelessness.

Shame also maintains the highly mythic, literary tone of *Midnight's Children*. Its unprepossessing hero, evocatively named Omar Khayyám Shakil, is a paunchy doctor of great promise with the name of the Persian poet known for the twelfth century *Rubáiyát*, the erotic lyric poems imitated in English by Edward FitzGerald in 1859. Rushdie's Omar is born in a crumbling house called Nishapur (also the town of the historical poet's birth), once the mansion of an Englishman, Colonel Arthur Greenfield, in a Pakistani backwater identified only as "Q," but perhaps Quetta.

The circumstances of Omar's birth are ambiguous. He has three mothers: Chhunni, Munnee, and Bunny Shakil. These three sisters all consider him their son, and none discloses which of them actually gave him birth, nor will they disclose the name of his father, though the reader learns that he is an Englishman. Omar's situation is thus a metaphor of the mixed cultural legacy Rushdie often describes. Indeed, Rushdie has often spoken of himself as a man with three mothers: India, Pakistan, and England. The house in which Omar is reared is a labyrinth, a relic of the British Raj; its corridors lead to rooms unoccupied for generations, and Omar, who in his early boyhood is prohibited from leaving the house at any time, is frightened out of his wits when he ventures too far and sees that the water-seeking roots of a tree have punctured the house's outer walls. All of this is Rushdie's metaphorical description of the state of mind of a person with mixed and hostile origins: alienated, loveless, relentlessly, fearfully traversing the labyrinth of the mind, and feeling shame. Omar's only glimpse of the world outside Nishapur is through his telescope, appropriately, given that the poet for whom he was named was also an astronomer.

The novel is filled with a wealth of characters whose backgrounds are similarly symbolic and complex. Rushdie draws them together both through family relationships and through their individually shameful actions as well as their capacity to feel shame. For example, Bilquìs Kemal Hyder is a woman reared in Bombay, India, by her father, Mahound "the Woman" Kemal, owner of a motion-picture theater. The epithet regularly applied to her father is simultaneously an indication of his motherly solicitude for his daughter and a jibe at his having lost his masculinity by assuming the burden of child rearing. After her father dies in a terrorist bomb blast that also destroys his theater, Bilquìs is rescued by Raza "Razor Guts" Hyder, Rushdie's version of Zia, an ambitious young military officer who takes her as his bride and returns to the family home in Karachi, Pakistan, the country created by partition of the Indian subcontinent. Thrust into an uncompromisingly Muslim environment, she finds herself shamed when she is unable to bear Hyder a son. Of their two daughters, Sufiya Zinobia Hyder and Naveed "Good News" Hyder, the first is perpetually childlike, the result of a mistreated case of meningitis. Bilquìs and Hyder's second daughter, "Good News," atones for her mother's relative infertility by bearing twenty-seven children.

The focus of *Shame* is the rise to power of Omar's companion in dissipation, Iskander "Isky" Harappa, based on Zulfikar Ali Bhutto. Isky gives up drinking and womanizing in middle age, adopts the veneer of a devout Muslim, and seizes power after the loss of Pakistan's east wing. For a time he remains popular, assisted by his beautiful unmarried daughter, Arjumand "Virgin Ironpants" Harappa, Rushdie's satiric depiction of Benazir Bhutto, who would later become prime minister of Pakistan. Isky's wife, Rani Humayun Hyder, remains out of the limelight on the family's isolated estate, where she weaves shawls that document all of her husband's acts of shame—a twist on the Penelope motif of Homer's *Odyssey* (c. 725 B.C.E.; English translation, 1614). By the time Isky is hanged in a military coup, Rani has completed eighteen of these shawls. (Rushdie enumerates the details of each in an angry excursus modeled on a Homeric epic catalog.)

When Hyder seizes power, he encourages the trial and conviction of Isky Harappa. After a curious combination of circumstances causes Harappa's death, Hyder orders the corpse hanged, ostensibly carrying out the court's sentence of execution. Hyder's increasing concern is, however, the deviant behavior of his daughter, Sufiya Zinobia. Though well past twenty, she has the mental age of less than ten. Hyder accepts Omar Shakil's offer to marry her, made out of shame for his past womanizing and platonic love for the young woman whose life he had saved. Sufiya Zinobia is, however, aware that some act about which she knows nothing regularly accompanies marriage. She twice escapes from the Hyder house, where she is literally imprisoned (recalling Shakil's own imprisonment in youth), allows herself to be raped at random by street-walking men, then decapitates the men who have raped her. The villagers who discover these decapitated corpses create the legend of a wild white panther to explain the murders, but Hyder knows that his daughter is the killer and fears that she will eventually decapitate him.

When Hyder's downfall appears imminent, he, his wife Bilquìs, and Shakil escape to the closed mansion of Shakil's youth, and Shakil's three mothers give them sanctuary. Shakil quickly realizes, however, that the three old women plan to kill Hyder in reprisal for his having ordered the death of their younger son, Babar Shakil, for his terrorist involvements. This they do, though not before the accidental death of Bilquìs. Shakil dies soon thereafter, shot by Talvar Ulhaq, Hyder's son-in-law and former state police chief. The pantherlike figure of Sufiya Zinobia observes the carnage, with Harappa's daughter Arjumand hovering as a vision of a future of "a new cycle of shamelessness."

Rushdie's point, developed through these and other complexities of plot, is that shame and shamelessness develop through religious and political failure; the images of Islam and Pakistan that he invokes are filled with parricide and cruelty, but never genuine and simple love. That those who destroy one another are related by family as well as national ties merely compounds the tragedy and the shame. Rushdie's Pakistan is presented as "a failure of the dreaming mind."

THE SATANIC VERSES

The Satanic Verses is Rushdie's strongest indictment of politicized religion, mixed cultural identity, and insensitive, arbitrary officialdom. Its tone is allegorical, picaresque, satiric, and irreverent. Those who know details concerning the founding of Islam, British politics, and contemporary London will recognize the objections made to the book; those unaware of these particulars will likely be puzzled by the novel's character and chronological shifts and may even wonder why the work has caused such consternation.

The novel begins with an explosion, a passenger airplane destroyed by a terrorist bomb as it flies over the English Channel. Only two passengers survive: Gibreel Farishta and Saladin Chamcha, two actors of Indian origin. Miraculously, they float to earth unharmed. Farishta, whose first name is the Indian form of that of the angel Gabriel, has made his reputation playing Krishna, Gautama Buddha, Hanuman, and other Indian deities in films known as theologicals. Chamcha, a complete Anglophile, has achieved fame by doing commercial voice-overs in England, though his face is unknown to his admiring audience. With this as background, Rushdie establishes the figure of the angel Gibreel (in Islam associated with bringing Allah's call to the Prophet Muḥammad) and the apparently diabolical Chamcha, who has traded his ethnic identity for a pseudo-British veneer.

When they land, Chamcha discovers that he has grown horns under his very English bowler, as well as cloven hooves and a huge phallus—this despite his mild demeanor, elegant manners, and proper British appearance. Farishta (whose surname means "sweet") finds that he has a halo, despite his being an unconscionable womanizer. His very trip to England was a pursuit of Alleluia Cone, the British "ice queen" of Polish refugee parents. Cone is an internationally famous mountain climber who has conquered Mount Everest. Rushdie thus mixes the imagery of good and evil, angel and demon; this is an exponential motif of the entire novel. It follows that the British police arrest Chamcha as an illegal immigrant and brutalize him terribly. Farishta, however, because of his angelic appearance, remains free, having charmed the police and having refused to identify Chamcha.

The narrative then abruptly shifts to introduce Mahound, a blasphemous name for Muḥammad, the founder of Islam. Edmund Spenser used the name Mahound in *The Faerie Queene* (1590, 1596) to represent a heathen idol reserved for oaths sworn by the wicked. Rushdie's Mahound profanely re-creates Muḥammad's call from Allah through the angel Gabriel. Mahound, like Muḥammad, is a businessman; he climbs Mount Cone and looks down on the city of sand that Rushdie calls Jahilia, a fictive town that corresponds to Mecca. Mahound's pursuit of his destiny on Mount Cone corresponds to Gibreel's pursuit of mountain climber Alleluia Cone; his dream-filled sleeps as he awaits the angel Gibreel resemble the trancelike seizures, ever increasing in severity, of Gibreel Farishta.

Mahound's companions are described as the scum of Jahilia (Muḥammad's companions were former slaves), and Rushdie puckishly names one of them Salman. They have the habit, dangerous in a city built entirely of sand, of constantly washing themselves (a parody of Muslim ritual purification). The twelve whores of Jahilia (which means "ignorance" or "darkness"), reminiscent of Muḥammad's twelve wives and known as Mothers of the Believers, reside in a brothel called the Curtain. Translated as *hejab*, this can be associated with the curtainlike veil worn by pious Muslim women.

Abu Simbel, the name of the village flooded in the 1960's when Egypt constructed the Aswān High Dam, is the name given here to the ruler of Jahilia, a city also endangered by water. Because he recognizes Mahound as a threat to his power, Abu Simbel offers him a deal. If Mahound's Allah will accept a mere 3 of Jahilia's 360 deities into the new monotheistic religion, he will recognize it and give Mahound a seat on the ruling council. It will not be much of a compromise, Abu Simbel insists, since Mahound's religion already recognizes Gibreel as the voice of Allah and Shaitan (Satan) as the spirit the Qur'ān records would not bow before Adam.

Mahound decides to compromise. He climbs Cone Mountain, consults with his Gibreel, then returns to Jahilia to announce the new verses: "Have you thought upon Lat and Uzza, and Manat, the third, the other?... They are the exalted birds, and their intercession is desired indeed." These are the so-called Satan-inspired inclusions of the goddesses of motherhood (Lat), beauty and love (Uzza), and fate (Manat) as daughters of Allah, which the Qur'ān rejects as heresy. Mahound later publicly recants this heretical insertion and flees to Yathrib (the ancient name for Medina), corresponding to the historical account of the *hegira*, Muḥammad's flight from Mecca to Medina. Gibreel reappears to announce: "It was me both times, baba, me first and second also me." One can draw implications that Islam was founded by rationalizing good and evil, that its founder was both a sincere mystic and a power-hungry entrepreneur, and that Gibreel, an actor who specializes in impersonating deities, had given at least one bravura performance that changed history.

Rushdie goes on to recount a masked sardonic version of the holy war to establish Islam, continuing to blur the distinction between ancient and modern times. A bearded, turbaned imam in exile in London (which he considers Sodom) is in exile from his homeland, called Desh. When a revolution begins in Desh and overthrows the corrupt empress, named Ayesha (ironically also the name of Muḥammad's favorite wife), Gibreel (perhaps the angel, perhaps the actor Farishta, perhaps one and the same) flies the imam to Desh on his back in time to see the carnage. This episode can be interpreted as the recall to Iran of the Ayatollah Khomeini, who was in exile near Paris until the overthrow of the shah. When the revolution succeeds, Ayesha metamorphoses into the mother goddess, Al-Lat, she whom Mahound had falsely named a daughter of Allah in the satanic verses.

In a parallel sequence, an epileptic peasant girl, also named Ayesha, arouses the lust of a landowner named Mirza Saeed, whose wife is dying of breast cancer. As Moses led the Israelites out of Egypt, so Ayesha, who declares that her husband the archangel Gibreel has told her to do so, leads the entire village, including Saeed's wife, on a pilgrimage by foot to Mecca. She declares that the Arabian Sea will open to admit them (recalling the parting of the Red Sea in Exodus); butterflies mark their privileged status, and they are Ayesha's only food (recalling the manna of the Israelites). All that the unbelievers see as they watch the pilgrims is their disappearance into the Arabian Sea. The implication remains that Ayesha parts the sea for those who believe; to everyone else, the entire enterprise ends as a cult suicide. This motif emphasizes the novel's focus on migration, which Rushdie has claimed is its central subject.

Much more happens in *The Satanic Verses*. London, called "Ellowen Deeowen" by Farishta, is beset by ethnic antagonisms. Its police and most whites are brutal racists; its Indians are rogues or displaced mystics. Still, nothing in Rushdie's novel is what it appears to be, and that is his point. Empires and religions alike arise from a combination of noble and sordid motives. It is impossible to admire or hate anything unreservedly; there is evil even in that which appears absolutely good, and, conversely, one can explain evil in terms of good gone awry. Such relativism is hardly new, but the notoriety *The Satanic Verses* has received has obscured the author's point. What is clear is that *The Satanic Verses* is the logical sequel to ideas Rushdie began to develop in *Midnight's Children* and *Shame*, as well as an allegory that strains narrative and religious sensibilities to the breaking point.

THE MOOR'S LAST SIGH

As a kind of permanent immigrant, a man who can neither return to a home country (India) nor feel really at home in any other land, Rushdie has, as Henry Louis Gates, Jr., has noted, presented a "vision of migrancy as the very condition of cultural modernity." A crucial aspect of this aesthetic position, however, has been an intense examination of the various homelands that formed—and continued to inform—the intellectual, spiritual, and political components of Rushdie's psychological being. Whereas *Midnight's Children* and *Shame* focus on India and Pakistan at specific, contemporary moments in their postcolonial history, *The Moor's Last Sigh* is an attempt to account for and understand the origins and evolution of the complex cultural matrix that Rushdie refers to as "Mother India." Its narrative combines the overall structure of the classic nineteenth century novel, projecting the epic sweep of history, with an episodic linkage of individual incidents and characters akin to the picaresque; it is also similar to Eastern story cycles.

The Moor of the title is Moraes Zogoiby, son of Aurora Da Gama, whose lineage is Indian Muslim, and Abraham Zogoiby, whose ancestors include Muslim and Jewish exiles who were banished from Spain in 1492. Through the course of the novel, Moraes tells the story of his family from the mid-nineteenth century to the present (the 1990's), where he, the lone survivor, has returned to Spain to continue a frustrating quest for his mother's legacy: the Moorish paintings that may reveal the essential truth and meaning of his life.

This intricate, swirling mix of history, myth, legend, personal feuds, ethnic rivalries, and disappointed love is the story of a man trying to make some sense of his life as well as the story of his fascinating, driven family. It is also the saga of a country with a long past, an interim as a semisubjugated colonial entity, and a turbulent, troubled present. While much of the narrative is written with the kind of vivid, detailed realism that is one of the marks of Rushdie's style—an abundance of descriptive images and evocative details—frequent infusions of mystic moments, almost hallucinatory states of being, apparent intrusions of the supernatural, and other features of Magical Realism contribute to a larger dimension than a historic record. This is especially apparent in the presentation of Aurora Zogoiby as a symbol for India itself, an equivalent to the *Mother India* (the name of a film released in 1957, the year of Moraes's birth) that represents all of the clashing, tempestuous qualities exerting an immense emotional pull on its inhabitants. It is also apparent in Moraes's (meaning Rushdie's) exhilarated response to and evocation of the city of Bombay, an urban masculine complement to the more pastoral, and historically traditional, feminine motherland.

Moraes states early in the novel that his account is one of regret, "a last sigh for a lost world," and the world that he re-creates or reimagines is a rich fusion of cultures, a hybrid set in sharp contrast to what Rushdie calls "the fundamentalist, totalized explanation of the world" that he has challenged throughout his work. The novel begins in the region of Cochin, where the West (Europe) and the East (India) met and mingled for the first time. It was the central site of the pepper crop, and among other extended metaphors that are threaded through the novel, spice—the source of the Da Gama family wealth—stands for passionate love. The shift from commerce in the spice trade to the contemporary economics of currency and technology underscores the separation of the human from its most significant strengths and is one of the primary causes of the downward course that the Da Gama line takes.

For Rushdie, love begins as an irresistible rush of physical feeling that overwhelms the senses but then is complicated by circumstances of family, ambition, and cultural forces beyond individual control. While Moraes maintains that "defeated love would still be love," Rushdie has observed that "the central story of Aurora and Abraham in the book is a story of what happens when love dies." Moraes struggles to fill the "dreadful vortex" of its absence, and though his life in retrospect reveals his failure in all the realms where love matters (nation, parents, partner), his efforts to understand love's power and to use it in accordance with a set of human values redeem his failure.

The loss of Moraes's family foundation due to love's blindness and treachery is balanced by the restoring capacity of the love for a place and by the invigorating experience of artistic consciousness as a means of illumination. *The Moor's Last Sigh* is a paen to a special place, the vanishing (perhaps never existent) India of Rushdie's heart's core, the "romantic myth of a plural, hybrid nation," which he lovingly describes in Aurora's paintings. A sense of loss permeates the narrative, as Moraes's three sisters, his treacherous lover Uma Sarasvati (possibly based on Marianne Wiggins), many acquaintances, and various semiadversaries die prematurely. Adding to this loss are his estrangement from his parents and his separation from the places he has known as home. As a compensation of sorts, India continues to glow in Moraes's mind, rendered indelibly in Rushdie's verbal paintings. It is the unifying concept for what Rushdie calls "the four anchors of the soul," which he lists as "place, language, people, customs." The sheer size of the India that Rushdie constructs, in addition to a palimpsest of its layers, makes it an elusive, almost chimerical country. *The Moor's Last Sigh*, laced with loss, disappointment, frustration, and anger, is not a pessimistic vision of existence, because even when place, peoples, and customs are removed, language remains, and Moraes—who exhibits all of the verbal virtuosity that is a feature of Rushdie's style—utilizes the powers of language in the service of truth, to his last breath.

THE ENCHANTRESS OF FLORENCE

The Enchantress of Florence is an ambitious work; though presented as a novel, it more closely resembles medieval romance. It is concerned with the storytelling process more than with telling a sustained story. Frame tales appear within frame tales, and the result is a work that resembles the fifteenth century collection of stories *The Arabian Nights' Entertainments* (also known as *The Thousand and One Nights*) or perhaps John Barth's *Chimera* (1972), his own resetting of the Scheherazade tales.

The central figure of *The Enchantress of Florence* is Akbar the Great, the liberal Mughal emperor of the sixteenth century, a historical figure. Akbar represents toleration of religion, no doubt an attractive symbol for Rushdie, given the precarious circumstances under which he has lived since publication of *The Satanic Verses*. Akbar sees the world in which he lives dissolving into hatred and violence. Though something of a philosopher king, he seems paralyzed by his inability to trust any of those around him, even his closest advisers.

A mysterious traveler from the West suddenly appears at Akbar's court. He too has a basis in history, though his identifications are several. The stranger is variously Agostino Vespucci (cousin of the explorer Amerigo Vespucci), though he also calls himself "Uccello." The immediate reference appears to be to Paolo Uccello, born Paolo di Dono (1397-1475), a Renaissance painter known for his application of mathematical principles to his art in conveying perfect perspective. It is also true, however, that this relatively common Italian surname, meaning "bird," implies someone wise but crafty and possibly untrustworthy. Vespucci-Uccello has a third identity, perhaps the most significant, that of Mogor dell'Amore, the "Mughal of Love." Vespucci-Uccello-Mogor dell'Amore claims kinship with Akbar and quickly becomes his closest adviser, though even Akbar is aware of the seductive quality of his new adviser's tale telling.

The Enchantress of Florence is a verbal arabesque with an enormous number of characters. Many of these are historical figures fictionalized and reworked, such as the Medicis and Niccolò Machiavelli. There is also a variation on the Pygmalion myth. Despite his extensive harem, Akbar is able to conjure up only one, Jodha, who is perfect, and he has done this through a dream. Jodha's opposite is Qara Köz ("Black Eyes") whose androgynous sensuality fills Rushdie's romance. Rushdie channels this sensuality into aesthetics, however, for this is his abiding concern.

Robert J. Forman
Updated by Leon Lewis

OTHER MAJOR WORKS

SHORT FICTION: *East, West: Stories*, 1994; "The Firebird's Nest," 1997; "Vina Divina," 1999.

PLAY: *Midnight's Children*, pr., pb. 2003 (adaptation of his novel; with Simon Reade and Tim Supple).

NONFICTION: *The Jaguar Smile: A Nicaraguan Journey*, 1987; *Imaginary Homelands: Essays and Criticism, 1981-1991*, 1991; *The Wizard of Oz: A Short Text About Magic*, 1992; *Conversations with Salman Rushdie*, 2000 (Michael Reder, editor); *Step Across This Line: Collected Nonfiction, 1992-2002*, 2002.

BIBLIOGRAPHY

Appignanesi, Lisa, and Sara Maitland, eds. *The Rushdie File*. Syracuse, N.Y.: Syracuse University Press, 1990. Collection of essays surveys critical reaction to *The Satanic Verses*. Includes the text of the Khomeini fatwa.

Cundy, Catherine. *Salman Rushdie*. Manchester, England: Manchester University Press, 1996. Provides a good, readable introductory overview of Rushdie's fiction.

Dascalu, Cristina Emanuela. *Imaginary Homelands of Writers in Exile: Salman Rushdie, Bharati Mukherjee, and V. S. Naipaul*. Youngstown, N.Y.: Cambria Press, 2007. Examines how exile, voluntary and involuntary, has affected the work of these three quite different writers.

Goonetilleke, D. C. R. A. *Salman Rushdie*. New York: St. Martin's Press, 1998. Focuses on Rushdie's long fiction, examining the author's technique, autobiographical and historical elements in his work, and his position as a writer between cultures, among other topics.

Gurnah, Abdulrazak. *The Cambridge Companion to Salman Rushdie*. New York: Cambridge University Press, 2007. Provides a comprehensive introduction to Rushdie's work for the general reader.

Hamilton, Ian. "The First Life of Salman Rushdie." *The New Yorker*, December 25, 1995. Excellent, illuminating presentation of Rushdie's life before the fatwa, written with Rushdie's assistance and including accounts from interviews with many of Rushdie's friends and peers.

Hassumani, Sabrina. *Salman Rushdie: A Postmodern Reading of His Major Works*. Madison, N.J.: Fairleigh Dickinson University Press, 2002. Presents close readings of Rushdie's five major novels from *Midnight's Children* through *The Moor's Last Sigh*.

Pipes, Daniel. *The Rushdie Affair: The Novel, the Ayatollah, and the West*. New York: Birch Lane Press, 1990. Recounts the controversy attending publication of *The Satanic Verses*, but examines the question from the Muslim point of view. Suggests that valid arguments against publication of the novel were lost in the wake of the Khomeini fatwa that decreed Rushdie's death, in effect giving credence to the stereotype of Muslims held by many Westerners.

Rushdie, Salman. *Salman Rushdie Interviews: A Sourcebook of His Ideas.* Edited by Pradyumna S. Chauhan. Westport, Conn.: Greenwood Press, 2001. Handy selection of Rushdie's many interviews provides insight into his thinking, writing, and life experience.

Taneja, G. R., and R. K. Dhawan, eds. *The Novels of Salman Rushdie.* New Delhi: Indian Society for Commonwealth Studies, 1992. Wide-ranging compilation of essays by contributors from the Indian subcontinent covers all of Rushdie's writing through 1992 except *The Satanic Verses.* Provides a perspective beyond the criticism of Anglo-American authors.

MIKHAIL SHOLOKHOV

Born: Kruzhilino, Russia; May 24, 1905
Died: Kruzhilino, Russia, Soviet Union (now in Russia); February 21, 1984
Also known as: Mikhail Aleksandrovich Sholokhov

PRINCIPAL LONG FICTION
Tikhii Don, 1928-1940 (partial translation *And Quiet Flows the Don*, 1934, also known as *The Don Flows Home to the Sea*, 1940; complete translation *The Silent Don*, 1942, also known as *And Quiet Flows the Don*, 1967)
Podnyataya tselina, 1932, 1960 (translation of volume 1 *Virgin Soil Upturned*, 1935, also known as *Seeds of Tomorrow*, 1935; translation of volume 2, *Harvest on the Don*, 1960; complete translation *Virgin Soil Upturned*, 1979)
Oni srazhalis za rodinu, 1943-1944 (serial), 1971 (book; *They Fought for Their Country*, 1959)
Sud'ba cheloveka, 1956-1957 (novella; *The Fate of a Man*, 1958)

OTHER LITERARY FORMS

Mikhail Sholokhov (SHAWL-eh-kawf) published collections of short stories, *Donskiye rasskazy* and *Lazorevaya Step*, in 1926. In 1931, *Lazorevaya Step* was expanded to include *Donskiye rasskazy* and was translated in 1961 as *Tales from the Don*. His short stories form volume 1 of his complete works, *Sobranie sochinenii* (1956-1960; *Collected Works in Eight Volumes*, 1984), which were first published in Moscow in eight volumes; war stories and essays form volume 8. They also are available in English as *One Man's Destiny, and Other Stories, Articles, and Sketches, 1923-1963* (1967) and *At the Bidding of the Heart: Essays, Sketches, Speeches, Papers* (1973).

ACHIEVEMENTS

Mikhail Sholokhov occupies a unique place in Soviet literature as the author of *The Silent Don*, the greatest novel to be published in the Soviet Union. He has been compared to Leo Tolstoy in his creation of a national epic, to Fyodor Dostoevski in his portrayal of Grigorii Melekhov, and to Nikolai Gogol and Anton Chekhov in his evocations of the steppe. In 1965, he was permitted by Soviet authorities to receive the Nobel Prize in Literature, a privilege denied to Boris Pasternak, who wrote a more profoundly philosophical novel. In addition, Sholokhov held numerous positions of honor in the Communist Party and the Union of Soviet Writers. He won the Stalin and Lenin prizes for literature (1941, 1960) and received honorary degrees from Western and Soviet universities.

In his two major works, *The Silent Don* and *Virgin Soil Upturned*, Sholokhov succeeds in bringing to life the Cossack world that he knew so well. Shrouded in legends, scorned for their barbarity, the Cossacks were little known to the Russians and totally unknown to

Mikhail Sholokhov
(Library of Congress)

Western readers. Sholokhov speaks in their dialect, clothes his characters in colorful Cossack traditions, and arms the soldiers with a spirit of courage and adventure. Part 1 of *The Silent Don* in particular and much of *Virgin Soil Upturned* shows them in their daily occupations, their celebrations and their interaction, much in their colorful and often crude language. Through his fictitious characters, all modeled on his own friends and acquaintances, the image of a people emerges.

Particularly in *The Silent Don*, Sholokhov skillfully combined Socialist Realism and art. Officially promulgated in 1934, Socialist Realism required that literature served the ideals of the Communist Party and portrayed a positive Soviet citizen. Early Soviet critics—with the exception of Aleksandr Serafimovich and Maxim Gorky—could not understand that *The Silent Don*, with its vacillating hero and its objective portrayal of both Reds and Whites, was a true proletarian novel, and they tried desperately to block its publication. Eventually, however, the critics accepted it because it showed the triumph of the Revolution through suffering and violence on both sides. Yet it was the artistic qualities of the novel, already evident in Sholokhov's early short stories, and to be continued in *Virgin Soil Upturned*, that won millions of readers in the Soviet Union and abroad. The humanness of suffering, the tenderness of love, and the uncertainty of truth touched them.

It was not without difficulty that Sholokhov acquired this reputation. Particularly in *The Silent Don*, the censors mercilessly changed and deleted some of his most brilliant passages. Joseph Stalin asked that the hero of *The Silent Don*, Grigorii Melekhov, accept Communism, but Sholokhov refused, saying that this was against the artistic conception of the work. Although *Virgin Soil Upturned* received less criticism, the death of Davydov was a concession to Stalin's wishes, since Sholokhov had planned a suicide. Yet the changes imposed on Sholokhov or accepted by him did not dim the original ideas that he had researched and reflected on painstakingly from 1925 to 1940 for *The Silent Don*, and from 1930 to 1960 for *Virgin Soil Upturned*. Outspoken like his Cossack hero Grigorii, Sholokhov says that an artist must follow his heart. He did not hesitate to criticize the inefficiency of the Soviet system and to express the depth of human suffering that accompanied the Revolution. On the other hand, as a dutiful Communist, he said that one's heart must follow the party. This was a difficult reconciliation, yet Sholokhov seems to have effected it more successfully than any other writer in the Soviet Union.

It should be noted, however, that ever since the publication of the first part of *The Silent Don*, Sholokhov's authorship of this masterwork, which clearly stands above the rest of his production, has been questioned. Among those to raise this charge was Aleksandr Solzhenitsyn, who believed that the actual author was a Cossack officer named Fyodor Krykov, who had written several books about the Don region before his death in the Civil War. This charge against Sholokhov has yet to be conclusively proved or disproved.

Biography

Born on May 24, 1905, in the Cossack village of Kruzhilino near Veshenskaya, Mikhail Aleksandrovich Sholokhov was himself not a true Cossack. His father, Aleksandr Mikhailovich, did not marry his mother, Anastasiya Danilovna Chernikova, until 1912, when Sholokhov's birth was legitimated and the Cossack status he had held from his mother's first husband was abrogated. Nevertheless, he grew up in the customs and traditions of the Cossack world that he was later to convey with such realism to his readers. His early education in his native village was minimal when he left for a year in Moscow in 1914. Financial reasons precluded his continuing, but he was subsequently enrolled in an eight-year *Gymnasium* (college-preparatory secondary school) in Boguchar. The German invasion of 1918 marked the end of his formal education but did not interrupt his love of reading and writing.

In the years between 1918 and 1922, Sholokhov worked for the new Soviet regime in many capacities, especially grain-requisitioning, and wrote plays for young people. His home was in an area controlled by the Whites. He saw much violence, participated in it himself, and was twice at the point of being killed. This experience is reflected especially in the violence and objectivity of *The Silent Don*, where Grigorii broods confusedly on the injustices committed by both sides.

In 1922, Sholokhov married Maria Petrovna Gromoslavskaya, the daughter of a well-to-do and long-established Cossack family. She was to prove an ideal "comrade" for him. The couple, who would have four children, moved to Moscow, where Sholokhov began his first serious commitment to literature. He published a number of short stories, uneven in literary value but extremely popular. In their vividness of language, diversity of speech, and lively dialogue, they anticipate the achievements of his mature fiction. Never at home in the capital, or in any city, Sholokhov returned to Kruzhilino in 1924.

Sholokhov began working on his masterpiece, *The Silent Don*, in 1925, amid innumerable difficulties with the censors. It was only the intercession of Aleksandr Serafimovich, editor of the monthly *Oktyabr'*, that permitted publication of the initial segment of the novel. Serafimovich's support, however, did not prevent the many attacks on the novel and on Sholokhov himself, who was first accused of plagiarism in 1929-1930. Later, Gorky's intervention, and ultimately Stalin's, permitted him to complete publication of the novel. Sholokhov worked on *The Silent Don* almost constantly from 1925 to 1930, the most productive years of his career. He interrupted *The Silent Don* in 1930 to begin *Virgin Soil Upturned*. In 1932, he gained admission into the Communist Party, and in 1934 he was elected to the presidium of the Union of Soviet Writers. He visited Sweden, Denmark, Great Britain, and France as a representative of the Writers' Union. His success did not prevent him from speaking out fearlessly against the bureaucracy, which ultimately placed him in a dangerous position, especially in 1938, when he narrowly escaped liquidation. His personal friendship with Stalin saved him, and he always remained loyal to his friend, even after Stalin's death.

During World War II, in which he experienced much personal suffering, including the loss of his manuscripts, Sholokhov became a war correspondent. His writings as a reporter are not his best; nevertheless, after the war he devoted himself mainly to journalism, with the exception of volume 2 of *Virgin Soil Upturned*; *They Fought for Their Country*, an unfinished novel in a war setting; and a very successful novella, *The Fate of a Man*. In the postwar era, he enjoyed unparalleled success in the Soviet Union, receiving many prizes, the most notable of which was the Nobel Prize in Literature in 1965. He became a staunch defender of party policies, attacking such dissidents as Pasternak, Solzhenitsyn, Yuli Daniel, and Andrei Sinyavsky, all of whom are superior to him as writers. Typical of his attacks on the West was an invective against Harry S. Truman, then-president of the United States.

Until his death in 1984, Sholokhov lived in the village where he was born. He hunted and fished, traveled widely in Europe, the United States, and Japan, and enjoyed his substantial wealth and international reputation.

Analysis

The critic Herman Ermolaev has observed that Mikhail Sholokhov's art embraces the epic, the dramatic, the comic, and the lyric; to this one might justly add the tragic, at least in *The Silent Don*. Helen Muchnic, for example, sees in the character of Grigorii the fatal flaw that marks the heroes of Greek tragedy: Grigorii is doomed by his failure to recognize the greatness of Bolshevism. His error lies in his independence. Like Oedipus, Grigorii cannot *not* know the truth, but unlike Sophocles' hero, Sholokhov's is destined never to know clearly. Even Soviet critics noted the tragic element in *The Silent Don*, and in 1940, Boris Emelyanov compared *The Silent Don* to Aeschylus's *The Persians* (472 B.C.E.), since both were written from the viewpoint of the vanquished. *The Silent Don* is of epic proportions because of its length and its scope in time (1912-1922) at a crucial period in Western history, World War I and the Soviet Revolution. It was serialized in *Oktyabr'* and *Novy mir* from 1928 to 1940. Volume 1 was published by Moskovskii Rabochii in 1928, volume 2 in 1929; Khudozhestvennaya Literatura published volumes 3 and 4 in 1933 and 1940 respectively.

THE SILENT DON

The novel is the story of the fall of a people seen through some of its most representative families: Melekhov, Korshunov, and Koshevoi in particular. Often compared to Tolstoy's *War and Peace* (1865-1869), *The Silent Don* unfolds a vast panorama of people and world-shaking events, and 1917 is to Sholokhov what 1812 was to Tolstoy. Yet Sholokhov is no Tolstoy. He lacks Tolstoy's depth of vision, moral intensity, and psychological analysis. Sholokhov's choice of a secluded and anachronistic prerevolutionary society places *The Silent Don* in the category of the primitive and popular epics, as David Stewart demonstrates through his analysis of action, character, language, and meaning in the novel.

Early in his career, Sholokhov was attracted to the theater, and thus it is not surprising that in both of his novels dialogue and action are of extreme importance. Sholokhov uses lively and spirited conversation, filled with dialectical and sometimes crude Cossack expressions, and often incorrect Russian. In fact, the major part of the novels is dialogue rather than narrative, and important events come to light through the characters rather than through the author. Sholokhov does not write reflective philosophical works. Grigorii Melekhov's search for truth is less evident in his thoughts than in his actions, as he vacillates constantly between Red and White, and between his wife, Natalia, and his mistress, Aksinia. Collectivization is not a well-thought-out plan in *Virgin Soil Upturned* but rather a process that occurs because each farmer moves in that direction.

Both people and nature are actors in Sholokhov's works, and he moves effortlessly and harmoniously from one to the other. The poetic evocations of nature that make up at least one-fourth of *The Silent Don* and a good part, though less, of *Virgin Soil Upturned* show Sholokhov's lyric mastery at its height. Most are placed at strategic positions, such as the beginning and end of chapters, and convey the union of people with nature. In somewhat pantheistic exultation, Sholokhov rejoices with nature in its cycle of birth, death, and resurrection. As one might expect from the titles of his novels, the Don mirrors human hopes and sorrows. Sholokhov's books convey the feel of the earth—the Russian soil—and evoke the rhythm of nature.

Nature is frequently associated with love in Sholokhov's fiction. Ermolaev, who has studied the role of nature in Sholokhov, identifies floral blooming with Aksinia; Easter, the spring, and rain, with Natalia. In Grigorii and Aksinia, one finds perhaps the tenderest love story in Soviet literature. Their passionate and fatal love recalls Anna Karenina or Dmitri Karamazov. As with Sholokhov's poetic lyricism, his love stories are close to the earth and show the deep bond of human beings with nature. The tenderness of maternal love also plays an important role in Sholokhov's works, as seen in the tender farewell of Ilinichna for her dead son, Piotra, and contrasts sharply with the brutality and violence of war.

Sholokhov's humorous vein is more evident in *Virgin Soil Upturned* but is not absent from *The Silent Don*, where one might cite Panteleimon Melekhov's wit. *Virgin Soil Upturned* abounds in comic characters and scenes: Shchukar's endless stories, the exuberance of the induction into the party, the initial reactions to collectivization at the village meetings. Sholokhov's dialogue is brisk and witty; his colloquial and dialectical language, always appropriate to the speaker, lightens the heavy subject and makes both novels highly readable.

Indeed, Sholokhov's style is brisk and light; the chapters, composed of short vignettes, leave the reader momentarily in suspense, for Sholokhov knows where to break his tale. His rapid transitions from humor to violence, from love to war, from nature to humanity, show the all-encompassing unity of life and the complexity of the Revolution and its effects. He shows the stark reality of war, the atrocities of both Reds and Whites, and humankind's inhumanity to others. On the other hand, he portrays the tenderness of love and the exultation of nature, as in his beautiful apostrophe to the steppe that rivals Gogol. He works in a linear manner, without flashbacks or foreshadowing, much in the tradition of the nineteenth century or indeed the ancient and medieval epic. He portrays life and love, the endless rhythm of birth and death, as seen in one great epoch, the Soviet Revolution.

The Silent Don was first conceived as an epic of the Don and of the role of the Don Cossacks in the Revolution, and Sholokhov projected the title *Donshchina*, later abandoning it because of its archaic allusions. The story begins in 1912 and ends in 1922. It shows the peaceful agrarian life of the Don Cossacks in the small village of Tatarsk. The domineering patriarch Panteleimon Melekhov and his independent and passionate son, Grigorii, clash often, especially in regard to Grigorii's liaison with the bewitching Aksinia. Neither the father's wrath and the arranged marriage with the beautiful and virtuous Natalia Korshunova, daughter of the prosperous Miron, nor the abuse by Aksinia's husband, Stepan Ashtakov, can break the liaison. The two lovers, defying all convention, finally choose to live together as hired help on the estate of Listnitsky.

The calm of the Cossack existence, broken only by such outbursts of passion, is shattered by mobilization in Tatarsk in 1914. Grigorii is called into battle, where his attraction and repulsion toward killing and violence are first evident. The war provides Grigorii's first contact with Bolshevism, for which he also feels both an attraction and repulsion. On leave in Tatarsk because of a wound, he learns of Aksinia's unfaithfulness and returns to his wife, who later gives birth to twins.

Like World War I, the Revolution is portrayed through the eyes of the soldiers and villagers and evoked through images of nature: "Above blood-soaked White Russia, the stars wept mournfully." The desertion of the troops, Kornilov's arrest, and the fall of Kerensky are moments of confusion to the Don Cossack soldiers. Grigorii embraces Bolshevism and becomes an officer but is incapable of the cold dedication exemplified by Bunchuk, whose brief idyll with the Jew Anna Pogudko softens the drama, and by Mishka Koshevoi, Grigorii's former friend and henceforth implacable enemy.

When Grigorii joins the Whites, his position becomes more dangerous. The violence grows more senseless and immediate, with victims such as Miron Korshunov and Piotra Melekhov, the latter killed by Mishka Koshevoi. Family tragedies also cloud Grigorii's existence and confuse his values. His sister-in-law, Daria, commits suicide; his wife, Natalia, dies as the result of an abortion after learning of Grigorii's return to Aksinia; his father dies of typhus. Parallel to Grigorii's uncertainty is Mishka's advance in the Soviet ranks and in coldheartedness. Even his marriage to Grigorii's sister, Dunia, does not dull his determination to kill Grigorii, which the reader surmises will occur when Grigorii returns home, having lost Aksinia to a stray bullet. Only his son, Mishatka, remains, and the implacable march of history will destroy the unwilling Grigorii, born to greatness at a point in history when only conformity can save him.

In 1930, Sholokhov interrupted his work on *The Silent Don* to address a contemporary problem: collectivization. He published part 1 of *Virgin Soil Upturned* in 1932, practically without any censorship difficulties. Part 2 was not completed until 1960 and is radically different in spirit. This novel is much more concentrated in scope, since it covers only the period between 1930 and 1932, has fewer characters, and is confined to the small Cossack village of Gremyachy Log. Although it does not have the epic sweep of *The Silent Don*, it is an on-the-spot documentary of a crucial phase in Soviet history.

VIRGIN SOIL UPTURNED

Also unlike *The Silent Don*, *Virgin Soil Upturned* has no main tragic character. Stewart observes that the heroes are dissolved by the party, so that the real hero is perhaps the collective people at Gremyachy Log. The logical hero is Siemion Davydov, a former factory worker and sailor, who was mobilized in 1930 to organize collective farms. He becomes chair at Gremyachy Log and manifests the zeal and inefficiency typical of early Soviet leaders. He is a colorless but not unlikable character. His death at the end of part 2 is far less tragic than Grigorii's return to Tatarsk. Although he shows his human side in his love affairs with Nagulnov's former wife, Lukeria, and with a gentle, shy seventeen-year-old, Varia Kharlamova, he is not convincing as a lover.

Siemon's associate, the passionate and impulsive Makar Nagulnov, secretary of the Gremyachy Log Party nucleus and still secretly in love with his former wife, is more attractive. Even better portrayed is Andrei Razmiotov, chair of the village Soviet. His one passion is his deceased wife, Yevdokia, and the novel ends as he visits her grave and wistfully mourns her absence. Stewart, however, regards Kondrat Maidannikov as the novel's most convincing character: A "middling Cossack," Kondrat joins the collective farm because he believes in it, yet his instincts draw him to his own property. He does not join the party until he has reflected carefully. In his simplicity, he is the most philosophical and intellectually convinced Communist in the novel.

The plot of the story is simple: the gradual conversion of the village to the collective farm. The beginning reflects Sholokhov's portrayal of violence and brutality, as entire kulak families are deported. Although collectivization is presented as voluntary, those who withdraw after reading Stalin's pronouncement are left with no animals and inferior land. The end of part 1 is indecisive though promising. In part 2, collectivization is complete, and a revolt is suppressed. Thus, this volume becomes mainly a series of sketches and stories, mostly in a humorous vein. It seems to be the work of a writer who has totally accepted party policies, writing about an accomplished fact no longer questioned.

Actually Sholokhov's best creative period ended before World War II, and part 2, written in 1960, weakens what promised to be a powerful, though limited, novel. Nevertheless, Sholokhov's treatment of collectivization has not been surpassed, and his wit and lyricism make *Virgin Soil Upturned* a valuable contribution to literature.

Irma M. Kashuba

OTHER MAJOR WORKS

SHORT FICTION: *Donskiye rasskazy*, 1926; *Lazorevaya Step*, 1926, 1931 (1931 edition includes *Donskiye rasskazy; Tales from the Don*, 1961); *Early Stories*, 1966.

NONFICTION: *Pisatel i vozhd*, 1997; *Pisma*, 2003.

MISCELLANEOUS: *Sobranie sochinenii*, 1956-1960 (8 volumes; *Collected Works in Eight Volumes*, 1984); *One Man's Destiny, and Other Stories, Articles, and Sketches, 1923-1963*, 1967; *At the Bidding of the Heart: Essays, Sketches, Speeches, Papers*, 1973.

BIBLIOGRAPHY

Clark, Katerina. "Socialist Realism in Soviet Literature." In *The Routledge Companion to Russian Literature*, edited by Neil Cornwell. New York: Routledge, 2001. Clark's essay includes discussion of *The Silent Don* and *Virgin Soil Upturned*, placing these novels within the broader context of Soviet Social Realism.

Ermolaev, Herman. *Mikhail Sholokhov and His Art*. Princeton, N.J.: Princeton University Press, 1982. A study of Sholokhov's life and art, philosophy of life, and handling of style and structure, with a separate chapter on the historical sources of *The Silent Don* and another on the question of plagiarism. Includes maps, tables of similes, notes, and a bibliography.

Klimenko, Michael. *The World of Young Sholokhov: Vision of Violence*. North Quincy,

Mass.: Christopher, 1972. The introduction discusses the Sholokhov canon as well as his life and his critics. Other chapters explore the genesis of Sholokhov's novels, vision of life, heroes, and treatment of revolution. Includes a bibliography.

Medvedev, Roy. *Problems in the Literary Biography of Mikhail Sholokhov.* New York: Cambridge University Press, 1977. A piercing examination of *The Silent Don*, exploring the issue of Sholokhov's authorship of the novel and how it poses problems for his literary biography.

Mukherjee, G. *Mikhail Sholokhov: A Critical Introduction.* New Delhi: Northern Book Centre, 1992. A bilingual study, in both English and Russian. Mukherjee analyzes the major novels and other writings of Sholokhov, considering them in relation to Soviet literature and ideology, and he discusses Sholokhov's critical reception.

Scammell, Michael. "The Don Flows Again." *The New York Times Book Review*, January 25, 1998. Scammell's review of a new translation of Sholokhov's best-known novel provides a useful overview of the writer's life and literary reputation, including an update on new evidence supporting Sholokov's claim to be the author of the book.

Stewart, David Hugh. *Mikhail Sholokhov: A Critical Introduction.* Ann Arbor: University of Michigan Press, 1967. Found in most university libraries, this is an accessible overview of Sholokhov and his works. Includes a bibliography.

UPTON SINCLAIR

Born: Baltimore, Maryland; September 20, 1878
Died: Bound Brook, New Jersey; November 25, 1968
Also known as: Upton Beall Sinclair, Jr.

PRINCIPAL LONG FICTION
  Springtime and Harvest, 1901
  The Journal of Arthur Stirling, 1903
  Prince Hagen, 1903
  Manassas, 1904 (revised as *Theirs Be the Guilt*, 1959)
  A Captain of Industry, 1906
  The Jungle, 1906
  The Overman, 1907
  The Metropolis, 1908
  The Moneychangers, 1908
  Samuel the Seeker, 1910
  Love's Pilgrimage, 1911
  Sylvia, 1913
  Sylvia's Marriage, 1914
  King Coal, 1917
  Jimmie Higgins, 1919
  100 Percent, 1920
  They Call Me Carpenter, 1922
  Oil! A Novel, 1927
  Boston, 1928
  Mountain City, 1930
  Roman Holiday, 1931
  The Wet Parade, 1931
  Co-op, 1936
  The Flivver King, 1937
  No Pasaran!, 1937
  Little Steel, 1938
  Our Lady, 1938
  World's End, 1940
  Between Two Worlds, 1941
  Dragon's Teeth, 1942
  Wide Is the Gate, 1943
  Presidential Agent, 1944
  Dragon Harvest, 1945

A World to Win, 1946
Presidential Mission, 1947
One Clear Call, 1948
O Shepherd, Speak!, 1949
Another Pamela: Or, Virtue Still Rewarded, 1950
The Return of Lanny Budd, 1953
What Didymus Did, 1954
It Happened to Didymus, 1958
Affectionately Eve, 1961

Other literary forms

Between 1901 and 1961, Upton Sinclair wrote or rewrote more than forty novels, but in addition to his longer fiction, Sinclair also wrote and published a massive amount of nonfiction, including pamphlets, analyses of diverse subjects, memoirs, twelve plays, and letters by the thousands. The bibliography of his works is testimony to his amazing fluency, but no one who is so prolific can escape being uneven, and this is indeed the case with Sinclair. His career, which spanned more than six decades, was unified in one respect, however, for both his fiction and his nonfiction were devoted to a single aim—the achievement of social justice. Everything he wrote was written primarily as a means to attain the end he sought, betterment of the conditions of life for all people. Much of what Sinclair produced is thus not belletristic in any full sense, but propaganda to spread his ideas about politics and economics. In books such as *The Industrial Republic* (1907), he tries to explain how socialism will be arrived at by a natural process in the United States; the theory is based on the premise that social revolutions are bound to be benevolent.

During the period following World War I to the onset of the Great Depression, most of Sinclair's writing was nonfiction. In a number of books that he called his Dead Hand series, in an ironic allusion to Adam Smith's "Invisible Hand" of laissez-faire economics, Sinclair deals with the destructive influence of capitalism on numerous American institutions: *The Profits of Religion* (1918) treats the abuses of institutional religions, showing how the established church supports the ruling classes in exchange for economic advantages; *The Brass Check: A Study in American Journalism* (1919) details the operation of class bias in American journalism; *The Goose-Step: A Study of American Education* (1923) reveals higher education's lackeylike relationship to capitalism, fostered by grants and endowments made to the universities by wealthy families and industry. In *The Goslings: A Study of the American Schools* (1924), the same kind of servile relationship with the capitalist status quo is exposed as existing in elementary and high schools, and in *Mammonart* (1925), Sinclair shows how artists and writers through history have been duped into serving oppressive economic and political power structures. Not even William Shakespeare, Fyodor Dostoevski, or Joseph Conrad was his own man according to

Upton Sinclair
(Library of Congress)

Sinclair's ideological criticism. Although the Dead Hand series is flawed by an excess of socialist polemics, Sinclair did extensive research to produce each book, and though the case is overstated, there is a grain of truth in his analysis of the all-pervasive influence of the economic and political structure of the United States on those areas that should be most independent of such pressure—the church, the press, the educational system, the arts.

Of more interest to the general reader are Sinclair's autobiographical works *American Outpost: A Book of Reminiscences* (1932) and *The Autobiography of Upton Sinclair* (1962), which updates his life for the thirty years intervening between the two books. In his accounts of his life, Sinclair reveals himself to be an honest but self-centered idealist. He chronicles his victories and defeats through childhood, youth, and marriage as the educational experiences of a genius; he offers in generally positive and optimistic terms his lifelong belief in progress and his hatred of social inequality and social exploitation.

Achievements

Upton Sinclair's literary remains weighed in at eight tons when they were collected for donation to Indiana University Library. Of modern American writers, Sinclair is among the most widely translated, his works having been published in forty-seven languages in thirty-nine countries, yet his literary reputation steadily declined after the 1940's, despite the fact that *The Jungle* was still widely read in high school and college classrooms. Moreover, Sinclair himself has historical importance for the role he played in the American radical movement.

Sinclair's recurring theme as a novelist was class conflict, the exploitation of the poor by the rich, of labor by management, of the have-nots by the haves. With few exceptions, the rich are depicted as useless, extravagant, and unprincipled, while the poor are essentially noble characters who are the victims of capitalistic society. Sinclair's literary method, which came to be called "muckraking," was intended to expose the evils of such a society. Apart from *The Jungle*, which is the best-known example of this genre, there is the Lanny Budd series—ten historical novels that trace the history of the world from 1913 to 1946. *Dragon's Teeth*, the third in the series, won the Pulitzer Prize for fiction in 1942 by virtue of its vivid portrayal of conditions in Nazi-dominated Europe. In addition to these, the most widely read of Sinclair's novels, he produced novels on almost every topic of then-current social history, including coal strikes in Colorado in *King Coal*, exploitation by the oil industry in California in *The Wet Parade*, and the legal injustices of the murder trial of Italian immigrants Nicola Sacco and Bartolomeo Vanzetti case in *Boston*. All of Sinclair's fiction was aimed at the middle-class liberal, whom he hoped to convert to his idealistic vision of a fellowship of labor. Sinclair was thus a spokesman for the progressive era of American history; a chronic protester and iconoclast, he tried to stir the conscience of his nation and to cause change. In only one case, *The Jungle*, was he successful in prompting the desired changes through legislation. As a propagandist writing in the spirit of Thomas Paine and in the idiom of Karl Marx, Sinclair made a permanent impact by what he said, if not by how he wrote, and to this day, he still serves as one of the chief interpreters of American society to other nations.

Biography

Upton Beall Sinclair, Jr., was born in Baltimore, Maryland, but reared in New York City. He finished high school at the age of twelve, but he was too young for college and had to wait until he was fourteen before he could enter the City College of New York. While an undergraduate, he helped support himself by writing stories and jokes for pulp magazines. In one span of a few weeks, he turned out fifty-six thousand words, an incredible feat even for a prolific prodigy such as Sinclair. In 1898, after taking his B.A. from CCNY, Sinclair enrolled as a special student in the Graduate School of Columbia University; he withdrew, however, after a professor told him, "You don't know anything about writing." In 1900, Sinclair married Meta Fuller and began work on his first novel, *Spring-*

time and Harvest, which was written in Canada. Shortly afterward, in 1902, he joined the Socialist Party. The reception of his early fiction gave Sinclair little critical encouragement, and the works gained him very little cash—his first four novels brought him less than one thousand dollars, and the threat of poverty put a strain on his marriage. In 1905, Sinclair, with Jack London, formed the Intercollegiate Socialist Society, an indication of his growing political radicalism.

Sinclair's first fame came with his fifth novel, *The Jungle*; he was even invited to the White House by President Theodore Roosevelt to discuss the book. With the thirty thousand dollars that *The Jungle* earned for him, Sinclair founded a utopian community, Helicon Colony, in New Jersey. In 1907, an arsonist burned down the colony and Sinclair's fortune with it. This was the first actual persecution that Sinclair had experienced for professing unpopular views. In private life, he faced further difficulties; his wife divorced him in 1911; he remarried in 1913 and moved West with his new wife, Mary Kimbrough, in 1915. Continuing to write at a furious pace, Sinclair became a publisher during World War I with the *Upton Sinclair Magazine*. He also issued a series of tracts on the effects of capitalism, objecting to its effects on education, art, journalism, and literature.

Not all of Sinclair's energies went into writing. He was instrumental in creating the League for Industrial Democracy and the American Civil Liberties Union. Three times he ran for the California state legislature and three times for governor, usually on the Socialist Party ticket but also as a Democrat. In *I, Governor of California and How I Ended Poverty* (1933), he set forth his platform, "End Poverty in California" or "E.P.I.C.," which explained the Depression as a result of private ownership and the economic insanity of limited production. His ideas found a large degree of public acceptance in the early days of the New Deal, and he came close to being elected despite the mudslinging of his opponent. Some critics believe that the chief reason for Sinclair's decline as a novelist was his involvement in electoral politics in the 1930's. His novels of that decade are about specific political situations. *The Flivver King* attacks Ford Motor Company and makes a case for labor unions. "Little Steel" is a story about the organization of steel-mill owners against unions. "Pasaram!" is another short story from the 1930's about the brave fight in the Spanish Civil War against right-wing dictators.

During World War II, Sinclair began the historical record of his times in the Lanny Budd series. The novels in this ten-book series show the metamorphosis of the hero, Lanny, from an espouser of socialist causes to an anti-Communist, a change that reflected Sinclair's own changed sympathies.

By the decade of the 1950's, Sinclair had entered semiretirement, during which he nevertheless managed to expand his autobiography and finish six books, including a clever parody of Samuel Richardson's epistolary novel *Pamela: Or, Virtue Rewarded* (1740-1741), titled *Another Pamela: Or, Virtue Still Rewarded*, and a biography of Jesus. In these years, Sinclair finally settled his quarrel with the status quo. In his old age, he came to approve of the American establishment's foot-dragging on civil rights and supported American intervention in Vietnam. The old radical had, like so many before him, softened his position.

Analysis

Upton Sinclair was a prodigy as a writer and wrote with great fluency and consequent unevenness. For him, the essential purpose of literature was to expose social evils and promote change; his end as a writer was the improvement of the condition of humankind. His literary reputation is thus not really germane to what he was trying to do as a writer. His fiction has more relevance when it is regarded in a political and historical light rather than as literature per se. As the social and economic issues of Sinclair's time recede into history, so does interest in those of his books that were simply propaganda.

Although Sinclair was regarded as a literary rebel for his iconoclastic attacks on the economic, intellectual, and political institutions of the United States, he was not in any way an avant-garde writer in terms of style and structure. His subject was society rather than the individual human consciousness. It is necessary in any analysis of Sinclair's fiction to admit at once the defects in his writing. Most of it is journalistic in quality rather than belletristic. In fact, Sinclair deliberately wrote against the genteel tradition in American letters. He employed his rhetoric for practical results rather than to achieve poetic effects. His polemics were couched in fictional form because he believed the novel to be a particularly effective medium for his idealistic radicalism.

Sinclair's first four novels were produced between 1900 and 1904. These early works were awkward but full of passionate idealism. In *Prince Hagen* and *The Overman*, which were written before Sinclair discovered socialism, there is already a conflict between the pure-minded and the corrupt oppressors, but no solutions for the problems are proposed. The ideology of socialism provided him with solutions, although Sinclair was not a traditional Socialist; to him, socialism was the purest expression of the American Dream. He did not see himself as an overthrower of American values but as a writer who was helping his fellow citizens return to a vision of human alliance.

Manassas

Prior to *Manassas*, Sinclair's fiction had been based on personal experience. In this novel about the American Civil War, a young Southerner, Alan Montague, the son of a Mississippi plantation owner, becomes a supporter of the abolition of slavery. The protagonist is present at many historic moments—the raid at Harper's Ferry, the bombardment of Fort Sumter—and encounters many historical figures, such as Abraham Lincoln, Jefferson Davis, Frederick Douglass, and John Brown. *Manassas* differed from Sinclair's early books in that it was more realistic and objective. As a work of art, however, *Manassas* is not remarkable. The plot is often an inert review of historical facts, the characterizations are shallow, and the story is too filled with coincidence to be plausible. Despite its flaws, *Manassas* marked a turning point in Sinclair's career. In this novel, he revealed attitudes that pointed toward his development as a writer of exposés.

THE JUNGLE

In 1904, Sinclair was asked by the editor of *The Appeal*, a radical newspaper, to write a novel about wage slavery and the oppressive conditions of industrial workers that would show that their plight was analogous to that of the blacks in the Old South. Responding to this offer, Sinclair spent two months in the meatpacking houses of Chicago talking to the workers; he visited the plants also as an official tourist, and in disguise as a worker. The impressions and information Sinclair gathered from this experience were extremely distressing to him. His personal reaction to the corruption he saw was outrage; it is his identification with the exploited workers and his naturalistic descriptions of the oppressive industrial conditions that make *The Jungle* so gripping.

As Sinclair explains in his memoirs, *American Outpost*, he returned to his farm in New Jersey after he had collected his data on the meatpacking industry in Chicago and started writing the novel on Christmas Day, completing it in the summer of 1905 after less than six months' work. Although it was published in serial form as it was being written, Sinclair had trouble finding a publisher for the book; it was refused by five houses before Doubleday and Company took it after their lawyers made a careful investigation to avoid any possible libel suits. When *The Jungle* was published in February, 1906, the public was horrified, not by the novel's account of the conditions of the workers as Sinclair and his socialist friends expected, but by the naturalistic descriptions of the slaughterhouses and the evidence of criminal negligence in meat inspection. *The Jungle*, like most of Sinclair's fiction, straddles genres; it is partly a novel and partly exposé journalism. Sinclair's purpose in writing the book was to protest the exploitation of the workers and to recommend socialism as a corrective ideology to capitalism; the revelations of unsanitary packing-plant procedures were only a means to those ends.

Hardly a dozen pages of this long novel are explicitly concerned with the repugnant details of the slaughterhouse, yet what remains in the reader's mind long after the plot line and thematic intentions fade are the scenes of grinding up poisoned rats, children's fingers, and carcasses of steers condemned as tubercular for canning meats; and the rendering of hogs dead of cholera for a fine grade of lard. Most dramatic of all, however, was Sinclair's report that men who worked in the cooking room occasionally fell into the boiling vats and were returned to the world transubstantiated into Durham's Pure Leaf Lard. The vividness of the author's descriptions had two effects: The first was an immediate drop in meat sales across the United States and Europe; the second was a summons to the White House to detail the abuses in the meat industry for President Theodore Roosevelt. The outraged public brought pressure to bear on politicians, and the U.S. Congress enacted the Federal Pure Food and Drug Act of 1906.

The sensational revelations of *The Jungle* have drawn attention from the book's literary qualities. *The Jungle* has been compared to the polemical late works of Leo Tolstoy and to the naturalistic fiction of Émile Zola because of its pessimistic determinism. The setting is the grim slums of Chicago and the gory stockyards. The novel tells the story of a group of recent Lithuanian immigrants who have been lured to the United States from their Old World villages with the promise of high wages.

Jurgis Rudkus, the novel's principal character, comes to the stockyard district, along with several of his friends and relatives, expecting to realize the American Dream, little aware that they have entered a jungle. Unable to speak English, the immigrants are exploited by almost everyone in power—the politicians, the police, the landlords, and the "Beef Trust" bosses. Jurgis has to pay his foreman part of his low salary to keep his job. He is cheated by a crooked real estate agent, who sells him a house with a hidden clause that allows the mortgage company to foreclose on him. After Jurgis and his family lose their house, they are further afflicted with misery. Jurgis loses his job after he is blacklisted, and he serves a jail term for slugging his wife's lascivious boss, who has compromised her honor. In turn, his father dies of disease, his wife and infant son die in childbirth, and, finally, he loses his last son in a drowning accident. Jurgis is left without anything; alone and in ill health, he is a broken man. He becomes a hobo, a petty criminal, and a strikebreaking scab—the lowest form of degradation for him.

In his extremity, Jurgis for the first time reflects on how unjustly he has been treated by society, which he begins to regard as his enemy, but his views are inchoate. One day, by chance he hears a Socialist speak. The lecture transforms his conception of the world; socialism is like a revelation, for now there is a way by which the workers of the world can win respect. With Jurgis's conversion, the novel as a narrative ends for all practical purposes. The last chapters are devoted to socialist propaganda and socioeconomic analysis. The optimistic conclusion of the novel contrasts sharply with the pessimistic naturalism of the first chapters. Ironically, and to Sinclair's disappointment, the novel's promotion of socialism and its protest against wage slavery did not win the hearts and minds of his audience, but his realistic portrayal of conditions in the meatpacking industry (as he once remarked) surely turned the stomach of the nation.

The Jungle will never be placed in the first rank of American fiction because of its mixture of fictional and journalistic elements, its unresolved contradictions in theme, and its melodramatic plot and bifurcated structure. Sinclair tried to do too many things at once, and he was only partially successful. Most readers think that the true significance of Sinclair's achievement in *The Jungle* lies in the uncensored presentation of the conditions of working-class life. Only Stephen Crane in *Maggie: A Girl of the Streets* (1893) had dealt with slum subjects with such integrity, and Sinclair had no models to follow in depicting this stratum of society. In his firsthand observations and deep compassion for the oppressed, he was breaking new ground for literary treatment, which Theodore Dreiser would follow to different purposes.

Following the success of *The Jungle* was difficult for Sinclair. He spent the next eight years trying to repeat what he had done with his first and best "muckraking" book. He produced a number of novels focused on specific problems, but at the other end of the social scale. *The Metropolis* is an exposé of conspicuous consumption among upper-class New York socialites. It is a poor book by Sinclair's own admission and is remarkable only for the absence of socialistic sermons by the author. Sinclair, like F. Scott Fitzgerald, apparently believed that money sets the very wealthy quite apart from the rest of society, but, rather than seeking rapport with his wealthy characters, as Fitzgerald did, Sinclair hoped to reform them. Another novel of this period, *The Money Changers*, is a story of the machinations of a high financier, obviously patterned on J. P. Morgan; the story tells of the exploits of Dan Waterman, the elderly head of the Steel Trust, who creates a panic on Wall Street purely for personal revenge against a rival steel magnate. Although *The Money Changers* is not very good fiction, it does have an interesting premise, suggesting a connection between sexual desire and the drive for financial power.

Another novel of this period that deserves mention for its subject is *Love's Pilgrimage*; neofeminist in theme, this work examines the pressures on Sinclair's own marriage because of his male insensitivity to his wife's personal, sexual, and intellectual needs. The novel is also interesting for the insight it offers into Sinclair's personality, for he implies that the divorce his first wife sought was deserved because he prudishly withheld from sexual relations on the theory that it would decrease his creative energy.

KING COAL

In 1914, Sinclair remarried and began living in California. The transition in his life resulted in a change in his writing. In the West, Sinclair was drawn back to the problems of the proletariat by labor strife in the Colorado coal mines. As a result of the attempt by the United Mine Workers to organize the miners, the governor of Colorado had called up the state militia to break up strikes. In 1914, in the town of Ludlow, National Guard troops fired into a camp of strikers and their families, killing eleven women and two children. This shocking event outraged Sinclair as nothing had since he had witnessed the brutal conditions of the stockyards.

Following the methods he had used to collect background material for *The Jungle*, he went to Colorado, visited the miners and their families, and talked with the mining officials and labor leaders. His direct contact with the working-class people stirred his emotions and gave him a more realistic point of departure for his next novel, *King Coal*, than any he had employed since *The Jungle*. In fact, *King Coal* was an attempt to repeat the same sort of muckraking performance that had succeeded so well in the former case. Unfortunately for Sinclair, *King Coal* did not create the response aroused by *The Jungle*, a fact largely resulting from the lag time in the publication of the novel. When *King Coal* appeared in 1917, the events in Ludlow were three years old and yesterday's news. The United States had just entered World War I, and the nation's mind was on "doughboys" rather than on coal miners.

The poor reception of *King Coal* was a great disappointment to Sinclair, because he knew he had produced the kind of novel he wrote best. *King Coal*, while not as powerful as *The Jungle*, has the rhetorical strength and the factual validity of the earlier book. Sinclair tells the story of a rich young man named Hal Warner, who impersonates a coal miner in order to investigate working conditions in the western coal camps. He becomes a union sympathizer and labor agitator after he becomes convinced that the mine owners are denying the miners their legal rights and are cheating them out of their wages by rigged scales. After witnessing the futility of getting justice for working men inside the legal system, the miners go on a wildcat strike. Hal convinces his coworkers to join the union, and the novel ends with the lines drawn between labor and management while Hal returns to college, vowing to continue his fight for the working people of America.

Although *King Coal* is not as powerful in its naturalistic details as *The Jungle* and lacks the pessimistic determinism of that novel, it is in the opinion of most critics Sinclair's second-best effort at muckraking. If very few Americans responded to Sinclair's account of the dangers of cave-ins, coal dust, and explosions, this result may be because they were never exposed to such perils, whereas all were subject to health hazards as a result of unsanitary food processing. For this reason, the exposé of negligence in Chicago meatpacking plants had a much more profound and practical effect than the exposé of the inhuman conditions in the coal camps of Colorado.

BOSTON

Between World War I and the start of the Depression, Sinclair wrote two remarkable novels based on topical social or political situations. *Oil!* delves into the Teapot Dome and other oil scandals of Warren G. Harding's presidential administration and thus has considerable historical significance as well as being one of Sinclair's most readable books. *Boston*, on the other hand, represents Sinclair's best use of a contemporary event for fictional purposes. This novel enfolds the drama of the Sacco and Vanzetti case, but it also encompasses the whole of Boston society, suggesting that the city itself was responsible for what happened in that tragic case. The central character is again from the upper classes, an elderly Back Bay aristocrat, Cornelia Thornwell, wife to a governor. Full of vitality and intelligence, she thinks that she has spent her life as an artificial adornment to a great family. She determines late in life to emancipate herself from the mores and manners of the mansion and moves out to board with the Brini family, who are honest Italian mill hands, and starts to earn her own living in a factory.

At this point, Vanzetti enters the story. During a strike in the mill, he plays an important role in keeping up the workers' spirits. He also prevents them from organizing, because as an anarchist, Vanzetti does not support unions. Afterward, Vanzetti and his friend Sacco are marked as "anarchist wops" by the police. They are picked up as suspects in a payroll robbery, and in the midst of the deportation mania of the postwar period, the city's reason and sense of justice are beclouded. The courts, judge, jury, and prosecutor seem determined to make the foreigners pay—if not for the crime, then for their politics. The climax of the novel comes when the cogs of justice bring the proletarian saints, Vanzetti and Sacco, to the electric chair with many doubts about their guilt still lingering.

Through a blending of fact and fiction, Sinclair is able to record a complex and tragic story of social injustice, although the story of the runaway grandmother does get lost in the final pages as the historical facts dominate the plot. As a novel, the two-volume *Boston* is too long except for readers with some special interest in the Sacco and Vanzetti case. As usual, Sinclair was writing for a mass audience, and the novel employs many stock characters and a melodramatic plot; furthermore, a statement of socialist doctrine forms a coda to the novel. Sinclair does, however, create a convincing portrait of Vanzetti. It is in Sinclair's account of the death of this man of dignity and intelligence that the novel gains its greatest power.

LANNY BUDD SERIES

The major literary effort of Sinclair's career was launched just before the outbreak of World War II: a ten-novel series offering a fictionalized history of the Western world in the first half of the twentieth century. The series is unified by its central character, Lanny Budd, and is known collectively by his name. One of the Lanny Budd novels, *Dragon's Teeth*, won for Sinclair a Pulitzer Prize in 1943. A chronicle of Germany's slide into Nazism, *Dragon's Teeth* is a scrupulous study of the fateful years between 1930 and 1934 and reflects an extensive research effort on Sinclair's part. In fact, several critics claimed that if the book were stripped of its fictional ingredient, it might well serve as a history text.

Sinclair creates an air of impending doom as he shows how quickly Europe was led to the abyss. His protagonist, Lanny Budd, is a neutral observer traveling the Continent with his millionaire wife, Irma, who is especially obtuse about economics, politics, and national traits. She is a foil to the sensitive and intelligent Lanny, who is aware of the coming crisis. Irma and her upper-class female friends refuse to believe that their smug routine of bridge and dinner parties will be disrupted. The reader in 1942 received these opinions with a great deal of dramatic irony. Meanwhile, Lanny grows increasingly concerned about the absence of morality in the political climate of Germany. Lanny has rather improbable meetings with the bigwigs of the Nazi regime. He goes hunting with Hermann Göring, has cocktails with Joseph Goebbels, and a discussion with Adolf Hitler about the Jewish question. His interest in this topic is not merely academic, since his sister is married to one of Germany's most prominent Jews. The Jews in Germany, however, are like Irma's circle; they refuse to face the realities of Nazism. The novel ends with Lanny's contriving to help his brother-in-law escape the dragon's teeth of the Nazi menace, closing the story on an exciting climax, somewhat like that of a cliffhanger film of the 1940's.

Sinclair continued the adventures of Lanny Budd, interweaving fiction with fact as he related the sequence of world events in *World's End*, which covers the years 1913 to 1919. *Between Two Worlds* deals with the events between the Treaty of Versailles and the stock market crash of 1929; the author then covers the Nazi "Blood Purge" of 1934 to the Spanish Civil War in *Wide Is the Gate*; the annexation of Austria, the invasion of Czechoslovakia, and the Munich pact in *Presidential Agent*; the fall of France in *Dragon Harvest*; and America's entry into the war in *A World to Win*. The years of Allied setbacks, 1941-1943, are covered in *Presidential Mission*; *One Clear Call* and *O Shepherd, Speak!* deal with the Normandy Invasion and the defeat of the German military machine; and in the sequel to the series, *The Return of Lanny Budd*, Sinclair brings events up to 1949 and the onset of the Cold War between the United States and the Soviet Union.

As a whole, this group of novels is interesting, in part simply because the series surveys a dramatic period of history in considerable detail. Throughout the series, Sinclair's careful research is evident, but the popularity of these novels was also a result of their appeal to patriotism. America's role as the savior of civilization is increasingly emphasized in the later novels in the series. During this period, Sinclair's confidence that progress was represented by socialism and communism was shaken by the example of the Soviet Union. Like so many early twentieth century political radicals, he became an anticommunist in the 1950's.

Sinclair was a propagandist first and a novelist second, if propaganda is defined as an "effort directed systematically toward the gaining of support for an opinion or course of action." He wrote millions of words trying to change, improve, or expose oppressive conditions. Because Sinclair so obviously used literature for ulterior purposes and because he was so prolific, serious critics have unduly neglected him; on the other hand, he has been overrated by those foreign critics who delight in finding indictments of the United States by American writers. As time puts Sinclair's contribution to American literature into perspective, it seems certain that he will never be regarded as a great novelist, but he will fairly be judged an honest, courageous, and original writer.

Hallman B. Bryant

OTHER MAJOR WORKS

PLAYS: *Plays of Protest*, pb. 1912; *Hell: A Verse Drama and Photo-Play*, pb. 1923; *The Millennium*, pb. 1924; *The Pot Boiler*, pb. 1924; *Singing Jailbirds*, pb. 1924; *Bill Porter*, pb. 1925; *Wally for Queen!*, pb. 1936; *Marie Antoinette*, pb. 1939; *A Giant's Strength*, pr., pb. 1948.

NONFICTION: *Our Bourgeois Literature*, 1904; *The Industrial Republic*, 1907; *The Fasting Cure*, 1911; *The Profits of Religion*, 1918; *The Brass Check: A Study in American Journalism*, 1919; *The Book of Life, Mind, and Body*, 1921; *The Goose-Step: A Study of American Education*, 1923; *The Goslings: A Study of the American Schools*, 1924; *Letters to Judd*, 1925; *Mammonart*, 1925; *Money Writes!*, 1927; *Mental Radio*, 1930; *American Outpost: A Book of Reminiscences*, 1932; *I, Governor of California and How I Ended Poverty*, 1933; *The Way Out—What Lies Ahead for America?*, 1933; *The EPIC Plan for California*, 1934; *I, Candidate for Governor, and How I Got Licked*, 1935; *What God Means to Me*, 1936; *Terror in Russia: Two Views*, 1938; *Expect No Peace!*, 1939; *The Cup of Fury*, 1956; *A Personal Jesus*, 1952; *My Lifetime in Letters*, 1960; *The Autobiography of Upton Sinclair*, 1962.

CHILDREN'S LITERATURE: *The Gnomobile: A Gnice Gnew Gnarrative with Gnonsense, but Gnothing Gnaughty*, 1936.

BIBLIOGRAPHY

Arthur, Anthony. *Radical Innocent: Upton Sinclair*. New York: Random House, 2006. Presents a well-researched, balanced, and thorough portrait of Sinclair that tracks the ups and downs of his career and personal life. Includes sixteen pages of black-and-white photographs.

Bloodworth, William A. *Upton Sinclair*. Boston: Twayne, 1977. Short, sympathetic, yet balanced literary biography examines Sinclair's place in American literary radicalism and the writer as social activist. Includes bibliography and index.

Colburn, David R., and George E. Pozzetta, eds. *Reform and Reformers in the Progressive Era*. Westport, Conn.: Greenwood Press, 1983. Collection of essays includes discussion of Sinclair's position as a muckraker and his role in inspiring Progressive reforms. Notes that, unlike other journalistic writers, Sinclair was personally and ideologically committed to reform.

Dell, Floyd. *Upton Sinclair: A Study in Social Protest*. New York: AMS Press, 1970. Treatment of Sinclair's career analyzes the apparent discrepancy between the author's literary position in the United States and his position throughout the rest of the world. Descriptions of personal incidents and psychological insights are intertwined with evaluations and interpretations of specific works.

Harris, Leon. *Upton Sinclair: American Rebel*. New York: Thomas Y. Crowell, 1975. Traces Sinclair's rise from obscurity to fame and his subsequent decline in popularity. Provides interesting information regarding source materials for some of his novels. Includes photographs, extensive notes, a list of Sinclair's books, and an index.

Mattson, Kevin. *Upton Sinclair and the Other American Century*. Hoboken, N.J.: John Wiley & Sons, 2006. Combines biography with a history of the American Left to place Sinclair's life and works within the context of the social, cultural, economic, and political events that surrounded them. Includes notes and index.

Mitchell, Greg. *The Campaign of the Century*. New York: Random House, 1992. Excellently researched work details Sinclair's 1934 California gubernatorial campaign from August to November, stressing the media's key role in defeating Sinclair and ushering in a new era of media politics. Includes notes.

Mookerjee, R. N. *Art for Social Justice: The Major Novels of Upton Sinclair*. Metuchen, N.J.: Scarecrow Press, 1988. Mookerjee, a critic of writers of the 1930's, provides a re-evaluation of *The Jungle*, *King Coal*, *Oil!*, *Boston*, and the Lanny Budd series, describing the pioneering role Sinclair played in creating the "documentary novel." Includes a selected bibliography.

Scott, Ivan. *Upton Sinclair: The Forgotten Socialist*. Lewiston, N.Y.: Edwin Mellen Press, 1997. Sound scholarly biography draws extensively on the Sinclair collection at the Lilly Library at Indiana University. In his introduction, Scott makes a good case for Sinclair's importance.

Yoder, Jon A. *Upton Sinclair*. New York: Frederick Ungar, 1975. Like some other critics, Yoder attributes Sinclair's "meager reputation" in part to his socialistic views. Five chapters in this volume examine various facets of the novelist's life and career. Includes chronology, notes, bibliography, and index.

ALEKSANDR SOLZHENITSYN

Born: Kislovodsk, Russia, Soviet Union (now in Russia); December 11, 1918
Died: Moscow, Russia; August 3, 2008
Also known as: Aleksandr Isayevich Solzhenitsyn

PRINCIPAL LONG FICTION

Odin den' Ivana Denisovicha, 1962 (novella; *One Day in the Life of Ivan Denisovich*, 1963)
Rakovy korpus, 1968 (*Cancer Ward*, 1968)
V kruge pervom, 1968 (*The First Circle*, 1968)
Avgust chetyrnadtsatogo, 1971, expanded version 1983 (*August 1914*, 1972; expanded version 1989, as *The Red Wheel*)
Lenin v Tsyurikhe, 1975 (*Lenin in Zurich*, 1976)
Krasnoe koleso, 1983-1991 (includes *Avgust chetyrnadtsatogo*, expanded version 1983 [*The Red Wheel*, 1989]; *Oktiabr' shestnadtsatogo*, 1984 [*November 1916*, 1999]; *Mart semnadtsatogo*, 1986-1988; *Aprel' semnadtsatogo*, 1991)

OTHER LITERARY FORMS

Although the literary reputation of Aleksandr Solzhenitsyn (sohl-zheh-NEET-seen) rests largely on his long prose works, this prolific writer experimented in numerous genres. The short story "Matryona's House" is an excellent example of Solzhenitsyn's attention to detail as well as his reverence for old Russian values as exemplified by the peasant woman Matryona and her home. In addition to his short stories, in 1964 Solzhenitsyn published *Etyudy i krokhotnye rasskazy*, a collection of prose poems (translated in *Stories and Prose Poems by Alexander Solzhenitsyn*, 1971), each of which generally conveys a single message by focusing on a solitary image. Solzhenitsyn also composed the long poem *Prusskie nochi* (1974; *Prussian Nights*, 1977), which he committed to paper only after his release from prison. Drama, as well, interested Solzhenitsyn from his early years as a writer. His dramatic trilogy was written between 1951 and 1954, but the plays were never published or staged in the Soviet Union. Solzhenitsyn's eagerness to experiment with different genres and to mesh them makes him an unusually interesting writer. Fairy tales, film scenarios, drama, poetry, and prose are continually found interwoven in Solzhenitsyn's works. A particularly striking example of his desire to mix genres is his history of the Stalinist labor camps, *Arkhipelag GULag, 1918-1956: Opyt khudozhestvennogo issledovaniya* (1973-1975; *The Gulag Archipelago, 1918-1956: An Experiment in Literary Investigation*, 1974-1978).

Aleksandr Solzhenitsyn
(The Nobel Foundation)

Achievements

The publication of Aleksandr Solzhenitsyn's first work, *One Day in the Life of Ivan Denisovich*—in Russian in 1962 and in English in 1963—sent shock waves throughout both the East and the West. Suddenly a new voice was heard in the Soviet Union, shattering the long, oppressive decades of silence and revealing forbidden truths of Stalinist society. In his preface to *One Day in the Life of Ivan Denisovich*, Aleksandr Tvardovsky, an established Soviet poet and editor of the journal *Novy mir*, notes that the talent of the young writer is as extraordinary as his subject matter. Tvardovsky states that *One Day in the Life of Ivan Denisovich* is a work of art. The decision to make this comment is revealing, for, from the outset, it has been difficult, if not impossible, for readers both in the East and in the West to evaluate Solzhenitsyn as an artist apart from his political views. Solzhenitsyn became a symbol of hope. Born after the Russian Revolution, educated in the Soviet system, and tempered by war and the Stalinist camps, he was in every sense a Soviet man.

With the publication of *One Day in the Life of Ivan Denisovich*, he also became a Soviet writer published in the Soviet Union—a writer who, through the actions and words of a simple peasant, unmasked decades of terror and tyranny.

Solzhenitsyn's focus on the peasant in *One Day in the Life of Ivan Denisovich* and in the short story "Matryona's House" contributed to the tremendous upsurge and success of the village theme in contemporary Soviet literature. "Village prose," as the movement has been called, treating the concerns of the Soviet Union's vast rural population, represents one of the dominant and interesting trends in the 1960's and 1970's. Solzhenitsyn's initial success undoubtedly encouraged other writers to turn to such subjects as a means of speaking the truth, a means of "acceptable" protest.

The nomination of Solzhenitsyn for the Lenin Prize in 1964 demonstrates the height of popularity and prestige that the author attained in his own country. Although he was not to receive his country's highest literary honor, six years later, in 1970, he was accorded worldwide recognition when he received the Nobel Prize in Literature. In his Nobel lecture, Solzhenitsyn stressed the writer's responsibility to the truth, a responsibility that he took seriously throughout his career. Solzhenitsyn took it upon himself to record—in both his fiction and his nonfiction works—events that would otherwise be lost to the world. His history of the Stalinist camps (*The Gulag Archipelago*) as well as his writings on the prerevolutionary politics of Russia (such as *August 1914*, *Lenin in Zurich*, and *November 1916*) and on the workings of the Soviet literary machine in *Bodalsya telyonok s dubom* (1975; *The Oak and the Calf*, 1980) will serve as historical sources for future generations. Solzhenitsyn's works had been translated into more than forty languages only ten years after his first publication. Popularity and politics aside, Solzhenitsyn will be remembered as a master of Russian prose whose works are among the finest of the twentieth century. His preoccupation with the profound issues confronting humankind and his search for a literary means to express these themes mark him as a great writer.

BIOGRAPHY

Aleksandr Isayevich Solzhenitsyn was born in Kislovodsk, a city in the north Caucasus, on December 11, 1918, one year after the Russian Revolution. His father, whose studies at the university were interrupted by World War I, died in a hunting accident six months before his son was born. Solzhenitsyn's mother, Taisiya Zakharovna Shcherbak, worked as an office clerk throughout Solzhenitsyn's childhood, earning very little money. In 1924, Solzhenitsyn and his mother moved to Rostov-on-Don, a city at that time of nearly a quarter million people. Because of financial considerations and the poor health of his mother, Solzhenitsyn was to continue his education there until he graduated in 1941 from the University of Rostov-on-Don, specializing in mathematics and physics. From an early age, Solzhenitsyn dreamed of being a writer. Having displayed a natural talent for math and finding no adequate literary institution in Rostov-on-Don, however, Solzhenitsyn studied mathematics and physics. Nevertheless, in 1939, Solzhenitsyn decided to pursue his literary interests and began a two-year correspondence course in literature at the Moscow Institute of History, Philosophy, and Literature while continuing his studies in mathematics and physics. He finished this course of study in 1940, the same year that he married Natal'ya Alekseyevna Reshetovskaya (the apparent prototype of Nadya in *The First Circle*). Reshetovskaya, a specialist in physical chemistry and biochemistry, taught at the Agriculture Institute in Rostov-on-Don. On October 18, 1941, Solzhenitsyn was drafted into the Soviet army; he hardly saw his wife for the next fifteen years.

Solzhenitsyn served in the army in various capacities, working his way up to battery commander. He was a decorated and inspiring leader, but his army duty was cut short in February, 1945, when he was summoned to his commanding officer's quarters and arrested. The charges, as was typical throughout the Stalinist era, were not made clear to Solzhenitsyn at that time. Later, he determined that he had been arrested for oblique, derogatory remarks concerning Joseph Stalin and his mismanagement of the war that he had made in a personal journal and in a letter to a friend. Upon his arrest, he was taken to the Lubyanka, the notorious prison in Moscow. On July 7, 1945, after four months of interrogation, he was sentenced to eight years of hard labor. Solzhenitsyn's novella *One Day in the Life of Ivan Denisovich*, his novel *The First Circle*, and his multivolume work *The Gulag Archipelago* are all based on his firsthand experience of the Stalinist labor camps. He, like countless other Soviet citizens, was sentenced, under section 58 of the Soviet penal code, for counterrevolutionary crimes. Solzhenitsyn spent the beginning of his term at Butyrka, a Moscow prison, laying parquet floors, as does Nerzhin, the protagonist of *The First Circle*. Later in 1946, because of his training in mathematics and physics, he was transferred to a *sharashka* (a prison where scientists work on special projects for the state) very similar to the one depicted in *The First Circle*. After one year in the *sharashka*, Solzhenitsyn was sent to a labor camp in northern Kazakhstan. During his stay there, he had a tumor removed; the prisoner was not told that it was malignant.

In February, 1953, Solzhenitsyn was released from prison only to enter perpetual exile (a common Stalinist practice) in Kok-Terek, Kazakhstan. There, Solzhenitsyn taught mathematics until his health deteriorated so severely that, in 1954, he was permitted to travel to Tashkent for treatment. In Tashkent, he was admitted to a clinic where he was treated for cancer and where he gathered material for his novel *Cancer Ward*. After his treatment, he returned to Kok-Terek to teach and began working on the play *Olen'i shalashovka* (pb. 1968; also known as *Respublika truda*; *The Love Girl and the Innocent*, 1969) as well as *The First Circle*. In June, 1956, as a result of the "thaw" that followed Stalin's death in 1953, Solzhenitsyn was released from exile, and he moved to Ryazan, where he taught physics and mathematics until the end of 1962. In Ryazan, he saw his wife for the first time in many years. She had remarried and had two children from her second marriage. In that same year, Reshetovskaya left her second husband and reunited with Solzhenitsyn.

Solzhenitsyn and his wife stayed in Ryazan, where they both taught and where

Solzhenitsyn continued to write in secret. In 1961, upon hearing Aleksandr Tvardovsky's speech to the Twenty-second Party Congress, in which he called for writers to tell the whole truth, Solzhenitsyn, in a bold move, sent his novella *One Day in the Life of Ivan Denisovich* to Tvardovsky's then-liberal journal *Novy mir* (new world). The literary battles waged for the publication of this work and subsequent works by Solzhenitsyn are documented by the author in *The Oak and the Calf* and by Vladimir Lakshin in *Solzhenitsyn, Tvardovsky, and "Novy Mir"* (1980). The response to the novel made Solzhenitsyn an immediate celebrity, and he was nominated for the Lenin Prize in 1964. The political tide was beginning to turn, however, and with it the possibilities for the future publication of Solzhenitsyn's works.

At this time, Solzhenitsyn's unpublished works were already being circulated in samizdat (a self-publishing underground network for literary, philosophical, and political works) and were being smuggled abroad. In 1964, his prose poems appeared in the West German journal *Grani* (facets). By 1966, when Solzhenitsyn's "Zakhar-the-Pouch" appeared in the Soviet press, the political and artistic tensions were further intensified by the highly publicized trials of Andrei Sinyavsky and Yuli Daniel. That same year, permission to publish *Cancer Ward* in the Soviet Union was denied. Finally, in 1968, both *The First Circle* and *Cancer Ward* were published in the West without authorization from Solzhenitsyn.

The following year, Solzhenitsyn was expelled from the Union of Soviet Writers, a fatal blow to his career in the Soviet Union, for without membership, publication there was impossible. The situation was quite serious in 1970, when Solzhenitsyn was awarded the Nobel Prize in Literature. The author did not travel to Sweden to accept the prize at that time for fear that he would not be allowed to return to his country. From that point on, Solzhenitsyn, recognizing the impossibility of publication within his own country, authorized the publication of some of his works abroad. Personal attacks as well as attacks from the Soviet press continued to mount, and, in 1974, after ignoring two summons from the State Prosecutor's Office, Solzhenitsyn was arrested and taken to Lefortovo prison. There he was interrogated, charged with treason, and placed on a plane. Only upon landing was he informed that he had been exiled. Six weeks later, Solzhenitsyn was joined in Zurich by his second wife, Natal'ya Svetlova (he had divorced Reshetovskaya in 1973), their three sons, and his stepson.

In October of 1974, the U.S. Senate conferred honorary citizenship on Solzhenitsyn (an honor bestowed only twice before—on the Marquis de Lafayette and Sir Winston Churchill). He soon settled in Vermont, where he continued to write, deliver occasional lectures, and promote the publication of materials dealing with the Soviet Union.

Living by choice in his Vermont isolation, Solzhenitsyn turned his attention to the past, writing historical works centered on the early twentieth century. His antipathy toward his adopted country was matched only by his lack of contact with his native land and his failure to stay in touch with the evolution of that complex country. He eventually returned to

Russia in 1994, a few years after the collapse of the Soviet Union. Somewhat to his surprise, instead of revisiting the land of the evil gulags and oppressed but saintly people, Solzhenitsyn arrived in a consumerized, highly commercial country striving to compete in European and global contexts. The gulags were remembered only by the oldest and were largely dismissed as uninteresting by the young. Irony had dealt Russian history a new blow by reinstating Russian Orthodoxy and removing secular saintliness—including the monastic, agrarian ideals propounded by Solzhenitsyn, Russia's self-conscious prophet.

Undaunted by his lack of popularity, Solzhenitsyn continued to pursue his platform with the support of many respectable nationalist factions. He tried to reach out to Russians of the post-Soviet era through a television talk show on which he propounded his ideals of a special Slavic nationality and its mission in the world. The program lasted only a few months, however, as objections to his verbosity and unwillingness to listen prevailed. On August 3, 2008, Solzhenitsyn died in Moscow after suffering heart failure.

Analysis

Aleksandr Solzhenitsyn and his novels are better appreciated and understood when the author's vision of himself as a writer is taken into consideration; he believed that a great writer must also be a prophet of his or her country. In this tradition of the great Russian novelists Leo Tolstoy and Fyodor Dostoevski, Solzhenitsyn sought to discover a place for the individual in history and in art. Solzhenitsyn viewed art, history, life, and people as continually interacting, forming a single pulsing wave that creates a new, vibrant, and oftentimes disturbing vision of reality and the future. From his first publication, *One Day in the Life of Ivan Denisovich*, to his cycle of historical novels, *Krasnoe koleso*, Solzhenitsyn concentrated on people's ability to survive with dignity in environments that are fundamentally inhumane. Whatever the situation of his protagonist—whether in a Stalinist prison camp, a hospital, the army, or exile—Solzhenitsyn demands from that character a certain moral integrity, a code of behavior that separates him or her from those who have forsaken their humanity. It is the ability or inability to adhere to this code that renders the protagonist triumphant or tragic.

Given the importance of the interrelationship of history, art, and life in Solzhenitsyn's works, it is not surprising that the works are often preoccupied with the larger issues confronting humanity. For the most part, Solzhenitsyn's novels are concerned less with action and plot than with ideas and ethical motivation. Radically different characters are thrown together into artificial environments, usually state institutions, which are separated from society as a whole and are governed by laws and codes of behavior that are equally estranged from society. Such institutions serve as a means of bringing together and equalizing people who would normally not have contact with one another; previous status and education become meaningless. Physical survival itself is usually at issue—prisoners and soldiers struggle for food, patients for treatment, and "free" people for continued freedom and integrity. For Solzhenitsyn, however, physical survival is not the only issue, or even the primary one. Several of his characters, including Alyosha in *One Day in the Life of Ivan Denisovich* and Nerzhin in *The First Circle*, actually welcome the prison camp experience, for they find their time in camp to be conducive to reflection on fundamental questions.

Nerzhin, like many of the other *zeks* (prisoners in the Stalinist camps), is also aware that, in contrast to the "free" members of Stalinist society, prisoners are allowed greater opportunity to speak their minds, to debate issues freely and openly, and to come to terms with the society and state that have imprisoned them. The freedom that some of the prisoners enjoy, the freedom that the ill-fated patients experience in the *Cancer Ward*, is the freedom encountered by those who have nothing left to lose. As the author indicates through one of the prisoners in *The First Circle*, society has no hold over a person once it has taken everything from him or her. Solzhenitsyn repeatedly returns to the theme of materialism as a source of manipulation and a potential evil in people's lives. According to Solzhenitsyn, those who maintain material ties can never be entirely free, and therefore their integrity can always be questioned and tested. Worldly possessions per se are not evil, nor is the desire to possess them, nor does Solzhenitsyn condemn those who do have or desire them. He is skeptical of their value, however, and ultimately holds the conscience to be humankind's single treasured possession.

Solzhenitsyn's insistence on integrity extends beyond the life of the individual. Solzhenitsyn asserts that because a person has only one conscience, he or she must not allow that conscience to be compromised on a personal level by justifying personal actions or the actions of the state by insisting that the end, no matter how noble, justifies the means. This single observation is the foundation of Solzhenitsyn's attack on the Soviet state. A brilliant, perfect Communist future is not motivation or justification enough for a secretive, censor-ridden socialist state, not in Stalin's time or in the author's lifetime. In Solzhenitsyn's view, corrupt means cannot produce a pure end.

Detractors of Solzhenitsyn in both the East and the West have claimed that his writings are too political and generally unconcerned with stylistic matters. Given the life and the times of the man, these objections fail to be particularly persuasive. Solzhenitsyn's language is rich and textured, and both a glossary (Vera Carpovich, *Solzhenitsyn's Peculiar Vocabulary*, 1976) and a dictionary (Meyer Galler, *Soviet Prison Camp Speech*, 1972) of his language have been produced. Prison slang, camp jargon, political slogans, colloquialisms, and neologisms all mesh in Solzhenitsyn's texts. His attention to language is often voiced by his characters, such as Ignatich in "Matryona's House" or Sologdin in *The First Circle*, and his prose is sprinkled with Russian proverbs and folk sayings that often summarize or counteract lengthy philosophical debates. A further indication of his concern for language can be seen in his insistence on commissioning new translations of many of his works, which were originally issued in hurried translations to meet the worldwide demand for them.

On another stylistic level, Solzhenitsyn employs two narrative techniques that enhance his focus on the exchange of ideas and debate as a means of attaining truth: *erlebte rede*, or quasi-direct discourse, and polyphony. Quasi-direct discourse involves the merging of two or more voices, one of these voices usually being that of a third-person narrator and the other the voice of the character depicted. Through this device, Solzhenitsyn draws the reader as close as possible to the thoughts, perceptions, and emotions of the character without interrupting the narrative with either direct or indirect speech. Similarly, polyphony, a term introduced by the Soviet critic Mikhail Bakhtin in regard to Dostoevski's narrative and structural technique and a term that Solzhenitsyn himself applied to his own novels, is employed in order to present more empathetically a character's point of view. Polyphony allows each character in turn to take center stage and present his or her views either directly or through quasi-direct discourse; thus, throughout a novel, the narrative focus continually shifts from character to character. The third-person omniscient narrator serves as a linking device, seemingly allowing the debates to continue among the characters alone.

In addition to these literary techniques, Solzhenitsyn's prose, particularly in *The First Circle*, is permeated with irony and satire. A master of hyperbole and understatement, Solzhenitsyn is at his best when caricaturing historical figures, such as Vladimir Ilich Lenin and Joseph Stalin, to name but two. Solzhenitsyn further deepens the irony by underscoring small physical and verbal gestures of his targets. The target need not be as powerful as Lenin or Stalin to draw the author's fire, and there are touches of self-irony that provide a corrective to Solzhenitsyn's occasionally sanctimonious tone.

ONE DAY IN THE LIFE OF IVAN DENISOVICH

Not all of Solzhenitsyn's works are dependent on irony and satire. *One Day in the Life of Ivan Denisovich* is striking for its restraint, verbal economy, and controlled tone. This *povest'*, or novella, was originally conceived by the author in 1950-1951 while he was in the Ekibastuz prison. The original draft, written in 1959 and titled "One Day in the Life of a Zek," was significantly revised, politically muffled, and submitted to *Novy mir*.

Set in a labor camp in Siberia, *One Day in the Life of Ivan Denisovich* traces an ordinary day in the life of a prisoner. The author reveals through a third-person narrator the stark, grim world of the *zek* in meticulous detail, including the daily rituals—the searches, the bed checks, the meals—as well as the general rules and regulations that govern his daily existence: little clothing, little contact with the outside world, little time to himself. Every detail of Ivan Denisovich's day resounds in the vast, cold emptiness of this remote camp. As György Lukács noted of the novel, "Camp life is represented as a permanent condition"; into this permanent condition is thrust a common person who quietly and simply reveals the essence of retaining one's dignity in a hopeless, inhumane environment.

Uncharacteristic of Solzhenitsyn's works, the tone of *One Day in the Life of Ivan Denisovich* is reserved, solemn, and dignified; irony surfaces only occasionally. The tone is probably somewhat attributable to the editing of Tvardovsky, whose language is felt here. Throughout the work, which is uninterrupted by chapter breaks, the focus remains on Ivan Denisovich and the passage of this one day. Secondary characters are introduced only insofar as they touch his day, and flashbacks and background information are provided only to deepen the reader's understanding of Ivan Denisovich's present situation. Unlike Solzhenitsyn's later novels, which focus largely on an institution's impact on many different individuals, *One Day in the Life of Ivan Denisovich* focuses on one man. Criticism of the camps is perceived by the reader, who slowly observes and absorbs the daily steps of this man. Only after Solzhenitsyn has revealed the drudgery of that one day, one almost happy day, does he place it in its context, simply stating that "there were three thousand six hundred and fifty-three days like this in his sentence, from reveille to lights out. The three extra ones were because of leap year."

CANCER WARD

Unlike its predecessor, *Cancer Ward* directly reveals the constant intense emotional pressure of its characters and its themes. Solzhenitsyn fixed upon the idea of writing this novel at his discharge from the Tashkent clinic in 1955. He did not begin writing the novel until 1963, and only after a two-year hiatus did he return to serious work on *Cancer Ward*. In 1966, having finished the first part of the work, Solzhenitsyn submitted it to the journal *Novy mir*; it was rejected by the censor. Meanwhile, Solzhenitsyn completed the novel, which soon began to circulate in samizdat. Eventually, *Cancer Ward* was smuggled to the West and published, first in excerpts and later in its entirety. It was never published in the Soviet Union.

On the surface, *Cancer Ward* depicts the lives of the doctors, patients, and staff of a cancer clinic. The two protagonists of the novel, Pavel Rusanov and Oleg Kostoglotov, are socially and politically polar opposites: Rusanov is a member of the Communist Party, well established, living a comfortable life with a wife and a family; Kostoglotov is a former prisoner who arrives at the hospital with no one and nothing. Because of the cancer that has afflicted them both, they find themselves in the same ward with an equally diverse group of patients. The novel is largely plotless and focuses on the contrasting attitudes of the patients in regard to the institution, their treatment, and life and death, as well as other philosophical and political issues.

The one plot line that runs through the novel centers on Kostoglotov, who, having been imprisoned and consequently deprived of female companionship for years, becomes an avid "skirt chaser," pursuing both his doctor, Vera Gangart, who ironically falls victim to the very cancer in which she specializes, and a young medical student, Zoya. Kostoglotov throughout the novel continually objects to the secrecy that surrounds his treatment and demands that he has a right to know. In a twist characteristic of Solzhenitsyn, Zoya informs Kostoglotov that the X-ray treatment that he is receiving will temporarily render him impotent. This serves as another reminder to Kostoglotov that, as in prison, his fate, his manhood, and in fact his life are beyond his control and in the hands of yet another institution. Throughout *Cancer Ward*, the abuses, idiocies, and tragedies of Soviet medical care are revealed, as terminally ill patients are released believing they are cured, patients are misdiagnosed, and hospitals prove to be poorly staffed and supplied.

Unfortunately, *Cancer Ward* suffers from its near absence of plot, its heavy-handed dialogues and debates, and its lack of focus, either on a genuine protagonist or on an all-encompassing theme. The reader feels little sympathy for Rusanov, a Communist Party member, or for Kostoglotov, despite the fact that he has been unjustly imprisoned and is a victim of cancer. Kostoglotov is generally impatient, intolerant, and at times completely insensitive to others. Nevertheless, he does grow in the course of the novel. In a discussion with Shulubin, another patient in the ward, Kostoglotov dismisses Shulubin's warning that happiness is elusive and only a mirage, but when he is finally dismissed from the clinic, Kostoglotov, wandering the streets free from prison and free from cancer, realizes that an appetite can be more easily stimulated than satisfied. By the conclusion of the work, Kostoglotov understands Shulubin's warning and abandons his dreams of love with Vera and Zoya.

Despite the work's significant shortcomings, there are scenes in *Cancer Ward* that remain unforgettable for their sensitivity and poetry. One such scene involves the two adolescents Dyomka and Asya. Dyomka is to lose his leg; Asya, a breast. Asya, a seventeen-year-old, worries about her appearance in a swimsuit and her future with men, lamenting that no man will ever touch her breast. In an act of both hope and despair, Asya asks Dyomka to kiss her breast before, as the narrator observes, it is removed and thrown into the trash. Throughout the novel, compassion, sensitivity, poetry, and philosophy are shamelessly interrupted by the reality of the cancer ward. The sharp contrast between the human spirit of hope and the ominous presence of death and destruction in the form of cancer simultaneously underscores the fragility of human existence and the immortality of the human spirit. It is this spirit that is admired and celebrated in this novel and that is also a feature of Solzhenitsyn's finest work, *The First Circle*.

THE FIRST CIRCLE

The First Circle, like *Cancer Ward*, is largely autobiographical, based in this case on Solzhenitsyn's experiences in the *sharashka*. The author began writing the novel while in exile in Kok-Terek in 1955. Between 1955 and 1958, Solzhenitsyn wrote three redactions of the novel, none of which has survived. After 1962, he wrote four additional redactions of the novel, the last of which appeared in 1978. The novel was first published abroad in 1968 and, like *Cancer Ward*, was never published in the Soviet Union. The 1978 redaction differs from the sixth redaction (the edition used for all foreign translations) largely in the addition of nine chapters. The discussion below is based on the sixth redaction.

The First Circle masterfully combines all of Solzhenitsyn's finest assets as a writer. It is by far the most artistic of his novels, drawing heavily on literary allusions and abounding with literary devices. The title itself is a reference to Dante's *La divina commedia* (c.

1320; *The Divine Comedy*, 1802), alluding to the first circle of Hell, the circle designated for pagan scholars, philosophers, and enlightened people, where the pain and the suffering of Hell are greatly diminished. The *sharashka*, as Lev Rubin indicates in the chapter "Dante's Idea" (chapter headings are particularly revealing in this novel), is the first circle of the Stalinist camps. Unlike Ivan Denisovich, who is in a hard-labor camp, the *zeks* in the *sharashka* have adequate food and livable working conditions. The *zeks* inhabiting the *sharashka* thus have a great deal to lose, for if they do not conform to the rules governing the *sharashka*, they may fall from the first circle into the lower depths of the Stalinist camps.

Three of the four protagonists of the novel, Gleb Nerzhin, Lev Rubin, and Dmitri Sologdin, face a decision that may endanger their continued stay at the *sharashka*. Each must decide whether he is willing to work on a scientific project that may result in the imprisonment of other citizens or whether he will retain his integrity by refusing to work on the project, consequently endangering his own life. The debates and discussions that permeate this novel are thus well motivated, playing a significant role in revealing the character and philosophies of these prisoners while drawing the reader deeply into their lives and minds. The tension of the novel arises as the reader attempts to determine whether each prisoner will act in accordance with his conscience. Placed in a similar situation, Innokenty Volodin, a free man and the fourth protagonist of the novel, decides to risk imprisonment by warning a fellow citizen that he may be in danger. Volodin decides to follow his conscience in the first chapter of the novel; in his case, suspense depends on the questions of whether he will be caught and punished for his actions and whether he will continue to endorse the decision that he has made.

The First Circle is a novel of characters and choices; the choices that must be made by nearly all the characters, primary and secondary, are of compelling interest to the reader, for each choice functions as an echo of another person's choice. The overall impact of nearly every character (free and imprisoned) being faced with a life-threatening decision based on moral issues vividly demonstrates the inescapable terror of the time. Furthermore, the multidimensional aspects of this novel—the wide range of characters from virtually every social stratum, the numerous plots, the use of polyphony, the shifting to and from radically different settings, the views of peasant and philosopher, the plethora of literary allusions, the incredible richness of the language—show the sophistication and remarkable depth of the author.

AUGUST 1914

Solzhenitsyn's historical works were first seen with the publication of *August 1914* in the West in Russian in 1971 and its English translation in 1972. This book was a greatly shortened variant of the intended whole book, and it was met with general perplexity. Paralleling the "literary experimentation" style of his nonfiction work *The Gulag Archipelago* (published in English 1974-1978), Solzhenitsyn casts his figures as embodiments of historical situations and ethical issues. Whereas in *The Gulag Archipelago* he wrote from personal experience, in *August 1914* he tries to reconstruct a past of which he was not a part, with varying results. The book's chapter on Lenin, deliberately withheld from publication in the first edition, was published separately in Paris in 1975 as *Lenin v Tsyurikhe* and translated in 1976 as *Lenin in Zurich*. Solzhenitsyn had expanded and reworked it after his 1974 exile. Many other chapters were written and added in 1976 and 1977.

KRASNOE KOLESO

August 1914 was republished in English in 1989, this time in its entirety. It was identified as a section, or "knot," of Solzhenitsyn's historical series *Krasnoe koleso* (words that translate into English as "the red wheel"). Confusingly, this version was published under the title *The Red Wheel* rather than *August 1914*. By the time of the 1989 translation, Solzhenitsyn had published two more knots of *Krasnoe koleso* in Russian, *Oktiabr' shestnadtsatogo* (1984; translated as *November 1916* in 1999) and *Mart semnadtsatogo* (1986-1988). A fourth knot, *Aprel' semnadtsatogo*, appeared in 1991. That same year the Soviet Union collapsed. The "evil empire" that had formed the fulcrum for the critical leverage of Solzhenitsyn's prose was gone, and Solzhenitsyn became a prophet without a cause. The work, while historical in nature and presumably impervious to the vagaries of political change, settled into Russian literary history almost like an anachronism. It had a very limited readership.

The structure of the work was intended to reveal the nature of Russia's history as Solzhenitsyn believed it to be. Unlike the first publication (*August 1914*), *The Red Wheel* and *Krasnoe koleso* as a whole used a framework composed of "knots," nodes at which historical events are compressed. Solzhenitsyn's philosophy, responding to Tolstoy's from *Voyna i mir* (1865-1869; *War and Peace*, 1886), conforms to the proposition that history is shaped not so much by great people as by all people striving to make the proper ethical choices when forced to take part in significant events. Tolstoy's ideas, however, are revealed in the narration; Solzhenitsyn uses narrative structure instead of describing the idea, leaving the narration in large measure beyond the ordinary means of artistic forms. His intention was to reveal the "full column" of historical actors, yet such a structure tends to obscure history at the same time that it loses literary form through diffusion of the plot.

Solzhenitsyn created an enormous role for himself as a prophet of Russian history with his first novella, *One Day in the Life of Ivan Denisovich*. In his later life, history granted him only a piece of the past. *Krasnoe koleso* fell outside the interest of the Russian readership it was intended to instruct. Moreover, Solzhenitsyn's ambitions and personal interests came under hostile scrutiny by the Russian literati, who questioned his motivation for returning to Russia in 1994. Solzhenitsyn remained unmoved by the criticism, however, and continued to work as before, motivated from within, defiant of the exterior world.

Suzan K. Burks
Updated by Christine D. Tomei

OTHER MAJOR WORKS

SHORT FICTION: *Dlya pol'zy dela*, 1963 (*For the Good of the Cause*, 1964); *Dva rasskaza: Sluchay na stantsii Krechetovka i Matryonin dvor*, 1963 (*We Never Make Mistakes*, 1963); *Krokhotnye rasskazy*, 1970; *Rasskazy*, 1990.

PLAYS: *Olen'i shalashovka*, pb. 1968 (also known as *Respublika truda*; *The Love Girl and the Innocent*, 1969); *Svecha na vetru*, pb. 1968 (*Candle in the Wind*, 1973); *Dramaticheskaya trilogiya-1945: Pir Pobediteley*, pb. 1981 (*Victory Celebrations*, 1983); *Plenniki*, pb. 1981 (*Prisoners*, 1983).

POETRY: *Etyudy i krokhotnye rasskazy*, 1964 (translated in *Stories and Prose Poems by Alexander Solzhenitsyn*, 1971); *Prusskie nochi*, 1974 (*Prussian Nights*, 1977).

SCREENPLAYS: *Tuneyadets*, 1981; *Znayut istinu tanki*, 1981.

NONFICTION: *Les Droits de l'écrivain*, 1969; *A Lenten Letter to Pimen, Patriarch of All Russia*, 1972; *Nobelevskaya lektsiya po literature 1970 goda*, 1972 (*The Nobel Lecture*, 1973); *Solzhenitsyn: A Pictorial Autobiography*, 1972; *Arkhipelag GULag, 1918-1956: Opyt khudozhestvennogo issledovaniya*, 1973-1975 (*The Gulag Archipelago, 1918-1956: An Experiment in Literary Investigation*, 1974-1978); *Iz-pod glyb*, 1974 (*From Under the Rubble*, 1975); *Pis'mo vozhdyam Sovetskogo Soyuza*, 1974 (*Letter to Soviet Leaders*, 1974); *Amerikanskiye rechi*, 1975; *Bodalsya telyonok s dubom*, 1975 (*The Oak and the Calf*, 1980); *Warning to the West*, 1976; *East and West*, 1980; *The Mortal Danger: How Misconceptions About Russia Imperil America*, 1980; *Kak nam obustroit' Rossiiu? Posil'nye soobrazheniia*, 1990 (*Rebuilding Russia: Reflections and Tentative Proposals*, 1991); *Russkii vopros*, 1994 (*The Russian Question: At the End of the Twentieth Century*, 1994); *Invisible Allies*, 1995; *Dvesti let vmeste, 1795-1995*, 2001.

MISCELLANEOUS: *Sochineniya*, 1966; *Six Etudes by Aleksandr Solzhenitsyn*, 1971; *Stories and Prose Poems by Alexander Solzhenitsyn*, 1971; *Mir i nasiliye*, 1974; *Sobranie sochinenii*, 1978-1983 (10 volumes); *Izbrannoe*, 1991.

BIBLIOGRAPHY

Bloom, Harold, ed. *Aleksandr Solzhenitsyn*. Philadelphia: Chelsea House, 2001. Collection of critical essays includes analyses of *One Day in the Life of Ivan Denisovich*, the representation of detention in works by Solzhenitsyn and Fyodor Dostoevski, and Solzhenitsyn's experiences as a creative artist in a totalitarian state.

Ericson, Edward E. *Solzhenitsyn and the Modern World*. Washington, D.C.: Regnery Gateway, 1993. Examines the reputation of Solzhenitsyn in the West in an attempt to clear up previous misunderstandings. Argues that Solzhenitsyn was never antidemocratic and that his criticisms of the West were made in the spirit of love, not animosity.

_____. *Solzhenitsyn: The Moral Vision*. Grand Rapids, Mich.: Wm. B. Eerdmans, 1980. Presents an analysis of Solzhenitsyn's work from the perspective of the author's Christian vision. Begins with discussion of Solzhenitsyn's theory of art, as enunciated in his Nobel Prize lecture, and then devotes chapters to his major novels as well as to his short stories and prose poems.

Ericson, Edward E., and Alexis Klimoff. *The Soul and Barbed Wire: An Introduction to Solzhenitsyn.* Wilmington, Del.: ISI Books, 2008. Two major Solzhenitsyn scholars provide a detailed biography of the writer and analyses of all of his major fiction.

Feuer, Kathryn, ed. *Solzhenitsyn.* Englewood Cliffs, N.J.: Prentice-Hall, 1976. Collection of thirteen essays includes discussions of Solzhenitsyn's uses of structure and symbolism, the theme of war in his works, and epic and dramatic elements in the works. Also provides an evaluation of the English-language translations of his writings.

Klimoff, Alexis. *"One Day in the Life of Ivan Denisovich": A Critical Companion.* Evanston, Ill.: Northwestern University Press, 1997. Useful guide for readers encountering Solzhenitsyn's novel for the first time. Provides primary source materials, a discussion of the novel within the context of Solzhenitsyn's body of work and of Russian literary tradition, and an annotated bibliography.

Lakshin, Vladislav. *Solzhenitsyn, Tvardovsky, and "Novy Mir."* New York: Oxford University Press, 1980. Presents an insider's view of the publication history of *A Day in the Life of Ivan Denisovich*, involving Aleksandr Tvardovsky, a poet and the editor of the journal *Novy mir.*

Mahoney, Daniel J. *Aleksandr Solzhenitsyn: The Ascent from Ideology.* Lanham, Md.: Rowman and Littlefield, 2001. Focuses on Solzhenitsyn's political philosophy and its impact on twentieth century thinking. Presents analysis of Solzhenitsyn's writings to demonstrate how they represent the political condition of humankind in the modern world.

Medina, Loreta, ed. *Readings on "One Day in the Life of Ivan Denisovich."* San Diego, Calif.: Greenhaven Press, 2001. Collection of critical essays is designed to assist students and other readers of the novel. Contributors interpret the novel from a variety of perspectives and provide biographical information about Solzhenitsyn.

Moody, Christopher. *Solzhenitsyn.* 2d rev. ed. New York: Barnes & Noble Books, 1976. Discussion of Solzhenitsyn's literary works to 1975 takes an essentially negative view, in contrast to the generally favorable reception of his early work.

Pearce, Joseph. *Solzhenitsyn: A Soul in Exile.* New York: HarperCollins, 1999. Generally uncritical biography chronicles Solzhenitsyn's evolution from pro-Marxist youth to anti-Soviet writer and, finally, to literary anachronism after the demise of the Soviet Union. Features exclusive personal interviews with Solzhenitsyn, previously unpublished poetry, and rare photographs.

Scammell, Michael. *Solzhenitsyn.* New York: W. W. Norton, 1984. Exhaustive and lively biography deals with practically all important aspects of Solzhenitsyn's life, but does not discuss his writings in detail.

Thomas, D. M. *Alexander Solzhenitsyn: A Century in His Life.* New York: St. Martin's Press, 1998. Personal portrait of the writer provides insights into Solzhenitsyn's struggle with Joseph Stalin and his successors as well as the author's relationships with the two women who provided strong support for his efforts to expose the evils of the Communist regime. Imaginative, well-documented, and at times combative biography includes a discussion of Solzhenitsyn's return to Russia in 1994.

YEVGENY ZAMYATIN

Born: Lebedyan, Russia; January 20, 1884
Died: Paris, France; March 10, 1937
Also known as: Yevgeny Ivanovich Zamyatin; Evgenii Ivanovich Zamiatin

PRINCIPAL LONG FICTION
Uyezdnoye, 1913 (novella; *A Provincial Tale*, 1966)
Na kulichkakh, 1914 (novella; *A Godforsaken Hole*, 1988)
Ostrovityane, 1918 (novella; *The Islanders*, 1972)
My, 1927 (wr. 1920-1921; corrupt text), 1952 (*We*, 1924)
Bich bozhy, 1939

OTHER LITERARY FORMS

The Russian literary lexicon includes a number of terms relating to prose fiction that have no exact equivalents in English. Among these is the term *povest'*, defined by Alex M. Shane in his study of Yevgeny Zamyatin (zuhm-YAWT-yihn) as "a fictional narrative of intermediate length"; as Shane notes, this term "frequently has been translated into English by the somewhat nebulous terms 'long short story,' 'short novel,' or the pejorative 'novelette.'" Shane himself prefers "tale" as a translation of *povest'*, but many readers will find "novella" the most useful equivalent.

Zamyatin published roughly a half dozen *povesti*, or novellas, in addition to several dozen short stories, including fables and other forms of short fiction. The dividing line between his short fiction and his long fiction is not always clear-cut, however, and to trace the development of his distinctive narrative techniques, one must consider his fiction as a whole.

Zamyatin was an influential critic and literary theorist as well as a writer of fiction, publishing articles on such writers as H. G. Wells, O. Henry, Anatole France, Andrey Bely, Anton Chekhov, and Maxim Gorky and devoting several broad essays to the evolution of art in general. In these essays, Zamyatin developed an interesting theory of artistic change based on a Hegelian dialectic.

Writing on Russian literature, Zamyatin perceived a "thesis" in the realism of the 1890's and early twentieth century, represented by writers such as Chekhov and Gorky. The "antithesis" came in the form of the Symbolist movement: The Symbolist writers delved into aspects of reality lying beneath the surface of everyday life; their literary techniques became more complex than those of the realists as they tried to capture the inner essence of things. Finally, a synthesis appeared in the form of neorealism, the representatives of which depicted everyday life with the knowledge that there is more to life than appears on the surface. While focusing on everyday reality, they utilized the complex techniques developed by the Symbolists to convey their visions with more power and verisimilitude. Zamyatin considered himself a neorealist along with Bely, Anna Akhmatova, Osip Mandelstam, and others. Zamyatin's observations on Russian art and literature help to illuminate a complicated period in the history of Russian culture.

In addition to his essays and prose fiction, Zamyatin also wrote several original plays, adaptations, and film scenarios. His first two plays, *Ogni svyatogo Dominika* (pb. 1922; *The Fires of Saint Dominic*, 1971) and *Attila* (pb. 1950, wr. 1925-1927; English translation, 1971), depict historical subjects: The former exposes the repressiveness of the Spanish Inquisition, while the latter deals with the epoch of the struggle between ancient Rome and its barbarian invaders. Later works include *Afrikanskiy gost* (pb. 1963; wr. 1929-1930; *The African Guest*, 1971), an original farce on accommodation to the Soviet system, and several adaptations of other writers' work for the screen. His most successful adaptation was of Gorky's *Na dne* (pr., pb. 1902; *The Lower Depths*, 1912) for Jean Renoir's film *Les Bas-fonds* (1936).

ACHIEVEMENTS

Yevgeny Zamyatin's most impressive contribution to world literature is his satiric antiutopian novel *We*, which he wrote from 1920 to 1921. A biting portrayal of a society in which the human spirit is curbed by a totalitarian state, *We* had an important influence on George Orwell's *1984* (1949). In his own country, however, Zamyatin's shorter prose works made a greater impact than his novel, which was not published in the Soviet Union until 1988. His innovative approach to narrative technique helped to shape the writing style of a number of contemporaries, and this impact was doubly enhanced by Zamyatin's role as literary critic and teacher in the post-Revolutionary period. Among those who attended Zamyatin's lectures on art and literature were writers Lev Lunts, Nikolay Nikitin, Veniamin Kaverin, and Mikhail Zoshchenko. Zamyatin's unique prose style and his unrelenting criticism of philistinism and human injustice have lost none of their power over the years, and his work continues to retain its vitality and relevance today.

BIOGRAPHY

The son of a rural schoolteacher, Yevgeny Ivanovich Zamyatin was born in the small town of Lebedyan on January 20, 1884. Located on the Don River, the town lies in the heart of old Russia, and Zamyatin notes that it was famed "for its cardsharpers, gypsies, horse fairs, and the most vivid Russian speech." Provincial Russia would figure prominently in Zamyatin's later fiction, but in his youth, he took little interest in it. Instead, his childhood was marked by a keenly felt isolation. Having few playmates, he regarded books as his real companions. Learning to read at the age of four, he called Fyodor Dostoevski and Ivan Turgenev his "elders" and Nikolai Gogol his "friend."

In 1896, after four years at the local school, Zamyatin enrolled in the *Gymnasium* (college-preparatory secondary school) in Voronezh. Six years later, he finished school with a gold medal, which he immediately pawned when he went to St. Petersburg to study naval engineering. During the next few years, he took classes at the Petersburg Polytechnic Institute, spending his summers working in shipyards and factories throughout Russia. He developed an interest in politics, and he soon joined the Bolshevik Party. During the frenetic political turmoil of St. Petersburg at the end of 1905, Zamyatin was picked up in a mass arrest and was forced to spend several months in solitary confinement; he spent his time in jail writing poetry and studying English. In the spring of 1906, he was released and exiled to Lebedyan, but he could not bear the torpor of the provincial town, and he returned to St. Petersburg illegally. It was not until 1911 that his true status was discovered, and he thus escaped renewed exile for several years.

In the interim, Zamyatin had graduated from the institute and had become a practicing naval engineer; in 1911, he was appointed lecturer at the institute. Moreover, he had just published his first stories: "Odin" (alone), which appeared in 1908, records the saga of an imprisoned student revolutionary who commits suicide because of frustrated love, and "Devushka" (1909; the girl) contains a similarly tragic theme of unfulfilled love. Neither story is the work of a mature artist, but both show that Zamyatin was already experimenting with prose technique. His first successful work was the novella *A Provincial Tale*, which he wrote from 1911 to 1912 during the weeks of seclusion in the country following his exile from the capital. This exposé of stagnation and cruelty in rural Russia sparked a glowing critical response upon its publication in 1913, while his next major novella, *A Godforsaken Hole*, so offended the authorities by its portrayal of inhumanity in a provincial military garrison that they confiscated the magazine in which it appeared.

In 1916, Zamyatin went abroad to work on icebreakers in England, where he wrote and gathered material for two satiric works, *The Islanders* and "Lovets chelovekov" (1922; the fisher of men), which depict the constrained reserve of the British with exceptional skill. After the abdication of Czar Nicholas II in 1917, Zamyatin returned to St. Petersburg and immersed himself in literary activities. During the years from 1917 to 1921, he completed fourteen stories, a dozen fables, a play, and the novel *We*. Zamyatin's works from this period exhibit a wide variety of styles and interests. They include stories that examine the undiluted passions still found in Russia's backwaters, such as "Sever" ("The North," 1966); stories that depict the struggle to preserve humanistic impulses in the difficult conditions of urban life after the Revolution, such as "Peshchera" ("The Cave"), "Mamay," and "Drakon" ("The Dragon"); and ribald parodies of saints' lives, such as "O tom, kak istzelen byl inok Erazm" ("The Healing of the Novice Erasmus").

In addition to writing fiction, Zamyatin gave lectures on writing to young authors in the House of Arts in Petrograd, held significant positions in literary organizations such as the All-Russian Union of Writers, and served as an editor for several journals and publishing ventures, including the World Literature publishing house. The immediate post-Revolutionary period was a time of intellectual ferment. In literature, all topics came under debate—the goals of literature, the proper style and technique for the age, and the relationship of literature to the Revolution itself. On one side of the debate were those groups that called for the creation of proletarian and socially useful literature; on the other were those who believed that literature should be free from any ideological direction. During this period, Zamyatin had considerable influence as a critic and literary mentor. His superbly written articles and speeches attracted a large audience and provoked a wide response.

Throughout his work, Zamyatin adopted the position of a perpetual opponent to the status quo. He attacked every kind of conformity and all attempts to channel a writer's output into an ideologically uniform direction. In his essay "Ya boyus" (1921; "I Am Afraid," 1970), he wrote that "true literature can exist only where it is created, not by diligent and trustworthy officials, but by madmen, hermits, heretics, dreamers, rebels and sceptics." Behind this stand lay a deep, humanistic concern for the individual's spiritual freedom in an era of growing absolutism. The spirit of defiance that had marked his student days in St. Petersburg had not faded, and in fact Zamyatin was in the process of developing a romantic philosophy of revolution that colored many of his articles, speeches, and fictional works.

In essence, Zamyatin believed in perpetual revolution, the ultimate effect of which is to combat what he termed "entropy"—stagnation, philistinism, static and vegetable life. All truths are relative; there is no final truth. It is the obligation of the heretic, the visionary, the imaginative writer to work for the revolution and the distant future. Attainment of one's goal paradoxically becomes defeat, not victory, because the result would be stagnation, not continuation of the struggle. Zamyatin never called for bloody revolution in the streets; on the contrary, he would protest at every manifestation of humankind's inhumanity to humans. His ideal seemed to be a balance of the rational and irrational in people, but his fear of stagnation and regimentation fired his imagination and resulted in his romantic concept of infinite revolution.

Yet, even if one dismisses these ideas as rhetoric, Zamyatin's earnest campaign for the rights of the individual was dangerous enough in a state that condemned individuality and glorified the collective. In 1922, Zamyatin was arrested along with 160 other intellectuals whose activities were considered undesirable. An order for his deportation was signed by the notorious head of the secret police, G. G. Yagoda. Unknown to Zamyatin, however, and very likely against his will, a group of writers and friends succeeded in having the order rescinded. When Zamyatin was released in 1923, he applied for permission to leave the country but was refused.

Zamyatin's production of prose fiction declined sharply after this incident, in part as a result of deepening involvement in his editorial and administrative duties, his growing interest in the theater, and the increasing influence of politics on the realm of literature. The political situation in the Soviet Union became more rigid during the mid-1920's. Joseph Stalin was then in the process of consolidating his dictatorial powers; he introduced the first Five-Year Plan into the economy late in 1928, and with it came a kind of Five-Year Plan in literature, too. A writers' organization named the Russian Association of Proletarian Writers (RAPP), headed by the strident critic Leopold Averbakh, began to dominate the literary arena and with the tacit approval of the party sought to discredit and harass all of those writers who deviated from their ideal of "artisans" producing ideologically sound works about the social benefits of the Five-Year Plan and collectivization.

Zamyatin, who had for some time been known as an "inner émigré," became one of the chief targets of this campaign of vilification. Productions of his plays were canceled, publishing houses were closed to him, and various writers' groups took turns criticizing him. In particular, he was reproached for "extreme individualism" and hostile attitudes toward the principles of Marxism-Leninism and class warfare. Yet Zamyatin, who had written in 1926, "a stubborn, unyielding enemy is far more deserving of respect than a sudden convert to communism," did not break down and confess his "errors" as others did.

Finally, in 1931, Zamyatin wrote a letter to Stalin asking permission to go abroad with the right to return "as soon as it becomes possible in our country to serve great ideas in literature without cringing before little men." Through the intercession of Gorky, Zamyatin's request was granted, and he left in November of that year with his wife. In Paris, he worked on translations, screenplays, and the first part of a novel, *Bich bozhy* (the scourge of God). He hoped to travel to the United States, where he could continue his work in drama and film, but his plans never reached fruition. He died on March 10, 1937.

ANALYSIS

In his essay "Sovremennaya russkaya literatura" (1956; "Contemporary Russian Literature," 1970), Yevgeny Zamyatin contrasts the narrative style of the realists to that of his own generation. He writes,

> By the time the Neorealists appeared, life had become more complex, faster, more feverish. . . . In response to this new way of life, the Neorealists have learned to write more compactly, briefly, tersely than the Realists. They have learned to say in ten lines what used to be said in a whole page.

His own work demonstrates how consistent he was in his search for a concise yet vivid narrative manner. Throughout his career, he experimented with language, imagery, colors, and sounds to craft his own personal narrative voice.

A PROVINCIAL TALE

The outlines of Zamyatin's mature narrative manner are evident in his first major prose work, the novella *A Provincial Tale*, written in 1911-1912. Zamyatin traces the life of a loutish brute named Anfim Baryba, from the moment he is thrown out of his house by his father, through an oppressive affair with a fat widow, a career of theft and dishonesty, and the attainment of a job as a police officer as a reward for betraying a close friend through perjury in a criminal court case. Zamyatin's treatment of Baryba's life highlights the callousness and ignorance that prevail in the primitive backwaters of Russia, and reflects his personal antipathy for stagnant, prejudice-ridden life. Heightening the verisimilitude of this dark vision is the colloquial narrative tone Zamyatin adopts in the story. This distinctive tone, in which the neutral language of an objective narrator is replaced by language drawing heavily on the vernacular of spoken Russian, is termed *skaz*, and Zamyatin's use of *skaz* reflects the influence of such writers as Nikolay Leskov and Alexey Remizov.

On the other hand, the devices that Zamyatin utilizes in character description already bear the hallmarks that later distinguish his mature work. A favorite method of characterization is the identification of a character with an object, animal, or distinctive physical attribute. With this device, Zamyatin can stress a character's personality traits and signal the presence of that character merely by mentioning the established association. When Chebotarikha, the widow with whom Baryba has an affair, first enters the story, Zamyatin notes that she was "spread out like dough." Later, when Baryba begins his liaison with her, Zamyatin writes, "Baryba turned around and . . . sunk his hands deep into something soft as dough." The scene concludes, "Baryba drowned in the sweet, hot dough." Finally, when the woman discovers Baryba's infidelity, she "shook like dough that's risen to the edge of the bucket." It is interesting to note that Zamyatin's penchant for concise yet striking forms of expression does not create a feeling of lightness in *A Provincial Tale*. His tone is somber, and images of stasis and grime prevail, as when the narrator sums up the life of his village: "And so they live in peace, sweating like manure in the heat."

By the end of the 1910's, Zamyatin had developed the vibrant, expressionistic style of *A Provincial Tale* to its fullest extent. His depiction in "The Cave" of Petrograd's urban landscape during the arduous winters following the Russian Revolution remains one of the most impressive representations of that city in Russian literature, which has a long tradition of exposing the unreal or fantastic aspects of the city. For this work, Zamyatin isolates the elements of darkness and cold on a winter night in Petrograd and weaves from them a broad "mother metaphor," to apply a term used by the critic D. S. Mirsky in his book *Contemporary Russian Literature, 1881-1925* (1926). Zamyatin once described his predilection for creating extended metaphoric images: "If I firmly believe in the image . . . it will inevitably give rise to an entire system of related images, it will spread its roots through paragraphs and pages."

The central image here casts Petrograd as a prehistoric, Ice Age setting and the city's inhabitants as cave dwellers who have regressed into a primitive lifestyle that includes worshiping the "greedy cave god: the castiron stove." Isolating one couple, Martin Martinych and his wife, Masha, Zamyatin records how the customs of civilization give way to the more primal instincts for survival. Needing fuel for the stove, Martin struggles with his urge to steal his neighbor's wood. As Zamyatin describes it, there were two Martins "locked in mortal combat: the old one, who loved Scriabin and who knew he must not, and the new one, the cave dweller, who knew—he must." In the frozen wasteland of this city, all choices are bad, and Zamyatin's taut narrative manner heightens the aura of entrapment and despair.

WE

Zamyatin's other memorable urban setting—the futuristic city of the novel *We*—transcends the boundaries of contemporary Russia and attains dimensions of universality. Influenced by his readings of H. G. Wells's utopian writings and repelled by the inflamed rhetoric of the new Soviet state, Zamyatin constructed an anti-utopian novel that both amuses the reader with its ironic humor and unsettles the reader with its startling prediction of totalitarian repression.

Written in the form of a journal by D-503, an engineer building a rocket ship to carry the ideals of the United State to less advanced worlds where people may still languish "in the primitive state of freedom," *We* describes a world in which nearly every action of its citizens is carried out according to strict schedules set by the government and its ruler, the Well-Doer. Even sexual activity is regulated by a rigid system of registration and appointments. Beneath the comic aspects of this society, however, lie such troubling phenomena as rigged elections, denunciations of one's fellow citizens, and the torture and execution of political dissidents.

The plot of the work centers on D-503's discovery of elements within himself that do not harmonize with his belief in order and control—the irrational emotions of love and passion. The object of his arousal is a female number, I-330, a member of a revolutionary group seeking to overthrow the government and to revitalize the world by reintroducing into society the energies of a primitive people who live beyond the Green Wall encircling the United State. I-330's conversations with D-503 contain the ideological message of the novel. An advocate of perpetual revolution, she articulates the fundamental concept that two forces exist in the world—entropy and energy: "One leads into blessed quietude, to happy equilibrium, the other to the destruction of equilibrium, to torturingly perpetual motion." She, of course, prefers the latter, but her revolutionary plans are uncovered by the secret police, the Guardians, and at the end of the novel, the forces of the United State seem to be winning the battle: I-330 has been arrested, and D-503 has undergone an operation to remove the source of his pain—his "fancy."

We unfolds at a rapid pace. D-503's journal entries are laconic, often breaking off in midthought; as in his other works, Zamyatin relies on bold imagery in characterization and description. Thus D-503 notes with shame that he has hairy, apelike hands—an indication of atavistic tendencies within him—while I-330 is distinguished by her black, slanting eyebrows, which form an X on her face—a kind of mathematical variable or unknown that troubles D-503. Zamyatin also makes use of vivid sounds and colors. At times, his manipulation of sounds recalls the prose of Andrey Bely, and his use of color creates an intense network of symbolic associations. Red, for example, is the color of blood and fire, and it is associated with the revolution and surging passion, while pink, a diluted version of red, is the color of the official forms through which the state regulates sexual contact. Zamyatin's handling of color and sound reflects his conviction that "a word has color and sound. From now on, painting and music go side by side."

Mathematics provides another major source of imagery in *We*. D-503 loves the precision of the multiplication tables and abhors imaginary and irrational numbers. Zamyatin's own support for the concept of the irrational in human affairs filters through D-503's opposition to it, and the reader recognizes that the writer owes a substantial debt to the works of Fyodor Dostoevski, particularly his *Zapiski iz podpolya* (1864; *Notes from the Underground*, 1913) and *Bratya Karamazovy* (1879-1880; *The Brothers Karamazov*, 1911). Reminiscent of the former work is the glass-enclosed world of the United State, in which human happiness is calculated according to exact mathematical formulas. This recalls the diatribe of Dostoevski's underground man against a world in which all human facts will be listed in something like logarithmic tables and people will be urged to live in an indestructible crystal palace. Zamyatin even invokes specific imagery used by Dostoevski. The underground man's animosity toward the "stone wall" of mathematics, symbolized in the simple equation $2 \times 2 = 4$, is echoed by D-503's ardent love for this same formula.

From *The Brothers Karamazov*, Zamyatin draws on the parable of the Grand Inquisitor to underscore his distaste for a self-serving ruling order that boasts of having eliminated individual freedom of choice for the sake of human happiness. *We* is a remarkably resonant piece of writing. Fusing dark dimensions of human oppression with light notes of affectionate satire, Zamyatin's novel remains an impressive model of the anti-utopian genre. After several years of working in the charged narrative mode of the early 1920's, Zamyatin gradually began to simplify his narrative techniques, and the tight austerity of his late fiction endows that body of work with understated power. The writer himself commented on the conscious effort he made to achieve this kind of effective simplicity: "It turned out that all the complexities I had passed through had been only a road to simplicity.... Simplicity of form is legitimate for our epoch, but the right to simplicity must be earned."

Zamyatin's evolution as a writer reflects the conscious striving of a dedicated artist, and the work he produced as a result consistently exhibits high quality. His innovative approach to narrative and descriptive techniques lends his fiction a special vibrancy and life, while his sensitivity to the demands of the human spirit and his aversion to all forms of repression add moral depth to his art. Although Zamyatin's work appeared as a draft of fresh air in the 1910's and 1920's, its appeal far transcends that time, and he has earned a place of lasting significance in the history of modern Russian literature.

Julian W. Connolly

OTHER MAJOR WORKS

SHORT FICTION: *Bol'shim detyam skazki*, 1922; *Nechestivye rasskazy*, 1927; *Povesti i rasskazy*, 1963; *The Dragon: Fifteen Stories*, 1966.

PLAYS: *Ogni Svyatogo Dominika*, pb. 1922 (*The Fires of Saint Dominic*, 1971); *Blokha*, pr. 1925 (*The Flea*, 1971); *Obshchestvo pochetnikh zvonarei*, pr. 1925 (*The Society of Honorary Bell Ringers*, 1971); *Attila*, pb. 1950 (wr. 1925-1927; English translation,

1971); *Afrikanskiy gost*, pb. 1963 (wr. 1929-1930; *The African Guest*, 1971); *Five Plays*, 1971.

SCREENPLAY: *Les Bas-fonds*, 1936 (*The Lower Depths*, 1937; adaptation of Maxim Gorky's novel *Na dne*).

NONFICTION: *Gerbert Uells*, 1922 (*H. G. Wells*, 1970); *Kak my pishem: Teoria literatury*, 1930; *Litsa*, 1955 (*A Soviet Heretic*, 1970).

MISCELLANEOUS: *Sobranie sochinenii*, 1929 (collected works); *Sochineniia*, 1970-1972.

BIBLIOGRAPHY

Brown, Edward J. "Zamjatin and English Literature." In *American Contributions to the Fifth International Congress of Slavists*. Vol. 2. The Hague, the Netherlands: Mouton, 1965. Discusses Zamyatin's interest in, and debt to, English literature stemming from his two-year stay in England before and during World War I.

Cavendish, Philip. *Mining the Jewels: Evgenii Zamiatin and the Literary Stylization of Rus'*. London: Maney, 2000. A thorough study of the folk-religious background of Zamyatin's sources of inspiration. It traces his attempts to reconcile the folkloric tradition and the vernacular through his artistic expression. In the process, drawing from the past and from the language of the people, he creates literature that is basically modernistic.

Collins, Christopher. *Evgenij Zamjatin: An Interpretive Study*. The Hague, the Netherlands: Mouton, 1973. In this ambitious study, Collins advances a rather complex interpretation of Zamyatin, mostly of *We*, based on Carl Jung's ideas about the conscious, the unconscious, and individualism.

Cooke, Brett. *Human Nature in Utopia: Zamyatin's "We."* Evanston, Ill.: Northwestern University Press, 2002. Cooke interprets the novel from the perspective of evolutionary psychology, analyzing its creation, style, content, and fascination for readers; he places the novel within the context of other works of utopian and dystopian fiction. Includes an index and a bibliography.

Kern, Gary, ed. *Zamyatin's "We": A Collection of Critical Essays*. Ann Arbor, Mich.: Ardis, 1988. A collection of essays on Zamyatin's magnum opus, covering the Soviet view of the novel, mythic criticism, aesthetics, and influences and comparisons. Edward J. Brown's essay "*Brave New World, 1984*, and *We*: An Essay on Anti-Utopia" offers a particularly incisive comparison of dystopian novels by Zamyatin, Aldous Huxley, and George Orwell.

Richards, D. J. *Zamyatin, a Soviet Heretic*. New York: Hillary House, 1962. An overview of the major incidents and issues in Zamyatin's life and work; an excellent, brief presentation of all facets of a very complex writer.

Russell, Robert. *Zamiatin's "We."* London: Bristol Classical Press, 2000. In the first part of the book, Russell discusses the novel within the context of the Russian civil war, when readers interpreted it as a satire on Soviet life; he also surveys major trends in modern criticism of the novel. The second part provides his own detailed analysis, based on a close reading of the "entries" in the protagonist's diary.

Shane, Alex M. *The Life and Works of Evgenij Zamjatin*. Berkeley: University of California Press, 1968. An unusually comprehensive overall study of Zamyatin in English. Shane covers Zamyatin's life and the most important features of his works, chronologically, in a scholarly but not dry fashion, and reaches his own conclusions. Includes extensive bibliographies.

Slonim, Mark. "Evgeny Zamyatin: The Ironic Dissident." In *Soviet Russian Literature: Writers and Problems, 1917-1977*. 2d ed. New York: Oxford University Press, 1977. Slonim offers a good portrait of Zamyatin as a leading literary figure of his time.

Bibliography

Every effort has been made to include studies published in 2000 and later. Most items in this bibliography contain a listing of secondary sources, making it easier to identify other critical commentary on novelists, movements, and themes.

Theoretical, Thematic, and Historical Studies

Altman, Janet Gurkin. *Epistolarity: Approaches to a Form.* Columbus: Ohio State University Press, 1982. Examines the epistolary novel, explaining how novelists use the letter form to develop characterization, further their plots, and develop meaning.

Beaumont, Matthew, ed. *Adventures in Realism.* Malden, Mass.: Blackwell, 2007. Fifteen essays explore facets of realism, which was critical to the development of the novel. Provides a theoretical framework for understanding how novelists attempt to represent the real and the common in fiction.

Brink, André. *The Novel: Language and Narrative from Cervantes to Calvino.* New York: New York University Press, 1998. Uses contemporary theories of semiotics and narratology to establish a continuum between early novelists and those of the postmodern era in their conscious use of language to achieve certain effects. Ranges across national boundaries to illustrate the theory of the development of the novel since the seventeenth century.

Brownstein, Rachel. *Becoming a Heroine: Reading About Women in Novels.* New York: Viking Press, 1982. Feminist survey of novels from the eighteenth century through the latter half of the twentieth century. Examines how "becoming a heroine" defines for women a sense of value in their lives. Considers novels by both men and women, and discusses the importance of the traditional marriage plot.

Bruzelius, Margaret. *Romancing the Novel: Adventure from Scott to Sebald.* Lewisburg, Pa.: Bucknell University Press, 2007. Examines the development of the adventure novel, linking it with the medieval romance tradition and exploring readers' continuing fascination with the genre.

Cavallaro, Dani. *The Gothic Vision: Three Centuries of Horror, Terror, and Fear.* New York: Continuum, 2005. Study of the gothic novel from its earliest manifestations in the eighteenth century to the early twenty-first century. Through the lenses of contemporary cultural theories, examines readers' fascination with novels that invoke horror, terror, and fright.

Doody, Margaret Anne. *The True Story of the Novel.* New Brunswick, N.J.: Rutgers University Press, 1996. Traces the roots of the novel, traditionally thought to have been developed in the seventeenth century, to classical Greek and Latin texts that exhibit characteristics of modern fiction.

_____. *Social Formalism: The Novel in Theory from Henry James to the Present.* Stanford, Calif.: Stanford University Press, 1998. Emphasizes the novel's special ability to define a social world for readers. Relies heavily on the works of contemporary literary and cultural theorists. Provides a summary of twentieth century efforts to identify a theory of fiction that encompasses novels of many kinds.

Hoffman, Michael J., and Patrick D. Murphy, eds. *Essentials of the Theory of Fiction*. 2d ed. Durham, N.C.: Duke University Press, 1996. Collection of essays by influential critics from the late nineteenth century through the twentieth century. Focuses on the essential elements of fiction and the novel's relationship to the world it depicts.

Lodge, David. *The Art of Fiction: Illustrated from Classic and Modern Texts*. New York: Viking Press, 1993. Short commentaries on the technical aspects of fiction. Examples from important and minor novelists illustrate literary principles and techniques such as point of view, suspense, character introduction, irony, motivation, and ending.

Lynch, Deirdre, and William B. Walker, eds. *Cultural Institutions of the Novel*. Durham, N.C.: Duke University Press, 1996. Fifteen essays examine aspects of long fiction produced around the world. Encourages a redefinition of the genre and argues for inclusion of texts not historically considered novels.

Moretti, Franco, ed. *The Novel*. 2 vols. Princeton, N.J.: Princeton University Press, 2006. Explores the novel from multiple perspectives, including as an anthropological, historical, and sociological document; a function of the national tradition from which it emerges; and a work of art subject to examination using various critical approaches.

Priestman, Martin, ed. *The Cambridge Companion to Crime Fiction*. New York: Cambridge University Press, 2003. Essays examine the nature and development of the genre, explore works by writers (including women and ethnic minorities) from several countries, and establish links between crime fiction and other literary genres. Includes a chronology.

Scaggs, John. *Crime Fiction*. New York: Routledge, 2005. Provides a history of crime fiction, explores key subgenres, and identifies recurring themes that suggest the wider social and historical context in which these works are written. Suggests critical approaches that open crime fiction to serious study.

Shiach, Morag, ed. *The Cambridge Companion to the Modernist Novel*. New York: Cambridge University Press, 2007. Essays explaining the concept of modernism and its influence on the novel. Detailed examination of works by writers from various countries, all influenced by the modernist movement. Includes a detailed chronology.

Vice, Sue. *Holocaust Fiction*. New York: Routledge, 2000. Examines controversies generated by novels about the Holocaust. Focuses on eight important works, but also offers observations on the polemics surrounding publication of books on this topic.

Zunshine, Lisa. *Why We Read Fiction: Theory of Mind and the Novel*. Columbus: Ohio State University Press, 2006. Applies theories of cognitive psychology to novel reading, explaining how experience and human nature lead readers to constrain their interpretations of a given text. Provides numerous examples from well-known novels to illustrate how and why readers find pleasure in fiction.

POLITICAL NOVELS

Bell, Bernard W. *The Contemporary African American Novel: Its Folk Roots and Modern Literary Branches.* Amherst: University of Massachusetts Press, 2004. Extensive historical examination of the development of African American fiction, focusing on distinctive elements and outlining the role of political and social influences in changing the focus of African American novels.

Clark, Katerina. *The Soviet Novel: History as Ritual.* 3d ed. Bloomington: Indiana University Press, 2000. Critical analysis of Soviet fiction by writers who followed the dictates of Socialist Realism, the only approved form of literature in the Soviet Union. Examines elements of this form of fiction and explains how the genre was intended to support larger political aims.

Cornis-Pope, Marcel. *Narrative Innovation and Cultural Rewriting in the Cold War and After.* New York: Palgrave, 2001. Systematic study of novels from the latter half of the twentieth century, considering how writers respond to the polarized political atmosphere of the time. Concentrates on American novelists, considering their work in the context of postmodern theories regarding the practice of writing.

Dineen, Patrick J., and Joseph Romance, eds. *Democracy's Literature: Politics and Fiction in America.* Lanham, Md.: Rowman & Littlefield, 2005. Essays on significant novels of the nineteenth and twentieth centuries outlining the political nature of American writing and the profound philosophical underpinnings of the best American literature.

Eagleton, Terry. *The English Novel: An Introduction.* Malden, Mass.: Blackwell, 2005. Surveys English fiction by concentrating on the work of major authors. Considers novels from various theoretical perspectives, giving primacy to Marxist readings that stress the historical and sociological aspects of fiction.

Gillespie, David. *The Twentieth-Century Russian Novel: An Introduction.* Washington, D.C.: Berg, 1996. Study of characteristics of selected novels that illustrate the political situation in the Soviet Union during the seven decades of Communist Party rule. Provides brief plot summaries and critical discussions of key texts; also focuses on the fate of writers during this period.

Hale, Dorothy J., ed. *The Novel: An Anthology of Criticism and Theory, 1900-2000.* Malden, Mass.: Blackwell, 2006. Collection of essays by theorists and novelists. Includes commentary on the novel form from the perspective of formalism, structuralism, poststructuralism, Marxism, and reader response theory. Essays also address the novel through the lenses of sociology, gender studies, and feminist theory.

Hart, Stephen M., and Wen-chin Ouyang, eds. *A Companion to Magical Realism.* London: Tamesis, 2005. Essays outlining the development of Magical Realism, tracing its roots from Europe through Latin America to other regions of the world. Explores the political dimensions of the genre.

Hsia, C. T. *A History of Modern Chinese Fiction.* 3d ed. Bloomington: Indiana University

Press, 1999. Analysis of Chinese fiction from 1917 to the end of the twentieth century. Examines the Chinese Communist Party's influence on the production of literature after 1949 and on the careers of writers. Also discusses the role of literature as a vehicle for political dissent.

Joshi, Priya. *In Another Country: Colonialism, Culture, and the English Novel in India.* New York: Columbia University Press, 2002. Applies contemporary theories of postcolonialism and political economy to a study of novels from the nineteenth through twentieth centuries. Also examines the influence of novels on readers in India and abroad.

Laurence W. Mazzeno

Glossary of Literary Terms

absurdism: A philosophical attitude, pervading much of modern drama and fiction, that underlines the isolation and alienation that humans experience, having been thrown into what absurdists see as a godless universe devoid of religious, spiritual, or metaphysical meaning. Conspicuous in its lack of logic, consistency, coherence, intelligibility, and realism, the literature of the absurd depicts the anguish, forlornness, and despair inherent in the human condition. Counter to the rationalist assumptions of traditional humanism, absurdism denies the existence of universal truth or value.

allegory: A literary mode in which a second level of meaning, wherein characters, events, and settings represent abstractions, is encoded within the surface narrative. The allegorical mode may dominate an entire work, in which case the encoded message is the work's primary reason for being, or it may be an element in a work otherwise interesting and meaningful for its surface story alone. Elements of allegory may be found in Jonathan Swift's *Gulliver's Travels* (1726) and Thomas Mann's *Der Zauberberg* (1924; *The Magic Mountain*, 1927).

anatomy: Literally the term means the "cutting up" or "dissection" of a subject into its constituent parts for closer examination. Northrop Frye, in his *Anatomy of Criticism* (1957), uses the term to refer to a narrative that deals with mental attitudes rather than people. As opposed to the novel, the anatomy features stylized figures who are mouthpieces for the ideas they represent.

antagonist: The character in fiction who stands as a rival or opponent to the *protagonist*.

antihero: Defined by Seán O'Faoláin as a fictional figure who, deprived of social sanctions and definitions, is always trying to define himself and to establish his own codes. Ahab may be seen as the antihero of Herman Melville's *Moby Dick* (1851).

archetype: The term "archetype" entered literary criticism from the psychology of Carl Jung, who defined archetypes as "primordial images" from the "collective unconscious" of humankind. Jung believed that works of art derive much of their power from the unconscious appeal of these images to ancestral memories. In his extremely influential *Anatomy of Criticism* (1957), Northrop Frye gave another sense of the term wide currency, defining the archetype as "a symbol, usually an image, which recurs often enough in literature to be recognizable as an element of one's literary experience as a whole."

atmosphere: The general mood or tone of a work; atmosphere is often associated with setting but can also be established by action or dialogue. A classic example of atmosphere is the primitive, fatalistic tone created in the opening description of Egdon Heath in Thomas Hardy's *The Return of the Native* (1878).

bildungsroman: Sometimes called the "novel of education," the bildungsroman focuses on the growth of a young *protagonist* who is learning about the world and finding his or her place in life; typical examples are James Joyce's *A Portrait of the Artist as a*

Young Man (1914-1915, serial; 1916, book) and Thomas Wolfe's *Look Homeward, Angel* (1929).

biographical criticism: Criticism that attempts to determine how the events and experiences of an author's life influence his or her work.

bourgeois novel: A novel in which the values, preoccupations, and accoutrements of middle-class or bourgeois life are given particular prominence. The heyday of the bourgeois novel was the nineteenth century, when novelists as varied as Jane Austen, Honoré de Balzac, and Anthony Trollope both criticized and unreflectingly transmitted the assumptions of the rising middle class.

canon: An authorized or accepted list of books. In modern parlance, the literary canon comprehends the privileged texts, classics, or great books that are thought to belong permanently on university reading lists. Recent theory—especially feminist, Marxist, and poststructuralist—critically examines the process of canon formation and questions the hegemony of white male writers. Such theory sees canon formation as the ideological act of a dominant institution and seeks to undermine the notion of canonicity itself, thereby preventing the exclusion of works by women, minorities, and oppressed peoples.

character: Characters in fiction can be presented as if they were real people or as stylized functions of the plot. Usually characters are a combination of both factors.

classicism: A literary stance or value system consciously based on the example of classical Greek and Roman literature. While the term is applied to an enormous diversity of artists in many different periods and in many different national literatures, "classicism" generally denotes a cluster of values including formal discipline, restrained expression, reverence for tradition, and an objective rather than a subjective orientation. As a literary tendency, classicism is often opposed to *Romanticism*, although many writers combine classical and romantic elements.

climax/crisis: The term "climax" refers to the moment of the reader's highest emotional response, whereas "crisis" refers to a structural element of plot, a turning point at which a resolution must take place.

complication: The point in a novel when the *conflict* is developed or when the already existing conflict is further intensified.

conflict: The struggle that develops as a result of the opposition between the *protagonist* and another person, the natural world, society, or some force within the self.

contextualist criticism: A further extension of *formalist criticism*, which assumes that the language of art is constitutive. Rather than referring to preexistent values, the artwork creates values only inchoately realized before. The most important advocates of this position are Eliseo Vivas (*The Artistic Transaction*, 1963) and Murray Krieger (*The Play and Place of Criticism*, 1967).

conventions: All those devices of stylization, compression, and selection that constitute the necessary differences between art and life. According to the Russian Formalists, these conventions constitute the "literariness" of literature and are the only proper concern of the literary critic.

deconstruction: An extremely influential contemporary school of criticism based on the works of the French philosopher Jacques Derrida. Deconstruction treats literary works as unconscious reflections of the reigning myths of Western culture. The primary myth is that there is a meaningful world that language signifies or represents. The deconstructionist critic is most often concerned with showing how a literary text tacitly subverts the very assumptions or myths on which it ostensibly rests.

defamiliarization: Coined by Viktor Shklovsky in 1917, this term denotes a basic principle of Russian Formalism. Poetic language (by which the Formalists meant artful language, in prose as well as in poetry) defamiliarizes or "makes strange" familiar experiences. The technique of art, says Shklovsky, is to "make objects unfamiliar, to make forms difficult, to increase the difficulty and length of perception. . . . Art is a way of experiencing the artfulness of an object; the object is not important."

detective story: The so-called classic detective story (or mystery) is a highly formalized and logically structured mode of fiction in which the focus is on a crime solved by a detective through interpretation of evidence and ratiocination; the most famous detective in this mode is Arthur Conan Doyle's Sherlock Holmes. Many modern practitioners of the genre, however, such as Dashiell Hammett, Raymond Chandler, and Ross Macdonald, have de-emphasized the puzzlelike qualities of the detective story, stressing instead characterization, theme, and other elements of mainstream fiction.

determinism: The belief that an individual's actions are essentially determined by biological and environmental factors, with free will playing a negligible role. (See *naturalism*.)

dialogue: The similitude of conversation in fiction, dialogue serves to characterize, to further the *plot*, to establish *conflict*, and to express thematic ideas.

displacement: Popularized in criticism by Northrop Frye, this term refers to the author's attempt to make his or her story psychologically motivated and realistic, even as the latent structure of the mythical motivation moves relentlessly forward.

dominant: A term coined by Roman Jakobson to refer to that which "rules, determines, and transforms the remaining components in the work of a single artist, in a poetic canon, or in the work of an epoch." The shifting of the dominant in a *genre* accounts for the creation of new generic forms and new poetic epochs. For example, the rise of *realism* in the mid-nineteenth century indicates realistic conventions becoming dominant and *romance* or fantasy conventions becoming secondary.

doppelgänger: A double or counterpart of a person, sometimes endowed with ghostly qualities. A fictional character's doppelgänger often reflects a suppressed side of his or her personality. One of the classic examples of the doppelgänger motif is found in

Fyodor Dostoevski's novella *Dvoynik* (1846; *The Double*, 1917); Isaac Bashevis Singer and Jorge Luis Borges, among others, offer striking modern treatments of the doppelgänger.

epic: Although this term usually refers to a long narrative poem that presents the exploits of a central figure of high position, the term is also used to designate a long novel that has the style or structure usually associated with an epic. In this sense, for example, Herman Melville's *Moby Dick* (1851) and James Joyce's *Ulysses* (1922) may be called epics.

episodic narrative: A work that is held together primarily by a loose connection of self-sufficient episodes. *Picaresque novels* often have episodic structure.

epistolary novel: A novel made up of letters by one or more fictional characters. Samuel Richardson's *Pamela: Or, Virtue Rewarded* (1740-1741) is a well-known eighteenth century example. In the nineteenth century, Bram Stoker's *Dracula* (1897) is largely epistolary. The technique allows for several different points of view to be presented.

euphuism: A style of writing characterized by ornate language that is highly contrived, alliterative, and repetitious. Euphuism was developed by John Lyly in his *Euphues, the Anatomy of Wit* (1578) and was emulated frequently by writers of the Elizabethan Age.

existentialism: A philosophical, religious, and literary term, emerging from World War II, for a group of attitudes surrounding the pivotal notion that existence precedes essence. According to Jean-Paul Sartre, "Man is nothing else but what he makes himself." Forlornness arises from the death of God and the concomitant death of universal values, of any source of ultimate or a priori standards. Despair arises from the fact that an individual can reckon only with what depends on his or her will, and the sphere of that will is severely limited; the number of things on which he or she can have an impact is pathetically small. Existentialist literature is antideterministic in the extreme and rejects the idea that heredity and environment shape and determine human motivation and behavior.

exposition: The part or parts of a fiction that provide necessary background information. Exposition not only provides the time and place of the action but also introduces readers to the fictive world of the story, acquainting them with the ground rules of the work.

fantastic: In his study *The Fantastic* (1970), Tzvetan Todorov defines the fantastic as a *genre* that lies between the "uncanny" and the "marvelous." All three genres embody the familiar world but present an event that cannot be explained by the laws of the familiar world. Todorov says that the fantastic occupies a twilight zone between the uncanny (when the reader knows that the peculiar event is merely the result of an illusion) and the marvelous (when the reader understands that the event is supposed to take place in a realm controlled by laws unknown to humankind). The fantastic is thus essentially unsettling, provocative, even subversive.

feminist criticism: A criticism advocating equal rights for women in political, economic, social, psychological, personal, and aesthetic senses. On the thematic level, the feminist reader should identify with female characters and their concerns. The object is to provide a critique of phallocentric assumptions and an analysis of patriarchal ideologies inscribed in a literature that is male-centered and male-dominated. On the ideological level, feminist critics see gender, as well as the stereotypes that go along with it, as a cultural construct. They strive to define a particularly feminine content and to extend the *canon* so that it might include works by lesbians, feminists, and women writers in general.

flashback: A scene in a fiction that depicts an earlier event; it may be presented as a reminiscence by a character in the story or may simply be inserted into the narrative.

foreshadowing: A device to create suspense or dramatic irony in fiction by indicating through suggestion what will take place in the future.

formalist criticism: Two particularly influential formalist schools of criticism arose in the twentieth century: the Russian Formalists and the American New Critics. The Russian Formalists were concerned with the conventional devices used in literature to defamiliarize that which habit has made familiar. The New Critics believed that literary criticism is a description and evaluation of its object and that the primary concern of the critic is with the work's unity. Both schools of criticism, at their most extreme, treated literary works as artifacts or constructs divorced from their biographical and social contexts.

genre: In its most general sense, this term refers to a group of literary works defined by a common form, style, or purpose. In practice, the term is used in a wide variety of overlapping and, to a degree, contradictory senses. Tragedy and comedy are thus described as distinct genres; the novel (a form that includes both tragic and comic works) is a genre; and various subspecies of the novel, such as the *gothic* and the *picaresque*, are themselves frequently treated as distinct genres. Finally, the term "genre fiction" refers to forms of popular fiction in which the writer is bound by more or less rigid conventions. Indeed, all these diverse usages have in common an emphasis on the manner in which individual literary works are shaped by particular expectations and conventions; this is the subject of genre criticism.

genre fiction: Categories of popular fiction in which the writers are bound by more or less rigid conventions, such as in the *detective story*, the *romance*, and the *Western*. Although the term can be used in a neutral sense, it is often used dismissively.

gothic novel: A form of fiction developed in the eighteenth century that focuses on horror and the supernatural. In his preface to *The Castle of Otranto* (1765), the first gothic novel in English, Horace Walpole claimed that he was trying to combine two kinds of fiction, with events and story typical of the medieval romance and character delineation typical of the realistic novel. Other examples of the form are Matthew Gregory

Lewis's *The Monk: A Romance* (1796; also known as *Ambrosio: Or, The Monk*) and Mary Wollstonecraft Shelley's *Frankenstein: Or, The Modern Prometheus* (1818).

grotesque: According to Wolfgang Kayser (*The Grotesque in Art and Literature*, 1963), the grotesque is an embodiment in literature of the estranged world. Characterized by a breakup of the everyday world by mysterious forces, the form differs from fantasy in that the reader is not sure whether to react with humor or with horror and in that the exaggeration manifested exists in the familiar world rather than in a purely imaginative world.

Hebraic/Homeric styles: Terms coined by Erich Auerbach in *Mimesis: The Representation of Reality in Western Literature* (1953) to designate two basic fictional styles. The Hebraic style focuses only on the decisive points of narrative and leaves all else obscure, mysterious, and "fraught with background"; the Homeric style places the narrative in a definite time and place and externalizes everything in a perpetual foreground.

historical criticism: In contrast to *formalist criticism*, which treats literary works to a great extent as self-contained artifacts, historical criticism emphasizes the historical context of literature; the two approaches, however, need not be mutually exclusive. Ernst Robert Curtius's *European Literature and the Latin Middle Ages* (1940) is a prominent example of historical criticism.

historical novel: A novel that depicts past historical events, usually public in nature, and features real as well as fictional people. Sir Walter Scott's Waverley novels established the basic type, but the relationship between fiction and history in the form varies greatly depending on the practitioner.

implied author: According to Wayne Booth (*The Rhetoric of Fiction*, 1961), the novel often creates a kind of second self who tells the story—a self who is wiser, more sensitive, and more perceptive than any real person could be.

interior monologue: Defined by Édouard Dujardin as the speech of a character designed to introduce the reader directly to the character's internal life, the form differs from other kinds of monologue in that it attempts to reproduce thought before any logical organization is imposed on it. See, for example, Molly Bloom's long interior monologue at the conclusion of James Joyce's *Ulysses* (1922).

irrealism: A term often used to refer to modern or postmodern fiction that is presented self-consciously as a fiction or a fabulation rather than a mimesis of external reality. The best-known practitioners of irrealism are John Barth, Robert Coover, and Donald Barthelme.

local colorists: A loose movement of late nineteenth century American writers whose fiction emphasizes the distinctive folkways, landscapes, and dialects of various regions. Important local colorists include Bret Harte, Mark Twain, George Washington Cable, Kate Chopin, and Sarah Orne Jewett. (See *regional novel*.)

Marxist criticism: Based on the nineteenth century writings of Karl Marx and Friedrich Engels, Marxist criticism views literature as a product of ideological forces determined by the dominant class. However, many Marxists believe that literature operates according to its own autonomous standards of production and reception: It is both a product of ideology and able to determine ideology. As such, literature may overcome the dominant paradigms of its age and play a revolutionary role in society.

metafiction: This term refers to fiction that manifests a reflexive tendency, such as Vladimir Nabokov's *Pale Fire* (1962) and John Fowles's *The French Lieutenant's Woman* (1969). The emphasis is on the loosening of the work's illusion of reality to expose the reality of its illusion. Other terms used to refer to this type of fiction include "irrealism," "postmodernist fiction," "antifiction," and "surfiction."

modernism: An international movement in the arts that began in the early years of the twentieth century. Although the term is used to describe artists of widely varying persuasions, modernism in general was characterized by its international idiom, by its interest in cultures distant in space or time, by its emphasis on formal experimentation, and by its sense of dislocation and radical change.

motif: A conventional incident or situation in a fiction that may serve as the basis for the structure of the narrative itself. The Russian Formalist critic Boris Tomashevsky uses the term to refer to the smallest particle of thematic material in a work.

motivation: Although this term is usually used in reference to the convention of justifying the action of a character from his or her psychological makeup, the Russian Formalists use the term to refer to the network of devices that justify the introduction of individual *motifs* or groups of motifs in a work. For example, "compositional motivation" refers to the principle that every single property in a work contributes to its overall effect; "realistic motivation" refers to the realistic devices used to make a work plausible and lifelike.

multiculturalism: The tendency to recognize the perspectives of those traditionally excluded from the canon of Western art and literature. In order to promote multiculturalism, publishers and educators have revised textbooks and school curricula to incorporate material by and about women, members of minority groups, persons from non-Western cultures, and homosexuals.

myth: Anonymous traditional stories dealing with basic human concepts and antinomies. According to Claude Lévi-Strauss, myth is that part of language where the "formula *tradutore, tradittore* reaches its lowest truth value. . . . Its substance does not lie in its style, its original music, or its syntax, but in the story which it tells."

myth criticism: Northrop Frye says that in myth "we see the structural principles of literature isolated." Myth criticism is concerned with these basic principles of literature; it is not to be confused with mythological criticism, which is primarily concerned with finding mythological parallels in the surface action of the *narrative*.

narrative: Robert Scholes and Robert Kellogg, in *The Nature of Narrative* (1966), say that by "narrative" they mean literary works that include both a story and a storyteller. The term "narrative" usually implies a contrast to "enacted" fiction such as drama.

narratology: The study of the form and functioning of *narratives*; it attempts to examine what all narratives have in common and what makes individual narratives different from one another.

narrator: The *character* who recounts the *narrative*, or story. Wayne Booth describes various dramatized narrators in *The Rhetoric of Fiction* (1961): unacknowledged centers of consciousness, observers, narrator-agents, and self-conscious narrators. Booth suggests that the important elements to consider in narration are the relationships among the narrator, the author, the characters, and the reader.

naturalism: As developed by Émile Zola in the late nineteenth century, naturalism is the application of the principles of scientific *determinism* to fiction. Although it usually refers more to the choice of subject matter than to technical conventions, those conventions associated with the movement center on the author's attempt to be precise and scientifically objective in description and detail, regardless of whether the events described are sordid or shocking.

New Criticism: See *formalist criticism*.

novel: Perhaps the most difficult of all fictional forms to define because of its multiplicity of modes. Edouard, in André Gide's *Les Faux-monnayeurs* (1925; *The Counterfeiters*, 1927), says the novel is the freest and most lawless of all *genres*; he wonders if fear of that liberty is the reason the novel has so timidly clung to reality. Most critics seem to agree that the novel's primary area of concern is the social world. Ian Watt (*The Rise of the Novel*, 2001) says that the novel can be distinguished from other fictional forms by the attention it pays to individual characterization and detailed presentation of the environment. Moreover, says Watt, the novel, more than any other fictional form, is interested in the "development of its characters in the course of time."

novel of manners: The classic examples of this form might be the novels of Jane Austen, wherein the customs and conventions of a social group of a particular time and place are realistically, and often satirically, portrayed.

novella, novelle, nouvelle, novelette, novela: Although these terms often refer to the short European tale, especially the Renaissance form employed by Giovanni Boccaccio, the terms often refer to that form of fiction that is said to be longer than a short story and shorter than a novel. "Novelette" is the term usually preferred by the British, whereas "novella" is the term usually used to refer to American works in this *genre*. Henry James claimed that the main merit of the form is the "effort to do the complicated thing with a strong brevity and lucidity."

phenomenological criticism: Although best known as a European school of criticism practiced by Georges Poulet and others, this so-called criticism of consciousness is also propounded in the United States by such critics as J. Hillis Miller. The focus is less on individual works and *genres* than it is on literature as an act; the work is not seen as an object but rather as part of a strand of latent impulses in the work of a single author or an epoch.

picaresque novel: A form of fiction that centers on a central rogue figure, or picaro, who usually tells his or her own story. The plot structure is normally *episodic*, and the episodes usually focus on how the picaro lives by his or her wits. Classic examples of the mode are Henry Fielding's *The History of Tom Jones, a Foundling* (1749; commonly known as *Tom Jones*) and Mark Twain's *Adventures of Huckleberry Finn* (1884).

plot/story: "Story" refers to the full *narrative* of *character* and action, whereas "plot" generally refers to action with little reference to character. A more precise and helpful distinction is made by the Russian Formalists, who suggest that "plot" refers to the events of a narrative as they have been artfully arranged in the literary work, subject to chronological displacement, ellipses, and other devices, while "story" refers to the sum of the same events arranged in simple, causal-chronological order. Thus story is the raw material for plot. By comparing the two in a given work, the reader is encouraged to see the narrative as an artifact.

point of view: The means by which the story is presented to the reader, or, as Percy Lubbock says in *The Craft of Fiction* (1921), "the relation in which the narrator stands to the story"—a relation that Lubbock claims governs the craft of fiction. Some of the questions the critical reader should ask concerning point of view are the following: Who talks to the reader? From what position does the narrator tell the story? At what distance does he or she place the reader from the story? What kind of person is he or she? How fully is he or she characterized? How reliable is he or she? For further discussion, see Wayne Booth, *The Rhetoric of Fiction* (1961).

postcolonialism: Postcolonial literature emerged in the mid-twentieth century when colonies in Asia, Africa, and the Caribbean began gaining their independence from the European nations that had long controlled them. Postcolonial authors, such as Salman Rushdie and V. S. Naipaul, tend to focus on both the freedom and the conflict inherent in living in a postcolonial state.

postmodernism: A ubiquitous but elusive term in contemporary criticism, "postmodernism" is loosely applied to the various artistic movements that followed the era of so-called high modernism, represented by such giants as James Joyce and Pablo Picasso. In critical discussions of contemporary fiction, the term "postmodernism" is frequently applied to the works of writers such as Thomas Pynchon, John Barth, and Donald Barthelme, who exhibit a self-conscious awareness of their modernist predecessors as well as a reflexive treatment of fictional form.

protagonist: The central *character* in a fiction, the character whose fortunes most concern the reader.

psychological criticism: While much modern literary criticism reflects to some degree the impacts of Sigmund Freud, Carl Jung, Jacques Lacan, and other psychological theorists, the term "psychological criticism" suggests a strong emphasis on a causal relation between the writer's psychological state, variously interpreted, and his or her works. A notable example of psychological criticism is Norman Fruman's *Coleridge, the Damaged Archangel* (1971).

psychological novel: A form of fiction in which *character*, especially the inner lives of characters, is the primary focus. This form, which has been of primary importance at least since Henry James, characterizes much of the work of James Joyce, Virginia Woolf, and William Faulkner. For a detailed discussion, see *The Modern Psychological Novel* (1955) by Leon Edel.

realism: A literary technique in which the primary convention is to render an illusion of fidelity to external reality. Realism is often identified as the primary method of the novel form: It focuses on surface details, maintains a fidelity to the everyday experiences of middle-class society, and strives for a one-to-one relationship between the fiction and the action imitated. The realist movement in the late nineteenth century coincides with the full development of the novel form.

reception aesthetics: The best-known American practitioner of reception aesthetics is Stanley Fish. For the reception critic, meaning is an event or process; rather than being embedded in the work, it is created through particular acts of reading. The best-known European practitioner of this criticism, Wolfgang Iser, argues that indeterminacy is the basic characteristic of literary texts; the reader must "normalize" the text either by projecting his or her standards into it or by revising his or her standards to "fit" the text.

regional novel: Any novel in which the character of a given geographical region plays a decisive role. Although regional differences persist across the United States, a considerable leveling in speech and customs has taken place, so that the sharp regional distinctions evident in nineteenth century American fiction have all but disappeared. Only in the South has a strong regional tradition persisted to the present. (See *local colorists*.)

rhetorical criticism: The rhetorical critic is concerned with the literary work as a means of communicating ideas and the means by which the work affects or controls the reader. Such criticism seems best suited to didactic works such as satire.

roman à clef: A fiction wherein actual people, often celebrities of some sort, are thinly disguised.

romance: The romance usually differs from the novel form in that the focus is on symbolic events and representational characters rather than on "as-if-real" characters and events. Richard Chase says that in the romance, character is depicted as highly stylized, a function of the plot rather than as someone complexly related to society. The romancer is more likely to be concerned with dreamworlds than with the familiar world, believing that reality cannot be grasped by the traditional novel.

Romanticism: A widespread cultural movement in the late eighteenth and early nineteenth centuries, the influence of which is still felt. As a general literary tendency, Romanticism is frequently contrasted with *classicism*. Although many varieties of Romanticism are indigenous to various national literatures, the term generally suggests an assertion of the preeminence of the imagination. Other values associated with various schools of Romanticism include primitivism, an interest in folklore, a reverence for nature, and a fascination with the demoniac and the macabre.

scene: The central element of *narration*; specific actions are narrated or depicted that make the reader feel he or she is participating directly in the action.

science fiction: Fiction in which certain givens (physical laws, psychological principles, social conditions—any one or all of these) form the basis of an imaginative projection into the future or, less commonly, an extrapolation in the present or even into the past.

semiotics: The science of signs and sign systems in communication. According to Roman Jakobson, semiotics deals with the principles that underlie the structure of signs, their use in language of all kinds, and the specific nature of various sign systems.

sentimental novel: A form of fiction popular in the eighteenth century in which emotionalism and optimism are the primary characteristics. The best-known examples are Samuel Richardson's *Pamela: Or, Virtue Rewarded* (1740-1741) and Oliver Goldsmith's *The Vicar of Wakefield* (1766).

setting: The circumstances and environment, both temporal and spatial, of a *narrative*.

spatial form: An author's attempt to make the reader apprehend a work spatially in a moment of time rather than sequentially. To achieve this effect, the author breaks up the *narrative* into interspersed fragments. Beginning with James Joyce, Marcel Proust, and Djuna Barnes, the movement toward spatial form is concomitant with the *modernist* effort to supplant historical time in fiction with mythic time. For the seminal discussion of this technique, see Joseph Frank, *The Widening Gyre* (1963).

stream of consciousness: The depiction of the thought processes of a *character*, insofar as this is possible, without any mediating structures. The metaphor of consciousness as a "stream" suggests a rush of thoughts and images governed by free association rather than by strictly rational development. The term "stream of consciousness" is often used loosely as a synonym for *interior monologue*. The most celebrated example of stream of consciousness in fiction is the monologue of Molly Bloom in James Joyce's *Ulysses* (1922); other notable practitioners of the stream-of-consciousness technique include Dorothy Richardson, Virginia Woolf, and William Faulkner.

structuralism: As a movement of thought, structuralism is based on the idea of intrinsic, self-sufficient structures that do not require reference to external elements. A structure is a system of transformations that involves the interplay of laws inherent in the system itself. The study of language is the primary model for contemporary structuralism. The structuralist literary critic attempts to define structural principles that operate intertextually throughout the whole of literature as well as principles that operate in *genres* and in individual works. One of the most accessible surveys of structuralism and literature available is Jonathan Culler's *Structuralist Poetics* (1975).

summary: Those parts of a fiction that do not need to be detailed. In *Tom Jones* (1749), Henry Fielding says, "If whole years should pass without producing anything worthy of . . . notice . . . we shall hasten on to matters of consequence."

thematics: According to Northrop Frye, when a work of fiction is written or interpreted thematically, it becomes an illustrative fable. Murray Krieger defines thematics as "the study of the experiential tensions which, dramatically entangled in the literary work, become an existential reflection of that work's aesthetic complexity."

tone: The dominant mood of a work of fiction. (See *atmosphere*.)

unreliable narrator: A narrator whose account of the events of the story cannot be trusted, obliging readers to reconstruct—if possible—the true state of affairs themselves. Once an innovative technique, the use of the unreliable narrator has become commonplace among contemporary writers who wish to suggest the impossibility of a truly "reliable" account of any event. Notable examples of the unreliable narrator can be found in Ford Madox Ford's *The Good Soldier* (1915) and Vladimir Nabokov's *Lolita* (1955).

Victorian novel: Although the Victorian period extended from 1837 to 1901, the term "Victorian novel" does not include the later decades of Queen Victoria's reign. The term loosely refers to the sprawling works of novelists such as Charles Dickens and William Makepeace Thackeray—works that frequently appeared first in serial form and are characterized by a broad social canvas.

vraisemblance/verisimilitude: Tzvetan Todorov defines vraisemblance as "the mask which conceals the text's own laws, but which we are supposed to take for a relation to reality." Verisimilitude refers to a work's attempts to make the reader believe that it conforms to reality rather than to its own laws.

Western novel: Like all varieties of *genre fiction*, the Western novel—generally known simply as the Western—is defined by a relatively predictable combination of *conventions*, *motifs*, and recurring themes. These predictable elements, familiar from many Western films and television series, differentiate the Western from *historical novels* and idiosyncratic works such as Thomas Berger's *Little Big Man* (1964) that are also set in the Old West. Conversely, some novels set in the contemporary West are regarded as Westerns because they deal with modern cowboys and with the land itself in the manner characteristic of the *genre*.

Charles E. May

Guide to Online Resources

Web Sites
The following sites were visited by the editors of Salem Press in 2009. Because URLs frequently change, the accuracy of these addresses cannot be guaranteed; however, long-standing sites, such as those of colleges and universities, national organizations, and government agencies, generally maintain links when sites are moved or updated.

American Literature on the Web
http://www.nagasaki-gaigo.ac.jp/ishikawa/amlit

Among this site's features are several pages providing links to Web sites about specific genres and literary movements, southern and southwestern American literature, minority literature, literary theory, and women writers, as well as an extensive index of links to electronic text collections and archives. Users also can access information for five specific time periods: 1620-1820, 1820-1865, 1865-1914, 1914-1945, and since 1945. A range of information is available for each period, including alphabetical lists of authors that link to more specific information about each writer, time lines of historical and literary events, and links to related additional Web sites.

Books and Writers
http://www.kirjasto.sci.fi/indeksi.htm

This broad, comprehensive, and easy-to-use resource provides access to information about hundreds of authors throughout the world, extending from 70 B.C.E to the twenty-first century. Links take users from an alphabetical list of authors to pages featuring biographical material, lists of works, and recommendations for further reading about individual authors; each writer's page also includes links to related pages on the site. Although brief, the biographical essays provide solid overviews of the authors' careers, their contributions to literature, and their literary influences.

The Canadian Literature Archive
http://www.umanitoba.ca/canlit

Created and maintained by the English Department at the University of Manitoba, this site is a comprehensive collection of materials for and about Canadian writers. It includes an alphabetical listing of authors with links to additional Web-based information. Users also can retrieve electronic texts, announcements of literary events, and videocasts of author interviews and readings.

A Celebration of Women Writers
http://digital.library.upenn.edu/women

This site presents an extensive compendium of information about the contributions of women writers throughout history. The "Local Editions by Authors" and "Local Editions by Category" pages include access to electronic texts of the works of numerous writers, including Louisa May Alcott, Djuna Barnes, Grazia Deledda, Edith Wharton, and Virginia Woolf. Users can also access biographical and bibliographical information by browsing lists arranged by writers' names, countries of origin, ethnicities, and the centuries in which they lived.

Contemporary Writers
http://www.contemporarywriters.com/authors

Created by the British Council, this site offers "up-to-date profiles of some of the U.K. and Commonwealth's most important living writers (plus writers from the Republic of Ireland that we've worked with)." The available information includes biographies, bibliographies, critical reviews, news about literary prizes, and photographs. Users can search the site by author, genre, nationality, gender, publisher, book title, date of publication, and prize name and date.

Internet Public Library: Native American Authors
http://www.ipl.org/div/natam

Internet Public Library, a Web-based collection of materials, includes this index to resources about writers of Native American heritage. An alphabetical list of authors enables users to link to biographies, lists of works, electronic texts, tribal Web sites, and other online resources. The majority of the writers covered are contemporary Indian authors, but some historical authors also are featured. Users also can retrieve information by browsing lists of titles and tribes. In addition, the site contains a bibliography of print and online materials about Native American literature.

LiteraryHistory.com
http://www.literaryhistory.com

This site is an excellent source of academic, scholarly, and critical literature about eighteenth, nineteenth, and twentieth century American and English writers. It provides numerous pages about specific eras and genres, including individual pages for eighteenth, nineteenth, and twentieth century literature and for African American and postcolonial literature. These pages contain alphabetical lists of authors that link to articles, reviews, overviews, excerpts of works, teaching guides, podcast interviews, and other materials. The eighteenth century literature page also provides access to information about the eighteenth century novel.

Literary Resources on the Net
http://andromeda.rutgers.edu/~jlynch/Lit

Jack Lynch of Rutgers University maintains this extensive collection of links to Internet sites that are useful to academics, including numerous Web sites about American and English literature. This collection is a good place to begin online research about the novel, as it links to hundreds of other sites with broad ranges of literary topics. The site is organized chronically, with separate pages for information about the Middle Ages, the Renaissance, the eighteenth century, the Romantic and Victorian eras, and twentieth century British and Irish literature. It also has separate pages providing links to Web sites about American literature and to women's literature and feminism.

LitWeb
http://litweb.net

LitWeb provides biographies of more than five hundred world authors throughout history that can be accessed through an alphabetical listing. The pages about each writer contain a list of his or her works, suggestions for further reading, and illustrations. The site also offers information about past and present winners of major literary prizes.

The Modern Word: Authors of the Libyrinth
http://www.themodernword.com/authors.html

The Modern Word site, although somewhat haphazard in its organization, provides a great deal of critical information about writers. The "Authors of the Libyrinth" page is very useful, linking author names to essays about them and other resources. The section of the page headed "The Scriptorium" presents "an index of pages featuring writers who have pushed the edges of their medium, combining literary talent with a sense of experimentation to produce some remarkable works of modern literature." The site also includes sections devoted to Samuel Beckett, Umberto Eco, Gabriel García Márquez, James Joyce, Franz Kafka, and Thomas Pynchon.

Novels
http://www.nvcc.edu/home/ataormina/novels/default.htm

This overview of American and English novels was prepared by Agatha Taormina, a professor at Northern Virginia Community College. It contains three sections: "History" provides a definition of the novel genre, a discussion of its origins in eighteenth century England, and separate pages with information about genres and authors of nineteenth century, twentieth century, and postmodern novels. "Approaches" suggests how to read a novel critically for greater appreciation, and "Resources" provides a list of books about the novel.

Outline of American Literature
http://www.america.gov/publications/books/outline-of-american-literature.html
   This page of the America.gov site provides access to an electronic version of the ten-chapter volume *Outline of American Literature*, a historical overview of prose and poetry from colonial times to the present published by the U.S. Department of State. The work's author is Kathryn VanSpanckeren, professor of English at the University of Tampa. The site offers links to abbreviated versions of each chapter as well as access to the entire publication in PDF format.

Voice of the Shuttle
http://vos.ucsb.edu
   One of the most complete and authoritative places for online information about literature, Voice of the Shuttle is maintained by professors and students in the English Department at the University of California, Santa Barbara. The site provides thousands of links to electronic books, academic journals, association Web sites, sites created by university professors, and many, many other resources about the humanities. Its "Literature in English" page provides links to separate pages about the literature of the Anglo-Saxon era, the Middle Ages, the Renaissance and seventeenth century, the Restoration and eighteenth century, the Romantic age, the Victorian age, and modern and contemporary periods in Britain and the United States, as well as a page focused on minority literature. Another page on the site, "Literatures Other than English," offers a gateway to information about the literature of numerous countries and world regions.

ELECTRONIC DATABASES

Electronic databases usually do not have their own URLs. Instead, public, college, and university libraries subscribe to these databases, provide links to them on their Web sites, and make them available to library card holders or other specified patrons. Readers can visit library Web sites or ask reference librarians to check on availability.

Canadian Literary Centre
   Produced by EBSCO, the Canadian Literary Centre database contains full-text content from ECW Press, a Toronto-based publisher, including the titles in the publisher's Canadian fiction studies, Canadian biography, and Canadian writers and their works series, *ECW's Biographical Guide to Canadian Novelists*, and *George Woodcock's Introduction to Canadian Fiction*. Author biographies, essays and literary criticism, and book reviews are among the database's offerings.

Literary Reference Center

EBSCO's Literary Reference Center (LRC) is a comprehensive full-text database designed primarily to help high school and undergraduate students in English and the humanities with homework and research assignments about literature. The database contains massive amounts of information from reference works, books, literary journals, and other materials, including more than 31,000 plot summaries, synopses, and overviews of literary works; almost 100,000 essays and articles of literary criticism; about 140,000 author biographies; more than 605,000 book reviews; and more than 5,200 author interviews. It also contains the entire contents of Salem Press's MagillOnLiterature Plus. Users can retrieve information by browsing a list of authors' names or titles of literary works; they can also use an advanced search engine to access information by numerous categories, including author name, gender, cultural identity, national identity, and the years in which he or she lived, or by literary title, character, locale, genre, and publication date. The Literary Reference Center also features a literary-historical time line, an encyclopedia of literature, and a glossary of literary terms.

MagillOnLiterature Plus

MagillOnLiterature Plus is a comprehensive, integrated literature database produced by Salem Press and available on the EBSCO*host* platform. The database contains the full text of essays in Salem's many literature-related reference works, including *Masterplots*, *Cyclopedia of World Authors*, *Cyclopedia of Literary Characters*, *Cyclopedia of Literary Places*, *Critical Survey of Long Fiction*, *Critical Survey of Short Fiction*, *World Philosophers and Their Works*, *Magill's Literary Annual*, and *Magill's Book Reviews*. Among its contents are articles on more than 35,000 literary works and more than 8,500 writers, poets, dramatists, essays, and philosophers, more than 1,000 images, and a glossary of more than 1,300 literary terms. The biographical essays include lists of authors' works and secondary bibliographies, and almost four hundred overview essays offer information about literary genres, time periods, and national literatures.

NoveList

NoveList is a readers' advisory service produced by EBSCO. The database provides access to 155,000 titles of both adult and juvenile fiction as well information about literary awards, book discussion guides, feature articles about a range of literary genres, and "recommended reads." Users can search by author name, book title, or series title or can describe the plot to retrieve the name of a book, information about the author, and book reviews; another search engine enables users to find titles similar to books they have enjoyed reading.

Rebecca Kuzins

GEOGRAPHICAL INDEX

AFGHANISTAN
  Hosseini, Khaled, 122
ALBANIA
  Kadare, Ismail, 128

CZECH REPUBLIC
  Čapek, Karel, 22
  Kundera, Milan, 145

ENGLAND
  Conrad, Joseph, 31
  Greene, Graham, 110
  Koestler, Arthur, 134
  Orwell, George, 172
  Rushdie, Salman, 200

HUNGARY
  Koestler, Arthur, 134

INDIA
  Rushdie, Salman, 200

KENYA
  Ngugi wa Thiong'o, 156

POLAND
  Conrad, Joseph, 31

RUSSIA
  Dostoevski, Fyodor, 50
  Gogol, Nikolai, 67
  Gorky, Maxim, 99
  Rand, Ayn, 193
  Sholokhov, Mikhail, 216
  Solzhenitsyn, Aleksandr, 239
  Zamyatin, Yevgeny, 254

SOUTH AFRICA
  Gordimer, Nadine, 78
SPAIN
  Blasco Ibáñez, Vicente, 9

UNITED STATES
  Hosseini, Khaled, 122
  Porter, Katherine Anne, 183
  Rand, Ayn, 193
  Sinclair, Upton, 225

SUBJECT INDEX

Aeschylus, 220
Age of Longing, The (Koestler), 141
Akhmatova, Anna, 255
Allegory
    Graham Greene, 118
    Khaled Hosseini, 125
    Ngugi wa Thiong'o, 166
    George Orwell, 172
    Katherine Anne Porter, 187
    Salman Rushdie, 204
And Quiet Flows the Don. See Silent Don
Animal Farm (Orwell), 177
Antagonists
    Fyodor Dostoevski, 59
    Arthur Koestler, 142
Apartheid, 81, 117
Apollinaire, Guillaume, 146
Arrival and Departure (Koestler), 140
Artamonov Business, The (Gorky), 106
Atlas Shrugged (Rand), 1, 197
Atmosphere, 18
August 1914 (Solzhenitsyn), 249

Bakhtin, Mikhail, 246
Between Two Worlds (Sinclair), 235
Biblical themes, 161, 169
Bildungsromans
    Khaled Hosseini, 124
    Ngugi wa Thiong'o, 160
Blair, Eric Arthur. *See* Orwell, George
Blasco Ibáñez, Vicente, 9-21
Book of Laughter and Forgetting, The (Kundera), 150
Boston (Sinclair), 234
Brecht, Bertolt, 105
Brighton Rock (Greene), 114

Broken April (Kadare), 131
Brothers Karamazov, The (Dostoevski), 62
Burger's Daughter (Gordimer), 90
Burgess, Anthony, 178
Burmese Days (Orwell), 175

Cabin, The (Blasco Ibáñez), 16
Call Girls, The (Koestler), 142
Camus, Albert, 52
Cancer Ward (Solzhenitsyn), 247
Čapek, Karel, 22-30, 147
Catholic themes
    Graham Greene, 113
    Arthur Koestler, 141
Censorship
    Ismail Kadare, 129
    Salman Rushdie, 200
Cervantes, Miguel de, 10
Cheat, The (Čapek), 28
Chekhov, Anton, 101, 216
Chesterton, G. K., 22
Coming Up for Air (Orwell), 175
Coming-of-age novels
    Nadine Gordimer, 82
    Khaled Hosseini, 124
Conrad, Joseph, 31-49
Conservationist, The (Gordimer), 88
Crane, Stephen, 33, 232
Crime and Punishment (Dostoevski), 57

Dahl, Roald, 203
Darkness at Noon (Koestler), 139
Dead Souls (Gogol), 69
Decadence. See Artamonov Business, The
Detective novels, 167
Devil on the Cross (Ngugi), 168

Subject Index

Devils, The. See *Possessed, The*
Dickens, Charles, 70
Doppelgängers, 176
Dostoevski, Fyodor, 50-67, 140, 216, 244, 261
Dragon Harvest (Sinclair), 236
Dragon's Teeth (Sinclair), 235
Dystopian novels
 George Orwell, 177
 Yevgeny Zamyatin, 260

Enchantress of Florence, The (Rushdie), 213
Esenin, Sergei, 149
Espionage fiction, 117

Fantasy fiction, 259-260
Farewell Party, The (Kundera), 149
First Circle, The (Solzhenitsyn), 248
Fitzgerald, F. Scott, 33, 233
Flashbacks
 Joseph Conrad, 33
 Arthur Koestler, 139
 Mikhail Sholokhov, 221
 Aleksandr Solzhenitsyn, 247
Foma Gordeyev (Gorky), 105
Foreshadowing
 Vicente Blasco Ibáñez, 17
 Mikhail Sholokhov, 221
Fountainhead, The (Rand), 196
Four Horsemen of the Apocalypse, The (Blasco Ibáñez), 20

Galdós, Benito Pérez, 13
Get a Life (Gordimer), 96
Gladiators, The (Koestler), 138
Gogol, Nikolai, 67-77, 216, 255
Goncharov, Ivan, 70
Gordimer, Nadine, 78-98
Gorky, Maxim, 99-109, 217, 258

Gothic novel
 Fyodor Dostoevski, 55
 Nikolai Gogol, 74
Grain of Wheat, A (Ngugi), 164
Great Depression, 2, 226
Greene, Graham, 110-121
Grotesque
 Fyodor Dostoevski, 55
 Nikolai Gogol, 70
 Katherine Anne Porter, 189
Guest of Honour, A (Gordimer), 87

Hašek, Jaroslav, 147
Heart of Darkness (Conrad), 37
Heart of the Matter, The (Greene), 116
Heller, Joseph, 176
Historical novels
 Vicente Blasco Ibáñez, 13
 Nikolai Gogol, 75
 Arthur Koestler, 138
 Upton Sinclair, 228
 Aleksandr Solzhenitsyn, 244
Hoffmann, E. T. A., 55
Holding, The. See *Cabin, The*
Homer, 130, 208
Hordubal (Čapek), 25
Hosseini, Khaled, 122-127
House Gun, The (Gordimer), 95
Howells, William Dean, 10
Human Factor, The (Greene), 117

Identity (Kundera), 153
Idiot, The (Dostoevski), 58
Ignorance (Kundera), 153
Impressionism, 37
Interior monologues, 16
Intertextuality, 123
Islam
 Khaled Hosseini, 125
 Salman Rushdie, 204

Joke, The (Kundera), 147
Jugo, Miguel de Unamuno y, 16
July's People (Gordimer), 92
Jungle, The (Sinclair), 231

Kadare, Elena, 129
Kadare, Ismail, 128-133
King Coal (Sinclair), 233
King, Stephen, 203
Kite Runner, The (Hosseini), 123-124
Koestler, Arthur, 6, 134-144
Korzeniowski, Jósef Teodor Konrad Nalecz. See Conrad, Joseph
Krasnoe koleso (Solzhenitsyn), 250
Kundera, Milan, 145-155, 203

Lanny Budd series (Sinclair), 235
Late Bourgeois World, The (Gordimer), 86
Le Carré, John, 203
Legal fiction, 57
Lermontov, Mikhail, 105
Letters from the Underworld. See *Notes from the Underground*
Lewis, Sinclair, 1
Life Is Elsewhere (Kundera), 149
Lord Jim (Conrad), 41
Lying Days, The (Gordimer), 82

McCarry, Charles, 5
Mailer, Norman, 5, 203
Malraux, André, 4
Manassas (Sinclair), 230
Mandelstam, Osip, 255
Man's Fate (Malraux), 4
Marx, Karl, 228
Marxism, 4
Matigari (Ngugi), 168
Mayakovsky, Vladimir, 149
Mayflower, The (Blasco Ibáñez), 14
Meteor (Čapek), 26

Midnight's Children (Rushdie), 204
Modern novel, 33
Moor's Last Sigh, The (Rushdie), 211
Mother (Gorky), 105
Motifs
   Joseph Conrad, 43
   Salman Rushdie, 206
Motivation, 148
My Son's Story (Gordimer), 94
Mysticism, 137

Naturalism
   Vicente Blasco Ibáñez, 14
   Upton Sinclair, 232
Negritude, 156
Neorealism, 254
Ngugi wa Thiong'o, 156-171
Nietzsche, Friedrich, 151
Nineteen Eighty-Four (Orwell), 1, 178
None to Accompany Me (Gordimer), 94
Noon Wine (Porter), 187
Notes from the Underground (Dostoevski), 56

O Shepherd, Speak! (Sinclair), 236
Occasion for Loving (Gordimer), 85
Old Mortality (Porter), 186
One Clear Call (Sinclair), 236
One Day in the Life of Ivan Denisovich (Solzhenitsyn), 246
Ordinary Life, An ({Ccaron}apek), 27
Orwell, George, 1, 172-182, 255

Palace of Dreams, The (Kadare), 130
Pale Horse, Pale Rider (Porter), 188
Pasternak, Boris, 216
Petals of Blood (Ngugi), 166
Philosophical novels
   Karel Čapek, 24
   Mikhail Sholokhov, 216
Picaresque novel, 70

Subject Index

Pickup, The (Gordimer), 95
Point of view
    Vicente Blasco Ibáñez, 19
    Fyodor Dostoevski, 55
    Nikolai Gogol, 71
    Nadine Gordimer, 94
    Graham Greene, 116
    Aleksandr Solzhenitsyn, 246
Porter, Katherine Anne, 183-192
Possessed, The (Dostoevski), 60
Power and the Glory, The (Greene), 118
Presidential Agent (Sinclair), 236
Presidential Mission (Sinclair), 236
Problem novel, 113
Proletarian novel, 141, 233
    Maxim Gorky, 101
    Russia, 257
Provincial Tale, A (Zamyatin), 258
Psychological novel
    Vicente Blasco Ibáñez, 13
    Joseph Conrad, 32
Pushkin, Alexander, 54

Quiet American, The (Greene), 118

Rand, Ayn, 1, 4, 193-199
Realism
    Vicente Blasco Ibáñez, 13
    Fyodor Dostoevski, 52
    Nikolai Gogol, 67
    Maxim Gorky, 103
    Ngugi wa Thiong'o, 156
    Salman Rushdie, 211
    Mikhail Sholokhov, 218
    Yevgeny Zamyatin, 254
Reeds and Mud (Blasco Ibáñez), 18
Religious novels
    Fyodor Dostoevski, 62
    Graham Greene, 113
    Salman Rushdie, 208

Return of Lanny Budd, The (Sinclair), 236
Rimbaud, Arthur, 149
River Between, The (Ngugi), 162
Romains, Jules, 22
Roman à clef, 136
Romanticism
    Katherine Anne Porter, 190
    Ayn Rand, 196
Rushdie, Salman, 200-215

Satanic Verses, The (Rushdie), 208
Satire
    Nikolai Gogol, 70
    Milan Kundera, 152
    George Orwell, 177
    Salman Rushdie, 206
    Aleksandr Solzhenitsyn, 246
Seeds of Tomorrow. See *Virgin Soil*
Shahnamah (Firdusi), 123
Shame (Rushdie), 206
Shaw, George Bernard, 22
Ship of Fools (Porter), 189
Sholokhov, Mikhail, 101, 216-224
Silent Don, The (Sholokhov), 220
Sinclair, Upton, 225-238
Sinyavsky, Andrei, 219, 243
Slowness (Kundera), 152
Solzhenitsyn, Aleksandr, 218, 239-253
Sophocles, 220
Sport of Nature, A (Gordimer), 93
Spring Flowers, Spring Frost (Kadare), 132
Storm in Shanghai. See *Man's Fate*
Stream of consciousness
    Nikolai Gogol, 71
    Nadine Gordimer, 89
Styron, William, 203
Symbolism
    Joseph Conrad, 33
    Yevgeny Zamyatin, 254

Taras Bulba (Gogol), 74
Thieves in the Night (Koestler), 141
Thousand Splendid Suns, A (Hosseini), 123, 125
Tolstoy, Leo, 51, 67, 101, 216, 244
Turgenev, Ivan, 52, 67, 255

Unbearable Lightness of Being, The (Kundera), 151

Victory (Conrad), 44
Virgin Soil Upturned (Sholokhov), 222
Voltaire, 2

War novels, 13
Warren, Robert Penn, 1
We (Zamyatin), 260
Weep Not, Child (Ngugi), 160
Wells, H. G., 22
Wide Is the Gate (Sinclair), 236
Wiggins, Marianne, 212
Wizard of the Crow (Ngugi), 169
World of Strangers, A (Gordimer), 83
World to Win, A (Sinclair), 236
World's End (Sinclair), 235

Zamyatin, Yevgeny, 254-263
Zoshchenko, Mikhail, 255
Zweig, Stefan, 100